BLANCHE BROWN ✠ SAN FRANCISCO

African Systems of Thought

General Editors
Charles S. Bird
Ivan Karp

Contributing Editors
Thomas O. Beidelman
James Fernandez
Luc de Heusch
John Middleton
Roy Willis

AFRICA'S
OGUN

OLD WORLD AND NEW

Edited by Sandra T. Barnes

INDIANA UNIVERSITY PRESS
Bloomington & Indianapolis

Manufactured in the United States of America

Library of Congress Cataloging-in-Publication Data
Africa's Ogun.
    (African systems of thought)
    Includes index.
    1. Ogun (Yoruba deity)—Cult—Africa, West.
2. Ogun (Yoruba deity)—Cult—America.   3. Yoruba
(African people)—Religion.   4. Blacks—America—
Religion.   I. Barnes, Sandra T.
BL2480.Y6A46   1989   299'.63   88-45452
ISBN 0-253-30282-X
ISBN 0-253-20505-0 (pbk.)
            2   3   4   5   93   92   91

Contents

PART ONE: The History and Spread of Ogun in Old and New Worlds

PART TWO: The Meaning of Ogun in Ritual, Myth, and Art

ILLUSTRATIONS

PREFACE

The ideas in this volume began to take shape in 1971 when I first began field research in Lagos, Nigeria, and they were periodically reinforced during subsequent research periods in the 1970s and 1980s. Each time I was struck by the vitality of certain religious ideas and practices and their adaptation to contemporary African life. Ogun, the ancient god of iron, warfare, and hunting, stood out in this respect, for his cult and the ideas espoused in it were alive, expanding, and flourishing. In present-day Nigeria his realm had extended to embrace everything from modern technology to highway safety—anything, in fact, that involved metal, danger, or, not incompatibly, political resistance.

In searching for an explanation for Ogun's vitality, I was led to his past, which, upon investigation, and certainly not surprisingly, revealed that Ogun embodied a core of Pan-African themes about human nature, conflict, and change that were basic to the construction of the world view of many peoples. In the Guinea Coast region of West Africa these ancient ideas remained as mere concepts in some societies whereas in others they eventually crystallized in the god Ogun and his cult. Later, as a result of the slave diaspora, some of these ideas were given a place in the reconstructed traditions of African descendants in the New World and, in time, in the lives of the peoples with whom they were coming in contact.

Ogun thus presented a challenging vehicle for examining issues that are categorized under the heading of continuity and change. Given the overwhelming dominance of global religions such as Islam and Christianity, how does a deity such as Ogun survive? How is it that he can appeal to an expanding audience? What does he mean to his followers? Is he the same in all contexts and at all time periods, or does he mean different things to different peoples?

These were the guiding questions in an earlier study, *Ogun: An Old God for a New Age* (Philadelphia, 1980), and at an Ogun colloquium held at the annual meeting of the African Studies Association in Los Angeles in 1979. The idea and encouragement for the colloquium and this volume came from Paula Girshick Ben-Amos and Dan Ben-Amos, who suggested that the international vitality of Ogun was in need of further exploration. Inasmuch as my early work came out of a mainly Yoruba experience, the obvious challenge was to examine Ogun elsewhere in West Africa and in the Caribbean and Latin America. In many places not only was Ogun a key figure in contemporary religious settings that had clear connections with the past, but he also was incorporated into new ideological systems and what might be called popular religions. Needless to say, it became increasingly clear that Ogun and others like him were not part of a disappearing world. In fact, Ogun and other divinities were beginning to play the same role that classical deities of the Greek and Roman world have long played in literature, drama, painting, and sculpture in Western civilization.

From its inception, putting together the essays about the *international* Ogun was a collective enterprise. It began with presentations by colloquium participants which became a core around which other contributions could be added. The U.S. Embassy in Lagos kindly provided a travel grant to Adeboye Babalọla so that he could participate in the colloquium. Others who gave papers and generously shared their own research and ideas about Ogun, but whose work is not included here, were William Bascom, who witnessed an Ogun festival in Ile-Ife, Nigeria, in 1938; Dan Ben-Amos, who studied the modern cult of Ogun in Benin, Nigeria; and Deirdre LaPin, who examined the extensive use of Ogun in the writings of Nobel laureate Wole Soyinka. Soyinka, moreover, attended the colloquium to offer his moral support. Finally, Ivan Karp met with participants to suggest further avenues for analysis and investigation.

The guiding principles for contributors were that their essays be original and based on their own research. With this in mind, some of the authors suggested others who they felt should be included, and in this respect John Pemberton deserves particular thanks. For other suggestions I am indebted to Deirdre LaPin, Candace Slater, Peter Frye, and Diana Brown.

A number of other people also contributed to the ideas that went into shaping the volume and its introduction. Miguel Barnet and Patricia Alleyne kindly helped me understand Ogun in Cuba and Trinidad, respectively, and Pierre Verger generously offered the benefit of his expertise in the People's Republic of Benin, Nigeria, and Brazil. Ivan Karp and Roy Sieber invited me to share my initial thoughts on the metaculture of Ogun with their Africa Seminar at Indiana University. Since then, at various stages and in various ways, I have benefited from the advice of Arjun Appadurai, Gregory Barnes, Paula Girshick Ben-Amos, Carol Breckenridge, Nancy Farriss, Ward Goodenough, Clifford Hill, Igor Kopytoff, Simon Ottenberg, and John Peel.

During the course of any long-term effort, changes occur. Thus it is with sadness that we met the passing of William Bascom, an original colloquium participant, and Robert Armstrong, whose linguistic analysis of Ogun in this volume provides valuable insights into this deity's origins. Each man devoted a lifetime to scholarship in West Africa and in Bascom's case also to African culture in the New World, and each in his own way is sorely missed. In tribute to their outstanding contributions to African Studies, this volume is dedicated to their memory.

SANDRA T. BARNES

A NOTE ON ORTHOGRAPHY

Several West African languages, but primarily the Yoruba language, are used in this volume. Spelling conventions make use of subscript markings (as in ẹ, ọ, and ṣ) and tone markings (as in à = low, ē = mid, or ó = high). Because conventions vary, each chapter is consistent unto itself. For the most part, subscript and tone markings are included in chapters where translations are important to the analysis, and omitted where they are not.

Africa's Ogun

Sandra T. Barnes

1

Introduction: The Many Faces of Ogun

There is a privileged class of supernatural and mythic figures who consistently grow in their renown and complexity. One thinks of such figures as Oedipus or Siva, each of whom plays a significant role in the traditions of many groups of people, to the extent that they have become metacultural, or international in scope. The contributors to this volume focus their attention on another such figure: Ogun,[1] an African deity, who thrives today in a number of West African and New World contexts, including the Caribbean, South America, and, more recently, North America.

Ogun was one of many deities carried to the New World by Africans during the slave diaspora which took place between the sixteenth and the mid-nineteenth centuries. More recently he, and the complex ideological systems of which he is a part, have been carried from Brazil to its neighboring countries and from the Caribbean to North America. In this more recent, twentieth-century movement of peoples and their belief systems, Ogun's appeal has transcended the boundaries of ethnicity, race, and class so that today's adherents are not simply people of African descent but people representing many walks of life. The story is equally dramatic in West Africa, where Ogun's popularity also has flourished and expanded.

As a consequence, more than 70 million African and New World peoples participate in, or are closely familiar with, religious systems that include Ogun, and the number is increasing rather than declining. Yet the claim that a god from a comparatively small religious faith, particularly one stemming from a nonliterate tradition, flourishes in spite of the overwhelming dominance of such large global religions as Islam and Christianity jars our expectations. Why does a deity like Ogun survive? How can he grow in popularity, especially when deities of global faiths are themselves gaining strength? Furthermore, how can we say that Ogun of the New World is still the same as Ogun of West Africa, given the limited interaction of peoples between hemispheres in the past century or more and the markedly different cultural influences that have obtained in each place during this period? Clearly, if we are to understand the Ogun phenomenon as more than a mere anomaly, a reassessment is needed of the way we view contemporary religious processes. This is a primary concern of my essay. As a first step, let me introduce Ogun in his more obvious manifestations.

Ogun is one of many gods and goddesses in West African pantheons. As such, he is embedded in belief systems of great complexity. It is not the intention of this volume to dwell on these systems in their totality, but it is important to know that, like the religions of the ancient Greeks and Romans or contemporary Hindus, Ogun always is one part of a larger whole. Perhaps because he has an uncanny ability to stay abreast of the times, Ogun has been a major figure in this larger picture for as long as historical records reveal.

Ogun is popularly known as the god of hunting, iron, and warfare. Today, however, his realm has expanded to include many new elements, from modern technology to highway safety—anything involving metal, danger, or transportation. In the minds of followers, Ogun conventionally presents two images. The one is a terrifying specter: a violent warrior, fully armed and laden with frightening charms and medicines to kill his foes. The other is society's ideal male: a leader known for his sexual prowess, who nurtures, protects, and relentlessly pursues truth, equity, and justice. Clearly, this African figure fits the destroyer/creator archetype. But to assign him a neat label is itself an injustice, for behind the label lies a complex and varied set of notions. As his devotees put it, "Ogun has many faces."

The many meanings of Ogun are revealed in a vast array of rituals, myths, symbols, and artistic representations. The same is true of other deities in the pantheon, who formulaically number from 201 to 401 and even more. Each deity has different features; for example, only Ogun devotees wear iron emblems, display fiery red eyes when possessed, and dance with swords. Such differences do not prevent deities from interacting with one another in the spirit world; they reproduce, have kinship relationships, and generally quarrel, love, help, and harm just as humans do. Rather, the differences perform a valuable service by separating one deity's meanings from another's.

The interactions of humans and deities take place in a varied range of contexts. They often involve several deities or groupings of deities. A devotee who venerates Ogun alone may retire to a private household corner to offer prayers and simple food sacrifices to his iron tools (see H. Drewal, this volume, Ch. 10). By contrast, communities stage public spectacles that are as complex in their staging as European opera; indeed, they are grander in scale than opera, since entire towns, from the king to the lowliest servants, participate for days and even weeks in their dramatic pageantry (Pemberton, Ch. 6). Between the extremes lie ritual encounters with divinities that take place during rites of passage and in a bewildering variety of family, occupational, and cult groups. These encounters are neither as solemn nor as standardized as those of Western missionary Christianity. Neither are they similar in substance. West African adherents put emphasis on sacrifice, divination, and possession as ways of communicating with deities, and they stress pragmatic, everyday concerns as the content of such communication.

Finally, ritual encounters put emphasis on emotions and personality traits. Ogun's devotees display fiery outbursts of anger to the extent that they may heedlessly injure bystanders; just as easily, they may dwell on Ogun's humanitarianism and self-reliance with poignant recitations of heroic deeds that require outstanding levels of courage and leadership. To a great extent, whether it is in thought, deed, or mood, humans and deities mirror one another in West African philosophies. Therefore, character strengths and character flaws are as divine as they are human.

Ogun plays a central role in these philosophies. Like all deities he advances understanding, unifies knowledge, and, as Durkheim and Mauss put it, creates "a first philosophy of nature" (1963:81). Stated more succinctly, he represents a theory of what life or part of life is about. To uncover this theory, however, we must return to a concern which I introduced earlier on.

If we are to appreciate Ogun's significance in contemporary religious life, any reassessment of that life must depart from past approaches that, by implication, relegated figures like Ogun to a dying tradition. The thesis here is that a deity's capacity to survive, flourish, and expand depends on the meanings he projects and, perhaps equally important, on the way those meanings are "packaged." Within the meanings of Ogun resides a philosophy of the human condition that can be stated as a theoretical proposition. The theory in Ogun embodies a profound and compelling observation of human nature. This theory enables us to examine a realm of ideas that explain, in deeply moving terms, certain strengths and weaknesses that are universal to the human condition. Still, there is no one source for these ideas.

The many manifestations of Ogun yield many meanings. Multiple meanings inevitably give rise to multiple interpretations and, by extension, multiple anomalies. Can we then claim there are common threads in Ogun traditions, particularly when these traditions are so geographically and historically separated? Clearly, if we are to understand what is unique to Ogun—or whether, in fact, he *is* unique—a reevaluation is needed of the way we treat meanings, particularly as they are reflected in a single cultural figure.

I will begin this endeavor—explaining why Ogun survives and by necessity what he means, since my thesis is that meaning and survival are connected—with a look at the scant but instructive historical evidence. The value of history lies in its ability to provide baselines from which to measure the deity's ongoing permutations. My excursion into Ogun's past is followed by a brief examination of the historical and contemporary processes that shaped, and continue to shape, his meanings and that also account for his expansion.

Any study of meanings, especially when they are attached to a deity whose history spans centuries and whose devotees span continents, is incomplete without a discussion of methods. This will form the next part of the essay. How can we uncover the deepest meanings of a metacultural figure? More particularly, how can we expect to uncover common meanings when there are wide variations in them? Fortunately, analytical tools for this kind of endeavor are beginning to reach a state of some refinement. By combining several of them we can grapple with complexities that previously stood in the way of our ability to generalize about culture on a grand scale and yet retain cultural uniqueness as part of that generalization.

Finally, I will return to Ogun's meanings, this time in search of his philosophical principles and how they are put together in ways that are easily but profoundly communicated. There is no single myth, ritual, or other context that captures his meanings in a comprehensive, unified way. Therefore, the theory of human nature that we encounter through Ogun and, I suggest, the thing that accounts for his survival, is drawn from the rich body of evidence provided in each of the chapters that follow.

The History of Ogun

No date can be assigned to the birth of Ogun, nor can a place be assigned to his origins. The ideas out of which Ogun emerged are undoubtedly ancient ones. In an earlier study it was proposed that many of the themes surrounding Ogun are rooted in a set of Pan-African ideas that probably accompanied the spread of iron-making technology throughout sub-Saharan Africa as far back as 2,000 years (Barnes 1980). I call these ideas the *sacred iron complex*. The three most commonly held ideas in the complex are that iron is sacred, that ironworkers are exceptional members of society with particularly high or low status (since their work makes them either feared or revered), and that iron workplaces (smelters and smithies) are ritual shrines or sanctuaries for the dispossessed (e.g., warrior refugees). A recent study suggests that sacred ritual and its attendant ideology may have been essential to iron-making as a formulaic way of remembering and perpetuating the steps and ingredients involved in the iron-making process (van der Merwe and Avery 1987:143). This being the case, the ideology attached to iron technology needed to be sufficiently flexible and general to be communicated easily and then adapted to various local cosmologies.[2] H. Drewal (Ch. 10) describes just such an adaptation in the iron-smelting ritual of a Yoruba community and shows how local ideology symbolically plays on the notions in the sacred iron complex.

Lévi-Strauss suggests (1966:16–22) that ideas such as those in the sacred iron complex are randomly distributed notions until people collectively join them together in ways that fit their own cultural contexts. He calls the people who engage in this collective enterprise *bricoleurs*, people who work with materials at hand. Each group of *bricoleurs* creates new patterns with random materials, making it difficult to compare cross-culturally the common denominators in the patterns without decontextualizing them and thereby reducing them to truisms. Although I return to this problem, it should be said here that in the forest-belt kingdoms of West Africa, a conventional pattern for dealing with extraordinary ideas, culture heroes, or anomalies in nature was to deify them. The genesis of Ogun, therefore, quite likely involved a deification that grew out of a set of commonly held notions about the mystical properties of iron and the powerful people who made or used it. But Ogun's beginnings need not have relied exclusively on iron-related notions.

Armstrong (Ch. 2) provides evidence to suggest that several equally fundamental, metaphysical ideas may have been involved in the genesis of Ogun. They center, first, on an association between pollution and killing—killers must be purified before they can be reintegrated into society—and, second, on the mystification of disorder—misfortune is supernaturally determined. These ideas are attached to a widely shared set of cognate concepts, Ògún-ògwú-ògbú, meaning "kill." Armstrong found that cognates of the term Ògún exist in six neighboring language groups in West Africa. Linguistic evidence led him to propose that the concept is at least as old as the beginning of the Iron Age and probably older. In two of the language groups, an Ògún-related term is the name of a ritual that is held to resocialize a dangerous hero—hunter or headhunter—by honoring his deed and, at the same time, cleansing him of the pollution of death with water from a blacksmith's forge.[3] Thus Armstrong takes issue with the hypothesis that Ogun arose out of Africa's iron revolution and its accompanying sacred iron complex. He proposes, instead, that earlier themes—hunting, killing, and the resultant disorder that killing brings—are more likely foundations on which an *ogun* concept, and later an Ogun deity, were constructed.

The actual apotheosis of Ogun—that is, transforming the concept into a divine being—appears to have occurred in a much later period than the creation of an *ogun* concept. The earliest reliable date that can be fixed to the existence of an Ogun deity is the latter part of the eighteenth century. The evidence comes from Haiti, where the cessation of slave imports from Africa by this date acted as a cutoff point for the introduction of the slaves' home culture. Brown (Ch. 4) indicates that Ogun had to have been firmly entrenched in Haiti by this time inasmuch as today he is a significant figure in its religious culture, and oral traditions tie him to a long series of Haiti's historical events. Clearly the god Ogun existed, and was widespread, before the 1700s in the West African societies whose peoples contributed to the slave diaspora, or he could not have emerged as strongly as he did in Haiti and elsewhere in the New World.

Yet dates for the emergence of this deity in West Africa must be inferred. One suggestion is that Ogun arose in eastern Yorubaland in the sixteenth century, when there was an increase in the supply of iron and an expansion of warfare (Williams 1974:83). The hypothesis is based, in part, on the fact that ritual objects made of iron, which can be dated because of their use of imported metal and which are commonly used by Ogun devotees, began to proliferate at that time. This hypothesis is pictorially reinforced by a brass plaque depicting a Benin warrior wearing miniature iron tools—the almost universal symbols of Ogun—that dates to the fifteenth or sixteenth century (fig. 3.1). An even earlier date for the emergence of Ogun is suggested by an annual ceremony, also in the Kingdom of Benin, which dates to the thirteenth or fourteenth century and which featured ritual battles and sacrifices of the type that today are appropriate only to Ogun (Barnes and Ben-Amos, Ch. 3). Both of these suggestions pin the emergence of an Ogun deity to activities associated with warfare. Furthermore, they pin the geographic area of his emergence to eastern Yorubaland and to the Kingdom of Benin, where ritual reenactments of battle between kings and town leaders have long figured in large civic pageants dedicated to Ogun. Ritual battles featuring Ogun also became significant in Dahomean kingship ceremonies, especially those honoring the military, and they have continued to the present day on a smaller scale elsewhere in eastern Dahomey (now People's Republic of Benin), western Yorubaland, and throughout the New World where Ogun appears.

A third suggestion is given by Babalọla (Ch. 7), who finds that songs and legends link the deity's origins to hunting. There are, of course, no dates for such mythological explanations, but the traditions themselves are concentrated within central and western Yorubaland, especially in the territory occupied by the Kingdom of Oyo, West Africa's largest precolonial empire. Their performance was tied to hunting and, by extension, to the military, since hunters were the vanguard of the army. A German surgeon aboard a Dutch merchant ship described a prewar sacrificial ceremony for a deity, specified only as "the Devil," that took place in 1603 and included seven dogs; today dogs are sacrificed exclusively to Ogun. The rites took place near Lagos (Nigeria), which at that time was under the Kingdom of Benin (Jones 1983:24). Oyo factors were present in the area, however, for Oyo controlled nearby trade routes linking its inland territory to the lucrative European sea trade.

As can be seen, all of the evidence for the emergence of Ogun is circumstantial. The suggested dates and regions for the genesis of this deity all rely on symbolic and ritual evidence that today is appropriate only to Ogun. But none of the evidence specifically names Ogun and therefore the connection between it and the actual deity cannot be confirmed.

Furthermore, because the evidence is fragmentary, no interpretation can be right or wrong. Little profit is to be gained from deciding whether sacred iron weapons from a blacksmith's forge or a successful yet polluted head-hunter comes first as an ideological building block in the making of an *ogun* concept. Similarly, little profit can be gained from trying to pinpoint the deity's origins to a specific geographical region. Great profit can be realized, however, from combining all pieces of evidence, for they strongly suggest that there is an extraordinary tenaciousness in the themes attached to both Ogun as a deity and *ogun* as a concept. For instance, the sacred iron theme is kept alive by Cuban migrants in the United States who, like their compatriots at home, sacrifice to cauldrons (*caldera de ogún*) filled with iron objects, and to which in 1979 New York devotees added a real pistol (Thompson 1983:55). Likewise, the purification/killing theme is reworked in Brooklyn when a Haitian devotee who feels responsible for her son's death is consoled by a priestess who is possessed by Ogun in an elaborate ceremony (Brown, Ch. 4).

The way to think about the beginnings of a deity such as Ogun, then, is to view his origins, *by necessity*, as indeterminate. At any historical point, the ideas reflected by Ogun, or the ideas out of which he is created, are a cultural assemblage. Rather than assign any one set of ideas to the genesis of Ogun, it is instructive to view his origins in a *bricoleur* idiom: many available notions were pieced together into patterns that began as a concept and eventually emerged in a cult group with Ogun as its symbolic figurehead. Taken together, the ideas associated with Ogun represent an ongoing process that, in human history, has consisted of the working and reworking of available themes—be they sacred iron, pollution from unnatural death, or a host of others that are uncounted and unrecoverable. There is neither a beginning nor an end to these reworkings, and for these reasons it is well to speak of historical processes rather than historical beginnings.

Historical Processes That Shape Ogun

The history of Ogun is made up of additions and subtractions. In the extensive areas where Ogun is a significant part of the religious culture, there are many contexts in which he is salient. Over time these contexts are layered, one on another, so that what appears today as a bewildering variety of beliefs, legends, and rituals is an historical accumulation.

Additions leave behind a kind of "stratigraphy," as Obeyesekere vividly puts it (1984:284–5). Unfortunately, cultural stratigraphy does not reveal principles of order in the ways geological or archaeological stratigraphies sometimes do. Rather, layers of ideas are combined in any way. If there is logic in cultural stratigraphy, it is not chronology, but patterns in the ways additions and subtractions come about. One way of making additions is through paradigmatic transfers. When Nigerians changed from driving on the left to driving on the right-hand side of the road in 1972 it was interpreted as an "Ogun"-type event. Radio and television stations alerted the public by broadcasting an Ogun chant, written in traditional style by a popular musician, that advised people to pay tribute to Ogun before going out on the dangerous highways, and transporters and mechanics gathered in motor parks to offer sacrifices so that they might avoid accidents caused by the change (Barnes 1980:41). In essence, there was an available paradigm to signal an unusual event. Once it was applied to the event, it became a layer in the history of Ogun's performance as an appropriate actor.

New layers also come about through fusions. This happens when the attributes of two figures overlap in significant ways. Nigeria's Nobel laureate Wole Soyinka merges Ogun with Sango, the god of lightning and thunder, in a poem drawing on the imagery of electricity. The union can be seen, he writes, "during an electric storm when from high-tension wires leap figures of ecstatic flames" (1967:86). This is a temporary fusion in that it works in some contexts and not in others. Other fusions, say the historically common mergers of heroic warriors or hunters and Ogun, may be permanent. Whether temporary or permanent, the merger legitimates new symbols, themes, or legendary tales (say of a warrior's prowess) that thereafter can be added to the repertoire of features that is attached to the deity in question.

Fusions also account for loss. A Xhosa praise singer once explained that acquiring skills involved learning the ways in which events that occur to prominent people recall events of past eras: "And then you just begin to join those things" (Scheub 1975:22–23). Babalola's analysis of Ogun's character (Ch. 7) treats this blending of past with present. Legends attribute to Ogun the founding of many communities and royal dynasties, especially when they are the result of conquest or civil war. At first an historical founder's name is linked to that of Ogun, the supernatural founder. One example is Ogundahunsi, the founder of Ire Town. Eventually the founder's personal name is dropped and only the title Ogun survives. This case and others like it constitute an ongoing process: what is once expanded eventually is compressed, obscured, then lost.

Other processes that are significant to the history of Ogun involve his perpetuation and spread. Possibly the most important mediums for transmitting information are rituals and oral traditions such as myths, songs, legends, or prayers. A relatively high level of intercommunity mobility in precolonial West Africa fostered the exchange of information (Barnes and Ben-Amos, Ch. 3). Trade, of course, was the most notorious vehicle for interaction. In addition, artists traveled explicitly to augment their repertoires (H. Drewal, Ch. 10). Hunters moved through wide territories spreading their Ogun chants (Babalola, Ch. 7 and Ajuwon, Ch. 8). Ogun devotees, in fact, were among the more mobile sectors of the populace, and thus Ogun was the patron deity of the road, the deity who "showed the way," and the founding father of new settlements. Needless to say, his followers spread their traditions as they moved. So, too, did itinerant priests, herbalists, and diviners, who were expected to introduce new religious practices and deities from one place to another. Ritual specialists were hosted by the more notable members of communities, who, as part of their strategy to increase their local power, adopted foreign mystical powers.

Oral traditions repeatedly tell of journeys undertaken by ordinary people to attend ritual festivals in far-off places. Native sons and daughters returned to their homes on these occasions, and representatives of rulers and chiefs also were delegated to attend them. In fact, representatives of the King of Ila, whose Ogun festival Pemberton describes (Ch. 6), had traveled fifty years earlier to the town of Ife (sixty miles away) to attend an Ogun festival. Their presence was noted by anthropologist William Bascom, who had just arrived in that city in 1938 for his first research. Bascom was struck by the stylized sword battles that were part of the rite (Bascom 1987), just as Pemberton was struck by similar battles staged, he was told, so that a town might have peace.

Ritual thus serves as a mnemonic formula for keeping knowledge alive and relatively predictable. Just as Africa's preindustrial ironworkers used sacred ritual as formulae for making iron, Ogun devotees use ritual as formulae for promulgating and perpetuating their deity. Reenactments of battle are foremost among these formulae today and are probably many centuries old.

All of these historical processes have been central concerns of researchers who study the African heritage in the New World. In one way or another their writings also ask to what extent the encounters between indigenous, European, and African systems of thought are obliterating the latter and to what extent such encounters leave them intact or altered. The transfer of African culture to the New World brought about the disappearance of many deities. In the slave trade, African populations were mixed together, and many were deprived of sufficient numbers to perpetuate their traditions; oppression and intolerance prevented many more from expressing them. As a result, some observers came to believe that the New World experience had virtually wiped out the African heritage.

In an influential study, Melville Herskovits attacked this position. "We have a tendency," he wrote, "to emphasize change and to take stability for granted." While Herskovits felt that it was essential to take account of both, he took a firm stand on the side of the "tenaciousness of tradition" (1958:xxxvii and 1937). To buttress his position he argued that the West African heritage was kept alive through the syncretic blending of Christian saints and West African deities. Thus in Brazil, Ogun was understandably merged with St. George the Warrior (Ortiz, Ch. 5), and in Cuba he became San Juan (Barnet 1968:80). Although Herskovits felt that West African meanings remained attached to the syncretized deities, he failed to give those meanings more than cursory attention in his writings and instead placed emphasis on the persistence of forms. Nevertheless, his emphasis on the tenaciousness of African culture left its mark on a generation of scholars.

One of them was Roger Bastide, who pointed out that African culture does not survive randomly, but only if there is a niche for it in the new society (1978:160). To his mind there is a dialectical relationship between the material conditions of life and the ideology that survives. Brown (Ch. 4) puts Bastide's notions to work on her Haitian case, where she points out that Ogun's roles as hunter and blacksmith have no favorable niche, since neither is a significant occupation in this Caribbean society. Instead, she shows that there is a functional relationship between the leader/warrior aspects of the *ogun* concept and the highly visible and powerful place military and political affairs have in Haitian life, and that this is the relationship that is elaborately worked out in Vodou traditions.

Not until recently have scholars who compare Old and New World Africanisms called for a significant shift of focus in the studies of continuity

and change. The most explicit agenda comes from Mintz and Price, who feel
that the study of African culture is empty until we uncover and then compare
similar cognitive orientations in the world views of people on both sides of
the Atlantic (1976:5–7). For them, comparing the form or function of supernatural elements does a disservice to our understanding of historical processes as these processes apply to human ideology. Rather, they suggest we
compare not the structural aspects of cultural representations but what the
representations mean, intend, and express. A byproduct of their approach
is that once carried to its logical conclusion—which is to understand cognitive
meanings—the findings can be used to explain why certain deities grow in
popularity. The key to making convincing comparisons thus rests with the
methods that are used to uncover the meanings of the cultural representations
in question. I will return to a discussion of those methods below.

Ogun in the Present

One of the unanticipated processes in Africa and the Western hemisphere
is, as indicated, that African-derived religious beliefs prosper rather than decline.[4] In Brazil alone, religious groupings that include Ogun have more than
30 million adherents, and they are spreading rapidly to Uruguay and Argentina, where there are scarcely any African descendants. The South American
cults are neither class-, race-, nor ethnicity-bound (Ortiz, Ch. 5), and the
same is true of Santería cults in Cuba (Barnet 1968:80). For instance,
100,000 Umbanda congregations have emerged in Brazil's southernmost
state settled largely by Polish, Italian, and German immigrants.[5] Ogun also
moves along with Haitian and Cuban populations to New York, Florida, California, and Texas (Brown, Ch. 4 and M. Drewal, Ch. 9). Participation in
Santería, Cuba's African-derived faith, is believed to be stronger since the
Cuban Revolution than Roman Catholicism, and it is especially strong in
North America, where it also serves as a support system for newcomers
(Hageman 1973:15). In fact, Miami police are briefed so as not to misinter-
pret some of the sacrificial rites of Cuban-American Santería devotees (*Wall
Street Journal* 18 Oct. 1984). Finally, Caribbean and West African religious
practices are spreading to a growing body of English-speaking North Ameri-
cans, and these new devotees hold ceremonies and have produced, after instruction by Cuban adherents, a theological treatise on African deities (M.
Drewal, Ch. 9).

The growth and vitality of a deity such as Ogun do not take place at the
expense of other faiths or other supernatural forces. Ogun does not coexist
with them in an either/or relationship. All of the societies where Ogun flourishes are culturally and religiously plural societies wherein religious faiths parallel one another.

The coexistence of several traditions poses few if any cognitive problems
for members of plural societies. What does pose problems to the Western

mind is that people often take part in and profess several faiths simultaneously. To some extent, the Western predisposition to think about deities in a monotheistic framework is extended into a monethetic way of classifying membership in cults, churches, temples, mosques, or shrines: a person is a Muslim or a Christian, not both. To many Western observers of West Africa, its peoples should be faithful either to their precontact religious systems or to Christianity, and either to precontact systems or Islam, but not to both. Participation in several religious faiths violates the Western tenet of exclusivity: thou shalt have no other gods before me. Dual or even multiple participation is not, however, contradictory to polytheistic thought, which by definition has an open, inclusive orientation to religious experience. In reality, dual participation is more common than studies of religion indicate, and the concept of "popular religion" also offers a vehicle for its study. Similarly, a category of bi-religiosity offers another vehicle for capturing many people's religious behavior. Many investigations fail to pick up dual participation, mainly because they focus on the faith itself rather than on the members and their practices, choices, or individual beliefs. The essential point about religious systems that parallel one another is that each of them is like an arena: participants come and go. People ordinarily assign one religious label to themselves, but there are no sanctions levied on those who move among several arenas simultaneously. Certainly, in many New World societies, exclusivity is not the norm. Ortiz (Ch. 5) offers many insights into the roles of Candomblé, Umbanda, Spiritism, and institutionalized Catholicism and their abilities to parallel one another and draw on one another's adherents. As in West Africa, Brazilian participants of all backgrounds move in and out of these arenas in increasing numbers.

Today's religious practices also give birth to new ideologies. In a classic study of religion in Java, Geertz (1960:355ff) shows the ways, despite the inevitable ideologic antagonisms that exist in any religiously plural society, in which boundaries between religious world views are blurred and new views come into being. The nub of his argument is that religion cannot be limited to certain times and places. Hence, social interchanges among peoples in Javanese society lead to interchanges of values and behaviors. The same is true in the societies discussed here. Among Yoruba-, Fon-, and Edo-speaking peoples, who figure so prominently in the West African cultural systems presented in this volume, Christianity and Islam have come to play strong parts in people's lives. Yet the blending of Christianity and precontact religious orientations is so marked that new forms have emerged that can loosely be described as African Christianity—a generic label that glosses a proliferation of well-developed and institutionalized, independent churches and their overarching governing bodies. The same is true of African Islam. The blendings range on a continuum that moves from the indigenous precontact religious systems to orthodox European, mission-type systems of Christianity or orthodox Islamic brotherhoods. There are even triple blendings of Christianity, Islam, and indigenous systems. To classify them would be to misrepresent the

nature of the phenomena or the abilities of adherents to layer ideas on one
another, make analogies, or otherwise subtract and add in a variety of ways.
Better to say that the present religious landscape is in flux—more complicated
than this brief summation indicates—and that the elements that make up ritual and belief overlap and intertwine in a bewildering complexity.

Be that as it may, the outcome so far as Ogun is concerned is that he remains firmly embedded in a repertory of mystical ideas that perpetuate ancient themes, yet contribute to the making of new combinations, new religious groupings, and new interpretations of the ultimate questions that have
puzzled humans since the beginning of time.

Methods for Uncovering the Meanings of Ogun

Earlier I indicated that devotees see Ogun as having a host of meanings
and that they came about historically through continued layerings, fusions,
and so on. In one West African community alone at least six separate Ogun
themes are developed by as many separate cult groups.[6] If we were to compare
meanings in various cult groups on both sides of the Atlantic, a more daunting
number of themes would emerge. Suffice it to say here that the variations
in meanings and themes are sufficiently marked that we may well ask if Ogun
is one god or many. The answer to dealing with variation lies in two proposi-
tions. First is the insistence by Durkheim and Mauss (1963:78) that a deity
collects and classifies information. The second, by Lévi-Strauss (1966:36), is
that information of this sort is not collected randomly.

Attributing certain things to a deity is like placing these things under the
same rubric or in the same class. Each class (or "domain" as it should be
called when one is dealing with a polytheistic religious system) is ordered according to logical principles. A typical one is the single common denominator
principle whereby phenomena are classed according to one feature. Using this
principle, one might propose that all things relating to iron belong in the
Ogun domain, and therefore this is *the* diagnostic principle for deciding
whether or not something is Ogun-related. In some New World contexts,
however, iron has receded compared to other elements (Brown, Ch. 4). Likewise, at Yoruba hunters' funerals iron is not a featured symbol (Ajuwọn, Ch.
8). How, then, do we find logic in the way Ogun classes information?

The principle by which Ogun information is classed accepts variation in
meanings. Rather than being an exclusive principle, it is inclusive. The technical term for this kind of classification is polythetic.[7] In a polythetic system
of classification, no one feature gives definition to a domain. A polythetic system identifies a domain through combinations of features. Again, no one
thing need be present to make a deity Ogun. Rather, a sufficient number of
features should be present to allow an identification to be made (Douglas
1978:15). A useful way of dealing with polythetic classification is to think,
as Wittgenstein proposed, of a chain of "family resemblances," where the

defining attribute changes from one link to the next (Needham 1975:350). Take, for example, the following sets:

ABCD
AB DE
A CDE
  BC EF.

There is no one monotypic feature that gives definition to all of the sets. Yet there is sufficient overlap in the features of each set to establish a family or a chain of overlapping resemblances. In polythetic classifications, stress is laid on each set's having a simple majority of the defining features, and not on assigning decisive weight to any one of them.

Thinking of Ogun as a system of classifying information—according to an inclusive, or polythetic, principle—shifts the discussion of meaning from singular to plural. It therefore relieves us of finding a single common denominator with which to identify and then compare this divine figure. Taken as a domain of related ideas, diversity and unity in meaning can then be thought of as being simultaneously present. One of the most useful implications of being able to think of meanings in the plural is that we can, by extension, visualize the processes by which some meanings remain unchanged while, at the same time, other meanings can be added, subtracted, or altered, little by little, over time and space. It allows us, further, to make order out of what seems to be contradiction, diversity, and unevenness. Needless to say, the logic used by insiders in assigning meanings to a deity's domain is intuitive. For the outsider, it is artificial and done mainly for heuristic purposes.

A problem for the outside analyst comes in drawing boundaries, since a chain of overlapping resemblances can, theoretically, extend indefinitely. Drawing lines around a domain is like giving a medical diagnosis: a certain amount of indeterminacy must be accepted. Nevertheless, when certain clusters of symptoms are present, there is a strong indication that the diagnosis is correct. The rule of thumb when dealing with cultural representations is to think of a deity's domain as sufficiently porous and adaptable to allow for creativity, but sufficiently stable to reject distortion.

Still, a deity does not absorb information randomly. The meanings in a domain do not shift and adapt to new stimuli without consequences. When the weight of distinctive features in any one domain tips too far in the direction of another domain we can say that a transformation has taken place. Orpheus may well have presided over the prototypical domain from which Christ emerged (Goodenough Vol. IV 1953:36), but over time the Christian messiah developed his own distinctive features to the extent that a new deity, and with it a new domain, emerged. Ortiz (Ch. 5) indicates a transformation may be occurring in the ideology of Ogun in Brazil's fifty-year-old Umbanda religion. Unlike the older (150 years) Candomblé, which adheres closely to its West African antecedents, Umbanda represents an authentically Brazilian world view—a coming together of African, European, and native American ideolo-

gies. As part of this synthesis, Ogun has gained sufficient stature to become
a symbol of Brazilian national identity. Ogun of Umbanda is familiar: an aggressive, violent defender in the fight for a just and balanced social order.
But more and more he represents the positive side in what Umbanda adherents see as a clear division between good and evil, something that is not done
in Candomblé or West African world views. The transformation of the
Umbanda Ogun into a force for good is not complete, for he is the only deity
in the new Umbanda pantheon who can still move freely between both evil
and good forces. Whether or not he will retain an ability to mediate between
the two sides, or be compelled to represent only one side, and thus represent
a major shift in cognitive orientations, only time will tell.

Given the problems with drawing boundaries, how can we, analytically, delineate domains? A first step is to find *redundance*. Needless to say, we are
looking for redundant clusters of meanings, not a single cluster of meanings.
A pioneering, but neglected, study that stresses the search for redundance
is Erwin Goodenough's twelve-volume examination of religious symbols common to the Mediterranean world in Greco-Roman times that derived from
the Old and New Testaments. In it Goodenough is deeply concerned with
the problem of bringing objectivity to the task of interpreting the value and
meaning of sacred symbols. He suggests that by accumulating scores of repeated cases, we establish a probability, a hypothesis, for assigning meanings,
in his case, to symbolic representations (1953 V.I:31). Since this study, but
independently, others have followed the same route. In his study of the meanings in Chinese systems of geomancy, Feuchtwang searches for *constant* symbols (1974:13). Obeyesekere's monumental work on the goddess Pattini,
found in Hindu, Buddhist, and Jain systems of belief, concentrates on *agreement* (1984:334). And Turner, in his study of the many legends and historic
and literary accounts of the twelfth-century tragedy of Thomas Becket, seeks
out sequences of events that add up to a *redundant paradigm*, which, he believes, is ultimately drawn from early Christian traditions (1974:60ff) to explain the meaning and experience of martyrdom.[8]

The studies mentioned share the decided advantage of relying on written
texts. Ogun is not, or was not until recently, associated with written traditions. His religious systems do not have priests, monks, or other specialists
who have regular channels for contacting one another or exchanging ideas.
They do not have overarching institutional bodies that standardize, perpetuate, or promulgate the ideology of Ogun. The redundancies that we see in
the representations of Ogun, whether Old or New World, are transmitted primarily by word of mouth, among cult priests, priestesses, and adherents,
through the repeated telling of traditions, the performance of rituals, and the
production and reproduction of emblems and icons. In this, Ogun defies
Weberian predictions which suggest that for global expansion to take place,
a religious system must have systematic and depersonalized modes for dis-
seminating its ideology. The unities that exist in the diverse body of Ogun
representations—as revealed by redundant themes found in many societies

of the two hemispheres—are achieved not with the help of a supporting bureaucratic, codified apparatus, but through the power of custom.

The study of custom in unwritten traditions, while conventionally the preserve of anthropologists, is concentrated in what is now more broadly known as the symbolic school. Like those who work with texts, humanist and social scientist adherents of this school try to do two things: interpret cultural representations found in oral traditions, rituals, metaphors, symbols, and artifacts in ways that are faithful to the actors and, then, translate their findings into terms that can be appreciated by outsiders. The foundations were laid by French structuralists, whose well-known work on myths erred in the direction of interpretations that were so general as to be truisms, and American ethnoscientists who in studying systems of classification remained too faithful to cultural context to generalize about what may be universal to these systems. For symbolists, the key to a middle-level analysis has come to rest primarily in their use of methods, recommended above, that elicit redundancies in cultural meanings and, thanks to the redundance, intepretations that can be verified.

M. Drewal's study (Ch. 9) of Ogun ritual dance is faithful to the symbolic school. She demonstrates that the meaning of Ogun is clearly displayed in the repeated qualities of movement—quick, direct, and forceful, with an explosive release—of dancers and devotees. Not content to limit the analysis to one level of experience, she also describes the ways performers bombard the senses—sight, sound, touch, and in some cases taste—with recurring reminders of their deity's distinctive qualities. Dancers carry iron weapons, especially sharp-bladed ones, and refer to a species of snake that is quick and deadly. The poetic chants that accompany performances contain percussive sounds and word-images—"he kills with one blow"—that evoke swift destruction. Over and again images of Ogun are impressed upon the observer.

In contrast, a pacific, not to say, poetic—"death has cut off our flower"—dimension of Ogun is revealed in Ajuwọn's presentation (Ch. 8) of Yoruba hunters' funerals. Ajuwọn, too, draws on a wide range of ethnographic evidence: chants of funeral musicians, actions of hunting-guild leaders who preside over the ceremonies, and items from the deceased's hunting kit that are conspicuously displayed. The portrait that emerges is not a ruthless figure, but a social role model from whom "the wise will draw inspiration." In funeral dirges Ogun is heroic leader—"lion of the thick forest"; provider—"one who never runs away on sighting a beggar"; protector—"my breadwinner alone"; and so on. An almost limitless repertoire plays on the nurturing side of the deity, repeatedly presenting the same themes to stress the point.

Clearly, eliciting the patterns from one context does not reveal the full meaning of a cultural representation. Thus, a second step is to ask *what* things people put together, *how* they are put together, and *why*. These questions are asked by O'Flaherty in an exhaustive study of the mythology of the Hindu god Siva, who, like Ogun but for different reasons, also is labeled as a creator/destroyer. These questions, she stresses, allow the outsider to comprehend a deity as subjects comprehend him or her (1973:2, 12). At the risk of oversimplifying a complex argument, it may be said that O'Flaherty asks why Hindu traditions consistently present Siva as erotic, virile, and passionate, on one hand, and as ascetic, pious, and withdrawn on the other. Earlier explanations of these seemingly contradictory traditions were that they either were anomalous or that one set of traits had been imposed on another and therefore was unfaithful to the ancient meaning of Siva. O'Flaherty argued, to the contrary, that both sets of traits are put together for a reason. Like love and hate, the "act of desire and the conquest of desire" are brought together to show that erotic and ascetic impulses are constantly interacting. Each set of impulses produces its own form of "heat" and each presents an unending play on the destructive and creative potential in desire (1973:5, 35).

Accordingly, when we look at Ogun it is not sufficient to extract one set of redundant patterns. If we elicit only the violent qualities of Ogun that are portrayed in the possession-dance context (M. Drewal, Ch. 9), our understanding of Ogun is incomplete. The same is true if, in analyzing Ajuwon's funeral context (Ch. 8), we stress only the nurturing and protective side of Ogun. Almost every context presents or in some way alludes to several dimensions of a deity. Babalola's study of Ogun songs (Ch. 7) uncovers themes that reveal many sides of the same unity, particularly the strengths and weaknesses that inevitably exist in a single being. And Pemberton's study of kingship ritual (Ch. 6) shows that Ogun is used as a symbol of political life and of many competing, but coexisting, agendas involving order and disorder.

Still in all, no single context explores all possible combinations of meanings that exist in Ogun's domain. Neither do they display the important creative dynamic that leads one set of combinations to generate another set.

When the several interpretations of Ogun in this volume are brought together and compared we find that each of them presents varying insights into the philosophy of life that Ogun embodies. Again, each interpretation is incomplete in some respect, for only in their totality do meanings and intentions become clear to the outside observer and, in some cases, to the insider as well. Drawing on the essays, then, let me offer an interpretation of the complete Ogun.

Interpreting the Meanings of Ogun

It is clear by this point that Ogun is repeatedly linked to positive and negative deeds. As a consequence of his harmful or beneficial acts he is viewed either as a lonely, isolated figure—the quintessential marginal man (Armstrong, Ch. 2)—or, in almost complete contrast, as a central force whose revolutionary and creative acts give birth to new social forms (Barnes and Ben-Amos, Ch. 3). Ogun kills and he creates. The two attributes are joined, for devotees are fully aware that all actions, especially those of leaders, warriors, or benefactors, are as advantageous to some as they are harmful to others.

One of the fundamental thematic combinations, therefore, is that Ogun is both destroyer and creator. These qualities are put together like two sides of an equation: destroyer = creator, or the obverse, creator = destroyer. From these equations it is possible to generate a series of permutations that are all faithful to Ogun. For instance, as a blacksmith, Ogun creates the tools and weapons that, when put to use by some occupational groups, increase productivity, but that also, when put to use by others, destroy the innocent. As a revolutionary warrior he eliminates an old order so that a new one can be established. To aid the powerless members of society, he takes from the powerful. Finally, as a hunter he depletes the natural world in order to nurture his own cultural world.

Rather than resolution, an unending tension is maintained between the two sides of either equation: destruction is creative and creation is destructive. The notion of an equation must be used here, rather than that of paradox or opposition, since the concept of opposition distorts the way devotees perceive their god. In African cosmologies where Ogun is a central figure, destruction and creation are two aspects of a unity that cannot be broken into opposing parts.

On a more abstract level, it can be said that Ogun is a metaphoric representation of the realization that people create the means to destroy themselves. He stands for humans' collective attempts to govern, not what is out of control in nature, but what is out of control in culture. He represents not so much what is inexplicable, unseen, or unknown, as what is known but not under control. He is a symbolic recognition of human limitations—human frailty, as Babalola (Ch. 7) puts it in his exploration of Ogun's character—and it is this kind of limitation that accounts for his lack of control.

Still the combinations are unfinished, because Ogun also represents human triumphs over limitations. This facet of the deity is exposed by many West African peoples who employ Ogun imagery to mark and celebrate each stage of their societal development. Ogun taught humans to use fire, make iron, build cities, centralize government, conquer neighbors, and create empires. At each step of the way, in this folk model of social change, Ogun is the metaphoric representation of a transformation brought about by human effort (Barnes and Ben-Amos, Ch. 3).

The meanings of Ogun are as rich in philosophy as they are in metaphor. The philosophic wisdom found in Ogun ideology treats the inner experience associated with both destructive and creative acts, and it is particularly poignant in its portrayal of the loneliness that inevitably accompanies either one of them. In a well-known legend and its many variations—all of which focus on civil war, rebellion, and other forms of political conflict—the warrior Ogun sentences himself to eternal isolation, in some versions going so far as to commit suicide, after unwittingly slaying his own people in a frenzy of rage over their lack of "hospitality" (Babalọla Ch. 7). The plight of the human condition is the punishment inflicted by self-insight and self-recognition. Humans realize that their actions have consequences that they cannot predict and, as a result, that no perfect balance can be brought between being in control and being out of control. The sole corrective comes in maintaining vigilance through self-contemplation, and inevitably this is an isolating experience. The message is reinforced in a popular Trinidadian myth in which a warrior-prince kills his favored, invalid brother in a fit of jealousy. As a punishment he is sentenced to guard forever the gates (meaning the morals) of his town and to serve as a solitary reminder to himself and others of the consequences of allowing power to fall out of control.[9]

The inventor or artist, like the warrior or leader, also lives on the margins of society in order to realize sufficient freedom to make the kinds of connections that lead to innovative expression. The dilemma is captured in H. Drewal's discussion (Ch. 10) of Yoruba body artists who struggle to avoid psychic and social isolation. Moreover, it is a recurring theme in the work of Soyinka, who identifies with Ogun and, in a series of essays, poems, and other writings, explores the meaning of the predicament posed by his alter ego. For him, Ogun is a tragic figure because he presides over humans' struggles to master themselves. The Ogun artist either labors to create explanation where there is none, or dooms himself to live in an unbearable void. The predicament is posed as an existential battle between being and nothingness. Balance is achieved through willpower. For Soyinka, *Will* triumphs when the individual is reconciled with "the paradoxical truth of destructiveness and creativeness in acting man" (1969:126).

We could not be humans, so the philosophy of Ogun goes, seeking control of ourselves and our social existence, if we did not experience the out-of-control phases that are necessary parts of reproducing and expanding the powers that make human existence possible. This is the constructive/destructive cycle that must be appreciated if we are to grasp the meanings of Ogun. In the Old World, one of the emblems of Ogun is a snake biting its tail, feeding on itself, and thereby engaging in an unending repetition of destruction in order to regenerate. The image of the snake is consistent with the Ogun world view, wherein what we do to ourselves in a self-destructive way is an inevitable aspect of the self-constructive process. This is our fate. This is what isolates us as a species and as individuals. We know ourselves as others never do. The helplessness that comes from self-knowledge coexists with the power—Soyinka's *Will*—to overcome that helplessness.

The Power in Meaning

The power in the Ogun philosophy of life resides in its plasticity and its transportability. Through a host of related notions, layered and fused onto one another, yet packaged as a single concept, the various creative/ destructive potentials of human existence are recognized and given force. Ogun is a profoundly satisfying symbolic expression of a human dilemma: how to balance the need for constraint against the need for freedom. In belief systems of West African origin, this dilemma is reconciled through a supernatural transformation. The power of the idea is given form, a named identity, for example Ogun, so as to control it and then draw inner strength from that control.

Ogun, and appropriately so for a deity, has an ability to bring together notions from worldly and spiritual realms. So in the old Kingdom of Ila, civic unrest brought about by competition among powerful segments of the community is interpreted as divine anger. Pemberton (Ch. 6) aptly sums it up as the sacrality of violence. The notions from each realm are presented as extremes, for this is the way, well-known to students of myth, that a people's preoccupations are heightened, given weight, remembered, and passed on. Extremes make the point. The universe, as we view it through a deity's eyes, is revealed by the ways in which extreme thoughts and extreme deeds complement and balance one another.

The meanings of a deity are revealed, in great measure therefore, by knowing which extremes are put together and why. In the case of Ogun, the notions of control/lack of control, sacrality/violence, or protection/destruction are brought into a perpetual state of interaction for a reason. Only when the pairs are complete is a balance of power reached.

In the world view of the peoples who include Ogun in their cosmic realm, power is a single, neutral force. There is a marked contrast here between West African and Western Christian modes of thought. In the West, positive and negative—familiarly glossed as evil and good—can be divided into opposing parts and symbolized by Satan and God. In West Africa, positive and negative power is not separate. Power is singular, and therefore what we in the West see as dual and capable of being divided into two mystical notions cannot be divided in African thought. For the latter, power exists in a single supernatural representation.[10]

Indeed, it is unthinkable that superhuman figures—mirroring as they do the human condition—display only one side of their character. The duty of devotees is not to appeal to one aspect of their divine benefactors. Their duty is to bring all of their aspects—their full supernatural equations, as it were— into balance through sacrifice and other ritual ministrations, just as they try to bring balance and harmony into everyday life.

In bringing together ideas from different levels of experience, and showing their complementarity, the African world view is designed to balance what is otherwise out of balance. In this way, a divinity suggests a theory of the way the world works. A theory of this type is significant in that it is stated metaphorically, viz., a creator is a destroyer.

Ogun is a metaphor, but not a simple metaphor. Simple metaphors liken one thing to another: "screaming headlines" or "heart of stone." They are applied for a specific purpose to a specific event, person, or thing. Thus they do a one-time job; they are ephemeral. They cannot be changed, for to change them is to lose them. Perhaps this is the reason that simple metaphors are used mainly in studies of world view that are limited to local, monocultural situations.[11]

Ogun is a root metaphor (see Pepper 1966:91–92). A root metaphor *names* the things that are likened to one another. The name gives the root metaphor permanence and therefore it can do its job many times over. When a psychiatrist says his patient is suffering from an *Oedipus* complex he can name and summarize what otherwise might take pages to explain, and he can use the label repeatedly. By the same token, when Haitian devotees call a despotic leader *Ogun Panama*, after a real figure, they condense into one label a complex historical essay on the uses and abuses of power (Brown, Ch. 4). *Ogun Panama* was first applied to one person; later other despotic leaders were given the same label. By naming the metaphor, Haitians were free to adjust or augment its content.

The concept of root metaphor is a middle-level analytical tool. Other such concepts are *emphatic symbol*, which is applied to the Christian cross; *root paradigm*, applied to Christian martyrs; *conceptual archetype* and *archetype*, applied elsewhere to Ogun himself.[12] Root metaphor, like the other concepts, focuses on cultural representations by hovering between two levels of analysis: one that stays close to the empirical ground, as does ethnoscience, and another that soars to the language of universal principles such as deep structures of the mind, as does structuralism. Root metaphor operates on a middle level because it is an abstraction. Yet it is an abstraction formulated by the minds that are being explored. As such, a generalization about the phenomenon under consideration already has been made. Furthermore, this generalization lends itself to interpretations that can be confirmed either by the actors or, on the basis of recurring patterns, by the analyst. Because it is created by the actors, the generalization retains its cultural uniqueness. But because it is an abstraction, it lends itself to being translated from the terms of one culture into those of another.

Ultimately, once a root metaphor is named it becomes a protected category within which many ways of replicating, restating, or reformulating an idea can be tried out. The greater its ability to incorporate and adapt to new experience, the more powerful it becomes. This is why a root metaphor such as Ogun has the power to operate cross-culturally. The meanings contained in the root metaphor are the result of interactions that, once energized, are capable of acting on their own to incorporate an ever-wider range of insights and meanings (Turner 1974:28–29). Hence the permanent, named quality of the metaphor is the package that makes a domain of ideas dynamic, and that allows the ideas to expand, spread, and change over time.

Discussion and Conclusion

I opened this chapter with the suggestion that reorientations are needed if we wish to explain the popularity of an African deity, and the growing strength of the religious systems in which he is a significant figure, in light of predictions that global deities and global faiths would eliminate small ones. Let me summarize the responses to this challenge by first indicating why previous orientations lead us astray.

One of the stumbling blocks in the study of contemporary religious processes comes from the fact that religious systems are still typologized. By now this is an implicit act. Perhaps the best known explicit typology was brought to life by Weber (1946:292–97; 1963:1–19) and elaborated by his followers as the great and little religious traditions (e.g., Marriott 1955:171–72). Because these categories were grounded in an evolutionary perspective, the tendency when the two types of system were studied in the same frame of reference was—and here is where the legacy persists—to give the great traditions, such as Islam or Christianity, a central position and the little traditions a peripheral one. The rationale for the dominance of great traditions is that they have highly developed bureaucratic organizations, standardized and written doctrines, institutionalized methods for promulgating beliefs, and highly developed systems of ethics. In comparison, little traditions are characterized as fragmented, localized, and largely associated with illiteracy. When these attributes are compared, global ideologies are seen to influence; little ideologies, to respond. Given the evolutionary bias, the very act of typing religious systems has the effect of predetermining the direction of change: participants of small systems are converted to, or their ideologies are merged with, or replaced by, world systems. As Weber put it, the stronger systems vanquish the weaker (1963:17).

Although I have reduced the arguments to their stark essentials—for they are more subtle in their totality than can be indicated here—I have done so to call attention to the role typologies continue to play in shaping our thinking about religious change. The kind of weighted typology that stems from Weber and great and little tradition writers clearly obscures the vitality of small religious ideologies even when they do survive and thrive. At least one scholar has attempted to rectify the problem by calling attention to an extraordinary migration and fusion of ideas, taken from all types of religious systems, which he goes so far as to call a contemporary worldwide religious revolution (Wilson 1976:42). We know that the changes associated with this revolution have no correlation with the types of system that are spreading or the types of ideologies that are mixed together. But in other respects, actual investigations of these recent ideological migrations and their implications are still in their infancy.

There is a need, then, to shift the point of reference away from studies that take as a starting point the fact that global faiths and their deities dominate the religious landscape. Instead, we need to start from the premise that several religious traditions may coexist in one context, and that participants may be bi-religious, and to work through the complexity that ensues from these reoriented perspectives.

Typologies offer a second challenge, in that they also classify deities according to the systems of which they are a part. Weber thought of them as urban and pagan (1963:xli). The stumbling block in this case is that deities are categorized according to the sphere in which they operate (universal or parochial) or their functional relationship with followers (personal or impersonal), but not according to what they mean. In an influential series of articles, Horton (1971 and 1975) takes a similar approach. He argues that the efficacy of the high gods of universal faiths derives from their being sufficiently abstract, all-explaining, all-knowing, and all-encompassing to provide ideological bridges between diverse peoples who seek a common code for their interactions. By contrast, the lesser deities are limited by their specificity. They fail to link diverse peoples together, because they are concrete, because they are parochial and therefore tied to concrete places and groups, and because they represent only part of the cosmos. They are like the ancient Roman god Mercury, who represented a few parts of the universe—commerce, manual skill, eloquence, cleverness, travel, and thievery—and who therefore depended on a full pantheon to provide a complete cosmological explanatory system for Rome's faithful. Finally, the deities of parochial religious systems focus on pragmatic functions, and in this they differ from most Western religious systems. African religions tend to dwell on predicting, explaining, and controlling day-to-day circumstances such as illness, poverty, infertility, or bad luck; Ogun followers focus particularly on their fear of accidents and other dangers. Stress on pragmatism is a part of non-Western traditions to a greater degree than in Western religious traditions, which put strong emphasis on transcendental functions, such as preparing for the hereafter or helping devotees gain faith or inner "grace."

While Horton's typology and others like it can be faulted in their inability to capture a vast middle range of supernatural types, or to explore the degrees to which transcendental or pragmatic levels of involvement are truly meaningful, the more fundamental problem is that the qualities used to compare and contrast divinities are inappropriate to the levels of explanation that are sought.

The power of an ideology or a deity to gain a privileged place in the world resides, in large part, in what it explains and in the way the explanation is communicated. This is the second point to which we need to be reoriented. The measure of universality of a supernatural figure need not be ascertained from qualities that define, say, a deity's impersonal or personal relationship to a follower, or a deity's ability to function in all or part of the cosmos, or even a deity's pragmatic or transcendental relationship with a devotee. The ability to appeal to a universal, by which I mean culturally plural, audience rests on what a deity means: what, in fact, a deity signifies, symbolizes, suggests, and intends and the ways these elements are expressed. As with many world figures—Oedipus, Siva, Aphrodite, or Thor—the abilities to capture and then communicate one part of the human experience are the very qualities that give such figures a metacultural appeal.

All deities provide a theory of what life is about and resolutions to the problems life raises. The more economically and profoundly a theory of life is expressed, the more likely it is to transcend the limitations of one place or one culture, that is, the more likely it is to become a world theory (Pepper 1966:92). Some theories of human nature, like scientific theories, are more profound than others in the ideas they bring together. The theory of relativity is one of them. Some theories, like metaphors, have great powers to explain life's mysteries because they combine notions from different levels of experience. They fill voids. They explain the ways the world works, in succinct, easy-to-comprehend and easy-to-apply ways. When it comes to the Oguns of the world, we need to know from what philosophical principles they derive, and what they express and do for the people concerned. Meanings can bring them to the forefront of our consciousness. The meanings attached to a divinity determine which explanations of life we reject and which explanations, to return to the point with which this essay began, we elevate to a privileged class.

NOTES

1. To be consistent, I use the Nigerian spelling of Ogun throughout. He is Gu in the People's Republic of Benin (formerly Dahomey), Ogum in Brazil, and Ogou in Haiti. Other variants are given in Armstrong (Ch. 2).

2. Local and general (metacultural) ideology need not be homogeneous, as Tambiah shows in his study of Thai Buddhist spirit cults. There is a constant interaction between the two levels, but there are quite specific, local ways of working through an idea. Looking at local traditions is useful, he suggests, for illuminating ancient ideologies, although the conclusions are never more than "inspired guesswork" (1970:369–72).

3. This ceremony is held by Igala and Idoma peoples, who live near the confluence of the Niger and Benue rivers in today's Nigeria. A similar ceremony was performed in Abomey, capital of the Old Kingdom of Dahomey. For a discussion of the latter, and a map showing locations of the three groups of people in question, see Map 3.1.

4. Evidence for Ogun's growth comes primarily from southwestern Nigeria. In 1939 a Yoruba scholar felt Ogun was one of the four or five most widespread deities (Fadipe 1970:261). By the 1960s researchers felt Ogun was possibly the most widely venerated national deity (Parratt and Doi 1969:112). It is significant to note in this respect that Ogun's popularity did not decline, but grew, at the same time there was a sharp decline in the numbers of hunters, smiths, smelters, and warriors, who were the core of Ogun's following in precolonial times but who were replaced by the introduction of Western technology and colonial restrictions on internal warfare. See also Barnes (1980:36–37).

5. The popularity of Umbanda is discussed by Hoge 1983, Pressel 1980, and Lerch 1980.

6. Deirdre LaPin, personal communication. See also Barnes (1980:20).

7. I am indebted to Ivan Karp for suggesting that the polythetic principle is applicable here.

8. Others who stress similar approaches are Keyes, who focuses on the ideology of Karma (1983), and Friedrich, who examines the goddess Aphrodite (1978).

9. I thank Patricia Alleyne for bringing this myth to my attention. See Elder (1972:25–26).

10. Watts treats the Western tendency to make separations and suggests that the illusion of opposition interferes with our ability to grasp essential continuities (1963).

11. Rosaldo and Atkinson (1975) make use of metaphors to show the relationship between beliefs about human health and principles of nature in Ilongot (Philippine) world view.

12. For more detailed discussion and application of these concepts see Firth (1973:91), Turner (1978:248), Black (1962:241), and Verger (1982:32–33).

REFERENCES CITED

Barnes, Sandra T. 1980. *Ogun: An Old God for a New Age*, Philadelphia: ISHI.

Barnet, Miguel (ed.). 1968. *The Autobiography of a Runaway Slave*, by Esteban Montejo, New York: Pantheon.

Bascom, William. 1987. "The Olojo Festival at Ife, 1937," in *Time Out of Time: Essays on the Festival*, A. Falassi (ed.), Albuquerque: University of New Mexico Press, pp. 62–73.

Bastide, Roger. 1978. *The African Religions of Brazil: Toward a Sociology of the Interpenetration of Civilizations*, H. Sebba (trans.), Baltimore: Johns Hopkins University Press.

Black, Max. 1962. *Models and Metaphors*, Ithaca: Cornell University Press.

Douglas, Mary. 1978. *Cultural Bias*, Occasional Paper 34, The Royal Anthropological Institute of Great Britain and Ireland.

Durkheim, E., and M. Mauss. 1963. *Primitive Classification*, Chicago: University of Chicago Press.

Elder, J. D. (ed.). 1972. *Ma Rose Point: An Anthology of Rare Legends and Folk Tales from Trinidad & Tobago*, Port-of-Spain: National Cultural Council of Trinidad and Tobago.

Fadipẹ, N. A. 1970. *The Sociology of the Yoruba*, Ibadan: University of Ibadan Press.

Feuchtwang, Stephan D. R. 1974. *An Anthropological Analysis of Chinese Geomancy*, Ventiane, Laos: Vithagna.

Firth, Raymond. 1973. *Symbols: Public and Private*, London: Athlone.

Friedrich, Paul. 1978. *The Meaning of Aphrodite*, Chicago: University of Chicago Press.

Geertz, Clifford. 1960. *The Religion of Java,* New York: The Free Press.

Goodenough, Erwin R. 1953. *Jewish Symbols in the Greco-Roman Period*, 12 vols., New York: Pantheon.

Hageman, Alice. 1973. "Santería in Black Experience," *Cuba Resource Center Newsletter*, V.2(6):15–20.

Herskovits, Melville. 1937. "African Gods and Catholic Saints in New World Negro Belief," *American Anthropologist*, XXXIX(4):635–43.

———. 1958. *The Myth of the Negro Past*, Boston: Beacon Press (first pub. 1941).

Hoge, Warren. 1983. "Macumba: Brazil's Pervasive Cults," *New York Times Magazine*, Aug. 21, pp. 30–33, 75–82.
Horton, Robin, 1971. "African Conversion," *Africa*, 41(2):85–108.
———. 1975. "On the Rationality of Conversion," Pts. I and II, *Africa*, 45(3):219–35 and (4):373–99.
Jones, Adam. 1983. *German Sources for West African History, 1599–1669*, Weisbaden: Franz Steiner Verlag.
Keyes, Charles F. 1983. "Introduction: The Study of Popular Ideas of Karma," in *Karma: An Anthropological Inquiry*, C. F. Keyes and E. V. Daniel (eds.), Berkeley and Los Angeles: University of California Press, pp. 1–24.
Lerch, Patricia B. 1980. "Spirit Mediums in Umbanda Evangelizada of Porto Alegre, Brazil: Dimensions of Power and Authority," in *A World of Women*, E. Bourguignon (ed.), New York: Praeger.
Lévi-Strauss, Claude. 1966. *The Savage Mind*, Chicago: University of Chicago Press.
Marriott, McKim. 1955. "Little Communities in an Indigenous Civilization," in *Studies in the Little Community*, M. Marriott (ed.), Chicago: University of Chicago Press.
Mintz, S. W., and R. Price. 1976. *An Anthropological Approach to the Afro-American Past: A Caribbean Perspective*, Philadelphia: ISHI.
Needham, Rodney. 1975. "Polythetic Classification," *Man* NS V.10(3):349–69.
Obeyesekere, Gananath. 1984. *The Cult of the Goddess Pattini*, Chicago: University of Chicago Press.
O'Flaherty, Wendy D. 1973. *Asceticism and Eroticism in the Mythology of Siva*, London: Oxford University Press.
Parratt, J. K., and A. R. I. Doi. 1969. "Syncretism in Yorubaland: A Religious or a Sociological Phenomenon," *Practical Anthropology*, 16(3):109–13.
Pepper, Stephen C. 1966. *World Hypotheses: A Study in Evidence*, Berkeley and Los Angeles: University of California Press.
Pressel, Esther. 1980. "Spirit Magic in the Social Relations between Men and Women (São Paulo, Brazil)," in E. Bourguignon (ed.), *A World of Women*, New York: Praeger.
Rosaldo, M. Z., and J. M. Atkinson. 1975. "Man the Hunter and Woman: Metaphors for the Sexes in Ilongot Magical Spells," in R. Willis (ed.), *The Interpretation of Symbols*, New York: John Wiley & Sons, pp. 43–75.
Scheub, Harold. 1975. *The Xhosa Ntsomi*, Oxford: Oxford University Press.
Soyinka, Wole. 1967. *Idanre and Other Poems*, London: Methuen.
———. 1969. "The Fourth Stage," in D. W. Jefferson (ed.), *The Morality of Art*, London: Routledge & Kegan Paul, pp. 119–34.
Tambiah, S. J. 1970. *Buddhism and the Spirit Cults in North-East Thailand*, Cambridge: Cambridge University Press.
Thompson, R. F. 1983. *Flash of the Spirit*, New York: Random House.
Turner, Victor W. 1974. *Dramas, Fields and Metaphors: Symbolic Action in Human Society*, Ithaca: Cornell University Press.
———. 1978. *Image and Pilgrimage in Christian Culture*, New York: Columbia University Press.
van der Merwe, N. J., and D. H. Avery. 1987. "Science and Magic in African Technology: Traditional Iron Smelting in Malawi," *Africa* 57(2):143–72.
Verger, Pierre F. 1982. *Orisha: Les Dieux Yorouba en Afrique et en Nouveau Monde*, Paris: Editions A. M. Métailié.
Watts, Alan W. 1963. *The Two Hands of God: The Myth of Polarity*, New York: Collier Books.
Weber, Max. 1946. *From Max Weber*, H. H. Gerth and C. Wright Mills (ed. and trans.), New York: Oxford University Press.

————. 1963. *The Sociology of Religion*, E. Fischoff (trans.), Boston: Beacon Press (first pub. in German, 1922).

Williams, Denis. 1974. *Icon and Image: A Study of Sacred and Secular Forms of African Classical Art*, London: Allen Lane.

Wilson, Bryan. 1976. *Contemporary Transformations of Religion*, Oxford: Oxford University Press.

PART ONE

The History and Spread of Ogun in Old and New Worlds

Robert G. Armstrong

2

The Etymology of the Word "Ògún"

The cult of Ògún is highly elaborated in Yoruba country and shows amazing vitality among people directly concerned with modern technology. In 1974, for example, the drivers of the Ibadan University Motor Transport system performed a sacrifice to Ògún in the presence of the Vice-Chancellor and a dozen or so of the other high officials of the university. One of the drivers, who came from Igara, an Igbira (or Ebira) town in the northwestern extension of Bendel State, was a particularly enthusiastic participant in the dances that followed the sacrifice of a dog. I cite this case as an illustration of the point made by Barnes that the Ògún cult continues to appeal to socially rather marginal men who are directly involved in the use of modern machines constructed largely of iron and steel. She goes so far as to call the Ògún cult "the cult of revolution," i.e., "the technological revolution brought about by the introduction of iron-making and the occupational specialization necessitated by that innovation" (1980:44).

As a deity, Ògún (and his cult, which is very male-oriented) was traditionally especially concerned with the smelting and forging of iron, with war, and with hunting. As Barnes says, it seems likely that the Yoruba cult is an amalgam and synthesis of originally separate cults. It has long been known that the cult is by no means restricted to the Yoruba. Indeed, an examination of the cult as it appears outside the Yoruba area (see Map 3.1) may well clarify its origins and some of the deepest meanings attached to it.

In Dahomey, now the Republic of Benin, Gǔ is the god of iron and of war. Herskovits (1938:105–107), in discussing the cult, does not mention a connection with hunting but says Gǔ is the god of metal, himself a smith, and the god of war. He is the third-ranking member of the pantheon, coming right after Mawú and Lísa. Fr. Segurola, a missionary with many years experience with the Fon of Dahomey, writes: "Gŭ, fétiche des forgerons, dieu des armes et de la guerre. C'est la déité de ceux qui travaillent le fer ou qui l'utilisent. On lui réserve la ferraille ainsi que les animaux tués accidentellement par le fer" (1963:194). I translate: "Gŭ: fetish of the blacksmiths, god of weapons and of war. The deity of those who produce iron or who use it. Scrap iron is reserved for him as well as animals accidentally killed by iron."

According to Herskovits (ii, 107), the god of hunters and the bush is Agè, who ranks immediately after Gŭ in the sky pantheon. Herskovits says of an earlier writer, "Le Hérissé . . . errs in making Agè the Earth god" (1938:107, note). On linguistic grounds we suspect that le Hérissé may not be wrong. In Idoma, which is a very conservative Kwa language, Earth is *àjè* or *àgyè*, and its cult is directly and basically concerned with the hunt. Segurola (1963:21) says: "Àgé, la Terre, divinité née de l'union de Lisa avec Mawu: on honore ensemble ces trois divinités," "Àgé, the Earth, divinity born of the union of Lisa with Mawu: these three divinities are honored together."[1] In Dahomey, it would seem, the cults of iron and of the hunt are separate; and the hunt is associated with the cult of the Earth, as in Idoma, east of the Niger.

In Benin, according to Melzian (1937), Ògún is "the god of iron, smiths, hunters and warriors; one of the highest gods in rank. . . . The sacrifices consist mainly of dogs, tortoises and snails, and oil must be used in them." This set of ideas and symbols is closely similar to the Yoruba cult.[2]

Barnes, after recognizing the role of "the hunter tradition" in the Ògún cult, speaks of "the earth tradition" as well. The main source is an old one (Ellis 1894), but this report, from Offa, seems well-founded. It fits with the myth of Ògún's disappearance, by sinking into the earth, and with the close association of the Idoma Earth cult with hunting. There is also the association of elephant symbolism with Ògún. Erinlè, "elephant of the earth," is regarded as the god of the bush (Williams 1974:91). He is also a hunter deity, and according to one story, he too disappeared into the earth, after turning himself into an elephant. Pa Adeniji (personal communication) says Erinlè was a follower of Ògún. A warrior who was a hunter too, Erinlè was also interested in agriculture, especially as a fertility god. He became an elephant and sank into the ground, reemerging as a river. Barnes (1980:23) thinks of him as a possible source of the elephant symbolism associated with Ògún. For an example of this, one may consider the myth of the hunter Tìmọyìn, who founded the city of Oshogbo. He was a priest of Ògún, and one day killed a female elephant who was in the act of giving birth—a very serious breach of taboo. Tìmọyìn established a shrine for the worship of the elephant calf and became Ògún Tìmọyìn, himself an incarnation of Ògún (Wenger 1980:134–38). (The artist Susanne Wenger created a large batik wall hanging on this theme, in which the elephant in parturition forms the central figure—a very bold artistic theme indeed!) It is interesting that at the central town of the Ògún cult, Ìré, no objects of Ògún worship are fashioned of iron (Williams 1974:84). It would appear that as we go east, the hunter symbolism becomes relatively more important in the Ògún cult.

East of the Niger, there is a quite different set of ideas and practices that, nevertheless, seem related to the Ògún cults of the Yoruba and the Edo peoples (including Benin). A fundamental difference is that groups like the Idoma, Tiv, and even the Igala do not have gods hierarchically arranged in pantheons like those of the Yoruba or the Bini. The really ancient Idoma religion consisted of Earth and Ancestors, rather like the religion of the Tallensi of northern Ghana, as described by Fortes (1945, 1949). The idea of a high god (Qwǫicō) came from the Moslems, according to one very knowledgeable elder. There are local spirits and "medicines" or charms, but these have restricted fields of effectiveness. We do not find gods with personalities and histories who interact with each other, who are represented in works of art, and who govern whole areas of life. It is perhaps fair to say that pantheons are more typical of hierarchically organized states than of stateless societies or societies where the state is a creature of the lineages.

A key concept in Idoma male society is ògwú (Armstrong 1968:122). It has not proved easy to define, but its various uses may be illustrated. The crowing of a cock is ògwú, used with the verb tá, "to throw": ó gē tógwú, "he is crowing." There is a special ògwú call accompanied by a handflap over the mouth. Using it is the privilege of a successful hunter or someone who has killed a man and taken his head. Such a person has "made his ògwú" (yógwú). When a man has killed a fierce animal, like a lion, a leopard, a bush-cow, or an elephant, or has taken a head, he must undergo the ceremony called èōgwóōnà, "washing ògwú from the face." For a long time we translated this as "washing pride from the face," since ògwú, or "making ògwú," is a high honor, rather like getting a medal for valor in European or American armies. Another reason for the ceremony is that without it, the spirit of the slain enemy or animal may trouble the victorious warrior or successful hunter, and he may cause trouble at home. From a sociological point of view, èōgwóōnà may be regarded as the resocialization of a dangerous hero, the acclamation of his brave deed, accompanied by the cleansing of the spirit of the dead animal or man from his face. It is significant that the washing is usually done by a blacksmith at his forge.

From a linguistic point of view, the word ògwú is as similar to "Ògún" as it can be, given the different sound systems of Yoruba and Idoma. The vowels and tones are identical, given the fact that Idoma has no nasal vowels. Both have the consonant "g"; and the "w" after "g" is inevitable before "u" in uncompounded words in Idoma. Both words are intimately connected with war, hunting, and ironworking. In other words, there is a strong case for regarding "ògwú" and "Ògún" as cognates.

The word ògú, in the same sense as Idoma ògwú, also occurs in Igala, according to my Igala colleague, Dr. Ìdáchàbá, of the Ibadan Department of Agricultural Economics. The near-mad behavior of a successful killer is called *é-dógū*: *é-*, infinitive prefix, *dá*, "to cut," *ògú*. The water of a blacksmith's forge is used to cool him down. Tom Miachi, an Igala postgraduate student of anthropology, adds that the Igala word may be *ògú* or *ògwú* in different subdialects. He too says the ceremony of "washing *ògwú* from the face" is practiced in Igala for the same reasons as in Idoma. He gives me the Igala phrase "*é-gwējóògwú*": analytically *é-*, infinitive prefix; *gwẹ̀*, "wash"; *éjú*, "eye, face"; *ògwú*. He agrees that an Igbo origin for the word seems plausible, and that "killing," as an abstraction, is a good translation for it. He also agrees that the Igala do not have "gods" in the Yoruba sense of "*òrìṣá*."

Sidney Kasfir has suggested (personal communication) that Idoma "*ògwú*" may derive from Igbo "*ògbú*," "killer." The verb "to kill" in Igbo is "*gbú*," probably cognate with Idoma "*ŋmó*."[3] Williamson, in her Igbo-English Dictionary (1972:153), says, "*ògbú ḿmādù*, 'man-killer'; a much coveted honour in the olden days; conferred on anyone who possessed a human head." The "*ò-*" prefix is for the agent, the doer of an act. The vowels and tones are identical with those of "*ògwú*"; the consonant, "*-gb-*," is a lightly imploded "*b*." It is produced by a movement of the back of the tongue toward the velum in combination with lip closure and is therefore to be regarded as a labio-velar consonant. The different articulation of Idoma "*-gw-*" is also labio-velar. The prima facie case for regarding Igbo "*ògbú*" as cognate with Idoma "*ògwú*" is strong, since both are used in the context of killing and taking a head.

Accepting this hypothesis, we may proceed to retranslate "*èōgwóōnà*" as "washing the killing from the face." Three Idoma informants agree that this translation makes excellent sense. The late King of Otukpó Land, speaking of the Lion Shrine (*Idu*) in the bush, said that it is the place where, "When one kills a person they wash it [i.e., the killing] from his face." He does not actually use the word "*ògwú*," but it is quite clear from the context that that is what he is talking about (unpublished tape-recorded interview, 1973, paragraph 24).

If we accept the hypothetical chain of cognation "*Ògún-ògwú-ògbú*," then in Igbo we arrive at a form that can be analyzed into other morphemes: *ò-gbú*, "killer," a verbal noun. Neither the Idoma nor the Yoruba forms can be analyzed further into meaningful parts.

Returning to the Idoma, we should also note that "*ògwú*" is an abstraction, not a god. It refers to hunting, to war, and to iron. Its relationship to iron-working is seen in the fact that it is usually the blacksmith who "washes the killing from the face" of the hunter or the warrior. He does it with medicinal leaves that have been dipped into the wooden trough of water in the forge which is used in the quenching of red-hot iron or steel implements after they have been heated, in contact with charcoal, to harden them. The following text was written, at my suggestion, in Idoma by a postgraduate student at the University of Ibadan, Ádā Ọkau, who comes from the Ọgllεwu district of central Idoma (Otukpó Local Government Area). He had inquired about *ògwú* at home. I have edited it linguistically and translated it. One can see from this text both the differences and the underlying similarities between the Idoma concept of *ògwú* and the Yoruba cult of the god *òrìṣà* Ògún. Ọkau says that this ceremony is not secret.

Eyī kÓgwúōna[4]

Ogwú wucē bɔ̄bí nɔ̄cɛ gboóōya eko nó lɔ́cɛ ŋmó ámāŋ eko nó lɛbé kíijile ŋmó. Ẹbé nōo wɛbé kíijile ā wɛyī, ɛjɛ, mlaágábá. Ucē bɔ̄bi nɔ̄coŋmɔ́ɔ̄cɛ gē yá ā wɛ ka hínĩ̄ī: ó gē kɛlā lɛ bɔ̄cɛ nōo le jɛélɛ́ āa. Ó gé yɔ̄ ī hīyē kɔ́ɔ̄cɛ nó ŋmó ɔ́māa (ɔ́dāŋ nó jíyē kúnū). Ó káa gē máācɛ dóodu lɛ bɔ̄dā né lɔfú bɛ̄ɛ kanúṁ māa. AcĪdɔ̄ma gē ka ka hínĩ̄ī: Ọcɛ ɔ́māa yɔ̄ ī jogwú. Eko dóodu nɔ̄cɛ gboóōjogwú lɛ āa, ācɛ géē ka kéé lɔ́cɛ ɔ́māa bī nyɔ̄ kéé lɔ́ eyī kógwú na céé kóō gboóōyúcōolɔhi. Ọdā nōo yá ɛ́ɛ́ nēeyī kógwúōna ī wā ā yɔ̄ɔ́.

Ẹdɔ kɔ́ɔ̄cɛ nōo gē naācɛ eyī kógwú ā waóonɔ̄wá (ábíije). Ọdā nūuwá gē bī le neyī ā wɛ: ēpū kókōpī, ɔbúgwū ámáŋ kidaŋbɔ, eŋ́ŋkpɔ̄. Uwá géē neyī nyāa ɛgɛ nábíije gē yúkĪ́lɔ̄ āa (ɔwá).

Eko nábíije gaáā neyī nyā ó le yɛ tɔ́ɔwá mlɔɔ́cɛ nōo ŋmɔ́ɔ̄cɛ ámáŋ kɛbé āa. Ó leŋ́ŋkpɔ̄ tāagbada nōo yīipɔ́wá āa. Ipéŋ́ŋkpɔ̄ nyā ó kwéēpū kókōpī í tá gɔɔ́. Ó lɔbúgwū ámáŋ kidaŋbɔ hɔ́ɔkɔ céé kóoyī kóō pé típéŋ́ŋkpɔ̄ āa. Eŋ́ŋkpɔ̄ nōo yɔ̄ nyā nábíije gē bī ɛ́ɛ́ nó gē noŋmɔ́ɔ̄cɛ eyī á. Ó géē bī eŋ́ŋkpɔ̄ nyā i nɔɔ́ eī (igbɛtá ēcɛ̄éi) jāā lɛ bɛ̄ŋ kɛ̄cɛ̄ɛnɛ ámáŋ kɛ̄cāhāpa. Ẹplléeko nōo yɔ̄ nyāa, ɔcɛ nōo ŋmɔ́ɔ̄cɛ ā géē gboóōyúcōolɔhi.

Ọdā nōo bī onɔ̄wá ipéyī kógwúōna ā wɛ ka hínĩ̄ī: anú wɔ̄cɛ nōo gē niyó kágbe nācɛ gē bī tɔ́té ámáŋ koōŋmɔ́ɔ̄cɛ ā á.

Washing *Ògwú* from the Face[5]

"*Ogwú* is the bad behavior that a person begins to display when he has killed a person or when he has killed a fierce animal. The animals which are fierce are the African buffalo ["bush-cow"], the leopard, and the lion. The bad behavior that the killer of a person displays is that he talks like a person who is crazy; he calls the name of the person he has killed (if he knows his name); and he regards everybody as not being as strong as he is. The Idoma people [then] say, 'That man is crazed by *ogwú*.' Whenever a man begins to be crazed with *ogwú*, people say that *ogwú* must be washed from his face so that he may begin to behave properly. It is this that brings [the ceremony of] washing *ogwú* from the face.

"The sort of persons who wash *ogwú* from a person's face are the blacksmiths (*ábíije*).[6] The things that they use for washing the face are leaves of the *okōpī* [meni[7] oil tree], a cock or a duck, and water. They will wash this face at the place where the blacksmith works [the forge].

"When the blacksmith is about to wash this face, he goes to the forge with the man who has killed a person or an animal. He pours water into

the trough[8] that is in the forge. Into this water he dips the leaves of *okōpī*.
He cuts off the head of the cock or the duck so that blood may flow into
the water. This water is what the blacksmith uses when he washes the
face of the killer. He will use this water to wash his face (three times
a day) for four, or even seven days. At that time, the man who has killed
a person will begin to behave well.

"The thing that brings the blacksmith into the washing of *ogwú* from
the face is the fact that it is he who forges the weapons that people use
in hunting or in killing a person."

A Yoruba authority, Pa Adeniji, reports that water for quenching iron is
similarly used in Yorubaland to "wash Ògún" (*Ó wẹ̀Gún*, "He washed
Ògún"; and *Ògún wíwẹ̀*, "washing Ògún"). The washing strengthens the
hunter or warrior and protects him from the spirits of the animals or enemies
he has killed. The water is kept at the forge in a basin called *ọpọ́n omi* or
ọpọ́n àgbẹ̀dẹ̀. The distinction between quenching and tempering (by air or
sand cooling) iron is well understood, as is also the case in Idoma—and in
Tiv, for that matter (Steve Tilley, personal communication).

Hunting is one of the oldest human activities, going far back into the Lower
Paleolithic. War probably comes in the Neolithic with agriculture, which provides the surpluses that make the organization of war possible and give it a
worthwhile target. Ironworking comes much later and produces the end of
the Neolithic. Each of these occupations is present in the Ògún concept,
which appears to be very ancient—given the presence of the cognate in Fon,
Edo (Bini), Idoma, Igala, Igbo, and Yoruba languages, although these must
be regarded as an ancient set of culture words associated with the spread of
the cultlike syndrome of ideas, probably westward from Igbo to Yoruba and
Fon. The forms "*ògbú - ògwú - ògú - Ògún - Gǔ*" are cognates by borrowing.
They are paralleled in all these languages by a series of older genetic cognates
for "kill," all of which begin with a labio-velar consonant: Igbo *gbú*, Idoma
ŋmó, *ŋmgbó*, Igala *kpa*, Benin *gbé*, Yoruba *kpa*, Fon *hù* (cf. the related Ewe
wù and *hù*; "*w*" and "*h*" before "*u*" are labio-velar articulations).

My point is that the hunting, and later the warrior, aspects that are so
significant in the Ògún cult of the Yoruba are not sufficiently emphasized by
Barnes, who looks to the more recent iron-making revolution (ca. 2,000 years
ago) as an event that may have stimulated the cult's beginnings. On linguistic
grounds, 2,000 years is not a bad guess for the phonetically eroded *ògbú-
Ògún* set. These words may be compared with such early Christian words in
English as "priest," from Greek "*presbyteros*," and "bishop," from Greek
"*epíscopos*." The symbolism of washing with the blacksmith's quenching
water gives us a kind of *terminus a quo*. The amalgam and synthesis of ideas
and practices that are found in the Ògún cult, however, may well have roots
that extend far more deeply into the past.

It would be interesting in the examination of Ògún's past to study the relation of hunting in the *Ògún-ògwú* syndrome to hunting in the various earth cults, since the latter are probably among the most ancient cults in this part of the world. In Yoruba culture, the Ògún cult has an earth aspect. In Idoma, the earth cult is concerned with the hunting of all animals and with the social relations of organized hunting activity. *Ògwú*, and very likely Ògún in Yoruba, are related to hunting as a masculine exploit—the hunting of fierce animals. Adeniji's comment that Erinlẹ̀ was concerned also with agriculture and fertility suggests a complex of ideas similar to that of the Idoma earth cult. The main Yoruba earth cult is controlled by the Ogboni Society. It is so secret that little is known publicly about it, but Adeniji says that it is not particularly concerned with hunting.

The meaning of all of this is cultural and psychological. Professional hunters are marginal men in any agricultural society, including Idoma. The best description of their marginal position that I know of was written by an Idoma poet, Samson O. O. Amali (1968:86–88), when he was still a Sixth Form schoolboy; it is reprinted below. The marginal position of hunters derives from many factors. They are wanderers and traditionally the founders of new settlements. Their interests, within limits, are worldly rather than domestic. They suffer from fatigue and loneliness, and in times when hunting is not very successful they may be hungry too. They achieve only a partial and temporary separation from village or town society, yet they may bring new ideas back home. Much of this pattern underlies the Yoruba Ògún cult and can be counted as additional psychological preparation for the latter-day transformation of Ògún into the god of vehicles and long-distance transportation. The implication is that in concentrating on the hunting aspects of Ògún, and by extension the marginal attributes of this occupation, the search for his origins can be broadened and, thereby, take a significant step forward.

The Hunter
by
Samson O. O. Amali

His weapons?
A dane gun
A product of
The village's blacksmith
A bottle of gunpowder
A tin of cartridges
His attire?
A piece of black cloth
Covering only his loins
He hung his cutlass
On his loins
He rubbed his protective

Charm upon his chest
And face.
Recited thrice
The blessing and protective
Incantations
He opened his door gently,
Peeped out gently
The night was still
It was very dark
No sign of any living being
Wind was blowing lightly
He walked backward
Out of his room
Raised his face
Into the sky,
The sky had no stars
A good omen.
He alone was awake
He stood still
In the still night
Studied the direction
Which the wind blew
And he began.
So he went alone
To hunt animals
In thick forest
In the heart
Of the still night.
This was his work.
He was a hunter
He followed
The foot-path
That passed
Through the forest
With his dane gun
Across his shoulder
All alone
In the dark still night.

He blew his
Hunting horn
Calling animals
In their tones
As he went along
Alone.

He arrived very close
To the hunting spot
Climbed the tree
Which stood very close
To the hunting spot
He had prepared
The spot
For the animals
To visit.
He clutched his gun
Ready to release
The trigger
At a moment's appearance
Of any animal
Sometimes he killed animals
Sometimes he killed no animals.
His was a tedious job
He had been beaten
By the rain
Many times
As he squatted
On the tree top
Armed
Awaiting his game
He had heard the voices
Of spirits.
Had met dangerous spirits
He could talk
With the animals
He was the mystery man
Of his land.

NOTES

1. The spellings of *Agè* and *Àgé* differ because neither is based on a modern linguistic analysis.

2. See also Bradbury (1973:257–58, 265).

3. The suggestion is that the *-gwú* syllable, with the sense of "kill," does not have an Idoma origin. Comparativists are likely to agree that *gbú* and *ŋmó* are cognate because both have a labio-velar consonant and a high, back vowel with a high tone; and they mean the same thing. The case is strengthened by the form *ŋmgbó* in the southernmost Idoma dialect, Yala (near Ikom on the Cross River), and by the form *ŋmgbέ*, "kill," in the closely related Ẹlɔyi language in Nasarawa. The ligature means that the "gb" is prenasalized, and the "ŋm" does not form a separate syllable.

4. High tone á; mid tone ā; low tone unmarked.

5. Literally, "washing the face of *ogwú*." (Dialect of Ādɔ́ká, which differs slightly from that of Otukpó.)

6. "*Ábīije*," the Igala word for "iron," used here as a blacksmith's title.

7. Meni appears to be *Lophira lanceolata*, a hardwood. The leaves have other medicinal and symbolic uses, such as cleaning the face of the gravedigger who has just buried someone who has died a "bad death."

8. "*Agbada*," the trough containing the water into which red-hot iron is plunged in order to quench it.

REFERENCES CITED

Amali, Samson O. O. 1968. *Selected Poems*, Ibadan: Privately published.

Armstrong, R. G. 1968. "Onugbo mlOko," *African Arts*, Vol. 1, No. 4.

Barnes, Sandra T. 1980. *Ogun: An Old God for a New Age*, Philadelphia: ISHI.

Bradbury, R. E. 1973. *Benin Studies*, London: Oxford University Press for International African Institute.

Ellis, A. B. 1894. *The Yoruba-Speaking Peoples of the Slave Coast of West Africa*, London: Chapman and Hall.

Fortes, Meyer. 1945. *The Dynamics of Clanship among the Tallensi*, London: Oxford University Press for International African Institute.

————. 1949. *The Web of Kinship among the Tallensi*, London: Oxford University Press for International African Institute.

Herskovits, Melville J. 1938. *Dahomey, an Ancient West African Kingdom*, New York City: J. J. Augustin.

le Hérissé, A. 1911. *L'Ancien Royaume du Dahomey*, Paris.

Melzian, Hans. 1937. *A Concise Dictionary of the Bini Language of Southern Nigeria*, London: Kegan Paul.

Segurola, Révérend Père B. 1963. *Dictionnaire Fon-Français*, Cotonou: Procure de l'Archidiocèse.

Wenger, Susanne. 1980. *Ein Leben mit den Göttern*, Wörgl, Austria: Perlinger Verlag.

Williams, Denis. 1974. *Icon and Image*, London: Allen Lane.

Williamson, Kay. 1972. *Igbo-English Dictionary, based on the Onitsha Dialect*, Benin City: Ethiope Publishing Corporation.

Sandra T. Barnes and Paula Girshick Ben-Amos

3

Ogun, the Empire Builder

During the years between 1400 and 1700 a cluster of conquest states rose to power along the Guinea Coast of West Africa and dominated large areas of this forest-belt region for several centuries. The expansion of these states was based on their many advantages, the most obvious of which was that each had a well organized and heavily equipped army, using a highly developed iron technology and, in a few cases, a mounted cavalry. The states included the Edo Kingdom of Benin, the Fon Kingdom of Dahomey, and a series of Yoruba kingdoms, the largest of which was Oyo (see Map 3.2). All of these states owed their political dominance to a policy of aggressive militarism.

It is no accident, we think, that each of these polities shared a symbolic complex which incorporated the three elements of iron, warfare, and state-building. This complex centered on Ogun (also known as Gu). For centuries there was close interaction between citizens of these states, thanks to migration, trade, warfare, and the itineracy of craftsmen and other specialists. Through this ongoing and intensive interaction, knowledge of a deity such as Ogun could easily have diffused.

It is well understood that symbols are adapted to, and then elaborated in ways that are unique to, or consonant with, the culture of the adopting groups. Certainly this was true in the cases discussed here. What is of interest, then, are not the differences but the similarities of underlying symbolic meanings which Ogun retained in each place. Basically, the Ogun concept encapsulated the progression from hunting to agriculture and the mastery of metallurgy, to urbanization and, ultimately, in these peoples' own view, to the development of empire. In one symbolic complex there existed a recapitulation of each kingdom's stages of growth and a statement about its basic nature.

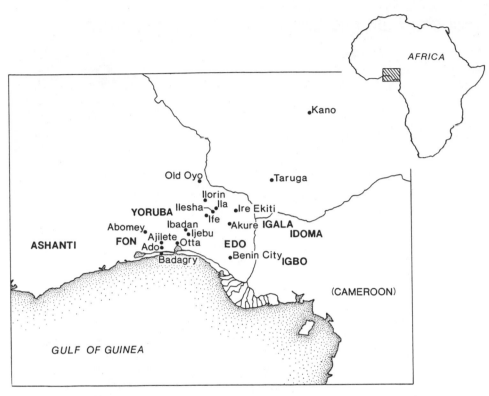

MAP 3.1. Significant linguistic groups (e.g., FON) and locations (e.g., Benin City) mentioned in chapters 2 and 3.

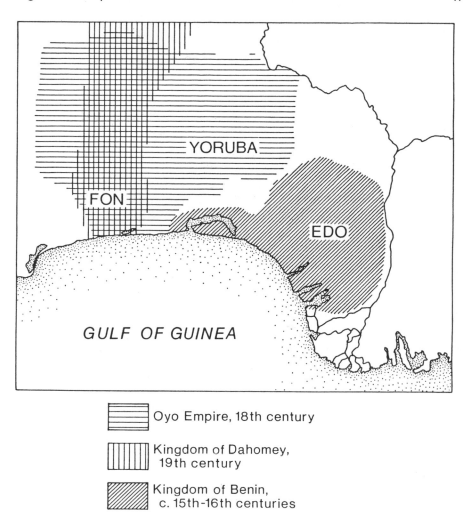

MAP 3.2. Three precolonial conquest states on the eastern Guinea Coast of West Africa where Ogun was a prominent deity.

In what follows, we examine some of the material and historical conditions that were relevant to the spread of a regional symbol. Then we demonstrate the ways in which basic symbolic meanings were shared, and, finally, we suggest that the myths and rituals of the Ogun complex served as a kind of "ideology of progress," devised by these peoples to explain their dominant position in the world.[1]

Iron Technology

The advent of iron in West Africa, as with all of sub-Saharan Africa, was "a catalyst which woke half a continent from the slumber of the Stone Age" (van der Merwe 1980:464). The diffusion of ironworking techniques was swift. If current calculations are correct there was a mere 800-year interval—500 B.C. to A.D. 300—between the earliest sub-Saharan smelting sites and the spread of iron to most areas of the subcontinent. During the early Iron Age, ending c. A.D. 1,000, population densities increased, and by its conclusion towns, kingdoms, and armies had emerged (Oliver and Fagan 1975:65).

The earliest known iron smelting in Western Africa is now believed to have occurred in what today is central Nigeria.[2] At the site of Taruga (see Map 1 for this and other places mentioned), an advanced iron technology existed as early as 600 B.C. (van der Merwe 1980:478; Calvocoressi and David 1979:10–11). By the end of the first millennium A.D., iron use and iron-making were widespread throughout Nigeria: in the northern savannah by the first or second century (Connah 1981:146–47; Shaw 1978:96–97), and in the southern forested area by the ninth (Shaw 1970:67, 260). Certainly at Benin by the thirteenth to fourteenth centuries iron smelting was well established (Connah 1975:34–35).

While the lateritic soils in much of West Africa made possible small-scale smelting of iron, large-scale smelting depended on the occurrence of rich ore-bearing sites. Several of the well-known sites in Nigeria, significantly, were concentrated around the capital city of Old Oyo and in more southerly parts of the kingdom, near the Awori and Egbado towns of Otta and Ajilete, respectively. In 1890, the Ajilete mine (20 miles north of coastal Badagry and the same distance west of Otta) was producing "excellent" ore from a series of many holes 8 feet in diameter and 50 to 60 feet deep (Mabogunje 1976:13). Ore deposits also lay nineteen-days' walk north of Abomey, capital of the Dahomean kingdom. During his travels in 1845–46, Duncan found that the hills north of Abomey "abound with iron," and that nearby smelters were willing to demonstrate their operations to him (1847:130–31). Similar sites occurred in western Nigeria and western Cameroon. The scale of smelting in these areas was impressive. At the end of the nineteenth century, for example, one Oyo site still had a smelting population of 100 to 120 (Bellamy

1904:101) and one Cameroon area had 270 smelters, whose production, exceeding the famous northeast Sudanic site of Meroe, was traded into Nigeria (Warnier and Fowler 1979:331). Whether or not these were the actual smelting sites which were producing iron when the forest-belt empires were formed is unknown. The point is that both the raw materials for large-scale production and the technical know-how for iron-making were in existence when the Guinea Coast kingdoms began to rise.

There has been considerable debate concerning the conditions necessary for the expansion of West Africa's large states. Some scholars believe that iron was an essential element (e.g., Davidson 1959:82–83; Goody 1971:46). This view coincides with folk ideology, for in speculating on their past political prominence, as represented in the ideology surrounding Ogun (discussed below), descendants of the Guinea Coast empires also equate state-building with the introduction and use of iron. Other scholars, however, hold that trade, a slow increase in population densities, or the control of labor and the subsequent ability to amass wealth and concentrate it in the hands of a privileged few were the conditions necessary to bring about state formation (e.g., Curtin et al. 1978:35–36; Horton 1976:103–113). This debate has been misleading, for two reasons. First, writers often confuse the search for conditions producing states with the search for origins of political centralization, whereas these are separate issues and must be examined separately. Second, they fail to take scale into account when comparing one case with another. Hence, arguments intended to apply to the building of kingdoms are countered with arguments that apply to the coalescing of sufficient power to operate a market center. Our concern is with the conditions necessary for the creation and expansion of states, that is to say, multi-community, stratified polities capable of centralizing the control and use of force.

Certainly iron was one of the elements that facilitated state building in West Africa. The weaponry that made territorial expansion possible was almost without exception made in whole or in part with iron and steel.[3] Iron production was concentrated in specific families or guilds that could be regulated and, therefore, as Goody points out (1971:46), the control of iron sources or its manufacture meant that military force also could be controlled. But iron was not solely responsible for the rise of large states in this part of the world. In addition to controlling weapons technology, it was essential that state-builders be able to organize and support large armies. Thus, in our view, iron, organization, and wealth were interdependent conditions, all necessary to the building of states.

Iron, Warfare, and Kingship

By the time Portuguese explorers arrived in Benin in the late fifteenth century, it was already an expanding warrior kingdom. According to an account by the Portuguese sailor Duarte Pacheco Pereira, "The Kingdom of Beny is about eighty leagues long and forty wide; it is usually at war with its neighbours and takes many captives" (Hodgkin 1960:93). While the Portuguese traded with the Benin kingdom intensively during this period, they sold it neither guns nor iron, possibly due to a papal ban (Ryder 1969:41), leaving Benin to continue its military expansion without the aid of imported weaponry or raw materials. Locally produced iron goods were not lacking, as this late sixteenth- or early seventeenth-century Dutch account indicates:

> They also have severall places in the Towne, where they keepe their Markets; in one place they have their great Market Day, called Dia de Ferro; and in another place they hold their little Market, called Ferro. . . . They . . . bring great store of Ironworke to sell there, and Instruments to fish withall, others to plow and to till the land withall; and many Weapons, as Assagaies, and Knives also for the Warre. This Market and Traffique is there very orderly holden. . . . ('D.R.' in Hodgkin 1960:121–22)

With their army using a variety of weapons—shields, javelins, spears, assegais, rapiers, bows and poisoned arrows—the Edo expanded their empire. The variety of weapons used by Benin warriors, and indeed their glorification of military prowess, were well represented in their sculpture. One example was a fifteenth/sixteenth-century brass plaque (fig. 3.1) from the royal palace illustrating the triumph of the Benin army over an enemy. The warriors are using shields, spears, and a variety of swords.

Seventeenth century Dutch sources indicate that the king of Benin could "mobilize 20,000 to 100,000 men. Thus he is the terror of his neighbours and an object of fear to his own peoples." Headed by a general, noble warriors and common soldiers were well disciplined and brave; "they never leave their posts, even when they have death before their eyes" (Dapper in Hodgkin 1960:128–29).

The motivations behind Benin's aggressive militarism are unknown, but it is clear that warfare was an accepted, ongoing aspect of the political system. It apparently was the custom for kings to declare war in the third year after their succession to the throne. Ruling princes of the empire who refused to pledge their allegiance at that time were considered rebels, and war was declared against them and their towns (Egharevba 1949:35). Economic factors were undoubtedly central to Benin's expansion, since, as Bradbury suggests, the Edo were intent on increasing their income from tribute, protecting and developing trade, and augmenting their army with captives and allies (1973:48). In Benin oral traditions, the commencement of their empire-building was associated with King Ewuare (c. fifteenth century), who was believed to have introduced major changes in the political structure of the kingdom, including centralizing royal authority, shifting the pattern of succession, organizing the urban population into corporate wards, and otherwise appropriating "a large measure of control over the means of administration" (Bradbury 1973:139).

FIGURE 3.1. Benin, Nigeria. Royal brass plaque from the palace at Benin. Warrior at far left wears miniature iron implements around his waist. 15th–16th century. H. c.17″. Photograph courtesy of the Museum für Völkerkunde, Leipzig.

The control of weapons production in Benin was part of this overall pattern of centralization. Iron craftsmen worked primarily for the king, but also for the nobles and, of course, for profit in the open market. There have been five guilds of smiths (sing. *ogun*; pl. *igun*) in Benin. The senior guild, Igun Eronmwon, consisting of brass-smiths, created the cast sculpture for which Benin is famous. Their objects decorated the royal palace and ritually enhanced the power of the king. Title-holders in this guild controlled great supernatural powers, which were used to protect the kingdom during important annual rituals. The other four, all ironworking guilds, produced herbalists' staffs, ceremonial swords, miniature emblems of Ogun, and assorted tools. All smiths were believed to control arcane knowledge, which they used for the enhancement and protection of the nation.

At its height, during the fifteenth and sixteenth centuries, the Benin kingdom reached its natural boundaries at the River Niger to the east and the sea to the south, and established suzerainty over Yoruba areas to the west and southwest up to the border of what was to become Dahomey. In the late sixteenth century it reached a common boundary with the Kingdom of Oyo.[4]

It is not known when the famed Yoruba Kingdom of Oyo got its start. Its foundation is variously set in the tenth to early fifteenth centuries, with the thirteenth being the most favored. We do know, however, that as a military power and empire it became important around 1600, and by 1780 it had attained its greatest size—greater than any other coastal African state—stretching from the Niger River to the sea and from Dahomey to the Benin border in the east (Law 1977:89; Obayemi 1976:255). Clearly Oyo's military policies were related to the desire for wealth, largely produced through commerce, especially long-distance trade. Not unrelated to Oyo's desire to expand and enlarge trade was its need for human labor to produce agricultural surpluses, and thus its need to take slaves both for domestic use and for foreign sale. Oyo's wealth also came from taxes on trade and from tribute, both of which were increased through expansion (Law 1977:202–236).

Like Benin, Oyo's power was dependent on military force; it was customary to stage expeditions every other year (Morton-Williams 1971:91). And like Benin, it expanded without the aid of firearms, which were not used effectively until sometime between the 1820s and the 1840s. Instead, Oyo's effectiveness in its military drives rested on two forces: a mounted cavalry numbering in the thousands, and a huge arsenal of iron weapons. So powerful was Oyo's military might that it defeated Dahomey in the 1720s, despite the latter's use of muskets, and forced it to pay tribute for nearly a century thereafter (Law 1977:164). The importance of cavalry, especially in savannah zones such as those occupied by Oyo, was captured by artists in many Yoruba kingdoms who idealized the equestrian warrior, and in fact portrayed Ogun as a mounted, spear-bearing soldier.[5] Edo artists, too, made extensive use of the horse and warrior theme in their bronze figures (Karpinski 1984). Yet the use of horses in both Benin and Dahomey was probably ceremonial and not military (Law 1980:22), since in the latter's forested environments horses were often subject to tsetse fly, and the expense of importing continuous replacements was high.

Oyo's army was well organized and led by a coterie of warrior chiefs whose senior members directly advised the king and acted as a strong check on his power. The size of its armed forces has been variously estimated at 10,000 to 100,000, with the lower number, even in the early nineteenth century, being the most reasonable (Law 1977:196–97). Its major eighteenth century adversary, Dahomey, was believed to have had no more than 12,000 warriors (Argyle 1966:89). The bulk of Oyo's army was made up of temporary recruits, although there were semiprofessional specialists, and its major strength came from the capital and not the provinces, tributary, or client states (Law 1977:183–97).

The main weapons of Oyo's cavalrymen and foot soldiers were spears, axes, and a variety of swords.[6] Special divisions of archers made use of bows and arrows (including crossbows), and both spears and arrows had iron heads that were often barbed. Other weapons included lances, cutlasses, daggers, knives, fighting bracelets, iron and wooden clubs, javelins, and even slings. To our knowledge, the only steel blades found on these antique weapons were on swords and knives (Smith 1973:232–33).

The government appears to have been less centralized in Oyo, where there was a separation of powers, than it was in Benin and Dahomey, and thus the relationship between that nation's highest civil authority and its smiths also was less centralized. In the nineteenth century, and no doubt before that time, the Alaafin (king) controlled his own weapon-producing smiths, who also supplied an allied power (Ajayi and Smith 1964:40). Additionally, a council of war chiefs led Oyo's military branch of government and, although the evidence is indirect, these chiefs probably had blacksmiths under their control (cf. Awẹ 1973:70). The official who commanded Oyo's citizen army and acted as prime minister of the kingdom, the Bashorun, worshipped Ogun; this god of warriors and smiths was his family deity, indicating that smithing was probably a family occupation (Johnson 1969:71; Morton-Williams 1967:54). The Bashorun presided over the Oyo Mesi, a council of state which not only advised the king but forced him to leave office (often by committing suicide) if his reign became unacceptable. Sitting with the Bashorun on the same council was the Ashipa, the official head of the Ogun cult in Oyo and his country's "minister of external affairs" (Morton-Williams 1964:254).

Dahomey, to the west of Oyo, traced its foundations to about 1625, and it became an important power near the end of that century. The unyielding pursuit of war was the hallmark of this kingdom, earning it the reputation of the Prussia of West Africa (Smith 1976a:51, 190). Yet Dahomey expanded gradually, not throwing off Oyo's yoke until 1818 and only then becoming the foremost power along the coast. In its rise to supremacy, Dahomey made use of guns, which it had received in trade as early as the late seventeenth century, and a few cannons, which were transported to the coast in the eighteenth century. The king monopolized trade in firearms and local production

of iron weapons. Likewise, the highly centralized army was under the immediate authority of the king, and included the famous divisions of women who
lived on the palace grounds and who, along with other powerful and well organized divisions of male warriors, brought Dahomey international fame as
a military power.

Dahomey's economy was based heavily on slave raiding and thus it
launched a fresh campaign each dry season on surrounding territories with
the intention of capturing as many slaves as possible for internal use and sale
to European merchants. Indeed Dahomey's fate was intimately bound up
with its militaristic, slave-raiding endeavors, and its oral traditions, which
looked back to earlier times, stressed this characteristic:

> The King has said that Dahomey is an enemy of all the world, and that his
> chiefs must use as much force in killing an ant, as they would to kill an elephant,
> for the small things bring on the large ones.

> The King has said that Dahomeans are a warrior people, and that, in conse-
> quence, it must never come to pass that a true Dahomean admit before an
> enemy that he is vanquished. (Herskovits and Herskovits 1958:480)

Dahomey's all-pervading interest in its militaristic mission was epitomized in
the motto of kings who saw war as the way to "make Dahomey always
greater" (Lombard 1967:72).

Dahomean traditions held that iron was the basis for its militaristic prowess. Iron must be looked after, said the king, or the careless owner would
become a lizard with a black tail (i.e., he would die), whereas the careful
owner would become a lizard with a red tail (i.e., he would live) (Herskovits
and Herskovits 1958:479–81).

The reliance of Dahomey on iron weaponry also was explicit in the relationship between smiths and the crown. All iron craftsmen were considered
to work under the control and at the behest of the king (Lombard 1967:80),
and blacksmiths' shops, occupying an entire quarter of the capital city, invariably caught the attention of foreign travelers (e.g., Burton 1864 V.I:291;
Forbes 1851:69). Smiths had high status, and even in the early twentieth century Herskovits found they still were among the most honored craftsmen
(1967 V.I:45). The king kept close watch on the production and the rituals
of all smiths in the kingdom. It was the duty of priests of Gu (the Dahomean
counterpart of Ogun) to report to the king's representatives the number of
smiths in each forge and the amount of their production. The king himself
set the date for annual sacrifices to Gu and transmitted it to the blacksmiths,
again, through Gu priests. Since smiths were worshippers of Gu, they were
expected to participate in these rites (Herskovits 1967 V.I:126–27, 181)
in addition to making their daily sacrifices, which, when Skertchly visited
Dahomey c. 1874, consisted of morning offerings to Gu of a water and corn-
flour porridge (1874:387–88).

Interaction

The amount of interaction between peoples of various political and cultural backgrounds during the period discussed here was extensive. Men and women traveled across boundaries by choice and by necessity for economic, political, social, and religious purposes. Despite intermittent hostilities, boundaries were relatively porous and it is likely, as Smith suggests (1976a:47), that ethnic differences simply had a different level of significance than they do today. For one thing, the three kingdoms of Oyo, Dahomey, and Benin all overlapped at one time or another during the 500 years between 1400 and 1900, and this overlap brought their peoples into various types of interaction. For another, the boundaries between the kingdoms, despite being hotly contested in the course of many regional wars, were frontier zones in which there was a great deal of intermixing.

Many eastern Yoruba communities were influenced by both Benin and Oyo. For instance, large areas of Ondo, Owo, Ekiti, Akure, and Otun fell into the orbit of Benin up to the seventeenth century and to lesser degrees to the nineteenth. Benin's influence took many forms, ranging from outright conquest to serving, as it did for Ondo, as a court of appeals in major land and succession disputes (Smith 1976a:193).[7] Its influence on nearby Owo was indirect, but no less effective, for in the reign of Ehengbuda, probably in the late sixteenth century, the heir to Owo's throne was sent to Benin to be trained and raised by the king (Egharevba 1960:33). During the seventeenth and eighteenth centuries, when Oyo reached its peak, much of the same area shifted into its orbit, again, in many ways but largely through military domination.

Similar shifts took place in western and southwestern Yorubaland. The buffer states of Egba, Egbado, and Ketu between Oyo and Dahomey were first part of the Oyo empire, but at the end of the eighteenth and nineteenth centuries they shifted into Dahomey's sphere of influence. Earlier in the seventeenth century the predecessor state to Dahomey, the coastal Kingdom of Allada (Ardra), was subject to the military operations of Oyo. Indeed, the origins of the Fon people were attributed to the intermarrying of Oyo immigrants with people of Allada (Lombard 1967:72). The Fon themselves had a policy of assimilating the ethnic groups under their suzerainty, and were known to intermarry with conquered peoples. Intermarriage, a subject to which we return, was common in the frontier zones, and as a result many people were no doubt able to claim dual identities (Obayemi 1976:235).

All three superpowers of the Guinea Coast also overlapped in the same areas, although at different times. In one case, Benin stretched its empire along the coast westward to Lagos, Badagry, and slightly inland to Ado (in the Egbado region of the extreme southwest of present-day Nigeria) in the sixteenth and early seventeenth centuries. Later, in the eighteenth century,

Oyo and Dahomey both vied for control of Badagry and its surrounding territory, with Dahomey openly attacking Badagry in 1737 (Law 1977:176–77; Smith 1976a:108). Today some residents of this once-contested area still trace ancestry to each of the ancient powers. A second case in which the three powers converged was in the southern Yoruba Kingdom of Ijebu. Benin and Oyo competed for control of the Ijebu in the seventeenth century, and Dahomey was believed to have attacked this kingdom a century later (Smith 1976a:93).

All three powers colonized their holdings. Whole families were sent by Oyo into Dahomey and elsewhere (Akinjogbin 1976:397; Law 1977:93). Benin usually sent its nationals to settle in newly conquered territory, whether it was annexed or tribute-paying; many of them intermarried, established businesses in trade or crafts (frequently smithing), and founded subcommunities that retained an Edo identity for many generations (Akintoye 1971:28–29). Dahomey, too, sent colonizers into conquered territories. In its holdings in Yoruba kingdoms, indigenous chiefs remained in office, but Dahomean "doubles" worked with them (Lombard 1967:75).

Military operations necessitated other types of interchange. Mercenaries sold their services from one kingdom to another (Smith 1976b:83); military alliances brought about exchanges of personnel; spies were sent to foreign lands (Akinjogbin 1976:393); and hostages were taken from country to country. A Dahomean prince thus spent many years in Oyo as a hostage (Smith 1976b:56–57). One of the major purposes of warfare, to take slaves, also brought about the inevitable interaction of people of different backgrounds. Foreign captives taken into domestic slavery were frequently recruited into the armies of their Oyo and Dahomean captors (Ajayi and Smith 1964:51–52; Argyle 1966:86).[8] Female slaves were known to have brought new religious practices, as for example the Aja woman, Hwanjile, who is said to have introduced the worship of the major deities Mawu, Lisa, and Age into the Dahomean pantheon (Bay 1983:347; Herskovits 1967 V.II:103–104).

People were included as tribute. Dahomeans gave their Oyo conquerors 40 (some accounts say 41) men and the same number of women per annum. If this tribute were paid during each of Dahomey's 70 years as a vassal state, then 5,600 foreign citizens were added to Oyo's population during that period. In addition to his usual payments, the ruler of Oyo demanded and was given 100 wives in 1779 (Law 1977:165–67).

Trade was a major source of interaction and infusion of new peoples into one another's territories. Fifteenth-century contacts between Benin and eastern Yoruba kingdoms were mainly for trading purposes and many Edo settled permanently in trade centers, such as Akure (Akintoye 1971:25–26). Similarly, colonies of Oyo traders are known to have established themselves in commercial centers, as far north as Kano, in the eighteenth century (Smith 1976a:51). The movement of people for trade also had a western dimension long before the 1600s when trade routes crossing Oyo territory passed through what would become Dahomey and extended as far west as Ashanti country (Morton-Williams 1971:83). Although it is usually believed that most long-distance traders were men, many transnational traders in precolonial eastern Yoruba and Edo areas were women (Akintoye 1971:24).

Ordinary migration from one polity to another, and particularly from outlying areas to prospering towns and kingdoms, appears to have been a common occurrence in the entire Guinea Coast region. Obayemi notes that there was "a period of relatively free interstate movement" before 1600 (1976:254); and oral traditions indicate that migrations were usual throughout the whole precolonial period (e.g., Akinjogbin 1976:377). Dahomean legends recount the migrations of royal princes and princesses outside the kingdom for many purposes (Herskovits and Herskovits 1958:377). In the Kingdom of Ilesha, noted for its migration traditions, two-thirds of the 21 leading chiefs claimed that their ancestors originated in other kingdoms (Obayemi 1976:253). Many migrants were refugees fleeing injustices, dynastic disputes, or civic turmoil, but others were simply seeking independence, wealth, and power in new places.

As indicated, intermarriage was a prime factor in the interaction of peoples of different kingdoms. There were many dynastic intermarriages. The kings of Oyo and Dahomey sent their daughters to one another as wives (Akinjogbin 1976:399; Law 1977:161), and Edo conquerors had a policy of intermarrying with subject peoples (Akintoye 1971:29). Yoruba women who married into aristocratic Fon families were responsible for much of the Yoruba cultural influence in nineteenth-century Dahomey (Bay 1983:347). Kings in the Yoruba and Edo kingdoms sent adulterous wives into exile by placing them under the care of other rulers; and they sent their children (and the children of adulterous wives) to live in the palaces of neighboring kings so as to protect them from jealous rivals (Akintoye 1971:23).

Itineracy also was common. Among the more mobile members of society were hunters, whose occupation dictated their movement (see Ajuwon, Ch. 8 this volume). Hunters in some areas were in charge of protecting roads, and therefore they were in constant contact with other mobile sectors of the population, among whom brass-casters, leather-workers, diviners, herbalists, tattooers, circumcisers, and artists (see H. Drewal, Ch. 10 and 1977:8–9) were prominent. Highly specialized individuals appear to have been in great demand, and oral traditions indicate that mobility for them was as much the rule as the exception. An early ruler of Ilesha, to give only one example, was said to have spent time preceding his ascendance to the throne as a medical expert in Benin (Obayemi 1976:254).

Interaction and Belief

The high level of mobility in the Guinea Coast region no doubt facilitated the sharing of belief systems, and the ideology of Ogun was no exception. If anything, the transmission of Ogun's symbolic complex was enhanced by the extreme mobility of his main devotees: warriors and hunters, as indicated, and also ironworkers.

Blacksmiths were notorious travelers. Many of them left Oyo during its declining years and settled elsewhere. In the city of Ibadan, which became a formidable military power in the mid-nineteenth century, many Oyo smiths attached themselves to military leaders and produced weapons under their protection and patronage (Awẹ 1973:70). Similarly, Edo smiths were well-known settlers throughout the eastern Yoruba kingdoms (e.g., Akintoye 1971:29). Iron-smelters also moved regularly, since ore-bearing sites were frequently depleted (Ojo 1966:97).

Ironworkers were given special treatment throughout West Africa (Barnes 1980:8–13). In some societies, it was a serious crime to kill a smith. In others, they could not be treated as prisoners of war but had to be given privileged care. Indeed, their capture may have been both a fringe benefit and an objective of warfare. Two of the metalworking guilds in Benin, for instance, traced their origins to the north of Benin and claimed they were forcibly brought to the capital of the kingdom during the reign of Esigie, one of the great sixteenth-century warrior kings (Bradbury 1957–61:BS276–77). Smiths, it might be noted, often traveled with armies; and this is believed to be one of the ways ironworking skills and perhaps iron-related rituals and symbols diffused. Smiths and soldiers, in fact, shared the same deity. Not only did ironworkers sacrifice to Ogun, but Edo, Oyo, and Dahomean soldiers all made sacrifices to Ogun and Ogun-related deities before battle (Ben-Amos fieldnotes 1976; Johnson 1969:136; Smith 1976b:49).

Wherever they settled, ironworkers acquired significant ritual status. Their forges and smelters were seen as ritual shrines or sanctuaries for anyone losing a fight or fleeing turbulence. The anvil was widely used for taking oaths and as a sacrificial altar. Moreover, ironworkers (and hunters) were organized into guilds, which served as cult groups organized around the worship of Ogun or Gu. Smelting and smithing were separate occupations, plied by separate professional groups. Yet both groups in Yoruba-speaking communities looked to Ogun as their patron deity and both sacrificed to him. Iron-smelters, who dug for their own ore, made sacrifices in order to find iron ore, to keep shafts from collapsing on them, and to prevent accidents while smelting (Adéníji 1977:9–11).

Clearly, the standardization of a cult system could be accomplished relatively easily with this high level of movement among ritually active devotees. There was, in addition, a conscious attempt to transmit and perpetuate sacred systems across boundaries. Oral traditions of Benin indicate that from the earliest period of the monarchy new deities and religious practices were constantly introduced into the state ritual system. One example was the mother of the late seventeenth-century heir apparent who brought the cult of Orunmila (Ifa divination) into the kingdom to protect her son and ensure his ascension to the throne (Ben-Amos 1983:82).

Cult activities drew people across state boundaries for festivals and ceremonies; many migrants returned on special occasions to their homes or went to well-known cult centers of the deities they worshipped (Morton-Williams 1964:259). This meant, among other things, that cult priests were potentially powerful figures, not only because they controlled supernatural powers but because they also organized and controlled groups of people. The kings of Dahomey were well aware of this power and made it a practice in conquered areas to incorporate foreign deities into the state pantheon and to place their priests under the control of a high priest centered in Abomey (Lombard 1967:76). Needless to say, such centralized control could only aid and abet the standardization of cult practices and beliefs.

Ogun Symbolism

The beliefs surrounding iron, centering on the god Ogun, were found throughout the Guinea Coast. The iron of Ogun was sacrificed to, sworn upon, subjected to stringent taboos, or made into a shrine. Its transformation into a sacred element extended from the least imposing scrap of metal to the most imposing decorative art form. Benin altars to Ogun, found in every forge and maintained by warriors and hunters, were "decorated with all kinds of scrap-iron objects" (Bradbury 1957:53). The same was true among Yoruba peoples; as one contemporary devotee explained, a shrine was called Ogun when two pieces of iron were placed together and a sacrifice performed. "As soon as it is put together it stays Ogun, and will be Ogun forever after" (Barnes 1980:37).

The Fon, Edo, and Yoruba peoples frequently used the warriors' iron weapons as the basis for aesthetic elaboration. In Dahomey, such an emblem was the *gubasa*, a ceremonial sword. According to myth, when the creator came to earth he held Gu in his hand in the form of a *gubasa* and with it he cleared the forest and taught people to build houses and till the soil. The creator then taught humans how to use metal so that they, too, could enjoy the power of Gu—a power that would enable them to secure food, cover their bodies, and protect themselves from the elements (Mercier 1954:233).

Among the more common iron objects that served as insignia of Ogun (Gu) were miniature iron implements (Williams 1973:148–52). They were sometimes hung on iron necklaces and bracelets worn by devotees, or attached to clothing (especially that of hunters and warriors), crowns, or standards—all to signify the power of the iron deity. This tradition may indeed go back 400 to 500 years, as evidenced by the miniature pincers on the belt of the Benin warrior depicted in the fifteenth-sixteenth century brass plaque referred to above (fig. 3.1). When he visited the Kingdom of Dahomey in the late nineteenth century, Skertchly found that emblems of Gu were decorated with miniature hoes, knives, and other tiny iron objects (1874:388); moreover, a life-sized iron statue of Gu, given in 1894 to Musée de l'Homme in Paris as a gift, had miniature sword, pincers, hoe, arrow tip,

FIGURE 3.2. Fon, Republic of Benin (formerly Dahomey). Iron statue of Gu. The deity formerly held a
sword in one hand and a bell in the other. Miniature
iron implements decorate the crown. H. 65″. Musée de
l'Homme, Paris, 94.32.1. Photograph courtesy of the
Musée de l'homme.

knives, and hook hanging from his hat (fig. 3.2). Nearly a century later Verger found in the frontier zone between the former kingdoms of Oyo and Dahomey that miniature iron tools still decorated the standards of Ogun (1957:90). These miniatures included blacksmiths' hammers, tongs, pincers, and pokers; farmers' hoes, cutlasses, or knives; warriors' swords, daggers, spears, or bows and arrows; and other items such as bells, gongs, state swords, scrapers, tattooing knives, and eventually guns. Each miniature carried supernatural force in that it protected and brought good fortune to the wearer or, conversely, harmed his enemies.

The tools of Ogun served as emblems of his various capacities; indeed, they became a kind of shorthand or code that extended into many domains. In Benin, for instance, miniature tools commonly appeared on wrought iron staffs used by herbalists. On the top of these staffs was a bird representing the mystical powers of the herbalist, and below the bird were depictions of hoes, swords, and other iron implements (Ben-Amos 1976:249). In former times an herbalist, taking with him such an iron staff as his means of protection, accompanied soldiers to war to assure success against their enemies. There was, as might be expected, a close relationship between herbalists, who provided war charms and medicines, warriors, who used them, and Ogun, whose supernatural powers were embedded in them. The clothing, and even the bodies, of warriors were heavily laden with medicinal and magical objects. Latoosa, a famous nineteenth-century warrior chief of the Yoruba city of Ibadan, went so far as to insert medicated iron objects in his body to gain added strength (Awẹ 1975:278).

Through their intimate connection with hunting, agriculture, crafts, and even warfare, iron objects served as metaphors for civilization itself. This is vividly portrayed in the patterning of an eighteenth-century Benin royal brass stool now found in the Museum für Völkerkunde in Berlin (fig. 3.3a). The seat of the stool (fig. 3.3b) is divided into three zones. At the top is the cosmos, represented by the sun, the moon, and the cross—a Benin symbol of creation. At the bottom are depictions of the powers of the forest, the untamed wilderness: monkeys with snakes issuing from their nostrils, an image indicating terrifying supernatural powers, and the trunks of elephants grasping leaves, representing the herbal knowledge possessed by creatures of the forest. In the middle zone are symbols of civilization, and these are—not surprisingly—the products of the smith. At the very center is an anvil—the ritual and technological heart of the smithy, the place where the heat of Ogun is tempered and controlled. On either side are the tools of the smith: hammer, knife, pincer, tongs, bellows, and blade. At the peripheries are two iron ceremonial swords, emblems of the social status and powers of the rulers, who control life and death (Ben-Amos 1980:30–31, 37).

Many oral traditions of the Guinea Coast kingdoms captured the essence of the Ogun concept through what we see as the paradoxical themes of aggression and civilization, but which for the cultures in question were united, not contradictory, themes. Thus Ogun was depicted as the aggressive, violent

FIGURE 3.3a and 3.3b. Benin, Nigeria. Royal brass stool. 18th century. H. 15 1/2″. Museum für Völkerkunde, Berlin, IIIc20295. Photograph courtesy of the Museum für Völkerunde, Staatliche Museen Preussicher Kulturbesitz, Berlin (West).

warrior whose sword struck swiftly and devastatingly, who "has water at home [civilization] but bathes with blood [aggression]" (Ibigbami 1978:48). In Benin shrines, he was depicted in a war costume, wearing or holding the tools and weapons of his varied occupations. Often his costume and, significantly, his eyes were painted red. To describe someone as having red eyes was a way of indicating his violent temper and capacity for causing harm (Ben-Amos 1980:51). The Yoruba, who also used red eyes for similar symbolic purposes, captured the ferocity of Ogun in the following praise poem:

> Where does one meet him?
> One meets him in the place of battle;
> One meets him in the place of wrangling;
> One meets him in the place where torrents of blood
> Fill with longing, as a cup of water does the thirsty.
> (Idowu 1962:89)

Although the deity was fierce and terrible, he was not evil, for as a civilized being he demanded justice, fair play, and integrity. If appeased, he was tolerant and protective, especially of the poor and dispossessed.

After all, Ogun was responsible for society's most important innovations. His praises were sung by many Yoruba-speaking groups as "Master of the World," the innovative deity who "showed the way" for others; the deity who brought fire; the first hunter; the opener of roads; the clearer of the first fields; the first warrior; the introducer of iron; the founder of dynasties, towns, and kingdoms. Each of these acts was in some way revolutionary. Each was in some way a "first." Indeed, fire was a first principle: it transformed ore into iron, just as it transformed raw food into cooked, and thus, as Lévi-Strauss would put it, nature into culture. Thereafter Ogun brought a new political order through civil war or conquest, a new economy through clearing the fields, a new technology through the introduction of iron, and a new way of life through the founding of towns and cities (Barnes 1980:42ff).

In similar fashion the Fon creator finished his work and then instructed humans to overcome the obstacles of nature, to civilize themselves, by learning to use iron. For Fon, the sword embodied their beginnings. Gu himself was, in some manifestations, perceived as a sword; he was a "force" with no head, only a great tool jutting out of a trunk of stone. From the day of creation onward the sword was given this praise name: *ali-su-gbo-gu-kle*, "the road is closed and Gu opens it." Thanks to Gu, "the earth would not always remain wild bush"; "Gu is the force which helped man adapt himself to the world" (Herskovits and Herskovits 1958:125, 134–35 and 1933:14–15).

The iron sword of Ogun was perhaps his most meaningful symbol, for it condensed the twin meanings of aggression and civilization. It cleared the forest and built the house. More significantly, it vanquished the enemy and crowned the king. The culmination of the coronation ceremony of the Alaafin

of Oyo occurred when the Great Sword, the Sword of Justice, was placed
in the king's hands. (A sword of this type is included among the weapons,
at the far left, on the Benin stool in Plate 3.3b.) Without it he could not wield
the supreme power over life and death. Before the King of Oyo could ascend
the throne, however, he was required to visit two shrines. The first visit was
to the shrine of Oranmiyan—son, father, or brother of Ogun (accounts vary),
and grandchild of the creator deity who founded Ife. According to legend,
Oranmiyan left the throne of Ife to found a ruling dynasty at Oyo and later
to rule at Benin, where his son soon succeeded him. Others of his "offspring"
are often said to be (legendary) founders of other Yoruba kingdoms. Certainly, no king was installed at Oyo or Dahomey without the Great Sword,
reconsecrated at Ife, being placed in his hands, or, in the case of Benin, without brass coronation objects from the Ooni of Ife.[9] The second visit, following
a five-day rest, was to the shrine of Ogun, whereupon, after making sacrifices,
the new ruler immediately entered the palace for the first time (Johnson
1969:45).

The relationship of Oyo's Alaafin to the iron deity was complex. Early
Alaafin worshipped Erin (Erinlẹ), a hunter deity who was related to Ogun
and whose devotees wore iron emblems.[10] Abiodun, who reigned as Alaafin
c. 1760–1789 and whose mother was of the Bashorun (head warrior chief)
line, adopted Ogun, his mother's deity, and was said to have merged the iron
deity with Erin (Abraham 1958:164, 482). Although we may only speculate,
it is possibly not accidental that Alaafin Abiodun made his tie to Ogun explicit
when Oyo's powers reached their zenith and when, history tells us, he tri-
umphed over his Bashorun in a civil war (Law 1977:54).

The relationship between kingship and the iron deity also was explicit at
Ife, the Yoruba kingdom which, as indicated, was believed to have provided
the founder, Oranmiyan (Oranyan), of Oyo's ruling house. In Ife, the Ogun
Laadin shrine, named for the first mythical blacksmith,[11] was housed within
the palace walls and was used by chiefs for debating judicial matters and
swearing oaths. The shrine consisted of a large tear-shaped lump of iron
called *omoowu*, the blacksmith's hammer, two stone anvils called *okuta
Ogun*, Ogun's stones, and, guarding them near the entryway, a stone fish and
a crocodile, described as domestic animals to Ogun.[12]

Symbols of Ogun, especially ceremonial swords and the dramatization of
warfare, were important features of kingship paraphernalia and ritual
throughout the region. The Dahomean King Glele, who reigned in the mid-
nineteenth century, adopted the *gubasa* (sword) for his coat of arms
(Waterlot 1926:Planche XXI); the blade was pierced with holes whose shape
signified Ogun. This identification with Gu was a way of explaining a king's
power (Mercier 1952:48, 59).

The sword presented to the king of Dahomey at his coronation provided
another avenue by which he could maintain contact with the power of Ogun.
Each time he returned from a campaign, the king, dressed in uniform and
holding the coronation sword, appeared with his retinue before hunter chiefs

and danced and pantomimed the actions of a warrior. The hunters were military reservists[13] who protected the capital city of Abomey during the annual campaigns. At the ceremony, the crowd praised Gu and the king, whereupon the king sent for the *guno*, chief priest of Gu, who took from each hunter a ritual knife, given to him at the start of the ceremony and to which sacrifices had been made, and placed the knives in Guzu (*guzume*), the forest sacred to Gu (Herskovits 1967 V.I:121–22).

The ritual relationship between Gu and the king was reaffirmed when the king ceremonially atoned for his warriors' deeds. In a rite called "washing the hands"[14] warriors were required to bring the heads of their victims to the king, who "purchased" them and then threw them to Guzu, the forest of Gu. The ceremony was intended to protect the king and his soldier "agents" from any supernatural vengeance that might ensue from their campaigns (Herskovits 1967 V.II:95–96).

In many eastern Yoruba kingdoms, such as Ife, Ila,[15] and Ire Ekiti (legendary home of the Yoruba Ogun), the annual Ogun ceremony was presided over by the king, who, holding a sword, joined in a mock battle. At Ife, the Ooni (king) made annual sacrifices during the Ogun festival at several Ogun shrines, one of which consisted of a heap of swords (Bascom 1987). Participants in the Ogun festival's mock battle at Ire Ekiti were believed to have once used machetes, and in accidental cases of overzealousness to have killed one another in an "act of war to remember the battling spirit of Ogun" (Ibigbami 1978:47).

In Benin, the annual Isiokuo ceremony, in honor of Ogun, was said to date to the first dynasty of kings, who ruled perhaps until the thirteenth or fourteenth century.[16] As prelude to the festival, and as it was recorded much later, participants made sacrifices at the shrines of Ogun and Efae (hunters' Ogun), and during the ceremony the king sacrificed to Ogun, praying for success in war. The *oba* and other participants, outfitted with war costumes, iron jewelry, and war weapons, then staged a series of mock battles. One of the highlights of the festival came when the *oba* received medicines from Ine Ogun, a titleholder, who held his ceremonial *ada*, sword, upright while the *oba* held his downward, "to show the power of Ogun."[17]

It is through this intimate relationship with kingship that the power and character of Ogun acquired a profoundly historic dimension. For these kingdoms of the Guinea Coast, Ogun—progenitor of iron and warrior king—summed up a long rise to political supremacy.

Conclusion

Ogun, as one scholar put it, was the symbol, par excellence, of the superior, conquering society (Beier 1959:43). The meanings attached to Ogun were abstractions that were *not* tied to a single place or a single cultural context. They conveyed a widely shared message, an evolutionary statement, perceived as such by these peoples and applied to themselves. Thus, throughout the region, this symbol provided a metaphor through which people reflected on the historical milestones of their development—from first clearing the land to living in a glorious Age of Empire.

NOTES

1. One of the surest dates that can be fixed to the existence of the Ogun cult in the Guinea Coast region is the later part of the eighteenth century. By this time the deity must have existed in Haiti, since the importation of slaves in sufficient numbers to establish Ogun as a local deity had by then ceased. (See Brown, ch. 4 in this volume, for a description of the Ogun cult in Haiti.) Williams suggests that the cult was present in an area that would have included Benin and eastern Yoruba kingdoms c. 1530 (1974:83–86). He bases his estimate on contemporary oral traditions and on the dating of (imported) iron used for ritual objects associated with the Ogun cult. Still another suggestion, as we state below, comes from the oral traditions of Benin that link Ogun to an annual kingship ritual that existed as early as the thirteenth or fourteenth century.

Most of the other Ogun traditions cited in this essay were gathered between the late nineteenth century and the mid-twentieth century. Their repeated references to warfare lead us to believe that these traditions were current among Edo, Oyo, and Fon peoples on the eve of colonial takeover, at the end of the nineteenth century, when warfare was prevalent and when they still lived in independent kingdoms.

2. The authors wish to thank Vincent Pigott and Ellen Sieber for assistance in examining iron technology and production.

3. In recent years it has become apparent that steel of medium to high carbon content was produced in West Africa as long ago as the first millennium B.C. The ancient site of Taruga yielded several steel objects (Tylecote 1975:54–55). The quality of locally produced steel, in the eyes of latter-day smiths, was "vastly superior to imported European hoop iron" (van der Merwe 1980:492–93; see also Bellamy 1904:118). The excellent quality of locally-made iron implements of the late eighteenth century was commented on by the French trader Landolphe who visited Benin (Quesné 1823:49).

4. Trees were said to have been planted to demarcate the boundaries of the two kingdoms (Smith 1976a:47).

5. In Oyo horses were symbols of royalty (Babayemi 1979:34).

6. According to Smith:

> Swords were of two main types: the heavier, single-bladed and eccentrically curved *agedengbe*, and the *ida*, usually double-bladed and either with an elongated leaf-shaped blade or approximating to European or Near Eastern types. Other varieties of swords and knives were also used, such as the short *jomo*, the *tanmogayi* (sabre), *ada, ogbo* or *ele* (cutlass), and *obe* (dagger). With the exception of the *obe*, all these were designed primarily for cutting rather than for thrusting or stabbing. (1976a:145)

The ceremonial sword was of the *ida* type.

7. A court of appeals such as this one had considerable importance, since it placed Benin officials in the position of deciding contested chieftaincy or kingship selec-

tions and thereby having a hand in choosing the highest officeholders of a neighboring kingdom.

8. War captives were also used for the well-known annual sacrifices made by the King of Dahomey to ensure the well-being of his kingdom.

9. See Bascom 1969:83; Herskovits 1967 V.I:121; Johnson 1969:7–12; Law 1977:30–31, 122; and Willett 1967:79.

10. The symbolism could be reversed. One emblem of Ogun, therefore, was the tusk or tail of Erinle, who also took the form of an elephant (Idowu 1962:89).

11. For a variation on the meaning of Ogun Laadin see Fabunmi 1969:12.

12. Barnes fieldnotes, 1984. See also Willett 1967:101.

13. In many Yoruba-speaking kingdoms hunters automatically served in the military during wartime.

14. See Armstrong ch. 2 in this volume.

15. See Pemberton ch. 6 in this volume and Bascom 1987.

16. This festival, like those at Ife, Ire Ekiti, and many other communities of the region, continues to be held each year.

17. Ben-Amos fieldnotes, 1976; Bradbury 1957–61:BS559 and 1958–59:OB10; and Egharevba 1949:88.

References Cited

Abraham, R. C. 1958. *Dictionary of Modern Yoruba*, London: University of London Press.

Adéníji, D. A. A. 1977. *Iron Mining and Smelting in Yorùbáland*, (translated and edited by R. G. Armstrong), Occasional Publication No. 31, Institute of African Studies, University of Ibadan.

Ajayi, J. F. A., and R. Smith. 1964. *Yoruba Warfare in the Nineteenth Century*, London: Cambridge University Press in association with the Institute of African Studies, University of Ibadan.

Akinjogbin, I. A. 1976. "The Expansion of Oyo and the Rise of Dahomey, 1600–1800," in *History of West Africa*, V. I (2nd ed.), J. F. A. Ajayi and M. Crowder (eds.), New York: Columbia University Press, pp. 373–412.

Akintoye, S. A. 1971. *Revolution and Power Politics in Yorubaland 1840–1893*, New York: Humanities Press.

Argyle, W. J. 1966. *The Fon of Dahomey: A History and Ethnography of the Old Kingdom*, Oxford: Clarendon.

Awe, Bolanle. 1973. "Militarism and Economic Development in Nineteenth Century Yoruba Country: the Ibadan Example," *Journal of African History*, 14(1):65–77.

———. 1975. "Notes on Oríkì and Warfare in Yorubaland," in *Yoruba Oral Tradition*, W. Abimbola (ed.), Ifé: Department of African Languages and Literatures, University of Ifé, pp. 267–92.

Babayemi, S. O. 1979. "The Fall and Rise of Oyo c. 1760–1905: A Study in the Traditional Culture of an African Polity," Ph.D. thesis, University of Birmingham.

Barnes, Sandra T. 1980. *Ogun: An Old God for a New Age*, Philadelphia: ISHI.

Bascom, William. 1969. *The Yoruba of Southwestern Nigeria*, New York: Holt, Rinehart and Winston.

———. 1987. "The Olojo Festival at Ife, 1937," in *Time Out of Time*, Alessandro Falassi (ed.), Albuquerque: University of New Mexico Press.

Bay, Edna. 1983. "Servitude and Worldly Success in the Palace of Dahomey," in *Women and Slavery in Africa*, C. C. Robertson and M. A. Klein (eds.), Madison: University of Wisconsin Press, pp. 340–67.

Beier, U. 1959. *A Year of Sacred Festivals in One Yoruba Town*, Lagos: Nigeria Magazine.

Bellamy, C. V. 1904. "A West African Smelting House," *Journal of the Iron and Steel Institute*, 66(2):99–120.

Ben-Amos, Paula. 1976. "Man and Animals in Benin Art," *Man*, N.S. II(2):243–52.

———. 1980. *The Art of Benin*, London: Thames and Hudson.

———. 1983. "In Honor of Queen Mothers," in *The Art of Power/The Power of Art: Studies in Benin Iconography*, P. Ben-Amos and A. Rubin (eds.), Los Angeles: Museum of Culture History, UCLA, pp. 79–83.

Bradbury, R. E. 1957. *The Benin Kingdom*, Ethnographic Survey of Africa, Part 13, London: International African Institute.

———. 1957–61. Benin Scheme Field Notes Series BS. On file at the University of Birmingham Library (England).

———. 1958–59. Benin Scheme Field Notes Series OB. On file at the University of Birmingham Library (England).

———. 1973. *Benin Studies*, London: Oxford University Press for International African Institute.

Burton, R. F. 1864. *A Mission to Gelele, King of Dahome*, Vol. I–II, London: Tinsley Brothers.

Calvocoressi, D., and N. David. 1979. "A New Survey of Radiocarbon and Thermoluminescence Dates for West Africa," *Journal of African History*, 20:1–29.

Connah, Graham. 1975. *The Archaeology of Benin*, Oxford: Clarendon.

———. 1981. *Three Thousand Years in Africa*, Cambridge: Cambridge University Press.

Curtin, P., S. Feierman, L. Thompson, and J. Vansina. 1978. *African History*, Boston: Little Brown.

Davidson, Basil. 1959. *Old Africa Rediscovered*, London: Victor Gollancz.

Drewal, H. J. 1977. *Traditional Art of the Nigerian Peoples*, Washington, D.C.: Museum of African Art.

Duncan, J. 1847. *Travels in Western Africa in 1845 & 1846*, London: Richard Bentley.

Egharevba, J. U. 1949. *Benin Law and Custom*, Port Harcourt: C.M.S. Niger Press.

———. 1960. *A Short History of Benin* (3rd ed.), Ibadan: Ibadan University Press.

Fabunmi, M. A. 1969. *Ifẹ Shrines*, Ile-Ifẹ: University of Ifẹ Press.

Forbes, F. E. 1851. *Dahomey and the Dahomans*, Vol. I, London: Longman.

Goody, J. 1971. *Technology, Tradition, and the State in Africa*, London: Oxford University Press for International African Institute.

Herskovits, M. J. 1967. *Dahomey: An Ancient West African Kingdom*, Vol. I and II, Evanston: Northwestern University Press (first pub. 1938).

Herskovits, M. J., and F. S. Herskovits. 1933. *An Outline of Dahomean Religious Belief*, Memoirs of the American Anthropological Association, No. 41.

———. 1958. *Dahomean Narrative*, Evanston: Northwestern University Press.

Hodgkin, T. (ed.). 1960. *Nigerian Perspectives: An Historical Anthology*, London: Oxford University Press.

Horton, R. 1976. "Stateless Societies in the History of West Africa," in *History of West Africa*, V.I (2nd ed.), J. F. A. Ajayi and M. Crowder (eds.), New York: Columbia University Press, pp. 72–113.

Ibigbami, R. I. 1978. "Ogun Festival in Ire Ekiti," *Nigeria Magazine*, No. 126–27, pp. 44–59.

Idowu, E. Bolaji. 1962. *Olodumare: God in Yoruba Belief*, London: Longmans.

Johnson, Rev. S. 1969. *The History of the Yorubas*, Lagos: C.S.S. Bookshops (first pub. 1921).

Karpinski, Peter. 1984. "A Benin Bronze Horseman at the Merseyside County Museum," *African Arts*, XVII(2), pp. 54–62.

Law, R. C. 1977. *The Oyo Empire c. 1600–c. 1836*, Oxford: Clarendon.

———. 1980. *The Horse in West African History*, Oxford: Oxford University Press for International African Institute.

Lombard, J. 1967. "The Kingdom of Dahomey," in *West African Kingdoms in the Nineteenth Century*, D. Forde and P. M. Kaberry (eds.), London: Oxford University Press for International African Institute, pp. 70–92.

Mabogunje, Akin. 1976. "The Land and Peoples of West Africa," in *History of West Africa*, V. I (2nd ed.), J. F. A. Ajayi and M. Crowder (eds.), New York: Columbia University Press, pp. 1–32.

Mercier, P. 1952. *Les Asé du Musée d'Abomey*, Catalogues VII, Dakar: IFAN.

———. 1954. "The Fon of Dahomey," in *African Worlds*, D. Forde (ed.), London: Oxford University Press for International African Institute, pp. 210–34.

Morton-Williams, P. 1964. "An Outline of the Cosmology and Cult Organization of the Oyo Yoruba," *Africa*, 34(3):243–61.

———. 1967. "The Yoruba Kingdom of Oyo," in *West African Kingdoms in the Nineteenth Century*, D. Forde and P. M. Kaberry (eds.), London: Oxford University Press for International African Institute, pp. 36–69.

———. 1971. "The Influence of Habitat and Trade on the Polities of Oyo and Ashanti," in *Man in Africa*, M. Douglas and P. M. Kaberry (eds.), Garden City, N.Y.: Anchor (first pub. 1969), pp. 80–99.

Obayemi, Ade. 1976. "The Yoruba and Edo-Speaking Peoples and Their Neighbours before 1600," in *History of West Africa*, V.I (2nd ed.), J. F. A. Ajayi and M. Crowder (eds.), New York: Columbia University Press, pp. 196–263.

Ojo, G. J. A. 1966. *Yoruba Culture*, London: University of London Press.

Oliver, R., and B. M. Fagan. 1975. *Africa in the Iron Age*, Cambridge: Cambridge University Press.

Quesné, J. S. (ed.). 1823. *Mémoires du Capitaine Landolphe*, Paris: Bertrand.

Ryder, A. F. C. 1969. *Benin and the Europeans, 1485–1897*, London: Longmans.

Shaw, Thurstan. 1970. *Igbo-Ukwu: An Account of Archaeological Discoveries in Eastern Nigeria*, V.I, Evanston: Northwestern University Press.

———. 1978. *Nigeria: Its Archaeology and Early History*, London: Thames and Hudson.

Skertchly, J. A. 1874. *Dahomey as It Is*, London: Chapman & Hall.

Smith, R. S. 1973. "Yoruba Warfare and Weapons," in *Sources of Yoruba History*, S. O. Biobaku (ed.), Oxford: Clarendon, pp. 224–49.

———. 1976a. *Kingdoms of the Yoruba* (2nd ed.), London: Methuen.

———. 1976b. *Warfare and Diplomacy in Pre-Colonial West Africa*, London: Methuen.

Tylecote, R. F. 1975. "Iron Smelting of Taruga, Nigeria," *Bulletin of the Historical Metallurgy Group*, 9:49–56.

van der Merwe, N. J. 1980. "The Advent of Iron in Africa," in *The Coming of the Age of Iron*, T. A. Wertime and J. D. Muhly (eds.), New Haven: Yale University Press, pp. 463–506.

Verger, P. 1957. *Notes sur le Culte des Orisa et Vodun*, Dakar: IFAN.

Warnier, J.-P., and I. Fowler. 1979. "A Nineteenth-Century Ruhr in Central Africa," *Africa*, 49(4):329–51.

Waterlot, Em. G. 1926. *Les Bas-Reliefs des Bâtiments Royaux d'Abomey*, Paris: Institut d'Ethnologie.
Willett, F. 1967. *Ife in the History of African Sculpture*, London: Thames and Hudson.
Williams, Denis. 1973. "Art in Metal," in *Sources of Yoruba History*, S. O. Biobaku (ed.), Oxford: Clarendon, pp. 140–64.
———. 1974. *Icon and Image: A Study of Sacred and Secular Forms of African Classical Art*, London: Allen Lane.

Karen McCarthy Brown

4

Systematic Remembering, Systematic Forgetting: Ogou in Haiti

Ogou is a central figure in Haitian religion. While little known in some areas of rural Haiti, in others he is one of the most important spirits[1] of African origin who are venerated in the Vodou religious system. In cities he has a more prominent role, so that in Port-au-Prince, where no temple neglects him entirely, Ogou frequently is the major spirit of priests and priestesses. Among Haitians who migrate to New York City, those who have Ogou as their *mèt tet,* "master of the head," may well be in the majority.[2]

Ogou in Haiti has his roots in the Gu or the Ogun of the Dahomean or Yoruba peoples, who (along with the Kongo peoples) seem to have contributed the largest concentrations of slaves to Haiti and consequently to have had the strongest influence on its culture. However, he is not simply a reproduction of these African deities. Certainly the Old World played a strong role. Large numbers of slaves were young men whose activities in the African homeland were often centered on the military, hunting, or ironworking—the areas where Ogun was a major patron (Barnes 1980:3, 17, 19–30, and personal communication). It was only natural, then, that this preponderant sector of the incoming population should bring ideas of Gu/Ogun to the New World. In Haiti, however, hunting and smithing were no longer crucial to everyday life, while the soldier took on new guises and added significance. Thus the Haitian Ogou became important to men, and women, of all ages. He also came into contact with Roman Catholicism, the religion of the slaveholders. Indeed, the Catholic saints penetrated the whole world of Vodou— its visual representations, where chromolithographs of the saints came to be used as images for Afro-Haitian spirits, and its naming system, where saint names and Afro-Haitian spirit names came to be used interchangeably. Also central to the development of the Haitian Ogou were several centuries of political and military upheaval, a historical legacy which transformed the African religious cosmos.

It is important to emphasize that any understanding of the centrality of Ogou in present-day urban Haitian Vodou must include an understanding of the history and of the social and political structures of Haiti. Bastide has written that the slave diaspora had the effect of separating "the world of symbols, collective representations, and values from the world of social structures and their morphological bases" (1978:155). In his view, the process by which African religious systems moved into the New World consisted of a search for appropriate social structural "niches" in which symbolic representations could survive.[3] In some cases, such as the match between Ogou and the military in Haiti, such niches were found. In others they were not. When they were found, the fit between cultural image and social structure was never perfect, and therefore the process by which the two came together was one of continuous negotiation, so that, over time, both were changed by virtue of their interaction.

The point I wish to stress about the continuation of African religions in the New World is that elements which are retained as a legacy from the past are subject to systematic and continuous redefinition and restructuring, and that out of this process new cultural forms emerge. The current Haitian Ogou is one such form.

I begin by placing Ogou in relation to the two major pantheons of urban Vodou. I then turn to analyze his various manifestations, mainly through sacred songs. This discussion focuses on military power and its transformations in a variety of political and social contexts. Finally, I will place the Ogou in relation to another group of spirits, the Gède, who occupy a parallel but clearly contrasting place in Vodou cosmology. I conclude that the emphasis given to Ogou in contemporary Haitian Vodou can be attributed to the fact that he is able to mediate between two diametrically opposed forces in Haitian life. These forces, represented by the two major urban pantheons, have gone through many incarnations in the course of Haitian history, but they are perhaps most succinctly named by pairs of contrasting terms such as insiders/outsiders, family members/foreigners, slaves/slaveholders, oppressed/oppressors.

The Rada and the Petro Spirits

The Vodou spirits, or *lwa* as the Haitians call them, were once divided into several *nanchon*, "nations"—Rada, Petro, Kongo, Nago, Ibo, and so on. In most cases, their names clearly indicate their African origins. This pattern is still used in some rural parts of Haiti. However, in and around Port-au-Prince, Haiti's major urban center, two pantheons, the Rada and the Petro, have emerged as dominant, largely by absorbing the other nations into themselves.

The Rada and the Petro groups express contrasting views of the world. One way of capturing this difference would be to say that the Rada pantheon articulates the ethos of insiders and family members, as opposed to the Petro pantheon, which describes that of outsiders and foreigners.[4] One of the most significant changes to take place in African religions as a result of the slave experience was what I call the socialization of the cosmos. For example, natural powers such as those of storm, drought, and disease paled before social powers such as those of the slaveholder. This caused a massive refocusing of the explanatory energies of the African religious systems. This characterization of Rada and Petro as respectively insiders and outsiders is thus in keeping with the general character of African religions in the New World.

The Rada spirits, whose name comes from the town of Allada in ancient Dahomey, are known as *lwa rasin*, "root *lwa*," or by a more general title, *lwa Gine*, "African *lwa*." The Rada are associated with the right hand, with the downward direction, and therefore directly with *Gine*, "Africa," a spiritual home for ancestors and spirits which the Haitians locate in the water under the earth. Hence the Rada pantheon connects the Haitians directly to their African homeland. Indeed, the names and characteristics of most of the spirits grouped in this pantheon have African counterparts.

The Rada *lwa* are intimate spirits who surround one with their protection on a day-to-day basis. Their protective power is of a noncoercive sort and is said to reside mainly in their spiritual knowledge. For example, they are often said to "know leaves," which means they are familiar with herbal healing. Their protective role is further articulated in the fact that they are socially familiar beings who are well known and trusted. They are the elders of the family, and therefore they are sometimes experienced as stern and austere; their fundamental benevolence, however, is never doubted. If a sacrifice is promised to a Rada *lwa* and there is not enough money this year, the spirit can be convinced to wait until next year. The Rada *lwa* thus represent one existential option. Their way of being-in-the-world is defined by family. The central consciousness of this mode of being is group consciousness and its highest value is the preservation of the group.

The origins of the Petro pantheon, and specifically the name itself, are obscure. Some writers have suggested the name can be traced to an eponymous hero, Dom Pedro, who was a Spanish Vodou priest, but there seems to be little historical evidence for this theory.[5] More promising is the suggestion that while few of the specific Petro spirit names indicate Kongo origins, the general ambiance of the group does (Thompson 1983:179–80).

The powers and symbols of the Petro *lwa* stand in marked contrast to those of the Rada group. They are associated with the left hand, with the upward direction, and with leaping flames and heat. In personality, the Petro *lwa* are fierce, severe, and uncompromising. Promises to them must be kept and services rendered with care. One does not break or even bend the rules when dealing with the Petro *lwa*. The ritual vocabulary of the Petro spirits is that of the slaveholders. These *lwa* are served with fire, small explosions of gun-powder, cracking whips, and shrieking police whistles. Some have argued that the Petro spirits represent an expression of rage against enslavement,[6] or an attempt to imitate the slavemasters. I prefer to state it another way: The Petro *lwa* represent an effort to expropriate the power of slaveholding and its con-temporary transmutations—oppression, prejudice, economic discrimination—and to use that power against itself.

The Petro *lwa* are the outsiders. Like stereotypic "strangers," the Petro *lwa* tend to look alike and act alike. When they possess their followers, they have personalities that are much less distinguishable from one another than the Rada *lwa*. For example, it is said of the Petro *lwa* that "if you feed one, you feed them all." In spite of this tendency to blend together, the Petro *lwa* are highly individualistic in their mode of being. Likewise, those who seek them out can do so for partisan, even individualistic, purposes. Furthermore, money, notorious for its ability to create social distance, is an area of life where the Petro *lwa* are thought to be particularly effective. The Petro *lwa* thus represent another existential option, a way of being-in-the-world which puts stress on the use of coercive power and the pursuit of self-interest. Be-cause these traits are considered by the Haitians to be too dangerous to be-come central in the conduct of life, the Petro *lwa* are never given so much emphasis as to displace the Rada *lwa*.

Vodou priests and priestesses in Haiti and in New York are careful to keep their service to the spirits balanced in favor of the right hand, the Rada *lwa*. Yet none is so foolish as to cut himself or herself off completely from the power of the Petro *lwa*.

In urban Vodou, the Ogou are recognized by all to be Nago spirits. This name is the ancient Dahomean title for the Ketu Yoruba (Thompson 1983:17). Nevertheless, these days it is felt that the Ogou should also be clas-sified according to the binary system set up by the Rada and Petro pantheons. The difficulty Haitians currently have in agreeing on how this is to be done points to Ogou's mediating role between the pantheons.

The Rada spirits are associated with water, the Petro with fire. From this perspective, Ogou appears to be clearly Petro. Ogou has a fiery nature: bon-fires are lit for him; those who serve him wear red; those who are possessed by him act aggressively. He is also said to fear water, the wisdom of this being captured in the Haitian proverb *Tizo difè di li fou men li pa janm fè nan chemen dlo*, "A firebrand, say it's crazy, but it will never get in the way of water." This otherwise neat picture is complicated by the existence of one Ogou—there are many—who is a water-dwelling spirit. This is Ogou Balendyo, escort of the Rada sea spirit, Agwe. Ogou Balendyo, who also can be identified with Ogou Batala (from the Yoruba Obatala), is known for his herbal knowledge, another Rada domain. For these reasons and because Ogou is clearly a root *lwa* with strong ties to the African homeland, some informants confidently state that the Ogou are Rada spirits. Métraux, who worked in the Port-au-Prince area in the late 1940s, just as confidently assigned at least one of the Ogou (Ogou Yamson) to the Petro pantheon (1972:89). And a Vodou priestess in New York claims that all Ogou are *en dèz o*, "in two waters"; by this she means that the Ogou can manifest themselves equally well in either the Rada or the Petro mode. From this we must conclude that Ogou's ambivalence in relation to the dominant Rada/Petro classification system is a significant dimension of his character.

Ogou's mediating role is further illustrated by the libations offered to the various groups of Vodou spirits. As we might expect, the central element in libations for the Rada *lwa* is water; for the Petro it is fire. Ogou is given libations of rum (fiery water), which are poured on the ground and set on fire, or, mimicking rain, sprayed upward through the air in a fine mist.

The significance of the opposition between Rada and Petro emerges clearly in the ritual rule that the two pantheons cannot be allowed to touch or mix. This principle is articulated in various ways within the Vodou system, including temple architecture, where Rada and Petro altars must be kept separate. Urban Vodou *ounfò*, "temples," consist of a large central space for ritual activities, and *dyevo*, small side-rooms where altars, offerings, and ritual clothing are kept. The number of *dyevo* varies with the financial resources of the temple. Usually the two pantheons are given separate altar rooms; however, even in *ounfò* where only one side-room is available, the Rada and Petro altars are separated by a partition such as a curtain or they are set at right angles to one another. In one temple outside Port-au-Prince where there are several *dyevo*, the separation is further reinforced by the location of an Ogou altar room in between the Rada and Petro chambers.

Ogou's mediating role finds further expression in ritual sequence. Large drumming and dancing ceremonies, of the sort that are common in urban Vodou, begin with an invocation of the Rada spirits in the order of their importance. A similar set of invocations for the Petro spirits follows. The transition from Rada to Petro cannot be accomplished without a shift in the ritual action. Sometimes this is accomplished by a short socializing break in which people eat, drink, and talk with their neighbors. At other times, Ogou will be called between the two pantheons, if only perfunctorily. In each of these examples, we have seen that Ogou mediates between two opposed ways of being represented by the Rada and the Petro pantheons, allowing movement from one to the other.

The urgent work of the various Ogou is to negotiate the social opposition represented in the two major pantheons. The Rada spirits delineate and reinforce familial bonds. They are treated as family and, in turn, treat their devotees with the indulgence and nurturing accorded to family members. The Petro *lwa*, by contrast, embody the individualism, effectivity, and power of foreigners. Petro spirits are not indulgent; they operate according to hard and fast rules that allow no exceptions. The Ogou model a way of being in the world that mediates between family members and foreigners, insiders and outsiders, the home and the larger world outside of it. They are intimate like the Rada spirits, yet powerful like the Petro. But Ogou power, in contrast to that of the Petro spirits, cannot be managed by faithful adherence to rule and principle. Ogou's power is rooted in feeling, specifically in rage, and so it is subject to all the complexities of emotion. As one Haitian put it: "Ogou loves to give people gifts even when he is very angry; he will reward at the same time as he punishes."

The center of Vodou worship, regardless of the classification of the spirits being addressed, is possession-performance. Singing and dancing are said to entice the spirits to possess a devotee. The *lwa* is then said to ride the person like a horse. Once possessed, the *chwal*, "horse," is treated exactly as if he or she were the spirit. Acts of obeisance are performed, gifts are proffered, and the spirit in turn gives advice to individuals and general admonitions to the community. The possession-performance of Ogou, like that of other *lwa*, has certain ritual constants around which the individual *chwal* can improvise. One such constant comes at the beginning of the ceremonial possession, when Ogou does a ritual dance with his sword. First he attacks the imaginary enemy: he rushes wildly about the temple clanging the sword on doorframes and brandishing it in the air. Then he threatens the immediate community: with smaller gestures, he brings the sword's point threateningly close to the bodies of those standing nearby. Finally he turns the sword on himself: lodging the point in his solar plexus, he poses. This performance is to body language what proverbs are to spoken language. In one elegant series of motions, it conveys the message that the same power which liberates also corrupts and inevitably turns on itself.

This exploration of the constructive and destructive uses of power is central to the character of each of the many different Ogou. In the following discussion we will be looking at several of the Ogou through one or more of their songs. It is not possible here to look at the entire range of Ogou symbolism; therefore, a word of caution is necessary. Rather than seeing one Ogou as illustrating a positive use of power and another a negative one, it is more accurate to see each as spinning out another version of the paradox of power expressed in a simple series of movements with the ritual sword.

The Power of Ogou: Against His Enemies

Military imagery is the perfect vehicle to handle the complex social negotiation which is the work of Ogou. Soldiers are given powers beyond those of the ordinary citizen. Ideally they use them to defend the group. Political and military emblems are conspicuously displayed in most Vodou temples. The Haitian coat of arms, with its palm tree, flags, and cannons, appears alongside images of the spirits in temple wall paintings and many temples decorate their ceilings with strings of tiny paper Haitian flags. Until the Duvalier regime fell in February of 1986, pictures of the ruling family often appeared along with the flags. It would be easy to see this as simply politically expedient, but it is not. The political and military imagery penetrates to the heart of Vodou symbolic language about the Ogou. The Ogou are soldiers (Ogou Feray, Sin Jak Majè, Ogou Badagri) or politicians (Ogou Panama, Achade Bokò, Ogou Chango). The military-political complex has provided the primary niche for Ogou in Haiti. It is partly Ogou who, over time, made the Haitian experience of these institutions manageable, and it has been the particular historical configuration of these institutions that, in part, gave life and definition to Ogou.

Sin Jak Majè (St. Jacques Majeur) is the senior Ogou. In ceremonies, he is saluted before all other Ogou. Haitians use the Catholic chromolithograph of Santiago, astride his horse crushing the enemy underfoot, to represent Sin Jak. One of the songs used to greet Sin Jak Majè has this refrain: *Sin Jak Majè/ Gason lagè ou ye*, "Sin Jak Majè/ You're a warrior."

Ogou Feray is head of all the soldier Ogou. An especially popular song for him is this one:

1	Seremoni Feray yo premye klas-o
2	Feray Layman, ki chita sou pè-a,
3	l'ap tire kanon. (Repeat)
4	Sa l'a di. Sa l'a fè avek zanfan la-vo.
5	Sa l'a di. Sa l'a fè avek timoun la-vo.

1	Ceremonies for Feray are first class.
2	Feray the Magnet, who sits on the altar,
3	he's firing the cannon. (Repeat)
4	That is what he will say. That is what he will do with his children.
5	That is what he will say. That is what he will do with his little ones.

The language of songs for the *lwa* is cryptic and multivalent. It is never possible to do a full translation or exhaustive exegesis of them. The word *seremoni*, for instance, can refer to healing work done in the name of Feray; to magical work similarly performed (and by implication almost any action done in a Feray manner); to a dancing and drumming feast held for Feray; or to a military parade, a ritual version of which is performed for Ogou. *Seremoni* also refers to the *vèvè*, abstract drawings which are executed on the floor of Vodou temples to call up the spirits from Africa. The *vèvè* for Ogou Feray is an abstraction of the Haitian coat of arms. So the reference in this song to the "first class" *seremoni* for Feray can be taken as an allusion to Haiti itself. Such chauvinism is understandable among a people who pride themselves on having carried out a successful slave revolution and founding the first independent Black republic in the Western Hemisphere.

It should also be said that Vodou military images always include, at some level, a reference to military culture heroes. One is Toussaint L'Ouverture, a brilliant military strategist and canny statesman who emerged as the leader of the revolution soon after it began in 1791. He was considered a saint in his time, and contemporary Haitians continue to venerate him. Subsequent soldier-kings of Haiti have sought to legitimize their rule by imitating Toussaint. Awestruck, unquestioning respect is one layer (among many) in the Haitian attitude toward soldiers, human and divine.

The title Feray the Magnet connects this Ogou to magical and healing powers. Magnets are valued for their ability to find lost objects, particularly pins and needles dropped on the ground. Because of these properties, magnets are often included in healing charms and lucky talismans. Feray Layman is therefore a magician-soldier "who sits on the altar" gathering the lost to himself and waging war in their name. A Vodou altar is the repository of the history of a people. In addition to images of spirits, it contains earthenware pots called *govi* in which reside the protective spirits of the ancestors. In this song, Ogou Feray is thus ensconced at the head of a vast battalion of spirits and ancestors, firing his cannon and launching a revolution on behalf of all his "children." The reference here is clearly to those who follow and serve him, for the Ogou have no children of their own. Through this multivocal symbolism, contemporary Ogou worship in Haiti shows itself to be a fecund marriage of experiences such as the slave revolution with memories of the African Ogun, warrior and forger of weapons. Added to this portrait, through a cryptic reference to Ogou's power to gather in the lost, is a hint at his nurturing or protective side.

The protective power of Ogou is revealed more explicitly in the following verse from a song in which he is called upon to guard the people against police harassment.

1   Aye, Aye.
2   Lapolis a rete mwen.
3   Jij pa kondane mwen.

1   Aye, Aye.
2   The police will arrest me.
3   The judge won't condemn me.

Arrest, often arbitrary, is a frequent fact of life in Haiti: "The police will arrest me"; however, Ogou's protection will suffice in the end: "The judge won't condemn me." Echoes of Ogou's ability to protect those who act in his name could be heard from many sources during the demonstrations and acts of civil disobedience that preceded Haiti's recent change of government.

For example, a fisherman in the northern town of Gonaïves, a center for anti-Duvalier protest, said he was able to stand up to the police only because of special protection given him by Ogou.

The Ogou operate in extreme social situations—in difficult, trying, perilous times—and so the strength they exhibit in themselves and call forth in their devotees is the strength of someone pushed to the limit. The Ogou call on one another and their followers to tap their deepest reserves of energy, as the next song indicates:

1   Ogou Badagri, sa ou ap fè la?
2   Ou sèviye, ou met envèye.

3   M-ta dòmi, Feray, m-envi dòmi-o.
4   M-ta dòmi, Feray, m-pase dòmi-o.
5   Se nan lagè mwen ye!
6   Ou met m-envèye, o Feray o.
7   Gason lagè mwen ye!
8   Yo met m-envèye.

1   Ogou Badagri, what are you doing?
2   You are on guard duty, you must wake up.

3   I would sleep, Feray, I need to sleep.
4   I would sleep, Feray, I am beyond sleep.
5   I am in the war!
6   You must wake me, oh Feray oh.
7   I am a soldier!
8   They must wake me.

In this song Ogou Feray, in his role as leader of all Ogou who are soldiers, calls out to Ogou Badagri, who threatens to fall asleep at his guard post. Badagri responds that he knows it is a situation of war, and even though he badly needs sleep, he is first and foremost a soldier and will stay at his post. The song's message is two-pronged. It first makes a realistic assessment of the situation: This is a situation of war and people are taxed beyond reason. In the second part of the message, it indicates people are up to the challenge. In the New World, in slavery, in the revolution and in the chaotic times that followed it, in the modern experience of political oppression, and for some, as we shall see, in the ghetto life of New York, war becomes the metaphor for life itself.

Ogou is a protective weapon for those who serve him. To wage war daily requires constant watchfulness and herculean energy. It is possible because Ogou taps the deepest source of human energy: anger, the final defiant refusal to admit defeat. Ogou's anger empowers those who serve him, as this song for Ogou Achade illustrates:

1   Baton pase nan men mwen,
2   Achade pou chè raje mwade mwen. (Repeat)
3   Achade, ki jen m-ap fè sa-ye?
4   Achade, ki jen pou-m fè sa-ye?

1   The club passes into my hand,
2   Achade, for the mad dog bites me. (Repeat)
3   Achade, how am I going to do that?
4   Achade, how am I going to be able to do that?

The same theme is echoed in a song for Ogou Feray which contains the line *Jou m-en kolè enryè pa sa fè mwen*, "The day I am angry nothing will happen to me." In situations of oppression, then, to touch one's anger is to reclaim one's power, position, and dignity in the world. This is the psychological maneuver at the heart of Ogou's message.

When Ogou is very angry, he can *chante pwen*, "sing a point song." The point song is another weapon against life's trials. *Pwen* means point, the point of a story, a comment, a complex human situation, as in, "Do you get the point?" In short, *pwen* is the condensation of a thing, its pith. When it is a spirit's power that is condensed, it becomes a talisman. Within Vodou, *pwen* refers to an object or a series of words or actions designed to focus the power of a particular *lwa* and thus enable a person to use that power by internalizing it. *Pwen* can be sung, swallowed, put under the skin, worn around the neck, or performed over a person. Thus, when Ogou sings a point song, at the same time that he is sending a pithy communication to his enemies he is also providing his followers with a talisman to use when they are angry. One of Ogou's point songs begins this way:

1   Ankò m-kay mèt-ye.
2   Bef mouri nan men mwen.

1   I am still the master of the house.
2   The bull dies by my hand.

This song evokes an image of rural Haiti where the father is both head of the household and head priest, controlling the family's access to the spirits by presiding over their sacrifices. As a point song, it provides a clear and poignant way of reminding those who cross Ogou that he is in charge, while assuring those who serve him that his power will prevail.

The Power of Ogou: Against His Followers

The anger of Ogou vacillates. It is directed outward toward the enemy, but can quickly turn toward his own people when they fail him. Ogou's discipline is severe. To serve Ogou is to be in an army where control of the self makes possible control of the enemy. Ogou's anger and his attacks on his wayward followers are key elements in the possession-performance of Ogou. When the ceremony is large enough and the space sufficient, rituals for Ogou include a kind of military parade, with flags and a sword bearer. After several revolutions around the sacred center pole of the temple, the sword bearer suddenly reverses directions and stages a mock attack on his own retinue. Ogou may even discipline his own *chwal*, "horse," the very person possessed by him. The following is a report of a conversation with a *manbo*, a Vodou priestess who lives in New York, where she has served the spirits for twenty-five years.

Manbo: When Ogou Feray is really mad, he takes his sword and he (gesture) breaks his own head.

Author: Why do you think he would do something like that?

Manbo: If you do something to make Ogou Feray angry, when he rides you, you suffer. If he is really mad at his *chwal*, when he leaves you have the pain to show for it.

The tendency of Ogou's anger to turn on his own people is captured in another song.

1   Ogou o.

2   Yo di ou ap sonde chwal mwen.
3   Jou m-en kolè m-a vante pwen mwen.

4   Ogou o.

5   Yo di ou ap sonde pwen mwen.
6   Jou m-en kolè enryè pa sa fè mwen.

7   M-di Feray, vre, ou Nago Feray.
8   M-di Feray, ou Nago Feray.

1   Ogou oh.

2   They say you are testing my horse.
3   The day I'm angry, I will boast about my point.

4   Ogou oh.

5   They say you are testing my point.
6   The day I'm angry nothing will happen to me.

7   I say Feray, truly, you are Nago Feray.
8   I say Feray, you are Nago Feray.

In Vodou songs, as in biblical psalms, the spirit is sometimes the speaker and sometimes the one spoken to. In this song, there is an intentional ambiguity about who is speaking. Thus the song communicates simultaneously that Ogou tests those who serve him and gives them protection, a *pwen*, in their time of trial.

Taken a step further, and it often is, Ogou's anger ceases to be about anything as rational as discipline. It becomes blind rage, which, lacking access to the real enemy, destroys whatever is at hand. This is the anger of a child throwing a temper tantrum. One song sung to Ogou with an unusually gay lilting melody captures both aspects of his rage.

1   Ki ki li ki o-ewa.
2   Papa Ogou tou piti kon sa.
3   Papa Ogou enrajè!

1   Cock a-doodle do.
2   Papa Ogou all little children are like that.
3   Papa Ogou enraged!

The song can be read as a caution to Ogou: "Don't be so angry with your followers; all 'children' are that way." Equally, it can be heard as saying, "Ogou throws a tantrum, just like all children."

The vacillation of Ogou's anger, its tendency to switch targets from his enemies to his followers, has historical precedent. This is a facet of his character which is present in the Yoruba tradition,[7] which the slaves no doubt brought to the Island of Hispaniola. It has been amply reinforced by experiences Haitians have had with their own soldiers and politicians. Time and again the Haitians have experienced their leaders turning on them. They are deeply ambivalent about their own military and political history, and that is why Ogou, who moves between constructive and destructive uses of power, has been a natural vehicle for making their history comprehensible.

Three chapters from Haitian history illustrate this point. Jean-Jacques Dessalines was the first Haitian head of state. He gained a place in history by striking the final blow for Haitian independence in 1804. He restored order and brought the economy out of chaos. He also gave the Haitians their revenge by slaughtering all of the whites who remained after the defeat of the French. But he then warned Haitians who resisted his rule of law that they would "merit the fate of ungrateful people" (Leyburn 1966:33). Dessalines built a large army and then began a practice, imitated since, of using it for domestic control. The economic order brought by Dessalines was based on forced labor, and, for the great majority, liberty came to be indistinguishable from slavery. Dessalines outlawed the use of the whip on plantations, but he said nothing when a local vine was used in its place. Laborers, Dessalines said, could "be controlled only by fear of punishment and even death" (Leyburn 1966:41). In spite of this record, some Haitians argue that Dessalines is the most revered of all Haitian heroes. In his own time there were those who felt otherwise. Dessalines was assassinated near Port-au-Prince in 1806.

A second Haitian leader, Guillaume Sam, took office in 1915. Less than a year after his election, and as a result of his execution of 168 political prisoners, Sam was set on by his own people and torn limb from limb. The United States government used this incident as an excuse to invade the country and to deploy its marines to occupy Haiti for nineteen years.

When the third figure, François (Papa Doc) Duvalier, was elected president in 1957, he called on the U.S. Marines to train his army. Like the others, Duvalier used force in pursuit of power.[8] On the one hand, he enjoyed the support of large sectors of the public. He used Vodou networks as a power base and spoke appreciatively of the folk culture of the Haitian people. His popularity was thus built in part on an appeal to Black pride. On the other hand, he established the *tonton makout*, a civilian militia, which exercised an unrestrained brutality toward those who questioned Duvalier's rule. The arrogance, efficiency, and power of the American marines added one more layer of experience to the imagery of Ogou. The Black pride mixed with brutality of the *tonton makout* added another.

Haitians have summed up this aspect of their historical legacy in the following song to Ogou:

1   Sin Jak pa la.
2   Se chè ki la.

1   Sin Jak is not there.
2   It's a dog who's there.[9]

While a previous song (page 74 above) has told us that it is Ogou who puts the club in our hands to deal with mad dogs, this one suggests that the mad dog could be none other than Ogou himself.

The moral, that power is easily abused and that leaders tend to destroy their own people, is stated most succinctly in the spirit known as Ogou Panama. Ogou Panama takes his name from a story told about Florvil Hippolyte, president of Haiti from 1889 to 1896. There were rumblings of political dissent from Jacmel in the South of Haiti, and Hippolyte, it is said, set out on a punitive journey in which he vowed to wipe out the entire town of Jacmel, leaving only one man and one woman to repopulate the area. As he mounted his horse to leave Port-au-Prince, Hippolyte's fashionable Panama hat fell off. The president's son took this as a bad omen and pleaded with him not to go. Hippolyte persisted. He was not yet out of the capital when he fell unconscious from his horse. Shortly thereafter he died. The falling Panama hat not only provided the Haitians with a jaunty refrain for secular songs of political satire (Courlander 1960:150–52), it also provided within Vodou a succinct and appropriately indirect reminder of the dangers of the misuse of political power. One of the songs for Ogou Panama has this refrain:

1   M-di Panama ye,
2   Papa Ogou se neg Panama ye.
3   O Panama ye,
4   Neg Nago se neg Panama ye.

1   I say Panama,
2   Papa Ogou is a Panama man.
3   Oh Panama,
4   The Nago man is a Panama man.

The Power of Ogou: Against Himself

Ogou's anger comes full circle and ultimately is directed against himself. This is the dimension of Ogou's character that reveals itself in the final movement of his ritual sword dance, when he points the weapon at his own body.

Hints of this self-destructive potential are found in Ogou Chango. A brief explanation of the history of this figure is necessary. In Yoruba contexts, Şango is the deity of lightning and thunder. As king, Şango indulged himself in an arrogant display of power, inadvertently calling down lightning on his own palace and killing his wives and children. In despair he hung himself (Pemberton 1977:20). Likewise, in Yoruba mythology Ogun inadvertently killed his own townspeople and, in despair, committed suicide by falling on his sword (Barnes 1980:28). Şango and Ogun, who are quite distinct among the Yoruba, have merged in Haiti.[10] Although Vodou mythology contains no stories about the suicide of Ogou Chango, the "point" of such stories is pre-served in his character, as the following song indicates:

1   Kapten Chango, Achade Bokò ye.
2   O Kapten Chango, Achade Bokò ye.
3   Achade li ki ye.
4   Kapten kenmbe, li pa kon lage-ou
5   Kapten Chango, Achade Bokò ye.

1   Kapten Chango. Achade Bokò is.
2   Oh Kapten Chango, Achade Bokò is.
3   Achade is who he is.
4   Kapten holds you, he won't let you go.
5   Kapten Chango, Achade Bokò is.

This song connects Chango to Achade, an Ogou who appears separately in other contexts. Achade is a *bokò*, "sorcerer," and this adds yet another facet to the complex mix of powers which are executed by the Ogou. The powers of the sorcerer, like those of the soldier and politician, are assertive, aggressive ones that are appropriate in confrontational situations. The arena of their action is an eminently social one in which people are divided into two camps: friends/enemies, insiders/outsiders. The inclusion of a sorcerer spirit in the pantheon of the Ogou suggests a situation in which power is un-evenly distributed, for sorcery is the weapon of the underdog. Haitians are wary of sorcery. While its effectiveness is accepted, it must be carried out with absolutely correct intentions or it will come back and destroy the one who unleashed its power. The "work of the left hand" is to be avoided be-cause one can easily become trapped in an escalating debt to the powers it calls upon. Finally the only way to pay that debt is with one's own life. The highly ambiguous line in this song, "Kapten holds you, he won't let you go," may speak of care and comfort on the surface, but its sinister meaning lies just below.

Yamson[11] exhibits another dimension of Ogou's penchant for self-destructiveness. Consider the next song:

1   Ogou Yamson sa kap pase?
2   M-ape mande Papa Ogou ki kote ou ye.
3   Lè nou bezwen ou, Ogou Yamson,
4   Nou pa bezwen ou saka tafya.
5   M-ape mande Papa Ogou ki kote ou ye.
6   Kote gildyev ou-a, saka-tafya?

7   Yo ap mande Papa Ogou ki kote ou ye, Ogou Yamson.
8   Lè yo bezwen ou, Ogou Yamson.
9   Yo pa bezwen ou saka tafya.

1   Ogou Yamson, what's happening?
2   I'm asking Papa Ogou where you are.
3   When we need you, Ogou Yamson,
4   We don't need you guzzling rum.
5   I'm asking Papa Ogou where you are.
6   Where is your rum-making apparatus, drunkard?
7   They are asking Papa Ogou where you are, Ogou Yamson.
8   When they need you, Ogou Yamson.
9   They don't need you guzzling rum.

In this song, self-destruction takes the form of degradation.

The degradation of Agèou Hantò,[12] another of the Ogou, comes not through liquor but through other forms of social disintegration, lying and begging.

1   Agèou, ou, o.
2   Agèou, ou hantò!
3   Agèou, ou neg Dahome.

4   Ou mande charite.
5   Ou fè di-set an,
6   T-ap manje youn sèl epi de mai.

1   Agèou, you, oh,
2   Agèou, you liar!
3   Agèou, you Dahomey man.

4   You beg for alms.
5   You passed seventeen years,
6   Eating only one ear of corn.

The direct point of this song speaks of the shame of hunger and the exaggerated stories beggars sometimes tell to move those capable of acts of charity, but the indirect point speaks of the breakdown of the family as the cause of Agèou's plight. In Haiti beggars are reminders not only of the failure of a particular individual to support himself or herself, but also, and more to the point, of the failure of a family to take care of its own. Many times Haitians giving alms will inquire first about the family situation of the beggar and then express more outrage at the absent or irresponsible relatives than at the immediate manifestations of the beggar's destitute condition. The large number of beggars in Port-au-Prince today is a direct reflection of the fracturing of the sustaining family structure that occurs as more and more people are forced to the cities by the soil erosion, drought, and political corruption that are wasting the Haitian countryside.

A poignant song for Ogou Achade captures at once the isolation of the urban migrant cut off from family support, and, reaching back in history, that of the slave cut off from ancestral roots in Africa.

1   Achade o,
2   M-pa genyen mama isit ki pou pale pou mwen.
3   Achade o, zami move o.
4   M-pa genyen fanmi isit ki pou pale pou mwen.

1   Achade oh,
2   I have no mother here who can speak for me.
3   Achade oh, friends are no good.
4   I have no family here who can speak for me.

The songs of Ogou suggest that power is isolating. While the Ogou are said to marry and have lovers from both the Rada and Petro pantheons, they have no children of their own. This biographical detail adds further to our understanding of their power. Theirs is a solitary, individual power, not the collective power of close-knit groups, not the power of the united family. It is true that the soldier is charged with the defense of his people, yet face-to-face with the enemy, he stands alone. Similarly, the politician is isolated in office; the sorcerer works apart and late at night; the city-dweller fends for himself or herself in the world of work; and the immigrant is thrown on his or her own resources. Loneliness is the other side of power.

The loneliness of those who seize Ogou power is thus another form of self-destruction or self-wounding. This kind of chosen isolation causes deep psychic wounds, wounds not easily seen or healed, as is recognized in a song to Sin Jak Majè.

1   Sin Jak o Majè,
2   M-blese, m-pa we san mwen.

1   Sin Jak oh Majè,
2   I'm wounded but I don't see my blood.

Broken families, lost pride, loneliness, alcoholism, indigency, anger without a clear object—these are the wounds of the oppressed and the underside of the self-assertiveness of the Ogou. The following song, which speaks collectively of the Ogou as the Nago *nanchon*, makes this point well. It suggests that while railing against one's fate may not bring success and surely will not bring peace, it provides, quite simply, the last line of defense against suffering. Short of God's miraculous intervention, Ogou-like defiance is the most effective response to hardship. Ogou's tendency to keep fighting in the face of overwhelming odds is thus seen as both an endearing trait and a character flaw.

1   Tout nanchon genyen defo pa-yo.
2   Se pa Nago-a kap pase mizè. (Repeat)

3   Mwen di ye, rele l-a ye.
4   Mwen di ye, rele l-a ye.

5   Kote defans sa-yo? Neg Nago genyen.
6   L-a rele Bondye.

1   All peoples have their flaws.
2   The Nagos don't know how to suffer.

3   I say it is, cry out it will be.
4   I say he is, cry out he will be.

5   Where is their defense? The Nago man has it.
6   He will call on God.

Ogou of the Haitian Diaspora

Haiti is the poorest country in the Western Hemisphere and one of the poorest in the world. The average annual income has been estimated at $260. When this is adjusted to take into account the considerable wealth of the elite, it appears that most people in Haiti get by on less than $100 a year. Eighty percent of the people are illiterate and unemployment in Port-au-Prince hovers around fifty percent.[13] Political repression, poverty, and the diseases associated with malnutrition, including a high rate of infant mortality, are everyday facts of life. Most wealth is controlled by less than ten percent of the population, and the power of this elite group is highly visible and oppressive. Tourism, an important part of the Haitian economy until tourists stopped coming because of the political and social unrest following Duvalier's departure, reinforced the perceived gap between the haves and have-nots of the world. Haiti's moment of glory lies in the past, when her armies and revolutionary heroes stood up to the French and won their independence.

For many Haitians, hope for the future means leaving Haiti. More than a million people, from a total population of 5.5 million, have left the island for the urban centers of North America, principally Montreal, New York, and Miami. Haitians have migrated on and off to the United States since the slave revolution began in 1791, but the present community in greater New York, estimated at 400,000, has been built largely since the late 1950s after François Duvalier came to power. Here the Haitian experience of being on the wrong side of the power balance takes new forms: ghettoization, with all of its attendant problems: racism and degradation at social service agencies; and exploitation on the job market. Those who migrate illegally live in constant fear of being found out and deported. They often work for less than the minimum wage at jobs that are exhausting, and even dangerous. Only a small percentage live with hope for a significantly better future.

Ogou plays a prominent role in the religious life of New York's Haitians. At a small ceremony in Crown Heights, Brooklyn in 1975, some twenty people crowded into the tiny room of a priestess who was carrying out a "headwashing" ritual. The young woman for whom the ceremony was being performed could not find a job and she was plagued by severe and frequent headaches. Her problem was diagnosed as spiritual. She needed to "baptize Ogou in her head" and the headwashing was the first step. When Ogou came to the woman, she had trouble stabilizing the possession. Young and inexperienced devotees sometimes have difficulty making the transition into a trance state. The struggle of this woman was violent and prolonged. When Ogou was finally and firmly in control, a live rooster was brought in. The spirit himself is expected to sacrifice the animal offered to him, but this small and flustered horse of Ogou could not wring its neck. Ogou's anger emerged and, uncharacteristically, it mixed with tears. In this state, Ogou's horse bit through the neck of the chicken.

This was not the only time I have seen Ogou cry in New York. At a much larger and more elaborate ceremony in 1980, Ogou possessed another woman—a strong, no-nonsense person for whom tears in any context would be uncharacteristic. During the course of the possession-performance, the Ogou, in this case Agèou Hantò, spoke with a woman who had lost her oldest child a few months before. The ten-year-old boy was sent back to Haiti to live with family and he died there after being beaten for misconduct. The tears rolled down Agèou's face and the faces of many who listened as he said "You know if I could have helped him, I would have helped him."

The tearful despair of these New York Ogou is a facet of the spirit's character that is difficult to imagine being acted out in Haiti. Perhaps a new dimension of the Haitian Ogou is emerging in the North American setting. Will he one day strut and attack, wave his sword about threatening those near him, turn the point of the weapon against himself, pose defiantly, and then col-

lapse in tears? At the end of the temper tantrum is the exhausted, teary child.
It could be said that the majority of Haitian people have always been oppressed, but only in the exile communities do they experience being a minority people on the wrong side of a gross power imbalance. This situation may
be bringing out something new in Ogou. Tears could never replace Ogou's
aggression, but it may be that immigrant life in New York has revealed another dimension of his anger.

Ogou's way of being-in-the-world provides a cognitive map for Haitians
who take up the challenges of contemporary life, whether in Haiti or in New
York. As we have seen, Ogou delineates both the possibilities and the potential hazards of doing battle in the modern urban world. This much the Haitian
Ogou shares with his contemporary Nigerian counterpart. However, the Haitian Ogou has not taken up the challenge of interpreting modern technology,
as he has in Nigeria. To the extent that this latter role has developed at all
in Haiti, a country that has experienced much less of modern technology than
Nigeria, it has accrued to a different group of spirits, the Gède.

Ogou and Gède

The only other group of spirits that functions in the ritual process as the
Ogou do, that is, as mediators between the Rada and Petro pantheons, is
the Gède. A Gède possession occuring between the Rada and Petro segments
of a ceremony makes a transition possible between these two otherwise anti-
thetical modes. To the extent that ritual process mirrors life process, the
Gède and the Ogou can be seen to represent the two major options that the
Vodou system provides for handling situations of transition or change.[14]

The Haitian Gède is quite similar to the Dahomean trickster figure Legba
and, in some of his aspects, to the Yoruba trickster Eshu (Elegbara). Legba
has survived in Haiti but as a venerable old man who has sloughed off his
sexuality and, along with it, his tricksterism. For a people so brutally cut off
from their ancestral roots, tricksterism may have been unbearable in the spirit
responsible for communication between humans and their protective spirits.
Legba's tricksterism and his sexuality appear to have been taken on by the
Gède. Gède is simultaneously the spirit of the dead, protector of small children, guardian of human sexuality, and irrepressible social satirist. The Gède
are licensed to beg, to steal, to tell dirty jokes, and to engage in various other
forms of antisocial behavior.

The Gède appear to be the most open and growing group of spirits.
Sponge-like, they soak up new roles that appear on the social horizon, many
of them having to do with newly introduced professions and technologies.
Among the Gède are an automobile mechanic, a dentist, a doctor, and a
Protestant missionary. The Gède, the Haitians say, are not a *nanchon* but
a *fanmi*, "family." The significance of this will emerge shortly.

As mediators between the opposing forces of Rada and Petro, family members and foreigners, the Ogou and the Gède represent two options for survival in the modern world—a world in which the interaction between insiders and outsiders is increasingly intense, dangerous, and complex. We have seen the option represented by the Ogou. They wage war in the modern world; they face challenges head-on. The devotee of Ogou leaves a starving family to make a living in the city, and ideally to send money home. The Ogou devotee leaves Haiti for New York to do battle with the welfare system and the business world. It is Ogou power that enables the individual to face the isolation inevitably involved in making these moves. It is the distilled wisdom of Ogou's complex personality that keeps an individual from going mad when faced, for example, with the wrenching choice of making progress in the new life or sending money to the family back in Haiti.

The Gède are quite different. Their mediating power comes from a different way of being-in-the-world. The Gède triumph over suffering through humor. Thus a raucous Gède laugh can emerge from a devotee who only an instant before was possessed by a somber, awesome Rada *lwa*. The same quick transition between moods occurs in the marketplace, in the home, and on the job. A tense situation is instantly flipped on its back by a sudden laugh, a quick joke, or a bit of clowning. This is not the confrontational power of Ogou; this is the power of redefinition. And, it always depends on the cooperation of the group.

The Gède are *fanmi*, "family," par excellence. As spirits of death and sexuality, they connect Haitians to their macro-family extending backward through time to the ancestors and forward in time to descendants yet unborn. They are the spirits to whom one can bring the smallest of life's problems. They are gossips who process neighborhood events and invoke in-group norms. Their powers are distilled homely wisdom and satiric humor that dissipate fear and level pretense.

Here lies the complementary centrality of Ogou and Gède. Life presents many problems, not the least of which are oppression, deprivation, and isolation. The social cul-de-sac represented by situations of extreme oppression does not necessarily lead to surrender. There are two possible human responses: rage or humor, Ogou power or Gède power.

Summary and Conclusion

For slaves in the New World, social conflict pushed issues that were traditionally emphasized in African religious systems into the background. The powers of nature paled in relation to the powers that some human beings exercised over others. The religious heritage of the African homeland shifted and blended in response to a need for emphasis on social problems. In Haiti Ogou emerged as central and important because he was effective in this perilous social negotiation.

Ogou's importance in urban Haitian Vodou is clearly demonstrated in his mediating role between the Rada and Petro pantheons. His position as a mediator is reinforced when we compare the Ogou to the parallel, but contrasting, Gède. The opposition between Rada and Petro is seen as an opposition between different ways of being-in-the-world. Familial modes of action appropriate to in-group situations are opposed to the partisan and coercive ways of the foreigner or outsider. Ogou's personality and his mode of action, imagery, song, and possession-performance provide a model for negotiating between these otherwise irreconcilable ways of being.

In Haiti, Ogou's central theme is power. Ogou the revolutionary hero frees his people and puts weapons in their hands for self-protection. He intervenes on their behalf before the civil authorities. He gathers his followers to him like precious lost objects. But he also exacts strict discipline and punishes those who tire or waver. Sometimes his anger turns to blind rage, irrationally attacking those close to him or even himself. His penchant for self-destruction is acted out in sorcery, alcoholism, and indigency. Ogou thus articulates the possibilities and the dangers of power as it is found in contemporary life. He shows the way to the self-assertion and self-respect necessary for success in the modern world. Yet each of his manifestations keeps the negative side of claiming power clearly in view.

Ogou in Haiti provides an accurate description of the social conditions of an oppressed people. In psychological terms, he presents an almost clinical diagnosis of what happens when people internalize anger. However, it would be naive to assume that the Vodou spirits simply mirror the Haitian people. All religions have a moral dimension that makes the transformation of human lives possible (Brown 1987). The transformative potential of Haitian Vodou does not reside in the capacity of the spirits to model morally appropriate behavior, but rather in their capacity to keep the full range of possibilities latent in any way of being-in-the-world before the eyes of the believers. The assumption is that people will choose a right way to behave (there may be many right ways) in a given situation when they have sufficient insight into that situation. Haitian military history yields rich moral lessons when filtered through Ogou. The metaphoric extension of military power to civil power, and beyond to all situations of willfulness and assertion, allows Ogou to give guidance in many troublesome areas of life.

Just as Ogou has interpreted the history and social structure of the Haitian people, so have those realities shaped him. The hunting and iron-smithing connections of the Old World Ogun have not survived in Haiti, because these occupations are no longer central to Haitian life.[15] Neither has the Haitian Ogou taken up the challenge of dealing with modern technology. The central conflict in Haitian life is social conflict. The defining imagery of the Haitian Ogou is military imagery. The Haitian Ogou's anger, alternately turning outward toward the enemy and inward toward his own people and even himself, has parallels in the African Ogun. However, these Ogou traits have been reshaped through interaction with Haitian history. Ogou therefore has new personae (Ogou Panama) and new dimensions of character (in New York, Ogou cries).

Any attempt to account for the changes that African religious systems underwent in the New World must be sensitive to the complex interactions between memory and the material conditions of life in that new place. Through the Middle Passage, into the life of slavery and on into the life of minority peoples, African culture searched for niches in the New World order. Some aspects of African culture found these niches; others did not and were forgotten; those that did were changed in the process. The point is to see these rememberings and forgettings, as well as the apparently new creations, as systematic. African religions did not survive in happenstance fragments in the New World. They blended, shifted, and took on new forms in response to new social conditions, and they continue to do so today.

NOTES

1. Haitians refer to the Vodou *lwa* (a Fon word) as *sin yo*, "the saints," and as *espri yo*, "the spirits," but never as gods or divinities. God, Bondye, is the one and only god and the *lwa* are his servants or messengers. I respect this distinction and follow their language in this paper.

2. Every Vodou initiate has a *mèt tet*, "master of the head." This is the Vodou spirit with whom that person is most closely related. To some extent, there is a mirroring between the personality of the spirit and that of the devotee.

3. "Niche" is the term Bastide uses to describe those parts of the New World social structure that were receptive to African cultural interpretations.

4. This particular formulation of the contrast between the Rada and Petro pantheons is my own. See my Ph.D. dissertation (1976:80–112) for a more detailed analysis of this point. Such precise and abstract language is not characteristic of the way Vodou is discussed among Haitians.

5. The earliest reference to this theory of the origin of the Petro name occurs in Louis Elie Moreau de Saint-Méry 1797–98: v.l, pp. 210–11. Moreau de Saint-Méry is questioned on this point, however, by Alfred Métraux (1972:38–39).

6. Maya Deren believes that the origins of Petro worship are found in "rage against the evil fate which the African suffered . . . to protest against it" (1970:62).

7. "There are stories of Ogun's intoxication with the taste of blood in battle. Such is his thirst that on occasion he kills his own followers as well as the enemy." See Pemberton 1977:17.

It is interesting that Pemberton, who uses the structural method of analysis in this article, also found Ogun to be a mediating figure between two major groups of Yoruba deities. He describes the opposition between these two groups as that between life and death, or culture and nature.

8. "The readiness of Duvalieristes to use force probably exceeds that of any Haitian government in more than a century." Sidney W. Mintz, "Introduction to the Second Edition" of Leyburn 1966: xvi.

9. Dogs are not sacrificed in urban Haitian Vodou, but the dog is a traditional sacrifice among the Yoruba for Ogun. See Barnes 1980:39 and Pemberton 1977.

Pemberton quotes an *oriki*, "praise name," for Şango which states: "The dog stays in the house of its master/but it does not know his intentions" (pp. 19–20).

10. The appropriateness of a union between Ogun and Şango is instinctively understood by the contemporary Yoruba poet Wole Soyinka. Their coming together, he says, would be "the ideal fusion . . . to preserve the original uniqueness and yet absorb another essence" (1967:86).

11. The name of the spirit Ogou Yamson is possibly derived from that of Oya Yansan, who among the Yoruba was a consort of both Ogun and Şango. However, the Vodou Ogou Yamson is male; there are no female Ogou in Haiti.

12. Agèou Hantò is an Ogou whose relationship to a Cuban spirit is instructive. In Cuban Santeria, Agaju is associated with the fire of dormant volcanoes. This fire connection provides one link to the Haitian Ogou. Another can be seen in the relation between the drought imagery in the song for Agèou Hantò (seventeen years and only one ear of corn to eat) and the barren and blighted landscape around volcanoes. Such a correspondence between Cuban and Haitian imagery could suggest an original African source for this spirit's connection to dry, uninhabitable terrain. Another name for the Cuban Agaju is Agaju Solo, the solitary one. In keeping with the strong social emphasis of Haitian Vodou, the image of natural desolation and solitude has been replaced with a social one. Agèou's solitary state arises from social ostracism; he is a beggar. Personal communication, Judith Gleason.

13. Such figures from Haiti are not precise since there are no accurate census data. However, most people who know the country would agree about the general accuracy of these figures taken from an article by Gilbert Lewthwaite in *The Baltimore Sun*, November 1981.

14. The link between Ogou and Gède is expressed in many places in the Vodou system. One such place is the initiation ritual. Each person is initiated "on the point" of their *mèt tet,* their major or controlling spirit. This means, among other things, that initiates literally lie down on the emblem of that spirit. When a person's *mèt tet* is a Gède, special measures have to be taken because the death and sexuality connections of the Gède forbid their presence in the initiation chamber. In those cases, it is Ogou who stands in for Gède.

Furthermore, in the chromolithograph of Santiago that is used for Sin Jak Majè, the knight behind Santiago is commonly understood to be Gède. His full armor, including helmet and visor, is said to make him resemble a skeleton.

15. While it is true that the iron-smithing connections largely have been lost to Ogou in Haiti, they survive in details of Ogou symbolism such as the name of Ogou Feray (*feraille*), "scrap iron," and the Nago shrine that is maintained at most urban Vodou temples. This shrine is a simple clearing on the earth near the temple entrance where bonfires are lit for Ogou. The fire is built around an iron rod thrust into the earth. Métraux notes that this rod is called Ogou's forge (1972:109).

REFERENCES CITED

Barnes, Sandra T. 1980. *Ogun: An Old God for a New Age*, Philadelphia: ISHI.

Bastide, Roger. 1978. *The African Religions of Brazil: Toward a Sociology of the Interpenetration of Civilizations*, Baltimore: The Johns Hopkins University Press.

Brown, Karen McCarthy. 1976. "The *Vèvè* of Haitian Vodou: A Structural Analysis of Visual Imagery," Ph.D. dissertation, Temple University.

———. 1987. "Alourdes: A Case Study of Moral Leadership in Haitian Vodou," in

Saints and Virtues, John S. Hawley (ed.), Berkeley: University of California Press.

Courlander, Harold. 1960. *The Drum and the Hoe: Life and Lore of the Haitian People*, Berkeley: University of California Press.

Deren, Maya. 1970. *Divine Horsemen: The Voodoo Gods of Haiti*, New York: Delta.

Leyburn, James G. 1966. *The Haitian People*, with an introduction by Sidney W. Mintz, New Haven: Yale University Press.

Métraux, Alfred. 1972. *Voodoo in Haiti*, New York: Schocken.

Moreau de Saint-Méry, Louie Elie. 1797–98. *Déscription topographique, physique, civile, politique et historique de la partie française de l'isle de Saint-Dominique*, 2 vols., Philadelphia.

Pemberton, John III. 1977. "A Cluster of Sacred Symbols: Oriṣa Worship Among the Igbomina Yoruba of Ila-Ọrangun," *History of Religions*, vol. 17, no. 1, pp. 1–28.

Soyinka, Wole. 1967. *Indanre and Other Poems*, London: Methuen.

Thompson, Robert Farris. 1983. *Flash of the Spirit: African and Afro-American Art and Philosophy*, New York: Random House.

Renato Ortiz

5

Ogum and the Umbandista Religion

To understand the role of Ogum in the Umbanda religion it is necessary to be familiar with the structure of the Umbandista universe as a whole and, above all, its meaning within Brazilian society. Umbanda is not an Afro-Brazilian religion; unlike Candomblé, the religion with which it will be compared here, Umbanda roots are neither black nor African. This does not mean that the African contribution has been unimportant to the formation of Umbandista religion. Quite the contrary, it is fundamental to the development of this new type of possession cult. However, the histories and the scope of influence of the two religions differ. Umbanda is a national religion; Candomblé is one cultural group's religion. Consequently, Ogum differs in each of them. The Ogum of Candomblé is one god among many; he is an unpredictable but accessible member of the spirit world. By contrast, the Ogum of Umbanda has been elevated to an inaccessible position in the cosmos, where he controls unpredictable spiritual forces; indeed, this Ogum has been elevated in some sectors of Brazilian society to the extent that he is a symbol of national identity.

Candomblé is a celebration of the collective African memory on Brazilian soil (Halbwachs 1968; Bastide 1971). The myths and the rites of Candomblé resurrect the gods and the mythic histories originating in Africa. I do not mean that this memory is faithfully reproduced in Brazil; it does suffer from gaps and lapses of memory, and it takes on new elements which are introduced through the process of syncretism. Meanwhile, even when syncretism occurs, the pole of reference continues to be the African continent. For example, even though he has been syncretized with Saint George, Ogum does not lose his original characteristics. Orixá (deity) Ogum possesses traits analogous to the Catholic saint: both are warriors and they combat their enemies.

But the analogy can only be taken so far; Ogum possesses a mythic history which in the minds of Candomblé acolytes cannot be confused with the Catholic hagiography. Syncretism is a form of *bricolage* that treats the Brazilian Catholic influences starting with a system of anterior classification, the collective memory (Bastide 1970). The changes which occur in the religious universe are filtered through the African system of classifying the world. Candomblé is a black religion, even when it is celebrated by mestizos and whites.

Umbanda, on the other hand, is a synthetic and not a syncretic religion. It makes use of the African element but it is not defined by it. Umbanda is a Brazilian religion in that it integrates various religious movements: Candomblé, Catholicism, and Spiritism (as introduced by Allan Kardec). It is a blend of many cultural elements, and for that reason I have referred to it as a synthesis. Without doubt, the African contribution is of fundamental importance, but the black element can be understood only when it is considered from the point of view of all Brazilian society. Umbanda is a national religion, even when practiced by mestizos, blacks, or whites.[1]

It is not easy to describe the history of Umbanda, for studies on this topic are few. There is agreement, however, that the religion emerged and was consolidated around the 1930s. One of the first *terreiros* (cult houses) of which we hear, the *Tenda Espírita Mirim*, was founded in 1924 in Rio de Janeiro. In this period many other cult houses appeared: *Cabana Espírita Senhor do Bonfim, Tenda Espírita Fé e Humanidade, Cabana Pai Joaquim de Luanda, Centro Espírita Religioso São João Baptista, Tenda Africana São Sebastião*, all in Rio (Bandeira 1970; 1961).[2] In 1926, the *Centro Espírita de São Jorge* was founded in Porto Alegre. Little by little, the *terreiros* were united as confederations, and in 1939, the first *Federation Espírita Umbandista* was formed in Rio de Janeiro: it subsequently served as a model for other federations in the rest of the country. In 1941, the First Umbandista Congress took place, with the sole purpose of systematizing the religion and codifying its rituals.

The emergence of the religion also can be documented through the change in meaning of the term *Umbanda*. Francisco Valente showed that the word *Umbanda* (of Kimbundo origin, an Angolan language) was initially used to describe both religious objects and the Kimbanda (an expert in spiritual matters), but was not used to identify a systematized religion that somehow differed from the rest (Valente 1970; Quintão n.d.). Brazilian historians, writing at the beginning of this century, also gave no indication that such an identification had occurred. The Afro-Brazilian syncretism, later Candomblé, was known by the names of *macumba* or *baixo espiritismo* (lower-level spiritism) (Rio 1976). Umbanda was not used in a more generic form until the 1930s, when it slowly became associated with the notion of a religious system. The eyewitness account of a participant in the First Umbandista Congress is very telling on this point. He writes:

> A name was necessary to baptize the religious modality which, even before
> forming its own personality, was proposed with so much prestige. Umbanda
> was chosen. But who chose it? No one can answer that. It is now known that
> it began to be used here in the Federal District and in the State of Rio de
> Janeiro. Much later, it was popularized, and spread to Bahia where it was in-
> corporated by northern Candomblés and Xangôs. (Bandeira 1961:81)

The emergence of Umbanda in the 1930s is not fortuitous. To understand
the importance of this timing, we must return to Brazilian history. Great social changes took place at the end of the nineteenth century: slavery was abol-
ished (1888) and free work was substituted for slave labor; the Republic was
proclaimed (1889); incentives for European immigration were established;
and urbanization and industrialization processes began to intensify. These
changes had an effect on the whole society, and particularly on the black segment of the population, which began to migrate from the countryside to the
city and, in the process, to occupy a marginal position at the very time a new
social order was being constructed.[3] One consequence was that, faced with
marginalization, Candomblé could survive only as a closed community opposed to the wider society. This did not happen with those practices of African origin which were disseminated into the wider population. Thus, on one
hand cults of African origin became more atomized, while on the other there
was a disintegration and dispersal of other aspects of the collective African
memory.

During this same period, Allan Kardec's Spiritism spread among the
poorer classes. Kardecism, which had a French origin, began to develop in
Brazil in 1865 in the middle class. From the very beginning, spiritualism in
Brazil was religious in form and distanced itself in a way from the rationalism
of Kardec. The first (1873) organized spiritualist movement, *Sociedade de
Estudos Espíritas do Grupo Confúcio*, the Society of Confucian Spiritual
Studies, of Rio de Janeiro, had the motto "true spirits do not exist without
charity," and it advocated the practices of homeopathy and faith healing. The
therapeutic orientation of the movement increased over time until it became
a focus of the religion. Consequently a schism developed between the "mys-
tics" and the rationalists. The latter remained close to the French tradition
of Kardecism, while the former moved away by considering the medium as
principally a healer. Spiritualism was disseminated among the popular
classes, especially blacks and immigrants, in this modified, therapeutic form.
Little by little, whites introduced it to the lower classes, mainly immigrants
and blacks. The interjection of this white element into popular religious
culture reinforced the process of separating black elements that existed
outside the closed Afro-Brazilian communities from the collective African
memory.

The role of "intellectuals" in forming the new Umbandist religion in the
1930s was crucial. The term *intellectual* is used here to designate individuals
who seek to systematize the religious universe. In this respect, Gramsci's con-

cept of the "organic intellectual," as it applies to the religious, not political, realm, is germane. The organic intellectual gave form to Umbanda, just as Weber's intellectual-priest systematized a world religion.[4] The new Umbanda religion emerged, therefore, as the *bricolage* of intellectuals, who "pieced" together elements of the past, including elements of Afro-Brazilian origin. As these elements were reinterpreted within the new religious future, they broke away from the collective memory of the past.

The 1930s, then, possessed a special meaning in the history of Brazil. A period of social disintegration which began at the close of the nineteenth century was followed by a period of consolidation and modernization out of which, by the 1930s, an urban, industrial society emerged. The rise of Umbanda, a new religious cult, taking place as it did in urban centers, thus paralleled the rise of a new socioeconomic order.

The Umbandista Intelligentsia

The role of the middle class in the formation of Umbanda is emphasized by several authors (Brown 1977; Ortiz 1975b). The intellectuals, who almost always come from that social class, are fundamental to its development. Intellectuals write books, establish Umbandista federations, hold congresses, and, above all, seek to systematize the religious beliefs. To a certain extent they act as "theologians" seeking to justify different aspects of their "doctrine." The explanations of the intellectuals retain a mystical quality, but at the same time contain an element of rationality that is characteristic, in the Weberian sense, of global traditions. Several examples illustrate the point.

In treating the principle of reincarnation, as regulated by the spiritual world, an Umbanda manual states:

> Reincarnation is a divine precept of the Father, through which he rewards or punishes, according to each one's merit, since reincarnation has the following as its predetermined ends: to rescue the individual from error and sins committed in previous lives; to furnish spiritual development for the individual; and to impose on each new arrival certain missions of great importance which must be fulfilled while on Earth. (Candido 1965)

As can be seen, this explanation provides a rationale to Umbanda followers for the ongoing intervention of the spiritual world in their lives. The influence of Kardec's Spiritism was a strong element in formulating this rationale. In his widely influential work, *Livro dos Espíritos* (*Book of the Spirits*), Kardec attempted to give the faithful principles by which they might understand the world and to justify the kind of ethical action that would make the salvation of souls possible (Kardec 1857 and 1870).

A second example concerns the justification of magic in Umbanda. A manual states:

All treatises on magic make reference to *pontas de aço* (*objetos com pontas* or steel points) which are the most effective means of dissolving certain agglomerations of larva, evil fluids, and miasmas. The ancients used swords and steel points in their magical operations, just as today steel points, particularly daggers, are used in Umbanda possession rites. The function of the steel point, i.e. sword and dagger, in possession is like a lightning rod in the thunderstorm. The principle is found in physics, and therefore it is a scientific function. (Magno 1952)

In this instance the scientific justification for magic is directed toward both an internal and an external public: the goal is to demonstrate that the religion is not a bundle of superstitions, as is frequently assumed by certain "cultivated" sectors of the population, but that the values of the modern scientific world are applicable to the values of Umbanda.

Similarly, the theology of Umbanda also functions to associate the new religion, as a whole, with modern (e.g., scientific) values. This permits Umbanda to define itself as a system of beliefs rather than of superstitions, and to attribute the latter to the Afro-Brazilian cults. The concept of science is used to justify the modernity of the Umbandista cult, which opposes, in principle, the traditionalism of Candomblé and what are considered to be its "backward" practices, that is, those which are said to pertain to an inferior stage in the development of civilization. Some examples will illustrate the point I wish to highlight. In referring to the Candomblé offerings that are made to the spirits of the river and the sea, one writer states:

It is common to see shallow bowls, bottles, ribbons, pig tails, bloody meat, and even pure blood from slain animals at offering sites. This is pure ignorance, pure cruelty. It exhibits a lack of knowledge of sacred, spiritual values. The Divine Umbanda does not accept such barbaric rituals which unfortunately display the backwardness of many creatures. (Oliveira 1971:46–50)

Referring to Candomblé sacrifices (*despachos*) associated with Exu, another writes:

Sacrifices placed in the middle of crossroads containing bottles or other materials which harm traffic and offer danger to children, aside from bringing scandal to the Afro-Brazilian cult, are hereby forbidden. (Freitas 1969:98)

Referring to the behavior of spirits at *terreiro* rituals, a third writes:

We call attention to the leaders of the *terreiros* in case possessed spirits use obscenities. This behavior makes them unworthy of our trust—*pretos-velhos* and *caboclos* become unworthy of trust—and lose the confidence of laymen. (Anonymous 1972:11)

Many warnings such as these are directed, above all, to the *terreiros* of the popular classes, where the practices of Afro-Brazilian origin are more evident than in the *terreiros* of the middle class. There is still a cleavage between "official" Umbanda precepts and their actual acceptance by the leaders of some cults. Just as there are two types of Catholicism—one of the priests and the other of the people—in Umbanda one can discern a distinction between the religiosity of the intellectuals and that of ordinary followers.

The thing which attracts attention in Umbandist discourse is the preoccupation with integrating new values which resemble a religion of the modern world and primarily the idea of "civilization." In the battle to legitimate their religion, Umbandists use moral values and scientific values to elevate their position. In using moral values, their attempts are not unlike those of Mary Douglas, who uses concepts such as purity and pollution to categorize various aspects of a society's value system. For Umbandists, the assignment of positive and negative values provides them with a way to differentiate themselves from the so-called backward practices of Candomblé. Thus the principle of reincarnation carries out an important cognitive function, for it allows adherents to assign Afro-Brazilian cults to an earlier stage of civilization and to place Umbanda at a more elevated position in the spiritual hierarchy.[5]

The Spirits, Good and Evil

Umbanda provides a religious "language" for the integration of human concerns with spiritual force. It is a cult of possession, and in this aspect it is similar to the variety of possession cults which exist in Africa or in Latin America. Communication between the sacred and the profane world comes about through trance during which a medium is "mounted" by a spirit which descends from beyond. The possessed devotee is the "horse of the saint"— the saddle in which spiritual entities ride to manifest their presence on Earth. All Umbanda sessions consist of invocations to the spirits, during which the spirits descend in order to understand and resolve the problems which afflict devotees. The problems include illness, unhappiness in love, or financial failure. The close of each session comes only after the spirits listen attentively to the problems of devotees and bestow charity on them. At this point, they return to the Kingdom of Aruanda.

The spiritual beings of Umbanda differ fundamentally from those of Candomblé. The Umbandist pantheon is, in principle, made up of four types of spirits, grouped into two categories: a) spirits of light: *caboclos, pretos-velhos, crianças*; and b) spirits of darkness: *exus*. The *caboclos* are spirits of Brazil's Indian ancestors, and they represent energy and vitality. They are vigorous spirits, who beat their chests strongly with their fists to offer greetings; they like cigars and smoke heavily during religious sessions. The *pretos-velhos* are spirits of old slaves who represent humility. When they descend, the bodies of the mediums curve, twisting as if they were old men or women overwhelmed with the weight of age. They speak with hoarse voices, but gently and affectionately, thereby transmitting a sensation of trust and familiarity to those who consult them. The *crianças* come in part from the notion of *erê* (spirits of deceased children), which is well-known in the world of Candomblé.[6] Compared to the *caboclos* and the *pretos-velhos*, the *crianças* have an evocative, rather than therapeutic, dimension. They represent the idea of purity and innocence and bring happiness to the cult in the form of folk games. When the children descend, the mediums adopt a childlike attitude; some, who do not know how to walk, crawl on the floor on all fours; others suck their thumbs; and still others speak in an infantile language.

The spirits of light are arranged in a hierarchy. According to Umbandistas there are seven *linhas* (sacred zones) in which the saints are grouped: Oxalá, Iemanjá, Xangô, Ogum, Oxossi, Crianças, and Pretos-Velhos. Each *linha*, headed by an *orixá* (the term is derived from the Yoruba, *orişa/orisha*, meaning god or goddess), is subdivided into successive spiritual divisions. Hence Orixá Ogum is the commander of a sector of the spiritual world in which there are a limitless number of *caboclos*. *Caboclo Ubiratã, caboclo Ubirajara*, and *caboclo Rompe-Mato* are Indian ancestor spirits who belong to the Ogum *linha*. Put in the language of Umbanda, Ogum is the chief of a phalanx of *caboclos*. In Umbanda, unlike Candomblé, the *orixá* does not descend; rather, the spirits who are his messengers come to Earth to listen to human problems.

The Umbandista universe is more extensive than Candomblé, in that the number of spirits is greater than the number of *orixás*. But, in logical terms, what the Umbanda system earns in extension, it loses in comprehension. Ogum is an *orixá* and therefore he does not make himself manifest in a "trance." His spirit messenger is present, but he is not. Consequently, the myths that envelop Ogum (and other spirits) tend to disappear. This allows a greater level of ambiguity to surround the interpretations and behaviors of the *caboclo*. In Umbanda the spiritual personality has a somewhat empty, indeterminate quality. For example, who are *caboclo Ubiratã, Ubirajara*, or *Rompe-Mato*? They simply represent an anonymous mass of Indians who played a generic role in the foundation of Brazilian society. The indeterminacy of the identity of each *caboclo* provides the adept with personal freedom in expressing what he feels the spirit's personality to be. The result is that a personality of a specific *caboclo* is, above all, an expression of the personality in whom it is incarnate, and not a personality taken from myth, as in Candomblé. Even if two *caboclos* possess the same name they never have the same attitudes, or behaviors, because they do not participate as part of the same mythic plot. Behind the *caboclo* stereotype the anonymity of history can be found.

The great difference between Umbanda and Candomblé is the division of the religious universe into compartments of good and evil. Candomblé does not separate the two, whereas Umbandistas define them as the conflict between Umbanda proper (good) and Quimbanda (evil). Ogum is a spirit of light and in this sense he radically opposes backward spirits who inhabit the Kingdom of Darkness. Yet it means that part of the religious world is outside the influence of Ogum's *caboclos*. For example, death and sex are two fundamental elements which exist on the side of darkness; the adept, who may by chance have a nocturnal desire, must seek out an *exu*—never a *caboclo*—in order to realize that desire. Any request to physically eliminate someone, or to realize a sexual desire for another person, can be accomplished only by *exus*. The *caboclos* are specialists in the Kingdom of Good, in other words, in healing illness or alleviating misfortunes, domestic problems, and so on. This does not mean that they do not possess the strength necessary to carry out requests connoted as deviant; it is simply that *caboclos* are considered "advanced" spirits, and undertaking such requests is incompatible with their position.

Among the African *orixás*, there is a special relationship in Umbanda between Ogum and the *exus*. The "point song" below helps to illustrate this relationship:

1	Que cavaleiro é aquele
2	Que vem cavalgando pelo céu azul
3	Ele é São Jorge Guerreiro
4	Que vem comandando a falange de Ogum
5	Traz um escudo no braço
6	Sua espada na cinta
7	E uma lança na mão
8	Ele é São Jorge Guerreiro
9	Que é defensor do cruzeiro do Sul
10	Ele é Ogum matinata
11	Que vem defender o cruzeiro do espaço
12	Em seu cavalo branco
13	Sempre montado
14	É um vencedor de demandas
15	Que na sua gira vem saravar.

1	That gentleman is the one
2	Who comes riding through the blue sky.
3	He is Saint George the Warrior
4	Who commands Ogum's phalanx.
5	He carries a shield on his arm,
6	His sword on his belt,
7	And a spear in his hand.
8	He is Saint George the Warrior
9	Who is defender of the Southern Cross.
10	He is Ogum, the early riser
11	Who defends the crossing place,
12	On his white horse,
13	Always mounted.

14   He is the conqueror of quarrels
15   Who salutes us in trance.

The idea of conquering quarrels (disputes or cases arising over illegitimate
requests) is associated with the warrior spirit Ogum, who, like Saint George,
combats his enemies. The requests in this case are evil and are only achieved
through the help of spirits of darkness. Like the *exus*, the spirits of darkness are strong entities who work with the dangerous dimension of night-
time. Only a stronger spirit can conquer them. Ogum has this superior energy, and at the last moment defends the order of goodness, the Kingdom of
Umbanda, against interference from the order of evil, the Kingdom of
Quimbanda.

Ogum's control over the Kingdom of Darkness is better understood after
one, first, apprehends certain facts concerning the dynamics of the religious
universe and, then, analyzes ritual sessions in which *exu* appears. The division
of the world into two compartments creates problems for Umbandistas, since
they are obliged to relate to the dangerous parts of the universe—albeit in
an ambiguous way.[7] The problem that arises for adepts is to deal with the
manifestations of *exu* without threatening the spiritual order of the Kingdom
of Light. Umbandists solve the problem by establishing a separation between
two types of *exu*: pagan and baptized. The religious literature and the practices in the *terreiro* (in this matter there is no cleavage between the intellectuals and ordinary devotees) are clear. The separation is explained as
follows:

> The different situations of the two *exus* are defined by their names. The pagan
> *exu* exists at the margin of spirituality—without light, without knowledge of
> spiritual development—working on evil magic in the full Kingdom of
> Quimbanda. The baptized *exu*—characteristically defined as human soul—has
> been made sensitive to good by working on the "road of spiritual develop-
> ment." The baptized *exu*, as it is said, works for good within the Kingdom of
> Quimbanda; he is obliged to live in his environment and serves as a policeman
> operating in a den of marginal characters. (Bandeira 1970:138)[8]

Accepting the concept of baptized *exu* allows Umbandists to incorporate into
their religious universe a moral dimension which is fundamental to any notion of completeness. The ambiguity of *exu* allows him to be characterized
sometimes as pagan and at other times as baptized. The behavior of the adept
in the *terreiro* reveals either one or the other characteristic. In the *terreiro*,
all spirits must abide by principles of religious morality, for example, they
must not use foul language. During possessions in which *exu* is present there
is a constant uncertainty and tension. Will the pagan *exu* explode at any moment? Will the expectations consistent with the Kingdom of Light be met?
To achieve the latter, Umbanda sessions must be carefully prepared and the

exus controlled. A "point song" about Ogum reveals this preoccupation with uncertainty:

1 O sino da capelinha faz belem, blem, blom
2 É meia-noite o galo já cantou
3 Seu Tranca Ruas [exu] que é dono da gira
4 O dono que Ogum mandou.

1 The chapel bell goes ding, dong, ding.
2 It is midnight and the rooster did sing.
3 Mister Tranca-Rua [an *exu*] is the owner of the trance,
4 The owner that Ogum did send.

This point song, a fairly familiar hymn in the *terreiros*, is sung as part of the opening of *exu* rituals. Each ceremony begins with an invocation to Ogum, the *orixá* who is well known for his dominating strength over the *exus*. He represents the separation between good and evil, and provides a symbolic expression of the fact that an inferior spiritual principle must give way to a superior principle. Through their song, adepts seek a diminished margin of ambiguity in the performance of ritual: the spirits that descend are baptized *exu*, they act under Ogum's control, and thus they adhere to the principles of Umbanda.

Umbanda and Brazilian Culture

Umbanda and Ogum play a particularly meaningful role in contemporary Brazilian culture. As I tried to make clear at the beginning of this essay, Umbanda is a national religion developed in Brazil at a particular point in its history. The main spirits, *caboclos* and *pretos-velhos*, are national historical legacies who are transformed into supernatural agents exclusively by Umbanda. The adepts of Umbanda are aware of these distinctive elements in their belief system. In fact, when seeking to enhance the qualities of their faith, many adepts unhesitatingly affirm that Umbanda is the only authentically national religion, in contrast to "imported" beliefs, such as Catholicism, Protestantism, Kardec's Spiritism, and even Candomblé.[9]

The theme of Brazilianness can also be encountered at other levels of the religious universe. One of these is the use of the *caboclo* as a representative of the Brazilian Indian. If we ask about the real influence of the indigenous Indian culture in Umbanda, we observe that it is secondary because the religion was formed in the great urban centers, where the presence of the Indian has been virtually nonexistent. The idealized model of the Indian adopted by Umbanda corresponds to the stereotypic vision which Brazilian society has of the Indian. Edison Carneiro is correct when he states that it was Romanticism which spread an image of the good, courageous Indian and stripped him of all traces of primitiveness (1964). The Romantic movement developed in mid-nineteenth century just as Brazil set itself free from the colonial Portuguese yoke. To establish ideological roots as a fledgling nation and to contrast itself with foreign countries, the movement's intellectuals tried to establish a symbolic model of nationhood. They were faced with unanswered questions. Who were the Brazilians? What was their identity, their race of origin? The answers were furnished by Romantic authors who transformed the Indian into a model of *brasilianismo*. There could be no other solution, since the two other dominant populations evoked images of the Portuguese colonizer or the African slave. Promoted to the rank of founder of the Brazilian people, therefore, was the Indian—however despoiled of his true features—whose resistance to the Portuguese colonizer was interpreted as being a catalyst for independence. In this way, *caboclo* spirits affirm the notion of Brazilianness inside Umbanda.

The issue of national identity goes beyond the frontiers of the Umbandist religious world, however. There is a long tradition of writers, journalists, academicians, and politicians dealing with the notion of Brazilianness. One of the influential mediums through which identity is defined and reinforced is the motion picture. For several film directors, the Afro-Brazilian Orixá Ogum, as represented in Umbanda, is a symbol of Brazilian nationality. Two films, *Antonio das Mortes: The Dragon of Evilness vs. the Warrior Saint* by Glauber Rocha, and *Amulet of Ogum* by Nelson Pereira dos Santos, center on Ogum. The first film tells the story of the battle between the poor and the rich and ends with the death of a large estate owner from the northeast (representing the dragon of evilness) who is eliminated by a black (Ogum) mounted on the white horse of Saint George. The second film tells a tale of crime and love, having as its center the world of Umbanda, but not, it should be stressed, Candomblé. In this film the hero, who has been dedicated to Ogum, is involved in the underworld, where, so long as he wears his deity's amulet, he can protect the innocent and eliminate dangerous gangsters. Ogum's role in both films is consistent with his role in Umbanda: in the war between the forces of evil and good, he defends those in need, rights social wrongs, and upholds the value system when it is threatened.

What must be underlined is that both films make political and social statements in an idiom consistent with Brazilian culture. In the 1960s, these two directors were part of the "New Cinema," whose mission was to create a national art form which projected an authentic Brazilian culture onto the screen, in contrast to the alien culture that was imported from outside. It is in this sense interesting to follow the destiny of Ogum, whose adventures and misadventures on Brazilian soil led him to be considered a medium for expressing the characteristics of national identity.

NOTES

1. For a more detailed study of the differences between Umbanda and Candomblé see Ortiz 1975a.

2. Brown considers the Umbandista religion was born in Rio de Janeiro during the middle 1930s. Her thesis seems questionable to me since the available historical data are insufficient to support it. There is no doubt that the Umbandista movement in Rio de Janeiro developed faster than in other states. However, it should not be forgotten that in Porto Alegre we know that *terreiros* have existed since 1926. See Brown 1985.

3. For further elaboration on the social changes that affected the black population in Brazil see Fernandes 1966; Fernandes and Bastide 1971; and Pinto 1953.

4. See Gramsci 1968 and Weber 1971. For a comparison between Gramsci and Weber on the topic of religion see Ortiz 1980.

5. Unfortunately, it is not possible in this article to cover the relationship between the intellectuals and the Umbandistas of the *terreiros* more thoroughly. It should be stated that the values considered legitimate by the global society have a greater penetration in the *terreiros* of the middle class than in the *terreiros* of the popular classes. This creates an internal conflict for the religion which has the characteristics of a battle over religious power.

6. On the role of the *erê* in Candomblé see Bastide 1958 and Cossard 1970.

7. For a more detailed study of the division between good and evil in Umbanda see Ortiz 1979.

8. See also Fontenelle 1952 and Scliar 1971.

9. See the series of articles edited by Pessoa 1960.

REFERENCES CITED

Anonymous. 1972. "Exu," in *Revista Mironga*, agosto-setembro.

Bandeira, Cavalcanti. 1961. *Umbanda evolução histórico-religosa*, Rio de Janeiro: Apostila apresentada, no. 11, Congresso Umbandista.

———. 1970. *O que é a Umbanda*, Rio de Janeiro: Editora Eco.

Bastide, Roger. 1958. *Les Candomblé de Bahia*, Paris: Mouton.

———. 1970. "Mémoire collective et sociologie du bricolage," *L'Année Sociologique*.

———. 1971. *As Religiões Africanas no Brazil* (2 vols.), São Paulo: Editora Universidade São Paulo.

Brown, Diana. 1977. "O papel de classe média na formação da Umbanda," *Religião e Sociedade*, no. 1.

———. 1985. "Uma história da umbanda no Rio," *Cadernos do ISER*, no. 18.

Candido, Felix. 1965. *A Cartilha da Umbanda*, Rio de Janeiro: Editora Eco.

Carneiro, Edison. 1964. *Ladinos e Crioulos*, Rio de Janeiro: Civilização Brasileira.

Cossard, Binon. 1970. *Contribution à l'étude des, candomblés au Brésil*, Ph.D. thesis, Ecole Pratique des Hautes Etudes, Paris.

Fernandes, Florestan. 1966. *Integração do negro na Sociedade de Classe*, São Paulo: Universidade São Paulo.

Fernandes, Florestan, and Roger Bastide. 1971. *Brancos e Pretos em São Paulo,* São Paulo: Editora Nacional.

Fontenelle, Aluisio. 1952. *O Espiritismo no conceito das religiões e a Lei da Umbanda*, Rio de Janeiro: Editora Espiritualista.

Freitas, Byron T. 1969. *Os Orixas e a Lei da Umbanda*, Rio de Janeiro: Editora Eco.
Gramsci, Antonio. 1968. *Os intelectuais e a Organização da Cultura*, Rio de Janeiro: Civilização Brasileira.
Halbwachs, Maurice. 1968. *La Mémoire Collective*, Paris: Presses Universitaires de France.
Kardec, Allan. 1857. *Le Livre des Esprits*, Paris: Librairie Spirite.
———. 1870. *Caractères de la Révélation Spirite*, Paris: Librairie Spirite.
Magno, Oliveira. 1952. *Umbanda e Ocultismo*, Rio de Janeiro: Editora Espiritualista.
Oliveira, Jorge de. 1971. *Umbanda Transcendental*, Rio de Janeiro: Editora Eco.
Ortiz, Renato. 1975a. "Du syncrétisme à la synthèse: Umbanda une religion brésilienne," *Archives des Sciences Sociales des Religions*, no. 40.
——— 1975b. *La Mort Blanche du Sorcier Noir*, Ph.D. thesis, Ecole Pratique des Hautes Etudes, Paris (published in Portuguese, Editora Vozes, 1978).
———. 1979. "Umbanda magie blanche, Quimbanda magie noire," *Archives des Sciences Sociales des Religions*, no. 47/1.
———. 1980. *A Consciência Fragmentada*, Rio de Janeiro: Brasiliense.
Pessoa, J. A. 1960. *Umbanda: religião do Brasil*, São Paulo: Editora Obelisco.
Pinto, L. A. Costa. 1953. *O Negro no Rio de Janeiro*, São Paulo: Editora Nacional.
Quintão, José. n.d. *Gramática de Quimbundo*, Museu de Luanda.
Rio, João do. 1976. *As Religiões no Rio*, Rio de Janeiro: Nova Aguilar.
Scliar, Marcos. 1971. *Umbanda Magia Branca*, Rio de Janeiro: Editora Eco.
Valente, Francisco. 1970. "Feiticeiro ou Quimbanda," *Ultramar*, ano 10, no. 39.
Weber, Max. 1971. *Economie et Société*, Paris: Plon.

This essay was translated from the Portuguese with the assistance of Maria Elena Viera Branco, Wilson Trajano Filho, and Charlene Flanagan.

PART TWO

The Meaning of Ogun in Ritual, Myth, and Art

6

The Dreadful God and the Divine King

1	Atótó! Arére!
2	Kéléjì ó má fò, kigbárája ó má lura ra wọn.
3	Àwa dé, ègbodò ilé kò gbọdò ṣọdọ poro.
4	Ìlògì kò gbọdò ṣọlo ṣúkúṣúkú.
5	Ọmọ kékeré ilé kò gbọdò sọkún kí ngbó.
6	Kí ọlómú ó fi ọmú bọ ọmọ rè lénu.
7	Ọjó Ògún tòkè bọ aṣọ iná ló fi bora, èwù èjè lówò.
8	Ọpò olókó ló fi òkò rẹ dáná;
9	Ọpò olóbò ló l'àbò rè dáná.
10	Ẹdun olú irin, àwònyè òrìṣà tíí bura rè sán wònyìnwònyìn.
11	Ifèèfèè lolè lebu, panlawọ, olùjèkà, má bù mí jẹ.
12	A mu sí Póngà; ó ba Póngà jé.
13	A mu sí Àkò-Ire, o là kò dànù.
14	A mú Ògún wọdò Ògún sì là omi lógbọgba.
15	Èrù jèjè tíí ba ará àdúgbò.
16	Ògún Ọgbórọ ló ni ajá; òun lapa já fún.
17	Ògún Onírè ló lèjè; Mọlàmọlà ló ni èkuru.
18	To ní gbàjámo, irun ló njẹ.
19	Ti òkọlà níí jẹ ìgbín.
20	Ògún gbénàgbénà igi lónjẹ.
21	Suminiwa, Ajọkẹopo.
22	Èrù Ògún mà ḿbà mí o.
23	Abi-ọwó-gbọgbọgbọ tii yọ ọmọ rè nínú òfin.
24	Yọ mí.
1	Silence! Silence!
2	Let no one talk: let no household utensil touch another.

3   We are here. Let no one pound any new yam.
4   Let no one grind anything.
5   Do not allow me to hear children crying.
6   Let every woman breastfeed her child.
7   On the day Ogun arrived from the hilltop, he wore a bright red
     dress, a cloth of blood.
8   He caused many a man to burn his penis;
9   He caused many a woman to slash open her vagina.
10   The owner of iron; the enraged òrìṣà who bites himself.
11   The fire that drives thieves away, that changes the color of iron and
     devours the wicked; do not harm me.
12   He was taken to Pọ́ngà; he ruined Pọ́ngà.
13   He was taken to Àkọ̀-Ire; he ruined Àkọ̀-Ire.
14   We took Ogun to the river, he divided the river in half.
15   The terrible one who strikes terror in men's minds.
16   Ogun of Ọ̀gbọ́rọ́ eats dogs and we give him dogs.
17   Ogun of Onírè needs blood; Ogun Mọlàmọlà eats mashed beans.
18   Ogun, who controls razors, feeds on hair.
19   Ogun, who controls those who circumcise, feeds on snails.
20   Ogun, who controls carvers, feeds on wood.
21   Suminiwa, Ajọkẹopo.
22   Oh! I am afraid of Ogun.
23   Ogun, whose long hands can save his children from the abyss.
24   Save me.[1]

Among the 20 million Yoruba people of southwestern Nigeria, Ogun is one
of the principal deities in the pantheon of òrìṣà (gods). The regional variation in the person and number of the gods is so great that the Yoruba say
that there are 401 òrìṣà. In this vast and complex religious system, only Ifa,
the deity of divination, and Eṣu, the deity who carries offerings and sacrifices
to the gods and to other spirit powers, are as widely known and worshipped
as Ogun; and in many communities only ancestral festivals rival in importance
that for Ogun in the annual liturgical calendar.

In the northern Yoruba town of Ila-Ọrangun[2] there are two civic festivals
in which Ogun is prominent. The one, Ọdun Ogun, is held for seven days
in early June.[3] The other, Ọdun Oro, also referred to as Ọdun Ọba (festival
of the king), is held for thirteen days in early September. In this essay I describe segments of the two festivals, but concentrate on the ritual segment,
which in the festival for Ogun is called "Iwa Ogun" and in the festival for
the king is called "Iwa Aṣọ." It is a rite of considerable complexity and dramatic action. Its importance in Ila is indicated by the fact that it is performed
three times in the annual liturgical calendar, once in the festival for Ogun
and twice in the festival for the king.

In many respects rituals and, by extension, festivals are like myths in that they may be "read" as textual statements and interpreted in terms of the images, motifs, and structural patterns of which they are composed. They may also be understood as religious metaphors as Fernandez has argued, and, following Geertz, as "enactments, materializations, realizations" of a particular religious perspective "that moves beyond the realities of everyday life to wider ones which correct and complete them" (Fernandez 1977:100–131; Geertz 1973:112). My reading of the ritual of Iwa Ogun, and of the material representations and oral traditions associated with it, suggests that Ogun symbolizes the reality and ambiguity of violence in human experience, a violence that creates through acts of destruction, but which can also destroy what it has created. The rites of Odun Ogun require the Yoruba to recognize the irony of cultural existence: death is essential to life. Yet these same rites reveal that if humans are to achieve social and political accord, then they must submit to a cultural power which can appease, even transcend the dreadful power of Ogun. That is what is acknowledged in the festival of Odun Ogun and affirmed in Odun Oro.

Odun Ogun: The Festival for Ogun

Odun Ogun is a community-wide celebration. The principal participants are associated with three distinct aspects of Ila society: kingship, chiefship, and occupation. The participants representing kingship include the *oba* (king, also called Orangun), the *olorì* (king's wives), the *omoba* (members of the royal family), the *omodégbélé* and *emese* (palace servants and messengers), the Baale Onilu (chief drummer), and the palace drummers. The chiefly participants are town, warrior, and lineage chiefs, who ordinarily inherit their titles through their kin groups. These chiefly groups are the *afóbaje* (seven senior chiefs, who are known as the kingmakers), an unspecified number of junior chiefs,[4] the Balogun and Ologun (warrior chieftaincy groups),[5] the Ikegbe (ritual chiefs who are associated with installing and burying the king), and the Ojuwa (heads of lineages who are affiliated with Chief Elemona, an *afóbaje* chief, who is the messenger between the senior chiefs and the king). The representatives of occupational groups include the Oloode (chief of hunters), the Oloriawo Onifa (leader of the divination priests), and the Oloriawo Onisegun (leader of the herbalist priests). Blacksmiths conduct essentially private rituals at their stalls during the festival. They do not participate in the public spectacles.

Days 1 through 6

In 1977, when I first witnessed Odun Ogun, the festival began with a ritual reenactment of the founding of the town of Ila-Orangun. On the morning of the first day, the six senior Ologun warrior chiefs, led by Chief Elekehan, paraded to the site of the ancient and abandoned town of Ila-Yara, which

lies about five miles to the south of Ila-Ọrangun; according to palace tradition, Ọrangun Igbonnibi in 1460 led the members of the Arutu family from
Ila-Yara to the site of the present Ila-Ọrangun.[6] Each warrior chief carried
an *ògbó* or an *òdùrọ* (a cutlass or an iron cudgel) to which *màrìwò* (fresh
palm fronds) had been tied. At the site of the abandoned town the chiefs tied
màrìwò around an *àràbà* (white silk cotton) tree, and there they worshipped
Ogun by sacrificing a dog and praying for peace. Just before sunset the warrior chiefs returned to Ila-Ọrangun, bringing with them a rock, which was
added to several hundred other rocks constituting the Ogun Ọja (one of the
town's Ogun shrines) located in the Ọba Ọja (the King's Market). Four
kolanuts were placed on the rock by Chief Ẹlẹkẹhan as he praised Ogun
and prayed for peace. Word was sent to the *ọba* that the rock from Ila-Yara
had arrived and the Ogun festival had begun.

On the following day, the blacksmiths hung *màrìwò* at the entrance to their
stalls and sacrificed dogs to Ogun at their smithy shrines (fig. 6.1). Together,
with all others who work with metal instruments—carvers, carpenters, barbers, circumcisers, facial scarifiers—they smeared their tools with sacrificed
blood and offered praises and prayers to Ogun. Each dog's head was added
to a collection of skulls, bits of metal, palm fronds, and *oògùn* (packets of
medicine) suspended above the large rock or cement mound that is Ogun's
shrine.

On the third day, the *ọba* joined the warrior chiefs in making three sacrifices to Ogun. The rite, called Iṣagun, was performed once in the morning
and twice in the afternoon. On each occasion the king, dressed in the robes
and wearing the beads of a chief, left the palace to meet the senior warrior
chiefs at the Ogun shrine opposite the palace gates. The Balogun warriors were represented by their chiefs, Otun Balogun and Osi Balogun, and
the Ologun warriors by their chiefs, Ẹlẹkẹhan, Oloyin, and Sagiku. The
king was accompanied by Chief Ẹlẹmọna, the Ojuwa chiefs, and the
ẹmẹsẹ̀.[7]

The king and warrior leader briefly confronted each other before making
their sacrifice. As the king approached the Ogun shrine, he and Chief Ẹlẹkẹhan rushed toward each other with raised cutlasses, but they stopped short
of a conflict as each touched his cutlass to the ground three times. Ẹlẹkẹhan
greeted the *ọba* and invited him to the shrine. The Ogun shrine was at the
base of what was once an enormous *àràbà* tree, around which *màrìwò* was
tied.[8] Here the *ọba* and Chief Ẹlẹkẹhan joined in offering kolanuts and
the following prayer:

1   Ògún! Obí re re o.
2   Fún wa ní àláafíà.
3   Ma da wahale silu.

1   Ogun! We give you kola.

FIGURE 6.1. A blacksmith's Ogun shrine. A devotee sits before the great stone for Ogun. From the rafters hang *màrìwò*, a dog's head, and other sacrificial items and sacred emblems.

2   Give us peace.
3   Do not make trouble in our town.

In the past, a dog was brought to the shrine by the king's servants and the warrior leader offered a second prayer:

I   Ògún, eran rẹ re o.
2   Ma pa wa o.
3   Gbà wá lówó ikú.
4   Ma jẹ́ k'ọ́mọ dé rí ewu ọkọ̀.
5   Ma jẹ́ k'ágbà rí aìsàn.
6   Ma jẹ́ káboyún sọ oyún nù.
7   Ma jẹ́ k'óde rí àgbàkó.
8   Jẹ́ ká ní àláafíà.

I   Ogun, here is your festival dog.
2   Do us no harm.
3   Keep us safe from death.
4   Do not let the young have accidents.
5   Do not let the elderly suffer disease.
6   Do not let pregnant women have miscarriages.
7   Do not let the hunter be killed.
8   Let us have peace.[9]

With a swift, deft swing of his cutlass, Chief Ẹlẹkẹhan severed the dog's head from its body. The head was tied among the palm fronds on the tree trunk so that the blood dripped on the stone of Ogun. (Although the sacrifice of the dog is omitted today, kolanuts are offered to Ogun and the participants carry out the other parts of the rite.)

Chief Ẹlẹkẹhan moved to the palace *gbẹ̀du* drums, on which the *ọmọ-dégbélé* (king's messengers) were beating the rhythms for Ogun, touched his cutlass to the ground three times, saying, "Ogun, we come to beg for peace!" and danced a few steps. The king and each of the warrior chiefs honored Ogun in the same fashion. Then to the multiple rhythms of the *gbẹ̀du, bàtá,* and *dùndún* drums, the *ọba*, and his entourage, led by the Ologun and Balogun chiefs and followed by the Ẹlẹmọna, the Ojuwa chiefs, the *olorì,* and the *ẹmẹsẹ̀*, paraded around the shrine. On the seventh time around, the rhythms quickened and the participants circled the shrine at a run. Before returning to the palace, the *ọba*, sword in hand, danced at length to the drum rhythms for Ogun (fig. 6.2).

Later in the evening of Iṣagun, the chiefs joined the king in the palace for a feast. They arrived in order of their seniority, knelt before the king,

FIGURE 6.2. The *ọba* dancing to the *gbèdu* drum at the Ogun shrine during the rite of Iṣagun.

and saluted him three times: "*Kábíyèsí. Ẹ kú Ọdún.*" ("Your Highness. Festival greetings.") The *ọba* replied, "*Àṣẹ.*" ("Let it come to pass.") Then the representatives of the Ikẹgbẹ chiefs, followed by the Balogun and Ologun chiefs, arrived, each saluting the *ọba* by touching his cutlass or cudgel to the ground three times and repeating the festival greetings. The king then led the chiefs to a banquet in the palace, but he did not eat with them. Throughout the next four days the Ologun chiefs feasted one another in accordance with their rank.

On the afternoon of the fourth day, Ila's hunters became active in the festival. The Ọlọọdẹ of Ore's compound, one of seven hunter chiefs for whom Ogun is the patron *òrìṣà*, came to the palace to greet the *ọba* on behalf of Ila's hunters. Accompanied by members of his family, hunters, dancers, and drummers, the Ọlọọdẹ escorted two *egúngún láyẹ̀wú* (masquerades for deceased hunters) into the outer courtyard of the palace. One of the masquerades, called *aláàrù láyẹ̀wú*, was entirely covered by a large, conical, tent-like construction made of antelope skins with four antelope horns protruding from the top. It was removed before the dancers approached the *ọba* and the Ojuwa chiefs, who were seated on the porch of the palace reception hall. The dancers were dressed in close-fitting cloth costumes designed to resemble a forest cat. A braided hairpiece of a type worn by hunters hung down the left side of the head. The hunter's flywhisk was carried on the left shoulder and leather pouches of protective medicine, similar to those worn by hunters, were tied about the waist and neck (fig. 6.3). The masquerades danced before the *ọba* and chanted *ìjálá*, (poetry associated with Ogun of the hunters). They sang the praises, not only of Ogun and the *ọba*, but also the *oríkì* (praise names), of the hunter chief and of the lineage and house from which the masquerades came. The king presented kola and money to the masquerades and asked that they convey his greetings to all of Ila's hunters.[10] That evening Ila's hunters gathered at the Ọlọọdẹ's house to feast and sacrifice a dog to Ogun.

There was now a two-day respite from the bloody sacrifices to Ogun before the festival was concluded.

Iwa Ogun (Day 7)

The final rite of Ọdun Ogun, a rite called Iwa Ogun, began in the afternoon on the seventh day. The king's servants prepared the veranda at the front of the palace, placing a rug, the king's throne, and a hassock before three elaborately carved panels at the center of the veranda wall. The panels frame a doorway which leads to a small chamber and, beyond it, the palace courtyard. A few townspeople moved slowly along the three roads which meet at the front of the palace.

Simultaneously, the chiefs assembled near the palace. The seven senior chiefs and representatives of the junior chiefs gathered on the veranda of the house of Chief Ọbale (the second-ranking senior chief and the head of the

FIGURE 6.3. The hunter's masquerades, *egúngún láyẹ̀wú*, chanting *ijalá* at the palace.

palace servants). The leaders of the Balogun and Ologun warrior chiefs and of the Ikẹgbẹ ritual chiefs assembled at the Ogun shrine, which was near Ẹlẹmọna's compound and halfway between the palace and Chief Ọbale's compound (see fig. 6.4). *Gbẹ̀du* drums were beaten at the Ogun shrine and at Chief Ọbale's veranda. They did not compete in volume or complexity of rhythm, however, with the *gbẹ̀du* and *dùndún* drums played in the palace courtyard.

The Ewe Ogun also took their place at the Ogun shrine. They are daughters of the Igbonnibi ruling house, whose son now occupies the throne.[11] The *ọmọba* (princes) and other members of the ruling house joined the townspeople in front of the palace veranda. The crowd had become quite large and the passage of traffic was brought to a halt.

The king's arrival was announced by the drums. Although royal umbrellas were raised above his head, he was dressed as a chief, in an embroidered red gown. After paying homage at an unmarked burial site of his predecessor, Ọrangun Igbonnibi,[12] the *ọba* left the palace courtyard and moved to the veranda with his servants and drummers, who sounded the rhythms reserved for the *ọba*. The king's wives and children sat on his right; beyond them sat the *ọba*. The *ẹmẹsẹ̀* and the *ọmọdégbélé*, armed with whips, stopped all traffic.[13] No one must cross the area between the palace and Ọbale's house, on pain of becoming a servant or wife of the *ọba*. Twenty minutes passed. The townspeople grew restless and the *ọba* impatient, and all looked in the direction of Ọbale's compound.

After long delays, the Ikẹgbẹ chiefs, Ọbasinkin and Ọdọọde, accompanied by a drummer, moved across the road from the Ogun shrine to Chief Ọbale's veranda.[14] They greeted Chief Ọbale and then, to the sharp, staccato rhythms of the *bàtá* drum, danced before the assembled senior and junior chiefs. In response to the Ikẹgbẹ dance, the chiefs left Ọbale's veranda and moved to the edge of his compound, where they sat facing the distant *ọba*. At the same time, the *ọba*'s chief drummer, Baale Onilu, left the palace veranda and moved in the direction of Chief Ẹlẹmọna's house, which is just beyond the Ogun shrine. He "called" Ẹlẹmọna by drumming his name, inviting him to join the *ọba*. The Ẹlẹmọna responded by leading the Ojuwa chiefs to the king.

The Ojuwa chiefs greeted the king with extreme deference. As they approached the *ọba*, they removed their hats, placed their fans on the ground, and rolled up the flowing sleeves of their gowns, knotting them behind their necks. They knelt, rubbed the palms of their hands together, and Ẹlẹmọna saluted the *ọba*:

1   Ẹ kú Ọdún.
2   Kábíyèsí, ẹbọ á fín.
3   Èrù á dà!

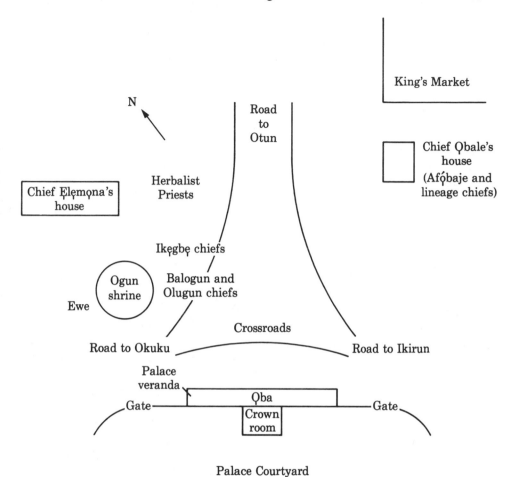

FIGURE 6.4. Iwa Ogun: Ritual Space and Participants

4   Agbèrù o gba ebo!
5   Alásekà o bá ọ sé!
6   Ilú á rójú.
7   Ilú á tòrò.
8   Ògún ò rí wòlú.
9   Ikú ọmọ wẹ́wẹ́ kòrí wòlú.
10   Èmí tí o se ọdún ní ni yóò se ẹ̀ẹmi.
11   Ìgbà yín á tù wá lára.
12   Ẹyin lao ṣà lẹ́ẹ̀mîi.
13   Kábíyèsí.

I   Festival greetings.
2   Your highness, may the sacrifice be accomplished.
3   It will happen!
4   Your predecessors will make it successful!
5   The ancestors will assist you.
6   May there be no disturbance in the town.
7   May there be peace in the town.
8   May war not come.
9   May death not take little children.
10   May you be able to perform this (rite) next year.
11   May your reign be peaceful for us.
12   May we be able to greet you again next year.
13   Your highness.[15]

Then the Ojuwa chiefs prostrated themselves before the king. In response the ọba rolled his flywhisk between the palms of his hands, touched it to the hands of the senior palace messenger, and instructed him to touch the upraised palms of the hands of Chief Ẹlẹmọna and the other chiefs, to present them with kola, and to beckon them to the throne. When Ẹlẹmọna presented himself to the king, the king instructed him to go to the chiefs at Ọbale's veranda and invite them to the palace front in order that the festival for Ogun might be concluded.[16]

When Ẹlẹmọna conveyed the king's request, the senior and junior chiefs remained aloof. In an effort to bring the chiefs into the proceedings, Baale Onilu drummed Ẹlẹmọna's name and again led him and the Ojuwa chiefs to Ọbale's compound. As before, Ẹlẹmọna greeted the senior and junior chiefs and invited them to the palace. They refused and the emissaries returned to the palace veranda, where they again saluted the king. With tension mounting, the emissaries returned a third time to the chiefs. This time, however, Baale Onilu stood in front of the Ẹlẹmọna and drummed with such power that he required Chief Ẹlẹmọna and the Ojuwa chiefs to dance the distance separating the ọba from the recalcitrant chiefs. Once again Ẹlẹmọna greeted the chiefs, but this time, as he stretched forth his hands, he pleaded: "This is the hand of the Ọrangun. He asks you to come nearer to him. There is no conflict between you and him." The Ẹlẹmọna then touched the hands of each chief. At last the emissaries persuaded the chiefs to accompany them as far as the center of the road, where they took seats in a line adjacent to the Ogun shrine.

At the moment the chiefs responded to the Ẹlẹmọna, the king left his throne. He entered the small chamber behind the carved panels of the veranda and changed from the clothes of a chief to royal robes and the conical beaded crown with veil called Ologun Ade (The Crown of the Warrior Chief). When Ẹlẹmọna and the Ojuwa chiefs returned from their successful mission, the ọba reappeared in his royal person (fig. 6.5). The king moved

FIGURE 6.5. The Ọrangun-Ila wearing the Ologun crown and greeting Ila's chiefs during Iwa Ogun.

rapidly to the Ogun shrine, where he was greeted by the Ologun warrior chiefs and where he offered kola to Ogun. Chief Ẹlẹkẹhan placed the offering on the shrine and, on behalf of the king, prayed:

1   Ògún, obì ọba re o.
2   O ńtoro àláafiá.
3   Ma pá o,
4   Jẹ́ kó s'àmódún kó mú.
5   Obì ẹ wá lẹ́ẹmi.

1   Ogun, here are the *ọba*'s kolanuts for you.
2   He asks for peace.
3   Do not harm him.
4   Let him live that he may return again to offer
5   you kolanuts next year.

The *ọba* then proceeded to the center of the road, where he stood silently before the seated senior and junior chiefs.

The climax was reached when a mock battle broke out between the palace servants and the warrior chiefs led by Ẹlẹkẹhan. The skirmish took place in the space between the king and the other seated chiefs. The antagonists clashed, striking one another with branches and making threatening gestures with cudgels and swords (fig. 6.6). Finally, at a signal from Chief Ọbale, the fighting stopped.[17] As the Ojuwa chiefs had done earlier, the senior and junior chiefs rolled up the sleeves of their gowns, placed their fans on the ground, and prostrated themselves before the Ọrangun (fig. 6.7). The *ọba* again rolled his flywhisk between his hands and touched the hands of Chief Ẹlẹmọna who in turn touched the hands of each chief, raising him up. When all were standing, the palace drummers began their rapid rhythms and the *ọba* danced along the line of chiefs before returning to the palace veranda. Once the Ọrangun was on his throne, the chiefs of Ila moved in a phalanx toward the king. They knelt and greeted him with the salutation: "*Ẹ kú Ọ-dún. Kábíyèsí. Ọba aláàṣẹ èkejì òrìṣà.*" ("Festival greetings, your highness! The king's power is like that of the gods.") The *afọ́baje* sat to the left of the king, opposite the Ojuwa chiefs, thereby creating an open stage between the palace and the Ogun shrine.

The chiefs and priests were then honored before the king. The chief drummer looked in the direction of the Ogun shrine, sounded the praise names of the various chiefs, who in sequence bowed, touched their cutlasses and cudgels to the ground, and danced before the king (fig. 6.8). Then the drum called the diviner and the herbalist priests. They too touched their staffs of office to the ground three times and danced before the king. Finally, the princesses left the Ogun shrine, chanting the king's praises as they approached

FIGURE 6.6. The mock battle enacted by the palace servants and the Ologun chiefs during the rite of Iwa Ogun.

FIGURE 6.7. The *afóbaje* and lineage chiefs greeting the *ǫba* at the palace in the rite of Iwa Ogun.

their kinsman; they knelt before the throne, and a servant gave each one a kolanut and a coin, as he had done to all others.

Finally, the king was honored before the chiefs. The palace drummers marched to the crossroads in front of the palace and the crowd fell silent. Baale Onilu faced the king and drummed the names and *oríkì* of the twenty-three kings of Ila from the time of Ọrangun Ajagun-nla, son of Oduduwa, to the present reigning *ọba*, Ọrangun William Adetona Ayeni, Ariwajoye I. The virtuoso solo performance, called *Ẹ̀kà kékà*, took fifteen minutes. As he completed the praises of the *ọba*, the crowd shouted: "*Kábíyèsí! Kábíyèsí! Kábíyèsí!*" and his highness left the throne to dance before the chiefs, in order of their seniority, and the townspeople. To the cheers of the crowd, the king, alone, entered the palace by way of the carved veranda door.

The public *ètùtù* (an obligatory ritual action) for Ogun had been performed. There was now a final, secret rite called Ikate (The Rolling Up of the Carpet) or Ikawa (The End of Iwa).

The *ẹmẹsẹ̀* cleared the entire area in front of the palace as far as the entrance to the king's market to the east and to the bends in the roads from the north and the south that converge at the palace front. No one was permitted to look upon the palace veranda or enter the outer courtyard as long as the palace *gbẹ̀du* drums were beaten by the *ọmọdégbélé*. While the senior *olorì* carefully rolled up the carpet and the palace servants removed the throne, hassock, and umbrellas, the *ọba* received Chiefs Ọbala, Ọbale, Ọbasinkin, and Ọbajoko in the chamber behind the veranda panels.[18] Each chief, stripped to the waist, wore a dark, strip-woven cloth (*aṣọ aláàro*) that was knotted on the left hip. Kneeling before the seated *ọba*, they greeted their king with the traditional salutation. The king gave the chiefs a calabash of palm wine, from which they pretended to drink. Observing that they did not drink the wine, the king chided them and asked why they refused to accept his hospitality. The chiefs' only response was to say "*Kábíyèsí.*" Each chief received a kolanut and was dismissed.

When the crown was removed from the king's head, he left the chamber and entered the outer courtyard and proceeded to the unmarked shrine of Igbonnibi. There he offered a prayer to the ancient Ọrangun, stepping upon the ground three times with his left foot. This festival for the *òrìṣà* of iron was now over.

Iwa Ogun: Analyzing the Ritual Action

Every ritual entails a use of space and has an axis along which the movement of the participants takes place and by which their movements are controlled. In Iwa Ogun, the axis is clearly the line of action between the veranda of the palace and the veranda of Chief Ọbale's compound. It passes through the point at which the three principal roads of Ila meet, and its midpoint passes the shrine of Ogun. Only the chief drummer and the people he calls

FIGURE 6.8. The ọba wears the crown *Ològún adé* as he sits on his throne. A woman chief dances before him.

and leads may walk along or cross the axis with impunity. It is a dangerous space, for it is charged by the tension of competing centers of power and, passing so close to Ogun, it is vulnerable to the eruption of violence.

The Ọbale's Veranda: Gathering Place of the Chiefs

Chief Ọbale is second in rank among the seven senior town chiefs of Ila. The title, Ọbale, is a contraction of *ọba ilé* (the one who is king in his own house). It refers specifically to the fact that the senior chiefs meet on Chief Ọbale's veranda each week, and whenever else necessary, to discuss the affairs of the town. From the veranda they may observe the movement of persons to and from the palace, at the crossroads, and in the marketplace. Here the town's senior chiefs talk with representatives of the junior chiefs and shape community policy. Hence, as the gathering place of the chiefs, Ọbale's veranda reflects the fact that Ila, like other Yoruba towns, is essentially an aggregate of descent groups. Senior and junior chieftaincy titles are hereditary among the lineages, which thereby become the basic representative units of the political system.[19]

At the outset of Iwa Ogun, the *ọba* must suffer the ritual affront of waiting for Ila's chiefs, who have assembled at Chief Ọbale's house. In this way, the king is made acutely aware of the fact that the people over whom he reigns have another allegiance, another locus of political identity than that which is expressed in his royal person. This is the primordial bond of kinship. Furthermore, as the king watches the chiefs gather on Ọbale's veranda, he is reminded of his own enforced residence of three months in Ọbale's compound prior to being crowned Ọrangun-Ila.[20] In those three months the king's person undergoes what might appropriately be called a substantive change.

The senior *afọ́baje* chiefs are kingmakers. At the death of a king, they consult the senior divination priests and select a new *ọba* from among candidates presented by the royal house whose turn it is to provide a king.[21] When the name of the *ọba*-elect is announced, the candidate "flees" and "hides" until he can be found by the palace servants. He is then taken to Chief Ọbale's house, stripped of his clothes, examined for physical deformities, and ritually washed and dressed in a new white cloth. For three months he remains in Ọbale's house, receiving visitors on the veranda, but never leaving the compound. During this period, the *ọba*-elect is instructed by the senior chiefs in his political and ritual responsibilities.

Among the many rites of enthronement, these are acts which set the king-elect apart from his own kin group and enable him to establish a new line of kinship relationships. In the past, one of these rites required the new *ọba* to eat the heart and drink maize gruel from the skull of the deceased Ọrangun, and to offer prayers to the *orí* (head or personal destiny) of his predecessor.[22] This ceremony signals a separation; the new *ọba* is indicating that his destiny is now defined through a new line of descent. This is a line of sacred kings—a line that has its origins in Oduduwa, the divine mythical king of all Yoruba. The ritual of eating the predecessor's heart and worshipping his *orí*, whose destiny can affect the success of his rule, is analogous to sacrificing to one's parents' *orí*, whose personal destiny can affect the course of a child's life. The man who is king may still sacrifice to the *orí* of his parent, but not as the king. Officially he belongs to a unique kind of descent group— that of the Ọrangun-Ila. This is a line of consanguineally-related sovereigns whose genealogy consists only of those who have held the office of king. The descent group is not of the same order as the lineages of the chiefs or the ruling house lineages, both of whose genealogies are reckoned according to a consanguineal parent-to-child relationship. Rather, the Ọrangun-Ila descent group is a separate line which—while being carved out of the ruling house lineages—has a separate, corporate life of its own.[23] Kingship may be analogous to chieftaincy in that it connotes high political office, but it must be clearly differentiated from chieftaincy because kingship, as we shall see, possesses an authority that transcends that of lineage chieftaincy.

The Palace Veranda: Images of Power

The Ọba's Crown

A transformation takes place on the veranda of the palace at the moment in the ritual when the chiefs move from Ọbale's veranda to the center of the road near the Ogun shrine. The king enters a small chamber, called Ori Ojopọ, behind the veranda door. There he removes the clothes of a chief (i.e., a lineage head), dons the beaded crown and royal robes of his office, and returns to the palace veranda as Ọrangun-Ila. In this manner, the authority and power of kingship arc graphically presented to the chiefs and the townspeople.

The *ọba*'s crown is the principal symbol of royalty. All kings who wear the crown trace their descent from Oduduwa. One tradition states that Oduduwa gave a beaded crown to each of his sixteen sons, the youngest of whom was Ọrangun, and each of them established his own kingdom.[24] Thus, the present Ọrangun has observed that the faces that decorate the conical portion of his crown "represent the face of Oduduwa and the sons of Oduduwa."[25] That is to say, the faces represent male power. But what about the large bird perched atop his crown, and the cluster of birds attached on the sides of the crown? Henry Drewal has noted that "bird imagery in many Yoruba art forms refers directly to the vital force possessed by females (living, ancestral, deified), collectively known as 'our mothers.'" He suggests, correctly, I believe, that the "birds surrounding the top of the crown signify that the king rules only with the protection of the mothers" (Drewal 1977:4). Thus, with reference to the great bird on the crowns of Ila's kings, the Ọrangun observed that it "represents the *ọba*'s *àṣẹ* (king's power)."[26]

The meaning of *àṣẹ* is extraordinarily complex. It is used in a variety of contexts, only one of which is kingship. Verger translates *àṣẹ* as "the vital power, the energy, the great strength of all things" (Verger 1966:35).[27] It also refers to a divine energy manifest in the process of procreation. *Àṣẹ* does not entail any particular signification, and yet it invests all things, exists everywhere, and, as the warrant for all creative activity, opposes chaos and the loss of meaning in human experience. Nevertheless, *àṣẹ* may be used for destructive ends. Its presence appears to vary throughout the universe. It is more manifest in the *òrìṣà* than in people, but it can be accumulated by humans.

The significance of *àṣẹ* is revealed in the Yoruba creation myth. One version states that when Olodumare, the High God, decided that the world should exist, he commissioned *òrìṣà* Ọbatala to take a calabash of sand and a five-toed cock, and, with the aid of a chain, to lower himself to the surface of the primeval waters.[28] Having poured the sand upon the waters, Ọbatala was to place the cock on the sand. As the cock scratched, sending the sand flying in various directions, the continents of the earth would take form. On his way to fulfilling his commission, Ọbatala passed a gathering of *òrìṣà* who were drinking palm wine. Accepting their invitation to join them, Ọbatala drank excessively and fell asleep. Oduduwa knew of the High God's commission, and, seeing the sleeping Ọbatala, he took the calabash of sand, the cock, the chain, and fulfilled Olodumare's wishes. The place of creation was the town of Ile-Ifẹ (spiritual center of the Yoruba). When Ọbatala awoke and saw what Oduduwa had done and heard his claim that he had authority over the earth, Ọbatala was enraged and a great struggle between the two *òrìṣà* ensued. At length Olodumare intervened. He gave Ọbatala the power to shape the bodies of the human beings who would populate the earth, and bestowed on Oduduwa the power and privilege of being the first king and founder of the Yoruba people.

The myth clearly distinguishes two types of creative power. There is biological power, which shapes the individual's physical existence for good or ill; Ọbatala is said to create albinos and hunchbacks, as well as beautiful and well-formed people. And there is political power, which shapes people as social and moral beings. In keeping with the creation myth, the present Ọrangun-Ila identified one of the faces on his crown as the son of Oduduwa who established the line of Ila kings. The crown and, hence, the Ọrangun himself are linked to both the powers of Ọbatala, which are also associated with "the mothers," and the powers of Oduduwa—the power of procreating and the power of establishing and preserving the body politic. The latter is identified with the distinctive urban life-style and political centralization of Yoruba peoples, apart from which, as the Ọrangun observed, "life would be like life in the bush."[29]

Other features of the crown suggest that royal power exceeds the powers expressed in the iconographic references to Oduduwa. The feet of the large bird on the peak of the crown are tied to the hidden *oògùn àṣẹ* (powerful medicines) which the chief herbalist placed in the crown when it was made. "It is the *oògùn àṣẹ* which gives me power. It makes the *ọba* powerful over all kinds of spirits, even over witches."[30] The ọba may look at the bird perched on the crown, but he must never look inside the crown. He must never see the hidden medicinal powers. To do so would risk blindness. Thus, when the crown is worn, it is placed on the ọba's head by the senior wife standing behind him, by one who possesses the àṣẹ of "the mothers."

The crown is a visual metaphor of the authority and power of the ọba. In its structure and iconography it refers to a power that relies upon and transcends the contrastive powers of male and female. It links, bridges, relates opposites. The crown is "looked on as an òrìṣà."[31] But the crown is "looked on" only in the performance of a ritual such as that of Iwa Ogun. It is in the ritual context that the Yoruba see and know the supernatural power of the crown.

The Carved Panels

The carvings on the panels at the rear of the palace veranda repeat the symbolism found in the crown. The carvings, it will be recalled, frame the doorway which leads to Ori Ojopọ, the chamber where the original crowns of the kings of Ila are kept. The carvings merit close attention (fig. 6.9).[32] They tell us and the people of Ila about the roles and the powers of the ọba in Igbomina society. The three panels, each 9½ feet high and 2½ feet wide, contain 79 human figures engaged in a variety of domestic and ritual activities. Animals such as snakes, lizards, dogs, or birds are used decoratively to subdivide the panels or as part of the activities portrayed.

The king dominates the central panel in size and position. The lower two-thirds of the central panel constitutes the door which leads to the chamber of the original crown. The upper portion of the door depicts a seated ọba wearing a crown and holding a royal staff and flywhisk. He is surrounded by wives and servants, all of whom look to him as they engage in various acts of service. Above his crowned head is an inverted U-shaped, serrated design, probably representing the royal umbrella.[33] The remainder of the door-panel is divided into three groups of figures. Immediately below the ọba is a warrior on horseback, accompanied by male servants who bear arms or blow flutes and horns, and women who kneel and lift up their breasts. The next band of figures portrays, at the left, an Ifa priest holding a divination chain and a woman holding a divining tray. In the center a couple engage in sexual intercourse. To their right a palm wine tapper is shown at work, while a man with a palm wine calabash and a woman holding her breasts wait below him. The third panel, containing hunters with captured animals and birds, decorates the lower portion of the door.

The panel immediately above the door is divided into two sections. Two couples, engaged in sexual intercourse, and the figure of a child form the upper section. The lower section contains figures of Aworo-ose, a priest of òrìṣà Ọbatala and òrìṣà Oṣoosi, dancing before the igbìn drums of Ọbatala and holding the bow and arrow of Oṣoosi. Other devotees carry libations for the two òrìṣà.[34]

FIGURE 6.9. The carved panels on the palace veranda. The door leads to
Orí Ojópò.

The panel to the left of the doorway concentrates on the emblems and devotees of various òrìṣà. Five equal sections depict Oṣun, deity of healing waters; Osanyin, deity of medicinal herbs; Ṣango, deified king of ancient Ọyọ; Ogun, deity of war and of iron; and Osumare, the deity whose emblems are the rainbow and the python.

The panel to the right is varied. The center section includes worshippers of òrìṣà Oko, god of the farm, and, once again, Ogun, whose devotees hold a sacrificial dog. Separated by joined snakes and lizards is the top cluster of figures in which an armed servant stands watch over two slave women who pound yam and a man who holds a rope tied to the waist of another female slave. The lower portion of the right panel is dominated by a man balanced at the top of a long bamboo pole, while musicians and acrobats, as well as a man holding his erect penis in one hand and a large staff in the other, perform to the left and below him. Another cluster of figures to the right includes a Muslim holding his prayer beads and Koranic slate and a man leading his son by the arm and shaking his cane in the direction of the circus performers. Finally, at the bottom of the panel two men lead a hobbled antelope.

The ọba of the veranda carvings is surrounded by images of generative or marginal activity and by figures whose status or activity of the moment places them on the margin of society: òrìṣà worshippers, warriors, hunters, couples engaged in sexual intercourse, palm wine tappers, slave women preparing food, diviners, drummers, captives, and acrobats. If we pursue the meanings conveyed by the carvings about the àṣẹ of the ọba, then we see that the palace is something more than the converging point of political activity. As in all Yoruba towns, the palace of the Ọrangun is located in the center of the town. The compounds of the senior chiefs are located in four of the five quarters into which Ila is divided; their houses more or less surround at varying distances the palace grounds.[35] Yet the carvings do not depict an ọba surrounded by chiefs, but an ọba at the center of a far more complex nexus of people and activities.

The palace is important in the ritual life of all people of Ila. There are shrines for many of the òrìṣà within the palace grounds; also, with one exception, every festival for an òrìṣà includes a time when the devotees come to the palace to dance before the Ọrangun, offer prayers to the òrìṣà for the king's well-being, and receive from the king offerings for the òrìṣà and gifts for the worshippers. The exception is the festival for Ṣoponna, the òrìṣà of smallpox and other dread diseases. The devotees of this fearsome god do not visit the palace or the marketplace; but they do receive offerings and gifts from the king, which are carried to them by one of the palace servants. At a distance, they too make prayers and offerings for the king's health and safety. It is not surprising, therefore, that the veranda panels should depict the Ọrangun surrounded on three sides by òrìṣà worshippers.

The fecundity of the community also is linked to kingship. It is no accident, the Ọrangun indicates, that the carving of the ọba is below that of the Ọbatala priest. Recall that in the creation myth, Ọbatala is given the power

to shape the human body. He "changes blood into a child, and causes defor-
mity in children when he is angry."[36] Hence on the veranda panel above the
dancing Ọbatala priest, couples engage in sexual intercourse and a child lies
at their side. Still, the same panel portrays the ọba's ability to deny life. Immediately below the king is a warrior on horseback. Like the warrior or
hunter, the ọba wields power which can kill in order to sustain life, and he
must do so for the sake of his people. In this role, too, the ọba is like the
òrìṣà, who take the sacrifices offered by humans so that the gift of life may
be given to them.

Drummers and acrobats are marginal people in Yoruba society. Like the
priests of the òrìṣà, they are privileged, for they are thought to be possessed
of unusual powers. Performers such as these violate conventional behavior
by moving, and enabling others to move, in their action and their imagination, across the social boundaries which separate people or which define socially acceptable activities. Nevertheless, they are granted privileged status
in the society and are often brought within the palace. The palace is an anomalous realm and its chief resident also is a marginal person. The presence of
performers, therefore, reinforces and reflects the uniqueness of the place.

The intertwined snakes and lizards which separate the human scenes on
the panels are more than decorative details. They symbolize the essential activity of the universe: the activity of generation and regeneration. The logic
of existence is that there is an interlocking interdependence of all things in
the continuous struggle of life and death. This logic is at work in both the
details and the larger scenes portrayed on the veranda panels, as well as in
the rituals of Ila's festivals.

If I have read the iconography of the panels correctly, then the message
they convey is that the person of the crowned ọba embodies a vital power.
The extraordinariness of this power is such that it plays a salient role in shaping peoples' perceptions of reality. According to the Ọrangun, when a man
passes through the veranda doorway, enters the room behind the carved panels, and receives the ancient crown of Ila on his head, "the *orí* [the destiny]
of the crown and the *orí* of the ọba are brought together. The *àṣẹ* of the
crown is bound to the head of the man. He becomes Ọrangun-Ila. Two
heads, two destinies, come together. That is what Ori Ojopọ means."[37] Ordinary people must not look on the face of the king who possesses such power,
just as an ọba must not look at the *oògùn àṣẹ* hidden within the crown.
For this reason, a veil of beads conceals the ọba's face, that is, the face of
the man, William Adetona Ayeni. As with all masks, concealment is designed
to disclose a power, a reality, not otherwise observable. It is the cluster of
faces and birds on the crown that are seen and that reveal the sacred power
of the ọba's *orí* (king's head). As the chiefs affirm in their salutation to the
king: *Ọba aláàṣẹ èkejì òrìṣà!* (The king's power is like that of the
gods).[38]

Dressed in the regalia of office, it is a formidable figure who leaves the

palace veranda and approaches the chiefs who are gathered in the road near
the Ogun shrine.

The Shrine for Ogun: The Owner of All Iron

The Ogun shrine is the place where the powers of the chiefs and the king
are brought into opposition. In the meeting of the chiefs and Ọrangun, mid-
way between the veranda of Ọbale's compound and the veranda of the palace, the Ọrangun's first act is to offer kolanuts and a prayer for peace at the
Ogun shrine. He then faces Ila's seated chiefs. The failure of the chiefs to
rise and pay respect to the king is an affront that can only lead to conflict.

The centrality of Ogun in this dramatic confrontation is consistent with the
deity's importance in Ila traditions. The praise name, "Ogun, god of war and
god of iron," indicates two of the realms in which Ogun's power is experienced by the community. As a warrior-god, Ogun brought the followers of
Ọrangun Igbonnibi to Ila. Later, his power aided other ọbas in defending
the town, sometimes at a terrible price, when Ogun seemed to turn against
his own. Consequently, his oríkì are filled with fearful lament:

1   Ọjọ́ Ògún,
2   Ṣí lo, ṣí lo, ṣiló, ní má ṣẹ aiyé.
3   Dùgbè dùgbè a gba óde oòrun kẹ̀kẹ̀.
4   Ipé ǹpé jú a si kùn fé kún.
5   Òtòpàkó a ṣí kùn fẹ jẹ̀.
6   Paranganda ní dà fọ́mọ ódó.
7   Abiri, abihun à ṣimu òrìṣà.
8   Mo rí fàájì rẹ.

1   On the days when Ogun is angered,
2   There is always disaster in the world.
3   The world is full of dead people going to heaven.
4   The eyelashes are full of water.
5   Tears stream down the face.
6   A bludgeoning by Ogun causes a man's downfall.
7   I see and hear, I fear and respect my òrìṣà.
8   I have seen your (bloody) merriment.[39]

In the sacrifices and prayers offered to Ogun by the warrior chiefs and the
king on the first and third days of the festival, and again in the rite of Iwa
Ogun, there is an acknowledgment of remembered violence which drank the
blood of men.

As the "owner of all iron," Ogun provides the tools which are essential to the community. In truth, Ogun's contributions to cultural existence are many. The praise poem which introduces this essay indicates that Ogun is the circumciser, scarifier, hair-cutter, or carver. Elsewhere he is known as "The possessor of two machetes: with one he prepares the farm, and with the other he clears the road" (Idowu 1962:86). By way of recognizing these vital contributions, blacksmiths and hunters sacrifice dogs to Ogun on the second and fourth days of the festival and bathe their iron tools in the blood of the animal. This sacrifice to Ogun emphasizes his dual nature. The dog is offered only to Ogun. All other òrìṣà who receive animal sacrifices taste only the blood of goats or rams, that is, the blood of herbivorous animals. The carnivorous beast belongs to Ogun. But the dog also is a carnivorous animal which can be domesticated. Thus Ogun receives what he is; he is the deity who eats flesh and drinks blood, yet his destructive work is culturally legitimated.

Cultural existence has its costs. It requires acts of violence, not only against the person who is the enemy but also against oneself and one's children, and against the forest, the land, and the animal. Circumcision or scarification, to name only two, are acts of violence—self-inflicted wounds which serve as marks of cultural and social differentiation.

Here, then, is revealed the irony of human existence: death is essential to life. This is the reality, the truth about themselves, with which Ogun confronts humans. But if death is essential to life, what kinds of death are necessary? What power justifies and limits acts of violence upon others, as well as upon one's own person? What saves one from the intoxicating power of blood and the beguiling self-justification that arises out of death's specter? The pathos of the Ogun worshipper is that neither the devotee nor Ogun can answer these questions, as the following praise song from another Yoruba community makes clear:

1   The light shining on Ogun's face is not easy to behold.
2   Ogun, let me not see the red of your eye . . .
3   Ogun is a crazy òrìṣà who still asks questions after 780 years!
4   Whether I can reply, or whether I cannot reply,
5   Ogun please don't ask me anything.[40]

If Ogun cannot resolve the question which his dilemma imposes upon people, then how are people to live with it? This, I believe, is what the rite of Iwa Ogun seeks to address, when it is celebrated after the respite of two days from the bloody sacrifice of dogs offered during the opening days of the Ogun festival.

The rite of Iwa Ogun is fraught with tension. Initially, the king faces the chiefs as a peer, dressed in the gown and beads of a chief. Later, he approaches the chiefs in a royal robe, wearing the great crown. At the Ogun shrine, and appropriately so, the tension provided by this shift in the king's persona produces conflict. Each side is saying to the other: "I shall make you come!"[41]

The ritual erupts into a reenactment of civil war when the two centers of power are pitted against each other. The senior and junior chiefs represent Ila as an aggregate of descent groups with their individual histories and myths of origin. Kinship is a centrifugal force in Ila's political life, which the chiefs represent. On the other side, the Ọrangun transcends ordinary blood ties and compound boundaries. He represents a centripetal force, the unity of Ila as a town. According to Chief Ọdọọde, it is important that the Ọrangun make the first move to resolve the conflict. When the Ọrangun leaves the palace veranda to stand before the chiefs, he is saying: "You chiefs have power (àṣẹ). You install the Ọrangun." This acknowledgment of chiefly power or authority by the ọba enables Chief Ọbale to respond by leading the chiefs to the ọba. Only when the chiefs collectively perform the nonviolent self-sacrificial act of homage to the king can peace be known and corporate life affirmed. Again, according to Chief Ọdọọde, the chiefs are saying: "You, Ọrangun, have power (àṣẹ). We no longer have authority over you. Your power and our power are different."[42]

The Palace Veranda: The Power of the Crown Acknowledged

Iwa Ogun concludes when the king returns to the palace veranda and receives representatives from various sectors of the community: chiefs, priests, royalty, performers. The movement of all of these groups, with the exception of the palace drummers, from the Ogun shrine to the ọba, stands as a collective appeal to a power which transcends, rather than thrives on, conflict. Iwa Ogun means "the essential character of Ogun." The rite extends the dimensions of the problem of violence and culture, the focus of the first four days of the festival, into the political realm. The problem of violence has been narrowed to civil conflict when society is defined solely in terms of lineage groups living in an urban setting. In such a context the problem of the locus of political authority becomes acute. While Ogun can create the implements of culture, Ogun's iwà, his essential character, does not let him control the destruction entailed in his creative power. That, as we have seen, is the pathos of Ogun: he cannot provide political order. Another power that transcends that of Ogun is necessary if there is to be community among the patrilineages. That power is to be found in the authority (àṣẹ) of the Ọrangun-Ila.

When the Ọrangun-Ila leaves his throne and dances before his people, he does so as one in whom there is a concentration of power. He dances not to a single drum, but to the multiple rhythms of all the drums of Ila and to the chanting of his praise names by the assembled crowd. Unlike the diversities and oppositions that lead to conflict in ordinary human experience, the sacred power of the *ọba* holds these oppositions in an awesome alliance. It would appear that the power of the crown is its capacity to bring the diverse and conflicting destinies of men together into a relatively peaceful accord. The Ọrangun's crown is the symbolic center and warrant for Ila's corporate life.

Once his power is publicly affirmed, the *ọba* retires to the palace. Before he places the ancient crown of Ila in the chamber where "destinies meet," the four chiefs who have accompanied the king into the chamber remind him of the essential mistrust of kingship by the lineage chiefs in the insulting obviousness with which they pretend to drink the palm wine and refuse to accept the king's hospitality. In Iwa Ogun the power which brings unity and peace is acknowledged as being possessed by the Ọrangun, but not quite. A more decisive affirmation waits for the festival called Oro.

Ọdun Oro: The Festival for the King

The rite of Iwa Ogun is performed again three months after Ọdun Ogun as part of Ọdun Oro, a thirteen-day festival also known as Ẹbọra Ila. On this occasion the rite, which is performed twice, is known as Iwa Aṣọ or Iwa Oro. Ọdun Oro is Ila's new year festival, since it marks the beginning of the new liturgical calendar.[43] The underlying concern shaping this festival which was expressed in the ritual of Iwa Ogun is whether political authority resides with the lineage chiefs or the king. For the people of Ila this is the essential question in terms of which the problem of violence and culture must be resolved.

A thirteen-day festival involves large numbers of people in many diverse activities. On some occasions the rites are collectively shared, on others they occur in private places and at random moments. Rather than attempt a full description of Ọdun Oro, I concentrate on the sequence of rituals, which reveals the structure, logic, and meaning in which participants share.

Rites of Preparation

Divination prefaced the Ọdun Oro festival. Six days prior to the actual rites, the senior priests of Ila gathered at the house of their chief priest to prepare for an all-night divination vigil to be held the following evening. The vigil, known as Ọdun Idafa or Ifa Ajọbọ (the communal worship of Ifa), was the longest and most carefully performed divination rite in Ila.[44] When I observed it, the rite took place in the presence of Chiefs Ọbale, Ẹlẹmọna, and Ọdọọde at the palace in the assembly hall of the chiefs. The purpose of the rite was to ascertain the sacrifices to be made by the king and the chiefs during the festival in order to assure the peace and well-being of the town in the year to come. When completed, in the early morning hours, the sounds of the hunters' gun shots rang out from the palace grounds. They signaled to the townspeople that every house must prepare sacrifices for Ǫdun Oro.

The day following the vigil was known as Ǫjǫ Aguntankojeja (The Day on which Sheep do not go to the Market to Eat), for the markets are closed and the fate of sheep was now linked to rites of sacrifice. Later in the day, the chiefs assembled at Chief Ǫbale's house to watch the procession of Ifa priests, as they returned the divination tray from the palace to the house of Oloriawo Onifa, the leader of the Ifa priests.

During the next four days, at four o'clock in the morning and again at seven in the evening, Ila's drummers assembled in front of the palace to hear Baale Onilu perform Ệkà Kékà. The fourth day of drumming marks the first festival day. The repeated drumming of the names and praises of the twenty-three Ǫranguns-Ila establishes kingship as one of the two major foci of the coming festival and indicates why it also is known as Ǫdun Ǫba, the King's Festival.

Isunsunlefa (Day 2)

There are seven important moments in the thirteen days of Ǫdun Oro. The first is called Isunsunlefa and actually occurs on the second day of the festival. The leaders of Ila's divination priests went to the palace to roast three new yams, portions of which were offered to òrìṣà Ǫbatala, Ǫsoosi, Osanyin, Ǫsun, Oko, Ṣango, Ogun, and Eṣu, and to sacrifice a goat to Orunmila, the god of wisdom, in order that the festival might be celebrated successfully.[45] In the past, similar rites were performed in many compounds. It is a day for remembering the lineage forefathers in stories told by elders and fathers to the children, in lamentation and praise songs sung by the wives and daughters of the house, and in the offering of kola and foodstuffs at the grave sites of the deceased.

Iwa Iyan (Day 3)

The following day, Iwa Iyan, is also known as Ǫjǫ Awejewemu (The Day for Eating and Drinking). The senior and junior chiefs proceeded to the palace, where they paid homage to the king and, according to rank, offered prayers for his well-being. As in the opening rites of the Ogun festival, the king was dressed in the simple regalia of a chief. As the chiefs knelt before him, the king touched his flywhisk to the hands of his servant, who in turn touched the hands of each chief. Having received the chiefs, the king invited them to a feast, which, as in the Ogun festival, he did not attend. The palace rite began a series of feasts that stressed lineage chieftaincy. In the days that followed, the seven senior chiefs feasted one another and the junior chiefs, according to rank.

Iwa Aṣọ (Day 7)

The third important moment was the rite of Iwa Aṣọ, which occurred on the seventh day of the festival. It began a sequence of rituals that more or less constituted a unit. Iwa Aṣọ is in every respect a repetition of the rite of Iwa Ogun, which concluded the Ogun festival, and I return to it below.

Isule (Days 8 through 10)

During the next three days, that is, from the eighth through the tenth days of the festival, the rite of Isule took place in every compound except those of the royal houses. "Isule" means the worship (*isu*) of the home (*ilé*). It offers an opportunity to petition the lineage ancestors through salutations and sacrifices for help with individual problems. Some pray to the deceased for children, others for a safe delivery, and still others for prosperity or protection from the power of witches. Families that have produced twins use this occasion to place offerings before their altar carvings for deceased twins and petition their favor.[46]

On the morning of the eighth day, the king, with his senior wives, went to his family compound, the House of Olutojokun. The king sacrificed a ram at his father's grave and requested the blessing of his genitor upon him and his family. He was feasted and honored by members of his family and for a brief time was once again a son in his father's house. It was a moment of utmost importance; for in the king's act of homage to his lineage ancestors he affirmed, along with the townspeople, the importance of the descent group in defining personal and social identity.

In the afternoon the king went with his wives to Ọbalumọ's compound to honor the first settler of Ila and also to sacrifice a cock at the grave of the mother of Ọrangun Igbonnibi. (All such rites are performed on the king's behalf by Chief Ẹlẹmọna and the palace servants.) Ila tradition recalls that when Ọrangun Igbonnibi arrived at the present site of Ila he found the house of Timo, a hunter. Timo welcomed the king and invited him to establish his palace opposite his house. In return Igbonnibi conferred the title of Chief Ọbalumọ on Timo on the condition that Timo would acknowledge Igbonnibi's authority and in recognition of the hunter's claim to have descended from a royal line in a distant town.[47] The rite, therefore, introduces political history into the festival, a "history" that may well preserve information about the past, but that also serves to establish a "character" for present relationships, legitimating the authority of the king and the status of the Ọbalumọ chieftaincy.[48] The rite thus purports to refer to a time when the political order shifted from one in which a lineage head was the highest authority to one in which a king became the central authority of the community's several lineages, that is, "a tribally structured kingdom."[49] Acknowledging the mother of Ila's founding king—for the ritual is called

Imuarugbo, "To Honor the Elderly Women"—acknowledges the depen-
dence of royal (masculine) authority upon the procreative power of
women.

Later in the afternoon the princes of the Igbonnibi and Arutu royal houses
brought rams and male goats to the palace to be sacrificed at the shrine of
Orangun Igbonnibi by the palace servants in the presence of the king. Two
days later the princes from the Okomo royal house did the same.

Iwa Aṣọ (Day 11)

On the eleventh day, the rite of Iwa Aṣọ was performed again. There
is no variation in the performance from Iwa Aṣọ of four days earlier, or
from the concluding Iwa Ogun rite of the Odun Ogun festival. But why is
it performed a second time in the Oro festival? And why is the ritual referred
to as Iwa Aṣọ rather than Iwa Ogun?

The two performances of Iwa Aṣọ, coming before and after the many rituals of Isule held throughout the town in the compounds of the lineages and
at the palace by the princes of the royal houses, are public actions that ritually
enclose the numerous private rites of Isule. Recall that the festival began with
divination rites performed in every compound to honor the ancestors and to
determine the sacrifices to be offered later in the rites of Isule. On both occasions the ritual emphasis was on the lineages and their primary significance
for defining the social identity of the participants. But in Iwa Aṣọ, as in Iwa
Ogun, an alternative referent for defining Yoruba social identity—namely,
the king—is acknowledged; and a deeply rooted conflict in Yoruba social experience is disclosed regarding the relationship between kinship and kingship
in defining the basic moral allegiance in Yoruba society. Hence, the conflict
and the possibility of its resolution are enacted in Iwa Aṣọ. It is that reality
which ritually encloses the celebrations of Isule performed by the lineages.
Even during the period of Isule the conflict is implicit as the royal houses
gather at the palace, not in their family compounds, to perform the sacrificial
rites to their royal ancestors.

The change of the name from Iwa Ogun to Iwa Aṣọ already indicates a
significant shift in the focus of the Oro festival as compared with the Ogun
festival. Aṣọ means "cloth." Hence, Iwa Aṣọ means "the character or essential quality of cloth." For the Yoruba, cloth is one of the principal modes
of cultural expression. For one thing, it expresses wealth and status. It is per-
fectly appropriate to admire the cloth a person is wearing by congratulating
him/her on the enormous amount of money spent for it. And it is often the
case that considerable sums disproportionate to other expenditures are spent
to purchase a man's handwoven, elaborately embroidered robe, or a woman's
wrapper and head-tie. Furthermore, cloth is rivaled only by oratory as the
principal means by which people reveal in a social frame of reference the
"positive" qualities of their individuality, that is, their character. At the ceremonies discussed here, the king and chiefs dress uniquely and sumptuously

to honor the community and thereby reveal their respect for its members. Hence, the shift in the ritual's title to Iwa Aṣọ represents a change in meaning away from violence and the uncertainty of cultural existence.[50]

Sakungbengbe (Day 12)

On the twelfth day of the festival the *olorì* (queens) of Ila, including the wives of former Ọranguns, as well as the older wives of the present king, process from the palace to Chief Ọdọọde's compound. The ritual is called Sakungbengbe. Chief Ọdọọde is one of three chiefs closely related to the palace. Specifically he supervises the ritual responsibilities of the queens. His position—along with that of Chief Ọbale, who is responsible for the palace servants, and Chief Ẹlẹmọna, who is the messenger between the king and the senior chiefs and who has access to the palace at all times—indicates that little can happen within the palace that is not known by the town's chiefs.

When the queens arrived at Ọdọọde's house, the chief greeted them dressed in the garments of a woman. Following the refreshment of palm wine, the queens led Chief Ọdọọde to the King's Market to dance and pay honor at the shrine of Amotagesi, the second Ọrangun. According to Chief Ọdọọde, Amotagesi possessed powerful herbal "medicines" (*oògùn*) and once transformed himself into a beautiful woman in order to marry the Olowu, another "strong man in medicines," who had repeatedly waged war on Amotagesi. After seventeen years, Amotagesi, having learned Olowu's secrets, transformed himself into a man and returned, only to find that his son had usurped the throne. With the help of several chiefs and a mask called Egunsanyin, which was endowed with magical medicines, Amotagesi regained his throne.[51] The ritual of Sakungbengbe thus introduces another aspect of Ila history. It recalls a situation in which the king's physical power to defend the town was inadequate and required the acquisition of hidden or covert power, a power analogous to that which women possess. Thus, Chief Ọdọọde, dressed as Amotagesi, yet carrying his sword of office as an Ikẹgbẹ chief, goes with the senior queens to the market shrine of Ila's second Ọrangun to honor him. The action also prepares for the concluding rite of the festival in Chief Ọdọọde's compound.

Isinro (Day 13)

The final ritual, called Isinro, which means "burial" or "completion of Oro," began in the afternoon when the king processed from the palace to the house of Chief Ọdọọde, a distance of just under a mile. The king was preceded by drummers and surrounded by his palace servants and wives. Chief Oloyin, representing the Ologun warriors, ran back and forth across the road in front of the *ọba* to warn people to clear the way. As the Ọrangun proceeded along the road to Ọdọọde's house, he paused before the house of Chief Ẹlẹmọna and the house of Chief Ọbale and performed ètùtù by touching his beaded staff to the ground three times and offered prayers for the chiefs and their families.[52]

The ceremonies were composed of elaborate displays of courtly etiquette. The king was dressed in a magnificent robe and appeared in public wearing a small beaded crown. He was seated in the courtyard on a large, circular dais. Attendees included town chiefs, the women of Ọdọọde's and of Olutojokun's house, and representatives of important groups, for example, the herbalists and the warrior chiefs. Chief Ọdọọde again appeared in women's clothes, carrying the Ikẹgbẹ cutlass. He invited the king to enter his house for refreshments. Once inside, the chief placed his cutlass on the ground between himself and the king as a sign of peaceful greeting. In a gesture of recognition of Ọdọọde's authority within his own house, the king picked up the cutlass and presented it to the chief with prayers for the house of Ọdọọde.

When the king reappeared in public, he wore the great conical, veiled crown called Ilawa (Ìlá Ìwà), the crown, as the Ọrangun-Ila described it, which reveals "the beauty of the Ọrangun-Ila, his character."[53] Ila's lineage chiefs took turns dancing before the ọba. The last to dance were the Ikẹgbẹ chiefs, who have a special role to play in the coronation and funeral rites of Ila's kings, and Chief Ọdọọde. The chief drummer repeated the Èkà recital, naming past kings, and the ọba concluded the event by dancing before the cheering chiefs and townspeople.

Interpretation

The ritual action of Ọdun Oro is twofold. On the one hand, the locus of ritual activity moves from many separate, private celebrations to a corporate, public ritual celebrated by all of the community. The logic of the movement is to be noted in the sequence of locations of ritual activity. From the perspective of the public, the movement from diverse places of ritual activity in the compounds to the single, shared space is essentially a shift in sacrificial attention from the family ancestors and descent groups to the king and the town.

On the other hand, the ọba moves from his seclusion in the circumscribed space of the palace into the public realm. Here, too, the ritual is governed by an underlying logic. The progression of rituals over the thirteen days moves the king out of the palace into the midst of the town, and in the process the role and authority of the king are affirmed. Recall that on the third day of the festival the chiefs gathered at the palace to pay their respects to Ila's paramount chief, for the king is dressed in the robes of a chief. They are feasted by the king, just as they feast one another in the days that follow. By contrast, in the celebration of Isinro, the king wears the richly embroidered robes and the beaded crowns of the Ọrangun. Throughout Isinro the chiefs treat him as one possessing a higher power, the sacred authority of the wearer of the crown.

Before the transfer of political authority to the king can take place, the struggle between kingship and kinship must be articulated and mediated. That is accomplished in the rituals of Iwa Aṣọ on the seventh and eleventh days. Both rituals begin with a mock battle near the shrine of Ogun and change course by concluding with the lineage chiefs' affirming the divine power of kingship. The fear that civil strife can erupt among the lineages requires that there be the recognition of another moral bond—a loyalty that unites persons and groups without denying their diversity and difference.[54]

Conclusion

As we have seen, festivals, as well as the rituals of which they are composed, have a structure and a logic that shape their meaning. The symbolism of the rituals expresses a shift from one source of political authority to another, and in the ritual process, deeply felt contradictions regarding culture and violence, political order and disorder, are acted out and, for the moment, resolved.

The logic of Ogun ritual in the Ila case is deeply intertwined with the realities of political history. In the study of the political structure of six eighteenth- and nineteenth-century Yoruba kingdoms, Lloyd argues that an inherent conflict of interest between kings and chiefs characterizes Yoruba political systems. He contrasts two types of political systems to make the point. Tribally structured kingdoms vest authority with a council of chiefs and the king acts as an arbiter, whereas strong centralized monarchies vest ultimate authority in the king and the chiefs act as advisors. Yoruba kingdoms are neither. None of them achieved full centralization, and therefore what shapes the Yoruba vision of history is a perpetual struggle for power (Lloyd 1971:1–8).[55]

Accordingly, the contest for political power dominates the ritual action of Iwa Ogun and Iwa Aṣọ. The rites reveal that from the point of view of society defined in terms of descent groups, kingship is alien to the sentiments, obligations, and allegiances of kinship. Furthermore, the centralization of power in a king poses the threat of tyranny and the denial of social differentiation through blood ties.[56]

Yet, without a king there is the threat of discord among the descent groups and the specter of death which accompanies civil strife. As Thomas Hobbes observed, ". . . during the time men live without a common power to keep them all in awe, they are in that condition which is called war; and such a war, as is of every man, against every other man" (1947:81–82).

Human conflict is therefore resolved with nonhuman power. In both festivals, the locus of the power is the crown. It is the gift of the first (divine) ancestor to his "sons"; it is bestowed on the wearer by the most powerful members of the community—the senior chiefs; it contains mystical power in the form of medicines prepared by priests; and on ritual occasions it is placed on the king's head by his senior wife, who possesses the covert power of "the mothers." Thus, when chiefs kneel before the king, they salute the fact that his power is "next to the gods." When townspeople look on the crown during ritual performances, they see the awesome power of sacred kingship, and they return to their compounds in peace.

The achievement of solidarity asks a price. Sacrifices, as well às prayers, must be made to the ancestors by the full community, and sacrifices must be made to the civic deities by the chiefs and king. In this pursuit, one deity stands out above all others. Repeatedly in the ritual cycle, the community's most prominent citizen appears at the shrine of Ogun, dancing for the *òrìṣà* of iron and war, honoring him, and asking for peace. In this way, and on behalf of his subjects, the king turns the powerful deity who can divide and destroy into a force upon whom they can rely to perpetuate their society.

NOTES

1. My translation of this *oríkì* (praise song) is based on Yoruba and English texts collected in the city of Ibadan and published by Simpson (1965:319; 1980:31–32). I am grateful to Jacob Olupọna of the Department of Religious Studies, University of Ọbafemi Awolowo, Ile-Ifẹ, Nigeria for his assistance with questions of translation and orthography of Yoruba passages throughout the essay.

2. Research on the Ogun festival was made possible from June to August 1977 by a summer stipend from the National Endowment for the Humanities. Previous research trips to Ila-Ọrangun in 1972 and 1974, which laid the groundwork for this study, were supported by grants from the Ford Foundation and the Social Science Research Council. Subsequent research in 1981 and 1982, the latter made possible by a basic research grant from the National Endowment for the Humanities (RO-20072–81–2184) shared with Henry J. Drewal, permitted further inquiry and the checking of earlier observations, notations, and interpretations. The research on Ọdun Oro in 1984 was supported by a National Endowment for the Humanities summer stipend and a grant from the Committee for Research and Exploration of the National Geographic Society. I am grateful to *National Geographic Research* for permission to use the data on the Oro festival previously published in their Scientific Journal (Spring 1986), Vol. 2, No. 2, pp. 216–233 in my essay on "Festivals and Sacred Kingship Among the Igbomina Yoruba."

I am indebted to His Highness, William Adetona Ayeni, Ariwajoye I, Ọrangun-Ila, for his support of my research in Ila in granting me permission to photograph the festivals and engaging with me in extended conversations regarding the festivals, the rituals of which they are composed, and the history of the royal houses of Ila. Lamidi Fakẹyẹ, master carver of Ila, introduced me to his hometown in 1971. His lively and sustained interest in my inquiries made access to the ritual life of the people of Ila, both in the privacy of their compounds and in public festivals, possible in a way that only the trust of family and friend could provide. I am also grateful to Sunday Adewumi and D. G. Taiwo for their invaluable and sensitive research assistance in Ila.

3. Although it is said that Ọdun Ogun is the oldest festival or the first festival in Ila, the dates for all festivals are determined in relationship to the concluding date of the new year festival, Ọdun Oro, and then in relationship to one another in an

established sequence. The liturgical calendar is the responsibility of Chief Lowa, who consults with the king and with various chieftaincy and cult groups. Chief Lowa is a descendant of Ọrangun Amotagesi, who was the junior brother of Ọrangun Ajagun-nla, son of Oduduwa. Ọrangun Amotagesi reigned in Ila-Yara and was father of Igbonnibi, who later led the people of Ila to their present town site. Chief Lowa: personal communication, *ilé* (house or compound) Lowa, August 12, 1982.

On Ogun festivals in the ritual life of Yoruba towns see Bascom (1987) on the Ogun festival in Ifẹ; Beier (1959) on the Ogun festival in Ilobu; Beier (1956); Ogunba (1977) for reference to the Ogun festival in Ondo; Ojo (1966:171) for a map of Yoruba towns where Ogun is the main civic deity; Peel (1983) for references to the Ogun festival in Ilesha; and Ben-Amos and Barnes ch. 3 on Ogun worship in Oyo.

4. The seven senior chiefs inherit named titles which reside in a specific lineage. The junior chiefs are simply lineage representatives.

5. Ila's warrior chiefs are divided into two groups, the Balogun and the Ologun. In the past, the Ologun chiefs were the defenders of the town. The Balogun chiefs fought beyond the town walls in expeditions of conquest or reprisal, or in alliance with the chiefs and kings of other towns.

6. The history of Ila-Yara appears to have been filled with strife between lineage groups, as well as among the royal houses over succession. Prince Arutu, having failed to gain the throne, left Ila-Yara in 1452 with his junior brother, Prince Igbonnibi, and his followers and settled in Ila-Magbon, where he was declared Ọrangun. Just before his death, Arutu gave the beaded crown of the Ọrangun to Igbonnibi and instructed him to lead the people of Ila to the place where Igbonnibi would "touch the ground with the Orere Staff." It would be known as Ila-Ọrangun (Adetoyi 1974:10–11).

7. Chief Ẹlẹmọna is one of the seven senior chiefs known as *afọ́baje* (kingmakers). Ẹlẹmọna is the first person in the morning and the last person in the evening from outside the palace to see the king. He may enter any part of the palace at any time. He is also the traditional head of the *ọmọdégbélé*, the palace slaves and servants. The Ojuwa chiefs are lineage chiefs associated with the Ẹlẹmọna who assist him in carrying out his official responsibilities.

The *ẹmẹsẹ̀* are messengers of the Ọrangun who come from the town's lineage groups other than the royal houses or Chief Ọbale's house, since he is the traditional head of the *ẹmẹsẹ̀*.

8. The tree was cut down in 1975 at the request of the chiefs because it was believed to be the gathering place of the witches, and it was feared that witches were preventing the prosperity known in other parts of Nigeria from coming to Ila. In 1976 electric power arrived in Ila, followed by a medical clinic, new markets, and in 1980 a teacher training college. In 1981 a large young *àràbà* tree was planted at the site of the Ogun shrine to serve as the appropriate focus of public rituals for the *òrìṣà*.

9. Chief Ẹlẹkẹhan: personal communication, *ilé* Ẹlẹkẹhan, June 7, 1977. According to Chiefs Ẹlẹkẹhan and Oloyin, a dog was sacrificed each time Iṣagun was performed. But protests from the Muslim and Christian communities in Ila regarding the public sacrifice became so strong, with threats of disrupting the ritual, that the practice was ended in 1973.

10. Ila's hunter chiefs, listed in the order in which their *egúngún láyẹwú* appear in the Ogun festivals, are Chief Odebiyi of *ilé* Lodo, Chief Ogundipẹ of *ilé* Osoo, Chief Ogundele of *ilé* Iyalode, Chief Babtunde of *ilé* Ore, Chief Raji Oladoyin of *ilé* Olode, Chief Ajide of *ilé* Ẹlẹkẹhan, and Chief Taiwo of *ilé* Alapo.

11. According to palace historians, there was one ruling house of Igbonnibi when Ila was founded. Over the years two others were recognized, the house of Arutu, which traces its line to Ọrangun Arutu, an older brother of Igbonnibi, and the house of Okomọ, which descends from Ọrangun Okomọ, a son of Igbonnibi. The kings of

Ila are alternately chosen from the lineage segments that make up each ruling house.

12. There are no marked grave sites for Ila's former kings. When an ọba dies, it is said that his body is escorted from the palace by the Ikẹgbẹ chiefs; but it is not known where the body is taken. Before this last rite, the deceased ọba's heart and skull are used in rituals of installation of the ọba-elect. Then they are buried at unmarked locations in the palace grounds. It is to these places that the king pays homage when he leaves and returns to the palace during the rituals of the Ogun, Oro, and Egungun festivals.

13. The ọmọdégbélé (palace servants) were slaves taken in intertribal wars by the warriors of the ọba or given by kings of neighboring towns to the royal family on the occasion of the death of an ọba. The slaves carried the clothes and other gifts to the family of the deceased and then remained as palace servants of the new Ọrangun and messengers to the courts from which they came. The kings most closely associated with the Ọrangun through the palace servants appear to have been the Owa of Ileṣa, the Alaafin of Ọyọ, the Ooni of Ifẹ, the Ajero of Ijero, and the Alara of Aramoko (Adetoyi 1974:24).

14. The Ikẹgbẹ chiefs are known as Irọnṣẹ ọmọ Odùdúwà (messengers of the son of Oduduwa). Their cutlasses are said to have been given to them by Oduduwa to clear the way to the town that the Ọrangun, son of Oduduwa, established. The Ikẹgbẹ chiefs escort the new Ọrangun from his installation in Ọbale's compound to the palace and accompany the remains of a deceased ọba from the palace to the burial ground. Chief Ọdọọde: personal communication, ilé Ọdọọde, July 11, 1977.

15. The prayers and salutations in the ritual were given by Chief Ẹlẹmọna: personal communication, ilé Ẹlẹmọna, March 12, 1981 and August 7, 1982.

16. As the salutation suggests, the ọba's person is sacred and therefore no one must touch him. Physical contact is made by the king placing his flywhisk in the hands of the senior palace servant (ẹmẹsẹ̀), who in turn touches the upraised hands of Chief Ẹlẹmọna and the other chiefs.

17. Chief Ọbale does not actually "signal" the end of the conflict, but simply "leads" the chiefs in the appropriate action. Chief Ọdọọde: personal communication, March 10, 1981. Ordinarily Chief Ọbala, a more senior chief, leads this part of the rite, but he was ill in 1977.

18. Chiefs Ọbala and Ọbale rank first and second among the senior chiefs, the kingmakers. Chief Ọbasinkin is the leader of the Ikẹgbẹ chiefs. Chief Ọbajoko ranks first among the junior lineage chiefs.

19. For discussions of Yoruba social and political structures see Eades (1980); Fadipe (1970); Law (1977); Lloyd (1962, 1971, 1973); and Peel (1979, 1983).

20. Ọrangun-Ila: personal communication, July 20, 1977.

21. The selection of candidates for ọba is overseen by Chief Alasan, second in rank among the twelve lineage segments of the Igbonnibi ruling house and leader of the ọmọba (princess of all three ruling houses). The Alasan presents the name(s) of the candidate(s) to the afọ́baje. According to palace historians, Ọrangun Amotagesi appointed Ila's kingmakers and assigned their functions (Adetoyi 1974:22).

22. When I inquired of the Ọrangun about this tradition, he answered: "There are some things about which I may not speak freely" (personal communication, June 28, 1974). When the question was put to the late Chief Ọbale, he answered: "No. That is no longer done in Ila. We have our own rites" (personal communication, July 3, 1974). It would have been difficult to have performed some of the rites other than in a token way at the 1967 installation of the present Ọrangun, since the conflict over a successor to the throne took seven years to resolve.

The acts of eating the deceased King's heart and drinking maize gruel from his predecessor's skull in the installation rites of an ọba are reported by Lloyd (1954:336–84), Morton-Williams (1960:354), and Ojo (1966:77). It is not clear whether Lloyd's inquiry is the sole source of information for the others or whether they have their own independent sources.

It should be noted that the Yoruba word *orí* may be translated either as "head," referring to one's skull, or as "personal destiny," depending on the context of use.

23. Ila kingship was once inherited according to rules of primogeniture. It now rotates among member-candidates put forward, in turn, by their royal houses (lineage segments).

24. Among Yoruba people, the right to wear a beaded crown is associated with the establishment of an independent kingdom (Agiri 1975:169–70). There has been a long history of challenges and conflicts over the claims of rulers and communities to wear or hold a beaded crown (Asiwaju 1976). Ila's claim to being an *ilú aladé* (crowned town) is an unchallenged tradition.

25. Orangun-Ila: personal communication, July 20, 1977.

26. Orangun-Ila: personal communication, July 20, 1977.

27. See also M. Drewal's discussion of *àṣẹ*, ch. 9.

28. For discussions of the cosmological and political variants of Yoruba creation and establishment myths see Agiri (1975), Bascom (1969), Idowu (1962), and Johnson (1969).

29. Orangun-Ila: personal communication, July 20, 1977.

30. Orangun-Ila: personal communication, July 20, 1977.

31. Orangun-Ila: personal communication, July 20, 1977.

32. The panels were carved during the reign of Orangun Oyinlola Arojojoye (1924–1936). Ogundeji (1870–1962), master carver of Aga's compound and the Baale of Ila's carvers, supervised the project. He assigned Akobiogun Fakẹyẹ (1878–1946) and his son, Adeosun, of Inurin's compound to carve the central panel, which includes the door to the chamber called Orí Ojópọ̀. The panels on either side of the door were carved by Ogunwuyi (c. 1890–1965) of Ore's compound and Oje (c. 1875–1960) of Aga's compound.

33. Henry Drewal suggests that the serrated design depicts the royal umbrella, since it always covers the *ọba* when he wears a beaded crown. Personal communication, January 15, 1979.

34. In Ila, the Aworo-ose is the chief priest of Obatala and also the chief priest of Oṣoosi, a hunter deity. Combining priestly roles for different deities is not unusual in Ila. Iya Oṣun, the chief priestess for Oṣun, is also the leader of the worshippers of *òrìṣà* Obalufon. The dual responsibilities reflect the history of a particular lineage group, which "brought the *òrìṣà* to Ila," but also suggest the complementarity of the gods in the ritual symbolism of *òrìṣà* worship. See Pemberton 1977:1–28.

35. Ila-Orangun is divided into five quarters: Isedo, Iperin, Eyindi, Okejigbo, and Oke-Ẹdẹ. The seven senior chiefs and the lineages composing the three royal houses are all located in the first four quarters, which surround the palace. The Oke-Ẹdẹ quarter lies to the south, its northern portion separated from the palace grounds by a narrow band of compounds included in the Okejigbo quarter. Oke-Ẹdẹ is famous for its herbalist priests. According to local tradition, no person from Oke-Ẹdẹ was ever taken into slavery or captivity during the slave raids and wars in the nineteenth century. It is also the quarter in which the *igbó egúngún* (forest of the ancestors) is located.

36. Obatala Priest Oyewole Akande: personal communication, *ilé* Aworoose, July 30, 1974. It is generally believed that the mingling of woman's menstrual blood with man's semen creates a child.

37. Orangun-Ila: personal communication, July 20, 1977. Henry Drewal notes that the literal meaning of the term *orí ojópọ̀* is "the collection or gathering together of heads" (personal communication, January 15, 1978).

38. The translation of *èkejì* in the salutation to the king poses an interesting problem. Abraham (1970:152) translates *èkejì* as "the second," but also as "companion," as in *èkejìimi* ("my companion"). In conversations with the Orangun-Ila and Chief Obala, as well as colleagues at the University of Ifę, it appeared that in the salutation to the Orangun-Ila *èkejì* may be translated as "like," "like unto," or "similar to," meaning that the power of the *òrìṣà* is employed as a simile for the power of the king. *Èkejì* may also be translated as "next to" or "second to," suggesting that the king's power is not simply like, but is of the same substance or nature as, that of the gods, although of a diminished order. Both translations and their distinctive connotations are, I believe, appropriate. While a king reigns, his *àṣę* (power or authority) and the sacredness of his royal person are dependent upon the crown, which "is (has the power of) an *òrìṣà*," as the Orangun-Ila observed. But when a king dies (although it is repeatedly affirmed that "kings do not die"), it is understood that the king becomes an *òrìṣà*. A king's death, therefore, is viewed as the movement from a wordly existence, in which his power is derived, to life in the fullness of *òrìṣà* power. For a king it is the transition from likeness to the identity of being as an *òrìṣà*. The salutation functions as an *orìkì* (a praise name or attributive name). It predicates to the king a power from a realm to which he, as a human, does not belong and within which he does not legitimately act. In the context of the ritual performance of Iwa Ogun, the metaphoric attribution of *òrìṣà* power to designate the power of the king is the culmination of a sequence of actions in which the person and authority of the king are distinguished from those of the chiefs.

39. Ade Anike: personal communication, *ilé* Iyalode, July 23, 1977.

40. Beier and Gbadamosi note that this praise poem was collected in "the area between Ędę, Ilobu and Oshogbo," which is 45 miles southwest of Ila-Orangun (1959:13, 21–22).

41. Chief Odọọde: personal communication, *ilè* Odọọde, March 12, 1981. Prince Adetoyi suggests that the mock battle might be a historical reference to a conflict between Orangun Adeyemi Okusu and the chiefs of Ila in the late sixteenth century. Orangun Okusu treated Ila's chiefs and elders with disdain and forced the people of Ila to dig fortification trenches around Ila. On hearing of a plot by the chiefs and townspeople to overthrow him, the king fled to his mother's home in Ipe, where he died (personal communication, August 7, 1982). See also Adetoyi 1974:13.

42. Chief Odọọde: personal communication, *ilé* Odọọde, March 12, 1981.

43. As Prince Adetoyi makes clear, the "celebration of Oro festival in Ila . . . is quite different from how it is being celebrated in other Yoruba towns," where Oro refers to a society through which the community's ancestors control and punish criminals and whose presence is known in the sound of the bull-roarer. Rather, "Oro festival at Ila is regarded as the time of Character Celebrations, the time for remembering the first Orangun of Ila, the other past *obas* of Ila, the important chiefs and our beloved fathers and mothers . . . who had passed away to eternity" (1974:27). Thus, as the Orangun-Ila explained, the festival's name, Ębọra Ila, is a conflation of *ębọ* (sacrifice) and *igboro* (town center), which means "sacrifice for the whole town" (personal communication, July 20, 1977).

44. I am grateful to the Oloriawo Onifa, leader of the Ifa priests, for permission to witness the rites of Odun Ifa and to Chief Odọọde for conversations about these rites.

45. Just seventeen days earlier, when Odun Idafa began, the Obatala festival had come to an end, marking the day on which new yams could be sold in the king's market.

46. Johnson refers to "a festival [in Oyọ] called Isule customarily held in the month of July, [when] all the members of the royal family gorgeously dressed go in procession

to a certain place to worship the spirits of their dead ancestors" (1969:213–14). For a discussion of the rites for deceased twins see Pemberton 1988.

47. In March, at the conclusion of the rite of Itadogun, when an announcement is made that a festival for the ancestors will begin in 17 days, a masquerade called Onise Timo, the Messenger of Timo, appears at Ọbalumọ's compound to instruct its chief and elders to prepare for the forthcoming festival. This rite reinforces the centrality of Timo in Ila tradition.

48. On history as "charter" and Yoruba historiography see Law (1973:25–40 and 1977:12–25), Lloyd (1973:205–23), Ogunba (1973:87–110), and Peel (1979: 110–11).

49. The phrase is used by Lloyd in his discussion of Yoruba kingdoms in the eighteenth and nineteenth centuries (1971:1–8).

50. Another way in which cloth is displayed socially is called aṣọ ẹbí, "family cloth." Aṣọ ẹbí is identical cloth, usually expensive, worn by family members (or other social groups) at public gatherings to express their solidarity and support of one another. On the occasion of Isinro, the women from Olutojokun's compound, the lineage "house" of the reigning king, wore aṣọ ẹbí, as did the women of Chief Ọdọọde's compound, where the rite of Isinro was performed.

51. Chief Ọdọọde: personal communication, ilé Ọdọọde, September 5, 1984.

52. Myths, rituals, and political responsibilities link Chiefs Ọbale, Ẹlẹmọna, and Ọdọọde. While Ọbale and Ẹlẹmọna are senior chiefs, Ọdọọde represents all of Ila's chiefs at rituals of divination performed on behalf of the king, the chiefs, or the town. Each of the chiefs has an ancestral masquerade called Olọbaloro, which includes as part of the costume a carved headdress depicting a leopard surrounded by human and animal heads. A story tells how each was a messenger to the mother of the ọbas of Aro-Ekiti, Ijero, and Ila. Only the Ọrangun-Ila was grateful for the small gift of a bead in a pot that the messengers brought with them from Ifẹ. When it was discovered that the pots were filled with beads, the Ọrangun-Ila showed his gratitude by establishing the chieftaincies of Ọbale, Ẹlẹmọna, and Ọdọọde and performing a ceremony in which he declared that the Ọrangun's prosperity would always be closely linked to their presence. Yet this presence denies privacy to the king and circumscribes his independent movement. (Chief Ọdọọde: personal communication, ilé Ọdọọde, March 12, 1981.)

53. Ọrangun-Ila: personal communication, March 14, 1981.

54. In his analysis of the sequence of dances in "the festival of the king," Ọdun Osu, in Owu-Ijẹbu, Ogunba observes that the festival begins with a series of "loosely connected events lasting for a few days, all in an atmosphere of general merriment. Then, there is a central event of a historical and military nature which is usually mimed. Then, the king may conclude the ceremony by dancing in full pomp and pageantry for the whole community." Ogunba believes that the Osu Festival is "typical . . . of the African 'royal drama' . . . [and] can serve as a paradigm for kings' festivals" throughout Yorubaland and West Africa (1977:368).

55. Yoruba kingdoms cannot be compared with the highly centralized Benin kingdom of the Edo to the southeast of the Yoruba (Bradbury 1957) or the Fon of Dahomey, which developed when Dahomey was a tributary state of Ọyọ (Akinjogbin 1967; Argyle 1966).

56. This is clearly the message conveyed in Ọdun Egungun, the festival for the ancestors, by the severely limited role of the king throughout the festival and by the ritual remembrance of Ọrangun Ijimogodo, who had the secret of the ancestral masquerades brought to Ila, but who was put to death by the chiefs in the forest of the ancestral masks for having betrayed the secret to his wife (Pemberton 1978, 1986). According to Wande Abimbọla, a similar story is told about Olufimo Adodo, a former

king of Akoko-Ekiti, in Ifa verses (personal communication, February 19, 1981). This ancient story is the basis for A. Isola's play, *Aye ye montan*.

REFERENCES CITED

Abraham, R. C. 1970. *Dictionary of Modern Yoruba*, London: University of London Press.

Adetoyi, A. 1974. *A Short History of Ila-Qrangun*, Ila-Qrangun, Nigeria: Iwaniyi Press.

Agiri, B. A. 1975. "Yoruba Oral Tradition with Special Reference to the Early History of the Qyọ Kingdom," in W. Abimbọla (ed.), *Yoruba Oral Tradition*, Ile-Ifẹ, Nigeria: Department of African Languages and Literatures, University of Ifẹ, pp. 157–97.

Akinjogbin, I. A. 1967. *Dahomey and Its Neighbors*, Cambridge: Cambridge University Press.

Argyle, W. J. 1966. *The Fon of Dahomey*, London: Oxford University Press.

Asiwaju, I. 1976. "Political Motivations and Oral Historical Traditions in Africa: the Case of the Yoruba Crowns, 1900–1960," *Africa* 46(2):113–27.

Bascom, W. 1969. *The Yoruba of Southwestern Nigeria*, New York: Holt, Rinehart & Winston.

———. 1987. "The Olojo Festival at Ife, 1937," in *Time Out of Time: Essays on the Festival*, Alessandro Falassi (ed.), Albuquerque: University of New Mexico Press, pp. 62–73.

Beier, H. U. 1956. "God of Iron," *Nigeria* 49:118–37.

———. 1959. "A Year of Sacred Festivals in One Yoruba Town," Lagos, Nigeria: A Special Issue of *Nigeria Magazine*.

Beier, H. U., and Gbadamosi, B. 1959. *Yoruba Poetry*, Ibadan, Nigeria: A Special publication of *Black Orpheus*. General Publications Section, Ministry of Education, Nigeria.

Bradbury, R. E. 1957. *The Benin Kingdom and the Edo-speaking Peoples of Southwestern Nigeria,* London: Ethnographic Survey of Africa, West Africa, No. 13. International African Institute.

Drewal, H. J. 1977. *Traditional Art of the Nigerian Peoples*, Washington, D.C.: Museum of African Art.

Eades, J. S. 1980. *The Yoruba Today*, New York: Cambridge University Press.

Fadipe, N. A. 1970. *The Sociology of the Yoruba*, Ibadan, Nigeria: Ibadan University Press.

Fernandez, J. 1977. "The Performance of Ritual Metaphors," in J.D. Sapir and J.C. Crocker (eds.), *The Social Use of Metaphors*, Philadelphia: University of Pennsylvania Press, pp. 100–131.

Geertz, C. 1973. *The Interpretation of Cultures*, New York: Basic Books.

Hobbes, T. 1947. *Leviathan*. New York: Oxford University Press.

Idowu, E. B. 1962. *Olodumare: God in Yoruba Belief*, London: Longmans.

Johnson, S. 1969. *The History of the Yorubas*. London: Routledge.

Law, R. 1973. "Traditional History," in S. O. Biobaku (ed.), *Sources of Yoruba History*, Oxford: Clarendon Press, pp. 9–24.

———. 1977. *The Qyọ Empire c. 1600-c. 1836*, Oxford: Clarendon Press.

Lloyd, P. C. 1954. "The Traditional Political System of the Yoruba," in *Southwestern Journal of Anthropology* 10(4):336–84.

————. 1962. *Yoruba Land Law*, London: Oxford University Press.

————. 1971. *The Political Development of Yoruba Kingdoms in the Eighteenth and Nineteenth Centuries* (Royal Anthropological Institute Occasional Paper No. 31), London: Royal Anthropological Institute of Great Britain and Ireland.

————. 1973. "Political and Social Structure," S. O. Biobaku (ed.), *Sources of Yoruba History*, Oxford: Clarendon Press, pp. 205–223.

Morton-Williams, P. 1960. "The Yoruba Ogboni Cult in Ọyọ," *Africa* 30(4):362–74.

Ogunba, O. 1973. "Ceremonies," in S. O. Biobaku (ed.), *Sources of Yoruba History*, Oxford: Clarendon Press, pp. 87–100.

————. 1977. "Traditional African Festival Drama," in O. O. Oyelaran (ed.), *Seminar Series* Number I (1976–77), Part II, Ile-Ifẹ, Nigeria: Department of African Languages and Literatures, University of Ifẹ, pp. 354–83.

Ojo, G. J. A. 1966. *Yoruba Culture: A Geographical Analysis*, London: University of London Press.

Peel, J. D. Y. 1979. "Kings, titles and quarters: a conjectural history of Ilesha. Part I, the traditions reviewed," *History in Africa* 6:109–35.

————. 1983. *Ijeshas and Nigerians*, New York: Cambridge University Press.

Pemberton, J. 1977. "A Cluster of Sacred Symbols: Orisha Worship Among the Igbomina Yoruba of Ila-Orangun," *History of Religions* 7(3):1–28.

————. 1978. "Egungun Masquerades of the Igbomina Yoruba," *African Arts* 11(3):40–47, 99–100.

————. 1986. "Festivals and Sacred Kingship Among the Igbomina Yoruba," *National Geographic Research: a Scientific Journal* 2(2):216–33.

————. 1988. "Yoruba Carvers of Ila-Ọrangun," in C. D. Roy (ed.), *Iowa Studies in African Art*, Vol. III.

Simpson, G. E. 1965. "Selected Yoruba Rituals: 1964," *Nigerian Journal of Economic and Social Studies* 7(3):311–24.

————. 1980. *Yoruba Religion and Medicine in Ibadan*. Ibadan, Nigeria: Ibadan University Press.

Verger, P. 1966. "The Yoruba High God," *Odu* 2(2):19–40.

Adeboye Babalọla

7

A Portrait of Ògún as Reflected in Ìjálá Chants

*I*jálá are Yoruba poetic chants used in entertaining and saluting Ògún. As those who are familiar with the Ògún tradition very well know, the *oríkì Ògún* (verbal salutes to Ògún) within *ìjálá* reveal, little by little, the nature of the deity. One of the most striking revelations of the *ìjálá* is the contradictions found in them. This paper addresses these contradictions and argues that Ògún symbolizes a universal contradiction: humans are strong and, at the same time, they are frail. The constant oppositions in the texts of *ìjálá* artists are therefore a necessary and explainable part of this poetic tradition.

The contradictions, and in some cases the variations, found in Ògún traditions as they are rendered by *ìjálá* chanters are of three kinds. First, the figure of Ògún displays opposing personality traits (e.g., he is fiery and cool) or symbolic traits (e.g., he represents death and healing). Second, the literary construction of the chants opposes metaphors and images thereby reinforcing, through structure, contradictions that occur in content and meaning. Third, the devotees of Ògún place him in a bewildering variety of contradictory mythical traditions. Ògún founds many towns, conquers many people, and pursues several occupations. The wide variation in traditions raises questions as to the authenticity or correctness of any of them. But this problem is resolved in the *ìjálá* verbal salutes to Ògún. As one *ìjálá* artist declares: "*Ògún méje l'Ògún-ùn mi*" (The Ògún that I know are seven in number). Thus, many forms are attributed to the god Ògún. But what is important is the total picture that the many contradictions and variations eventually create. It is the sum of the parts that provides insight into what Ògún actually represents to the Yoruba.

Ìjálá-chanting[1] is a tradition found primarily among the Ọyọ Yoruba, though pockets of *ìjálá* artists exist among the hunters in some of the communities adjacent to the Ọyọ-Yoruba.

One of the Yoruba legends accounting for the origin of *ìjálá* well illustrates the contradictions found in this tradition. In the book *The Content and Form of Yoruba Ìjálá*, I reproduce in English four legends that claim *ìjálá*-chanting was originated by Ògún during his lifetime (Babalọla 1966:4–7). There is no need to repeat them here. Instead, I have a recently collected legend on the same theme, a legend that attributes the origin of *ìjálá* not to Ògún but to Erinlẹ̀, a hunter deity who also has a place in the Yoruba pantheon.[2] This variation seems remarkable in that the informant is a well-known devotee of Ògún,[3] yet he gives to another god the credit for originating *ìjálá*-chanting, which is traditionally referred to as *aré Ògún* (Ògún's entertainment). To Ògún he ascribes only the popularizing of *ìjálá*-chanting. The legend, told with some commentary, runs thus in English translation:

> Erinlẹ̀[4] was the very originator of *ìjálá*-chanting. He was a hunter who used to go on frequent hunting expeditions from his hometown, Àjàgbùsì, to the forests within a day's journey on foot. As he had no wife he decided one day to make his abode in the forest. So he built a hut with stakes for walls and leaf-thatch for roof under a mighty *gbìngbin*[5] tree near the bank of a river. The monkeys in the forest were his favorite game and he used to sell their carcasses, fresh or roasted, in Àjàgbùsì on market days.
>
> To amuse himself during his lonely sojourn in the forest he began to chant utterances in Yoruba in a peculiar style featuring a nasal twang. Whenever he was in the market he also used to invite prospective buyers of his bush meat, with sentences chanted likewise. Thus he drew special attention to himself, until one day some stalwart medicine men followed him from the market to his forest abode to ascertain where he came from. Erinlẹ̀ welcomed his guests with utterances in his peculiar chanting style and bade them wait for him in his hut while he went into the forest to get some fresh bush meat for them to take home. He made good his promise before the visitors departed.
>
> This was how Erinlẹ̀'s fame quickly spread in Àjàgbùsì town. The people regarded him as an uncanny man who had befriended the spirits living in the forest.
>
> Soon, some men decided to make farms near Erinlẹ̀'s hut. They got his permission not only for this but also for making their own dormitory huts near his. Soon, a village developed. Erinlẹ̀ taught the people his special style of chanting and they gave it the name *ìjálá* from the notion that the chanting style was best described as "*ohun tí à ń já tí a sì ń lá*" (that which is chanted on and on protractedly and is also licked up or relished with gusto).
>
> One day Ògún, a blacksmith, farmer, and hunter born and bred in

Sakí, came to Àjàgbùsì in the course of his wanderings and met Erinlẹ̀ in the marketplace. It was Erinlẹ̀'s chanting that attracted Ògún, and Ògún went with him to his village in the forest. Thus began their friendship, which deepened on account of their common occupation, hunting.

Ògún's favorite pastime then was drumming and dancing. In the course of his friendship with Erinlẹ̀, Ògún taught Erinlẹ̀ how to make drums, how to produce lively drum music, and how to dance to the music. On the other hand Erinlẹ̀ taught Ògún how to chant *ìjálá* and Ògún really took a fancy to it, mastering it, and excelling in it.

As Ògún was an itinerant hero, he quickly spread the knowledge and love of *ìjálá* all over Yorubaland, so much so that people thought he was the originator of *ìjálá*-chanting with singing, drumming, and dancing at intervals, and started to describe it as *aré Ògún* (Ògún's entertainment).

After Erinlẹ̀'s death by accidental drowning in the river that flowed past his forest village, his corpse was never recovered and this led to his being deified. His first worshippers were people closely associated with him in his lifetime. They therefore commenced a tradition of profuse chanting about historical events, interspersed with drumming and dancing, during their acts of worship. Until this day the Erinlẹ̀ devotees are recognizable by iron or brass neck chains that they wear along with matching bracelets. When they dance, the initial rhythm of the drumbeat tallies with the following words if uttered repeatedly with increasing speed:

> *Pinkún! Pinkún!*
> *Àjànbìtì!*[6]

When these drumbeats reach their fastest point, the drumming switches over to that of the hunters (Ògún devotees) and so does the dancing. This is a reflection of the friendship between Erinlẹ̀ and Ògún during their earthly lives.

The tradition that Erinlẹ̀ can also be considered a legitimate originator of *ìjálá*-chanting and not contradict the legends which attribute this task to Ògún, or *vice versa*, is explained by the close relationship of the two deities. Both Erinlẹ̀ and Ògún are hunters, as are most *ìjálá* artists. Erinlẹ̀ is a solitary figure who, at the beginning of the legend, lives alone in the forest. Later his fame draws others to join him, and he becomes the founder of a new settlement. Some of the *ìjálá* texts reproduced in the following pages reveal that Ògún, too, is a solitary figure who not only lives and travels alone but also founds new settlements. In other respects, devotees of the two deities share similar attributes: both use iron as a symbolic emblem, and both draw on the same drum rhythms and dance steps in their rituals. The attributes of the two figures are interchangeable in several dimensions, and this then justifies the liberties taken in the legends that, on the one hand, attribute the origin of *ijálá* to Erinlè and, on the other, to Ògún. In short, they are separate deities who in significant respects occupy a large overlapping segment of the same cosmological domain.

Before turning to some excerpts from texts of *ijálá* performances, it is important to point out that an *ijálá* artist, like every Ògún devotee, is expected to keep faithful to the transmitted texts of verbal salutes which he has learned in the course of both his training and his practice. He is forbidden to make improvisations on the verbal salutes to Ògún, or to incorporate counterfeit topics of his own creation into his performance. Ògún is a god whose symbol, iron, is used voluntarily in law courts in Yorubaland for the taking of oaths by witnesses to affirm that the truth will be told. Therefore, only the truth about Ògún is to be told in the *ijálá*. Although an artist sometimes resorts to euphemisms in the presentation of Ògún's fiery temper, there are no skeletons hidden away in Ògún's cupboard.

In the following exchange, the many-sided character of Ògún is reflected. Two *oníjalá* (*ijálá* artists)[7] make use of stark contrasts as a way of building a general picture of the deity and the ideology that supports his cult. Ògún is given what, at a glance, seem to be contradictory attributes but which, on further consideration, are reconcilable as two sides of the same coin. Since the Creator made the world, both good and evil are now noticeable in it; therefore, the recognition of the opposing personality traits in Ògún's character is regarded not as an abnormal thing but just as a thing in consonance with humankind's lot.

Ìjálá Excerpt 1

(Gbàdàmǫ́ṣí)

1   Ìbà oooo ni ng ó f'ǫjǫ́ òní jú ooo.
2   Lákáayé, mo wáà d'ójú-òòde.
3   Pàá mo wáà dé fúnràami Àkàndá—
4   Abójòsúpǫ̀ arǫmǫbíeji.
5   Aká mulukú-yígi-dí-'nà-ęgàn.
6   Èmi Aríbùkí Gbàdàmǫ́ṣí mo dé tìkálárààmi.
7   Gbàdàmǫ́ṣí ǫdęę̀'lú Ǫ̀fààà.
8   Ògún mo ríbàà, k'íbàa mi k'ó mǫǫ ṣę.
9   Oñlé-owó ǫlǫ́ǫ̀dęę-'mǫ̀.
10   Awónúwóto ìjà náà kankan re.
11   Ǫ̀kárá f'idà hayín.
12   Labalábá kan'mí akǫ ętà, ó tú gììrì.
13   Ṣòóñlé-Ìwó ǫkǫ Adéǫlá, olúwaa'yáà mi.
14   Asínrín aboojulęnu.
15   Ǫ̀gę̀dę̀ àgbagbà tí í s'ǫmǫ 'ę̀ kǫ́ dę̀ngbę̀rę̀.
16   A-bùn-ún-ni-má-gbà-á.

17   Ogunlabí tí í wín ni í kún t'ọwọ́ ẹni.
18   Òrìṣà tí í gbà lọ́wọ́ ọlọ́rọ̀ tí í fi í fún òtòṣì.
19   Ògún ó f'owóo'lé ọlọ́rọ̀ ṣ'ọ̀ọ̀dẹẹ gbogbo wa.
20   Ikin adádéjọba.
21   Àwàlàwúlú òrìṣà tí í jẹ'gba ekòló mọ́ bì.
22   Òrìṣà t'ọ́ bá sọ pé tÒgún ò sí, Lákáayé.
23   Òrìṣà náà ní'ó f'eyín araa rẹ̀ hóò'po iṣu jẹ ni.
24   Abẹ́rẹ́ mú tojútimú.
25   Ẹjẹ o t'ibi ire wọ̀run.
26   Ẹgun òṣùṣú tí i kọ'ra'ẹ̀ lébè.
27   Ọkùnrin yalayala ní'gbó enígbó.
28   Ọkùnrin yàlàyàlà ní'jù ọlọ̀tẹ̀.
29   Ọkùnrin gìdìgbà n'ígbóò 'Jẹbú.
30   Atóónàlórógùn ọdẹ atàpárìnyẹ́nkú.
31   Alá-ta-pa, afòkúsàmìọnà.
32   Gbáláuntàwi iná gbá'lẹẹ 'jù gẹrẹrẹ.
33   Ògún nì ng kéé sí, bẹ́ẹ ni ng ò p'Óbòkun.
34   Ògún nì ng kéé sí, bẹ́ẹ ni ng ò p'óògùn.
35   Ìbà ni ng ó f'ọjọ́ òní jú.
36   K'áí t'òní lóórin délẹ̀,
37   Áá tó'jọ́ méje.
38   Fágbèmí ìbà lọ́wọ́ọ̀ rẹ ooò.
39   Àjànàkú, ìbàà lọ́'ọ̀ rẹẹẹ.
40   Àràbà ni bàbá,
41   Ẹni a bá l'abà náà ni baba ẹni.
42   Ọmọ Lágúnádé, mo ríbà.
43   K'íbàà mi k'ó mọ́ọ ṣẹ.
44   Ọmọ Lágunárèe t'Àmàdú,
45   T'Alùtótó t'Ègbẹdi Òwu t'ọba Arọ́wáyan.
46   Arọ́wáyan lọ́tùn-ún a-bààlè-èyí-lósì.
47   Ọ̀kàn kunkun tí wọn ń fi méjì í pààrọ̀.
48   Ọmọ ọba ọ̀rọ̀ tíí bẹ́ṣin lọ́nà múgùn.
49   Ọba dimudimu lórí ẹṣin.
50   Ọmọ Ìtáǹdógún.
51   Ọmọọ Táa-o-rẹ́fọ̀n.
52   Ọmọ Ògúnróunbí.
53   Ọmọ Ìtáǹdógún.
54   Ọmọọ Ta á o rẹ́fọ̀n.
55   K'ágbàà'wo Ọya lórí ẹran.

1   It is in homage, homage profuse that I intend to render all my chants today.
2   Lákáayé,[8] I have now arrived at the open-air social gathering.
3   I have come fully prepared, I Àkàndá[9]—
4   A man laden like rain clouds with forthcoming precipitation.

A man who drenches people like rain.

5   A man as big as a barn, who one day pushed a log
Across the footpath leading to the distant farm.

6   I, Aríbùkí Gbàdàmọ́ṣi, have arrived in top form.

7   Gbàdàmọ́ṣi a hunter who hails from Ọ̀fà Town.

8   Ògún, I pay you homage.
May my homage prove beneficial to me.

9   Your house is full of wealth though its roof is thatch.

10   Destroyer of the human-frame who thereby causes an uproar.
An uproar involving accusation and counter-accusation.

11   A bellicose man who scrapes his teeth with a sword.

12   A butterfly chances upon a civet-cat's excrement
And flies away very fast.[10]
Such is the dread in which Ògún is held.

13   Ṣòónlé-Ìwó,[11] husband of Adéọlá,[12] my mother's divinity.

14   A veritable *asín*[13] rat whose mouth is defaced with a nasty ulcer.

15   You are a plantain tree,[14] keeping its fruits aloft in safe custody.

16   When you give out gifts you give them for good.

17   You are Ogunlabí,[15] who gives one loans to supplement one's resources.

18   You are the divinity who takes from the rich to give to the poor.

19   Ògún shall guard the dwelling place of each one of us
With money from the rich people's homes.

20   Ikin,[16] who became a king and wore a crown.

21   Rugged and rough divinity who eats two hundred earthworms
Without feeling sick at all.[17]

22   Any divinity who scoffs at Ògún Lákáayé

23   Will use his teeth in place of a knife for peeling boilt yam pieces
Before eating the yam.

24   A needle is sharp at both ends.

25   When blood comes out to gaze at the sky,
It does not issue from a good incident.

26   You are the *òṣùṣú*[18] thorny plant which casts itself in a series of heaps.

27   You are the swift warrior moving to battle in the enemy's bush tract.

28   You are the waddling fighter cautiously advancing in enemy forest territory.

29   You are the stalwart assailant confronting the enemy in Ìjẹ̀bú[19] woodland.

30   Hefty hunter who walks haltingly.

31   Hunter who shoots at game and kills hunted animals galore,
Thus marking his way with animals' carcasses.

32   The forest fire that completely destroys the undergrowth
Together with the mass of shed leaves on the ground.

33 I am addressing Ògún, mark you, it's not Obòkun.
34 I am addressing Ògún, mark you, it's not óògùn.[20]
35 I will devote all my chants to homage-paying today.
36 Starting to chant from my repertoire today,
37 I can go on for a full week.
38 I pay homage to you, Fágbèmí.[21]
39 I pay homage to you, Àjànàkú.[22]
40 You, Àràbà,[23] are our father,
41 Just as the man who precedes one in settling in a farmstead
    Virtually becomes one's father.
42 Offspring of Lágúnádé,[24] I pay homage to you.
43 May my homage prove beneficial to me.
44 Offspring of Lágunárè of Àmàdú,[25]
45 Of Alùtótó,[26] of Ègbèdi Òwu,[27] of king Arówáyán,[28]
46 Whose palace had two parts, the right-hand one which he used for pub-
        lic affairs,
    The other on the left-hand side, which he reserved for his private life.
47 Whenever a valuable object of his was lost by someone,
    Two such objects were to be provided in replacement.
48 Offspring of a king who used to mount any horse
    That he found on his way.
49 A king who used to appear heavily clad on a horse.
50 Person associated with firing a gun twenty times.
51 Person associated with the tradition of hunting buffaloes.
52 Offspring of Ògúnróunbí.[29]
53 Person associated with firing a gun twenty times.
54 Person associated with the tradition of hunting buffaloes.
55 With a view to procuring her favorite horns for the goddess Oya.[30]

Ìjálá Excerpt 2

(Omo Kowéè)

56 Ìbàa bàbá, ìbàa yèyé.
57 Olójó-òní mo júbà orin ìn mí ki ng tóó máa lo.
58 Ojó orún ìbà.
59 K'íbàà mi ó máa se ní olclc ní olele.
60 Mo ríbà mo ríbàa bàbáà mi.
61 Fajúfúwolé Ògún babaà mi káre.
62 Sùsùká-rù'pá-Ògún-kèdukèdu.
63 K'á múra oko jàgàjígí Ajíté-pepe-Ògún-gbèngèdè.
64 Ò-gb'órí-ègún-rán won-níyò-lójà-gágá.
65 A-gb'óri-igi-sò'kòò-'jàà'lè.

66   Ọkọ Ọ̀gbẹ̀gún, Alóṣòópọ̀bọ.
67   A-d'orí-orókè-má-kọ̀'-rọ̀ọ̀-jà.
68   Òun náà l'ó kọ́ mi lórin.
69   Bẹ́ẹ̀ ni kì í kuku kọ ìpa orin wò.
70   Tí a bí ni mọ́ o leè hun ni.
71   Kò ní í hun mí.
72   Èkúkúú'ṣu kì í kúkúú họ̀bẹ.
73   Mo ríbá mo ríbàa bàbáà mi.
74   Ìbàa bàbá ìbàa yèyé.
75   Àràbà ni bàbá.
76   Ẹni a bá lábà náà ni baba ẹni.
77   Ọba Akọ́dá, mo júbà orin-in mi ng tóó máa lọ.
78   Aṣẹ̀dá mo júbà orin-in mi.
79   Kódẹ̀ǹlẹ̀gẹ́, mojúbà orin-in mi ng tóó máa lọ.
80   Akọ́dá ní í dá tiẹ̀ ní eréwé.
81   Aṣẹ̀dá ní í dá tirẹ̀ ní'lẹ̀ pẹ̀pẹ̀.
82   Kódẹ̀ǹlẹ̀gẹ́ náà ní í dá tirẹ̀ ni òfuru jágá dọba.
83   Kódẹ̀ǹlẹ̀gẹ́ ọba Àkórì, ọbayíga a-kẹ̀-bí-àlà.
84   Ọlálọmí ọ gbà á l'ẹ́nu mi ọ lọọ tójú orin.

56   Homage to my fathers, homage to my mothers.
57   O Creator of this day, I pay you my homage before proceeding with
         my chant.
58   O four-day week, I pay my homage to you.
59   May my homage prove beneficial to me resoundingly.
60   I dutifully pay homage to my father.
       I stylishly pay homage to my father.
61   My father who used to carry with him a handbag
       Whenever he was going into the Ògún shrine; I salute him.
62   He who used to carry with a pad on his head,
       The parcel containing a deceased hunter's hunting gear
       And walk becomingly with it to where it should be deposited.
63   Who used to wear from the house to the farm
       A tunic bedecked with sheathed knives, medicinal charms, and a mini-
         ature gun.[31]
       Who daily prepared a low framework for roasting animals' carcasses
         to glorify Ògún.
64   He who used to hand down instruction from his hunter's platform
       High up among a tree's leafy branches—
       Instruction that someone should go and buy salt from the marketplace
         in town.
65   He who used to throw down, from high up on the tree,
       Stones of combat.
66   Husband of Ọ̀gbẹ̀gún,[32] he who used to kill monkeys

With his gun fired from a squatting position.
67   He who dared to engage in combat while on a hillock.
68   'Twas he who taught me the *ìjálá*-chanting technique.
69   He never, even as a joke, chanted hostile words.
70   What one has inherited from one's parents does not harm one.
71   *Ìjálá*-chanting will not harm me.
72   For a partly rot-infected yam tuber
     Does not harm the knife used in cutting off the rotten part.
73   I dutifully pay homage to my father.
74   Homage to fathers, homage to mothers.
75   The Àràbà is our father.
76   Just as the man who precedes one in settling on a farmstead
     Virtually becomes one's father.
77   Priest Akódá,[33] I pay you my homage before proceeding with my chant.
78   Priest Asèdá,[34] I pay due homage to you in respect of my chant.
79   Priest Kódènlègé,[35] I pay you my homage before proceeding with my chant.
80   'Twas Akódá who used to do his work of divination on the leafy boughs.
81   'Twas Asèdá who used to do his work of divination on the earth.
82   And 'tis Kódènlègé who usually does his own work of divination in the air.
83   Kódènlègé, King Almighty, Highest King attired in radiant white.
84   Olálomí,[36] do take over from me now and sing a song.

After introductions, the first *ìjálá*-chanter turns to Ògún, calling attention to his nurturing qualities and then to his destructive qualities. He has a house "full of wealth," i.e., general prosperity, which he shares with those who need his help, while at the same time he is a hot-tempered, belligerent deity who is capable of destroying "the human frame." One of the most intriguing aspects in this juxtaposition of qualities is Ògún's zeal in protecting the oppressed. He is an Aeneas or a Robin Hood-like figure, who is good to the poor and needy, using the abundance of the rich to help those in want, and thus acting as a crusader against injustice. One canon of good conduct that is strongly held by the Yoruba is that the rich should help the poor. The wealth of a rich person is believed to be basically the result of a good *orí*[37] (predestined lot), though it is also partly due to self-application. A Yoruba adult who is really an *omolúàbí*, a person of good character and conduct, habitually uses money unselfishly, caring for the family and helping people in need. In Yoruba society, sharing is an important virtue and Ògún stands ready to see that justice, in terms of rectifying imbalances in wealth, is carried out. Indeed Ògún is a stickler for justice. He is looked to as a protector who will promptly respond to the appeals of the oppressed in their encounter with an unjust fate. In this respect, Ògún is a warrior against injustice within his own society, just as he is a warrior in battles against outside enemies or in forests against animals unwilling to be killed for human food.

The protective and nurturing aspects of Ògún's nature are also strong themes in the *ijálá* chanted by the second artist. This is demonstrated by the homage paid to Ògún. The homage calls attention to, and establishes, a dependent relationship. In return for homage, Ògún, like a father, elder, ancestor, or founder, is expected to protect his faithful dependants. The *oníjulá* is explicit in his exhortation: "May my homage prove beneficial to me." Just as a good parent responds justly to a dutiful child, a deity is expected to respond justly to a supplicant who properly performs his duty to the deity.

Ògún's relationship to justice is also revealed in a keen sensitivity to deceit. As a result, his devotees call on him for oath-taking (see *Ìjálá* excerpt 3). Upon a sword, a piece of iron, or a measure of earth[38] (any of which signals the deity's presence), no devotee of Ògún dares swear falsely. If one breaks an oath, one may be castigated with "*Ògún l'áá jẹ' rí ẹ*" ("Ògún shall afflict you with a fatal accident").

Ògún's hot temper makes him a dreaded figure. Yet it is this very characteristic which renders him powerful enough to protect and defend the outcasts of society with whom he in fact identifies. Ògún, therefore, wields a double-edged sword: "The needle is sharp at both ends." While protecting some, for example the honest, the innocent poor, or the victims of military attack, Ògún inevitably inflicts pain on others—the deceitful, the miserly rich, or one's enemies in warfare. The paradoxical nature of this beneficent/destructive deity is contained, without contradiction or condemnation, in the symbolic emblems associated with his cult. The cutlass, to name but one, is a useful implement that serves humans by cutting paths, felling trees, or clearing new farm plots. Yet, accidentally or on purpose, the cutlass causes wounds that can "destroy the human frame."

The same paradox is revealed in Ògún's actions. In an attempt to mete out justice, Ògún is sometimes unwittingly unjust. The dilemma is well illustrated in a famous legend in which the people of Ìrè refuse to answer Ògún's call for palm wine (Babalọla 1966:5). Annoyed with what is interpreted as a deceitful response, Ògún slaughters many of the townspeople, only to learn later that they are observing a traditional taboo that enjoins them to refrain from speaking on a particular festival day. Ògún's response, while varied in the oral traditions, usually makes use of the double-pointed needle theme. Filled with remorse for perpetrating injustice, Ògún either falls on his sword and kills himself (see *Ìjálá* excerpt 3) or in a nonviolent gesture retreats to a remote hilltop (see *Ìjálá* excerpt 6) to lead a solitary life, brooding in isolation from society.

The incident at Ìrè which causes Ògún to make "his own blood flow" is recalled in the following *ijálá* excerpt.

Ìjálá Excerpt 3

(From a performance by Aláwodè Ògúnòwe at the
Òwe Sector of Abẹokuta town)

1   Ògún ni ng ó sìn, ng ò s'n Eégún.
2   Ògún ni ng ó sìn, ng ò sìn-ìn'ṣà.
3   Ògún ni ng ó sìn, ng ò s'n ẹbọrakẹbọra.
4   Ògún jèéwó tán
5   Ògún yọ́ ṣubúlulẹ̀
6   L'ágbẹ̀dẹ.
7   Wọ́n l'"Ògún-ùn,"
8   Wọ́n ní, "Kín ní ṣe ọ́
9   T'ọọ yọ́ ṣubúlulẹ̀
10 L'ágbẹ̀dẹ?"
11 Ó l'éwòó tí òún jẹ
12 L'òun yọ́ ṣubúu'rẹ̀ l'ágbẹ̀dẹ.
13 Òdínu òòṣà
14 Tí í bu'ra 'ẹ̀ ṣán wòn-ìn-wòn-ìn,
15 Yánkan-n'Írè.
16 Ọm'AAdìgbòlẹ̀gbọ̀.
17 Ọ́ já ń'nú okó pamọ́.
18 Ó bù ń'nú òbò sọfà.
19 Wọ̀lọ̀wọ́lọ́
20 Ùn-un ní í ta dúndùn mọ́bẹ̀.
    Orin:
21 *Lílé:*   Òrìṣà l'Ògún, ẹ má dalẹ̀.
22   Ẹní bá mÒgún, e má dalẹ̀.
23 *Ègbè:*   Òrìṣà l'Ògún.

1   I will always worship Ògún, I won't worship Eégún.[39]
2   I will always worship Ògún, I won't worship any other divinity.
3   I will always worship Ògún, I won't worship any of the embodied
      spirits.[40]
4   After eating a meal of *èéwó*[41]
5   Ògún slowly fell off his seat to the floor
6   In his smithy.
7   People present asked him,
8   "What went wrong with you
9   And caused your slowly falling off your seat to the floor
10 In your smithy?"
11 Ògún in reply said that 'twas the *èéwó* eaten
12 That he celebrated by slowly falling off his seat.[42]

13   A reticent divinity
14   Who bites off and noisily munches parts of his own body,
15   Thus making his own blood flow at Ìrè.[43]
16   Offspring of Adìgbòlẹ̀gbọ̀.[44]
17   He cuts off and keeps part of the penis.
18   He breaks off and gives away part of the vagina.
19   'Tis snippets of meat
20   That contribute most to the flavor of a nice stew.
      Song:
21   *Lead*:   Ògún is a divinity, so don't break your oath.
22   Whoever knows Ògún, don't break your oath.
23   *Refrain*:   Ògún is a divinity.

The next *ìjálá* excerpt continues to reveal the many facets of Ògún that his Yoruba devotees are aware of.

Ìjálá Excerpt 4

(From a performance by Àjàní Ògúnkànmí Jóògún of Ẹdẹ town)

1   Ǹlẹ́ oo !
2   Ògún Eníràn, o le o.
3   Ògún Oníré ní í jajá.
4   T'Enirèè ní í jàgbó.
5   Ògún-ùn kọ̀làà òun ní í jẹgbín-ín.
6   Ògún onígbàjámọ̀ irun orí ní í jẹẹ.
7   T'Àgalamọ̀sà a jẹ ọ̀ tọ̀ tọ̀ èèyàn.
8   T'odè wọn a si jẹ ahun.
9   Ògún-un mi, ǹlẹ́ !
10   'Tó' bí ẹní b'aró méjì, aṣọ̀nbọ̀ọ̀kò.
11   Apòòṣàmá-pÒgún ara'ẹ̀ l'ó tanjẹ,
12   Ọ́ dá m'lójú gbangba.
13   Èmi ọmọ Mọnílọ́lá mo ti mọ̀ bẹ́ẹ̀.
14   Ògún tó mi í sìn ní tèmi, Ajugudunírin.
15   Ògún mo fi ọ́ bọ párá, ọ la párá.
16   Ògún mo fi ọ́ bàkọ̀, ọ làkọ̀ pẹ̀rẹ̀.
17   Ògún l'ó pọkọ 'ójúu'ná.
18   Ògún payà s'ẹ́yìn àràrò.
19   Ògún palárinà s'íta gbangba.
20   Ó dá m'lójú mo ti gbà báàun.
      Orin:
21   *Lílé*:   Ògún jọ́ọ́ bá m'gbéjò dí i mọ́lé.
22   Ògún jọ́ọ́ bá m'gbéjò dí i mọ́lé.

23		Ẹni s'ọ̀rọ̀ mi tí ò jẹ́ kí ng gbọ́.
24	*Ègbè*:	Ògún bá m'gbéjò di i mọ́lé.
25		Ògún-ùn mi ńlẹ́ o !
26		Ó tó ná onílù orin-ìn mi.
27		Àrìpọ̀ l'à á rì'Gún àjọbọ.
28		Ẹni inú ń bí o ri tirẹ̀ lọ́tọ̀.

1	I greet warmly!
2	Ògún Eníràn,[45] you are stern.
3	King Oníré's Ògún eats dog meat with relish.
4	That of king Enirè[46] fancies ram meat.
5	The circumcisers' Ògún eats snail meat.
6	The barbers' Ògún eats human hair.
7	That of Rebels eats full-bodied human beings.
8	That of rivers eats tortoise flesh.
9	I greet you, my Ògún!
10	In reverence for you, I say "Tó," which sounds like the dripping of indigo dye.
	You are the owner of a mighty, lidded straw basket.
11	Anyone who, while shouting praises to the divinities,
	Omits praises to the god Ògún,
12	Is certainly wallowing in self-deceit.
	I am very sure of this.
13	I, a son of Mọnílọ́lá,[47] know that for a fact.
14	Ògún, possessor of a massive stock of iron, suffices me as a divinity to give worship to.
15	Ògún, when I placed you in the roof's interior, you made a gash in it.
16	Ògún, when I put you in a scabbard you split the scabbard in a jiffy.
17	'Twas Ògún who once killed the bridegroom on the fire.
18	Then Ògún killed the bride behind the fireplace.
19	Finally Ògún killed the go-between in the courtyard of the compound.
20	I am sure of this, this is what I believe.
	Song:
21	*Lead:* Ògún, please send a snake to confine him to his room.
22	Ògún, please send a snake to confine him to his room.
23	The man who speaks ill of me
	While I am not present.
24	*Refrain:* Ògún, please send a snake to confine him to his room.
25	My god Ògún, I greet you!
26	That will do for now, dear drummer to my song.
27	We customarily come together to set up Ògún emblems
	To represent our communal Ògún.
28	Whoever does not like this should set up his own Ògún.

The *ijálá* artist begins with a greeting to Ògún and quickly switches to a full-blown verbal salute addressed to the deity. This verbal salute expands our knowledge of the diverse spheres in which Ògún is the appropriate supernatural figure. Thus authority figures, the king of Ìrèé (Oníré) and the king of Ìrè (Oníré), worship Ògún by offering a dog or a ram to him in sacrifice. Ògún's favorite sacrifice is believed to be a dog but the artist mentions a ram as a play on the idea that Ògún actually "eats"[48] more than a single thing. The barber's razor made of steel is Ògún who eats hair. The axe-wielding logger and the sculptor using an axe and chisel use instruments made of steel, which represent Ògún eating the sap of trees. The rebel's or warrior's sword wielded in battle is Ògún eating humans.

Ògún is also the patron deity of circumcisers, who rely on iron implements in pursuit of their trade. The phrase "the circumciser's Ògún" refers to "the circumciser's knife." Ògún becomes the knife. Hence it is Ògún who cuts the foreskin of the penis or part of the clitoris from a person. "The circumciser's Ògún eats snail meat" because usually the snails whose fluid has been used on the circumcision wound are buried in the ground as an offering to Ògún. The snail's clear, light grey liquid also has masculine associations and symbolic connotations of peace and coolness. The snail liquid is used medicinally to heal the wound caused by the circumciser's knife, and therefore Ògún is said to "drink the liquid from the snail."

For each of these occupational groups, Ògún is a special, patron deity, since their livelihood is dependent on iron technology. In the case of kings, Ògún's patronage is highly valued because the general welfare and safety of their subjects is their responsibility. Because they share common symbols, the various groups of Ògún devotees can all come together as a single ritual body, or they can form separate cult societies wherein each makes use of a slight variation on the overall Ògún theme. This freedom of association for worshippers of Ògún is made clear in the last line of *Ìjálá* Excerpt 4: "Whoever does not like this should set up his own Ògún."

The verbal salute is concluded with utterances extolling the power of Ògún and calling attention to the accidents such power can cause. In this respect it returns to the double-pointed needle theme. The *oníjalá* describes iron implements and then notes that they can make a gash in the grass roof, split a scabbard, or kill bride, bridegroom, and the matchmaker.[49] The song with which the artist rounds off his performance returns to the theme of Ògún as a crusader against injustice. The song is presented as being sung by a morally injured party. Someone is backbiting against him; he therefore invokes Ògún, in the form of a poisonous snake, to attack the backbiter in his home.

In the next *ijálá* excerpt, the chanter laments the ignorance of those people who underestimate the power of Ògún that can be unleashed when the occasion calls for it.

Ìjálá Excerpt 5

(From a performance by Ráájí Ògúndìran Àlàó on a
ritual occasion in his hometown, Ẹripa)

1	Ọ́ wáá tó oooo:
2	Ògún l'èmi í sìn ìn, igi lásán l'ará-oko ń bọ.
3	MÒgún l'à bá k'Ìrè.
4	Mogbe l'á bá k'ará Ìlákùkọ.
5	Àwọn tí ò gbọ́n,
6	Àwọn tí ò dà,
7	Wọn a ní k'Ógùn-ún ó l'áwọn l'ọ́nà-odò.
8	Ẹní bá sọ bẹ́ẹ,
9	Ma l'áwọn ògìnnìjọ̀ginnijọ nù un.
10	Àwọn gòngọ̀gọñgọ àwọn ràwìnnìrawinni.
11	Àwọn tí ò gbọ́n tí ò dà.
12	Ni 'ọ́n-ọ́n p'Ógùn-ún ọ́ l'áwọn l'ọ́nà-odò.
13	Ògún mọ́ lèé mi n'íbìkọ̀ọ̀kan.
14	Ní 'jọ́ Ògún gba'lé Ìlógbò lọ ariwo ẹkún wáá gbẹnu.
15	Orí ọmọdé rí bí ẹdá odó.
16	Orí aagbalagbà rí bí èso àfọ̀n.
17	Èbẹ̀ l'à ń b'Ògún k'ọ́ mọ́ sọọ'léè 'Lógbò dahoro.
18	Ògún mọ́ bínúu 'jókan n'íléè mi.
19	Ẹ ẹ́ gberin àb'ẹ́ẹ́ gberin?
20	(Orin tẹlùúkú bá dá l'ọmọọ rẹ̀ẹ́ gbè.)
	Orin:
21	*Lílé:* Àrà l'èmi ń f'Ògún-ún dá.
22	Àrà nì ń f'Ògún-ún dá.
23	Gbogbo ìṣòwò ibi mo b'ọdẹ dé rèé o.
24	*Ègbè:* Àrà nì ń f'Ògún-ún dá.

1	It is now high time indeed for me to say as follows:
2	It is the god Ògún that I worship,
	But the country bumpkins worship mere trees.
3	MÒgún[50] would be a fitting epithet for Ìrè.
4	Mogbe[51] would be a fitting epithet for Ìlákùkọ[52] citizens.
5	Those who are not wise,
6	Those whose mental development was arrested in childhood,
7	Say they want Ògún to drive them back on their way to the river.
8	Whenever some people say this,
9	I comment, drawing attention to them as foolish people.
10	Absolute nincompoops they are.
11	Complete morons, thorough simpletons.

12   Only unwise people whose development stopped in childhood
        Request Ògún to drive them back on their way to the river.
13   Ògún, please don't drive me from anywhere.
14   On the day Ògún passed through Ìlógbò[53] town,
        The inhabitants were thrown into wailing.
15   Children's heads lay scattered on the ground like broken pestles.
16   Adults' heads lay scattered about, like African bread-fruits.
17   We started appealing to Ògún, begging him not to ruin Ìlógbò town.
18   Ògún, please don't grow angry in my home any day.
19   Will you now sing the refrain to my song?
20   [Whatever song the Ẹ̀lúkú[54] starts, his followers sing its refrain.]
        Song:
21   *Lead*:   Innovations are my stock-in-trade with my Ògún.
22   Innovations are my stock-in-trade with my Ògún.
23   All you fellow-hunters, this is how far I have come with hunting.
24   *Refrain*: Innovations are my stock-in-trade with my Ògún.

The *ijálá* artist first declares the superiority of Ògún—whose emblems are iron implements or slabs of rock—over the trees that are worshipped by rustics when they are on the farm.[55] He then pokes fun at "unwise people" who unwittingly invite Ògún's wrath by asking him to "drive them back on their way to the river." Little do they know of the destruction Ògún can cause. To illustrate this the chanter describes the terrible holocaust that occurred when "Ògún passed through Ìlógbò town."

The *ijálá* concludes on two notes. The first is a prayer that Ògún in the form of violent strife may never visit one's own home. The second, at a tangent to the destructive Ògún, is an assertion that the *ijálá* artist's devotion to Ògún led him to giving innovative performances of Ògún's entertainment.

The unfolding of Ògún's character is continued in the next *ijálá* excerpt, where solitariness is a prominent theme.

Ìjálá Excerpt 6

(From a performance by Olókòtó-ìbọn, an *onijalá*
from Ile Olu Ọdẹ in Oṣogbo town)

1   Ìbà l'á ó f'òní jú, aré Ògún dọ̀la o.
2   Ìbà Ògún Lákáayé, ọsìn imọlẹ̀.
3   Ògún aládàáméji t'ó mú bí iná.
4   B'ó ti ń f'ìkan ṣánko.
5   Bẹ́ẹ̀ l'ó ń f'ìkan yènà.
6   Ní'jọ́ Ògún ń t'orí òkèé bọ̀ mo m'aṣọ t'ó mú bora.

7   Aṣọ iná l'ó mú bora, ẹ̀wù ẹ̀jẹ̀ l'ó wọ.
8   Mọ̀rìwò l'aṣọ Ògún.
9   Aṣọ t'Ógùn-ún ní l'ó fi fún'galà.
10 At'ijọ́ náà àt'ìjọ̀ nàà o,
11 Tí wọ́n bá pàgalà wọn a l'Ogùn-ún,
12 L'ó t'òde wáá gbaṣọ l'áraa rẹ.
13 Ògún oníléowó, ọlọ́nàọlà.
14 Ògún onílékańgunkàngun-ọ̀run.
15 Ògún t'ó pọnmi silé tán t'ó wáá fẹ̀jẹ̀-wẹ̀.
16 Ògún awọ́nlẹ́yinjú.
17 Ègbè lẹ́yìn ọmọ òrukàn.
18 Ògún méje l'Oogún-ùn mi !
19 Ògún Alárá ní í gb'ajá ńlá.
20 Ògún Onírè a gb'àgbò gàgàrà.
21 Ògún Ìkọ̀lé a gbàgbín.
22 Ògún Ẹlẹ́mọnà ní í gb'ẹ̀sun-un'ṣu.
23 Ògún Akìrun a gbà'wo-àgbò.
24 Ògún-un gbẹ́nàgbẹ́nà oje igi ní í mu.
25 Ògún olóólà ní í jẹ̀jẹ̀.
26 Ǹjẹ́ níbo l'a ti pàdé Ògún ?
27 A pàdé Ògún n'íbi-ìjà.
28 A pàdé Ògún n'íbi-ìta.
29 A pàdee rẹ̀ n'íbi-àgbàrá ẹ̀jẹ̀.
30 Àgbàrá ẹ̀jẹ̀ tí í de ni lọ́rùn bí omi Ago.
31 Òrìṣa t'ó ni t'Ògún ò tó ǹkan rárá,
32 Òrìṣà náà yóò f'ọwọ́ hó'ṣu rẹ̀ jẹ ni.
33 Bàbáà mi Ògún Onírè ọkọ Àjíkẹ́.
34 Agbórí-igi-sọ̀kòìjà-sílẹ̀.
        Orin:
        Lílé: Òrìṣà l'Ògún.
                 Òrìṣà l'Ògún.
                 Ẹní bá mÒgún k'ó ma fÒgún ṣiré o.
        Ègbè: Òrìsà l'Ògún.

1   We shall devote all our chants today to homage-paying.
2   Ògún's entertainment will commence tomorrow.
3   I pay homage to Ògún Lákáayé, a divinity worthy of worship.
4   Ògún who had two very sharp cutlasses, sharp as fire.
5   He used one for clearing an area for making a farm in the forest.
6   The other he used for cutting a path in the forest from one place to
        another.
7   The type of clothing that Ògún wore,
    On the day he made his descent from the hill to the plain,
    I know very well.
8   He wore a flame-red coverlet over a blood-red tunic.

Fresh palm fronds were also part of Ògún's clothing.

9   These he passed on to Mr. Bush-Buck, *Ìgalà*,[56] one day.
10   Since that day until today,
11   When a bush-buck is killed in a hunting raid,
12   The hunters say Ògún has called on it and forcefully recovered his clothes.
13   Ògún has plenty of money in his house.
     Ògún acquires plenty of wealth on the road.
14   Ògún's dwelling is a polyhedral house in heaven.
15   'Twas Ògún who, after storing water in abundance in his house,
     Then proceeded to have a bath of blood.
16   Ògún whose eyeballs are of a rare type.
17   Supporter and provider for any orphaned youngster.
18   The Ògún that I know are seven in number!
19   King Alárá's[57] Ògún demands and is given a big dog.
20   King Onírè's[58] Ògún demands and is given a huge ram.
21   The Ògún at Ìkòlé[59] is appeased with snails.
22   The Ẹlẹ́mọnà's[60] Ògún demands and is given roasted yam tubers.
23   King Akìrun's[61] Ògún fancies rams' horns which he is given.
24   The wood carvers' Ògún enjoys drinking the vital juice from trees.
25   The circumcisers' Ògún feeds on blood.
26   I now ask: "Where is Ògún to be found ?"
27   Ògún is found where there is a fight.
28   Ògún is found where there is vituperation.
29   Ògún is found where there are torrents of blood.
30   Torrents of blood, the sight of which nearly strangles one,
     Like the water of River Ago[62] in flood.
31   Any divinity who belittles Ògún outright,
32   Will use his teeth in place of a knife for peeling boilt yam pieces.
33   My sire, Ògún, lord of Ìrè, Àjíkẹ́'s[63] husband.
34   He who used to throw down, from high up on the tree,
     Stones of combat from his gun.

Song:
Lead: Ògún is a divinity.
          Ògún is a divinity.
          Whoever knows Ògún should not mock Ògún.
Refrain: Ògún is a divinity.

The solitariness of Ògún is a prominent theme in this and other *ìjálá* texts. He is presented as a traveler whose wealth gained on the road is used, as mentioned earlier in other *ìjálá* excerpts, to help those in want. Specifically mentioned here are orphans, who, like himself, are alone in the world and who, because they are without the usual social supports, are categorized as antisocial or asocial. The theme is reinforced in the image of Ògún, who de-

scends, from his home on a hilltop where he lives alone, to the plain below. In another legend, Ògún lives in solitude on a hilltop near Ìrè, also
called Ìlú Iná, Town of Fire (Babalọla 1966:5). While such antisocial behavior is no doubt recognized as unnatural by the *ijálá* artists, they do not condemn it. Rather, they and their communities accept it as part of the extraordinary quality that a supernatural figure is expected and allowed to display.

Ògún's clothing provides further insight into his character. The robes are
blood-red or fire-red, signaling his fiery, belligerent comportment and furious
temperament. As in Western culture, red is a color indicative of danger.
However, Ògún's clothing also includes an overlay of *màrìwò*, fresh palm
fronds, worn round the waist over the red garments. The significance of this
màrìwò may be discerned from the contemporary survival of its connotation
in Yoruba society. *Màrìwò* is used along footpaths as a signal that a shrine
is nearby; it serves as a special decoration on sacred trees at the time of annual worship; some *egúngún* have their costume draped with *màrìwò* and on
a motor vehicle fresh palm fronds signify either that a corpse is being conveyed in the vehicle or that the driver of the vehicle is proclaiming his loyalty
and homage to Ògún at the time of the annual Ògún festival. In each case
màrìwò has supernatural associations and indicates to passersby that they are
close to a divinity. There is no doubt that the fresh palm fronds inject a pacific
image into the picture of Ògún drawn by the verbal salutes addressed to him.
On the other hand, the fiery red clothing renders him a dreaded, supernatural
personage.

Ògún's face also reflects his character. His eyes are fiery and "of a rare
type"; they are radiant, resplendent, and so penetrating that Ògún is capable
of reading the inmost thoughts of a person he meets by chance. And he
mostly meets people "where there is a fight . . . where there is vituperation."

Like the other *ijálá* excerpts already used in this essay, this text also turns
to the theme of the many-sided Ògún. He has seven manifestations, just as
his dwelling is seven-sided. Most of the aspects recounted here have been previously discussed. However, one addition to the occupational catalogue for
Ògún is agriculture. Ògún uses his cutlass for farming and for cutting out a
path in the forest. He also provides the iron from which blacksmiths forge
agricultural implements (hoes, cutlasses, or knives) for farmers to use.

In the final *ijálá* excerpt, Ògún is praised as a universal deity.

Ìjálá Excerpt 7

(From a performance by Adédìran Ògúnmólá of Ondo,
who learned the art while living in Ọyọ)

1   Àgbàrá-òjò l'Ògún.
2   Ibi gbogbo ní í gbéé rìn.

3   Ògún l'ó l'ọdẹ ọdẹ l'ó ni'igbó.
4   Ògún l'ó l'Òrìṣà-Oko.
5   Ògún Lákáayé.
6   Ògún aládé, aládé-Ifẹ̀.
7   Òkérè-ọmọ.
8   Ògún Onírè tí ò jehoro,
9   T'ó j'éhoro ó yan ka'nú-oko.
10   Ògún Oníre tí ò jẹ kọ̀ǹkọ̀,
11   T'ó jẹ́ kọ̀ǹkọ̀ ó máa j'ọlá abiyamọ l'ómi.
12   Ajá l' ońjẹ Ògún.
13   Ọkọ́ l'Ògún fẹ́ràn jù, ó dájú gbangba.
     Orin:
14   *Lílé*:   A ì í jọ̀kọ́ọ́ gbélé.
15   A ì í jọ̀kọ́ọ́ gbélé.
16   B'ẹ́ẹ bá j'ajá Ògún tán,
17   Ẹ kálọ s'íjù.
18   *Ègbè*:   A ì í jọ̀kọ́ọ́ gbélé.

1   Ògún is a torrent of rainwater.
2   He goes everywhere.
3   Ògún is the hunter's lord and master.
     The hunter is the forest's lord and master.
4   Ògún is Òrìṣà-Oko's[64] lord and master.
5   Ògún Lákáayé.
6   Ògún, a crowned king, wearing an Ifẹ̀[65] crown.
7   King who enjoyed his offspring's offerings.
8   Ògún, king of Ìrè, who, not fancying the hare,[66]
9   Allowed the hare to swagger about among the crops on a farm.
10   Ògún, king of Ìrè, who, not fancying the bullfrog,[67]
11   Allowed the bullfrog to enjoy a mother's privileges in the pond.
12   Ògún's special food is dog meat.
13   'Tis dog meat that Ògún fancies, this is very sure.
     Song:
14   *Lead*:   'Tis forbidden to stay at home after eating dog meat.
15   'Tis forbidden to stay at home after eating dog meat.
16   As soon as you've finished eating Ògún's dog,[68]
17   Do come along to the high grass parkland.[69]
18   *Refrain*: 'Tis forbidden to stay at home after eating dog meat.

Far from being worshipped in a single town, Ògún is worshipped throughout Yorubaland. And just as "a torrent of rainwater" flows everywhere, so
too does Ògún impinge upon the lives of all Yoruba.[70] *Ògún Lákáayé* is the
praise name that proclaims: "Ògún's fame is worldwide." The same theme

is developed in a slightly different way when the *oníjalá* declares that Ògún is not simply the lord and master of a single sector of society but that he is important in the lives of many people: hunters, farmers, and even kings. All in all he is a universal, well-traveled personality.

The association between Ògún and kingship is stressed in this and other *ijálá* chants. Ògún is the king of Ìrè who relishes the fact that in his veins flowed Oduduwa's blood from Ifè, the legendary cradle-city of all Yoruba. As a crowned king of Ifè origin, Ògún is a legitimate ruler in the eyes of the Yoruba.

There is an important connection between kingship and beginnings. This takes the form of Ògún's involvement with royal dynasties. This association also extends to the divine world. The legend which opens this essay likens Ògún to another deity, Erinlè, who founded a village in the forest. Other legends state that Ògún was the first deity to descend to the earth from heaven. He led the way with his cutlass, clearing a path for the other gods as they followed him into the world.

Linking Ògún with kingship, and particularly the first king of a dynasty, is one of the many ways communities make symbolic use of this figure. There is a marked tendency to link a settlement's ancestry and historical events to Ògún. This is especially apparent if, in towns such as Ìrè, the ruling dynasties are in power through military conquest or civil war. Elsewhere the association can be related to the blacksmith status of Ògún and the fact that the introduction of ironmaking is associated with or under the patronage of the ruling lineage, since itinerant smiths (or even iron traders) needed the protection of authority figures to work safely in a new place. Finally, if hunting was significant in a place, Ògún also could be associated with its beginnings. While each settlement builds its own Ògún traditions, there is a preference for the ancestral tie between the ruler and Ògún because, as a blood relative, it connotes the greatest degree of social proximity. A blood relationship gives credence to a story. If a royal lineage has Ògún as an ancestor or offspring, and this can be traced to the founding period of the settlement, this will boost the prestige of the town. No one will speak lightly of the place. Ògún brings honor and fame to a place. If iron is an important part of the economy, Ògún's presence gives that endeavor blessings which result in prosperity. Ògún's presence gives historical depth to a town, and deep roots are more highly valued than shallow roots.

The important point is that people are talking about their origins and the involvement of the divinity in the process. Often there is a parallel legend, accompanying the cosmological legend, that involves a historical human figure. So the origins are explained on two levels: the supernatural and the human. Hence, there are founding legends and oral traditions that may credit both Ògún and a named king with founding the same town. The two types of traditions—mythological and historical—can collapse the two figures into a single founder, such as *Ògún Onírè*, Ògún and the first king of Ìrè. The human founder also brings prestige, authenticity, and legitimacy to a community, adding to the fact that there are deep roots. The supernatural figure brings protection, peace, and prosperity. It should be stressed that this use of a supernatural founder does not mean that other divinities will not be worshipped both in civic ritual and in separate cult groups. Rather, crediting a deity such as Ògún with founding a place means that this patron deity will be given preeminence. The people of a town use whatever divinity (or divinities) fits their way of life and history.

When people account for their origins or explain their view of the world, they tend to use the most appropriate symbolism to achieve these ends. Symbols, of which Ògún is exemplary, have many meanings and interpretations. All symbolic forms the deity takes are correct forms; all variations in founding legends are correct variations; and all of the personality traits or characteristics are correct, despite their seeming oppositions. Ògún is neither good nor bad. There is no moral evaluation of the deity's many characteristics in terms of right and wrong. As a larger-than-life figure he is expected to reflect the contradictions of human nature. A deity such as Ògún condenses a broad range of human experience into a single figure and serves as a means by which contradictions in that experience can be resolved.

It is inconsequential that Ògún is the founder-king of several places, the founder-blacksmith of others, or the founder-hunter of still others. What is consequential is the composite picture each of these tales provides: Ògún is a legitimator of beginnings, foundings, and innovations, and each *oríkì Ògún* is a folk etymology, relevant to the specific place in which it is performed. Together the etymologies delineate a symbolic "space" over which Ògún "presides." When human events or circumstances fall into this space, Ògún serves as a metaphor for the experience being related. When events fall outside that space, another deity may be the more appropriate metaphor or symbolic figure.

The overall picture, presented by the *ìjálá* artists' *oríkì Ògún*, depicts an Ògún that is linked to beginnings, especially those in which iron technology or hunting is prominent. He is a heroic figure, who is strong enough and violent enough to bring dread into the hearts of people, yet protective enough to render them grateful for the benefits that are a product of his strength. He is just and unjust at the same time, not because he is capricious but because the two are inseparable. In the world of humans, actions must be given values, whereas in the world of the gods these values can be withheld. This is why the picture of Ògún presents an ambivalent deity. The verbal salutes to Ògún in *ìjálá* chants remind us that in highly-placed men strength and frailty are often inseparable, and they recognize that this dilemma brings loneliness and solitude. This, then, is one of the fundamental aspects of the human condition that the *ìjálá oríkì Ògún* texts collectively portray, and as the *oníjálá* tell us, this condition, like a torrent of rainwater, is universal.

NOTES

1. For detailed and systematic literary analysis of *ijálá*, see Babalọla 1966, 1968, and 1975.

2. Erinlẹ̀ is one of the beneficent water divinities. He is believed to be on earth in the River Erinlẹ̀, whose source is close to a small town called Ìlobùú near Oṣogbo. However, Erinlẹ̀ has devotees spread all over Yorubaland; some worship Erinlẹ̀ as a goddess.

3. His name is Gbàdàmọ́ṣí Aríbùkí, whilst his praise name is Ọlọ́ọ́dẹ Ìlú Ọ̀fà. He hails from the famous northern Ọyọ Yoruba town of Ọ̀fa, but now lives at Ebutemẹta, Lagos.

4. *Erinlẹ̀* is a name whose etymology, like that of Ògún, is lost in antiquity. However, Erinlẹ̀ is a name given to a male child whose umbilical cord at birth was found to be twined round an arm.

5. *Gbìngbin*: a tree (resembling the chestnut tree) with dense evergreen foliage that provides good shade.

6. *Pinkún* and *Àjàṅbìtì* are onomatopoeic words, imitating the sounds of the drum beats.

7. One of the artists is Gbàdàmọ́ṣí Aríbùkí, who told me the Erinlẹ̀ legend given in this paper. He performed the *ijálá* with a junior companion, Ọmọ Kowéè, at a monthly social gathering of a society in Ebutemẹta on July 27, 1962.

8. *Lákáayé* is a praise name for Ògún, meaning "He whose fame is worldwide."

9. *Àkàndá* is a personal praise name given by the father to this *ijálá* artist when an infant. The name means "One uniquely created."

10. The image here is based on the belief that the odor emanating from a civet-cat's excrement is obnoxious to a butterfly. It is used to convey the Ògún devotee's belief that Ògún's anger is offensive and dreadful, not to be contemplated.

11. *Sòónlé-Ìwó*: "Straight-bound for Ìwó Town." This is an allusion to the fact that iron (Ògún's symbol) is mined in the environs of Ìwó, in a village called Ìsundúnrin.

12. Husband of Adéọlá: Adéọlá is the personal name of the *ijálá* artist's mother. Ògún is referred to as the woman's husband because the word 'ọkọ' in Yoruba, meaning "male partner in marriage," implies also "lord and master." Ògún is the woman's divinity, and therefore her lord and master.

13. *Asín* is a type of rat having a foul smell and a pointed mouth. Ògún is called a veritable *asín* rat because some of the things offered in sacrifice on his emblems (iron prongs or granite slabs) become rotten and give off a foul odor.

14. A plantain tree: This is a metaphorical picture of Ògún used when many tiny gourds, containing magical medicine, are fastened to his tunic across the breast.

15. *Ogunlabí* is a nickname for Ògún; it means "We've given birth to war." It is a way of calling Ògún "War Personified" on account of his bellicose nature.

16. *Ikin*: This term is used metaphorically here, whereas it literally refers to the collection of sixteen sacred palmnuts of Ifá divination invariably kept by an Ifá priest in an ornamented, lidded bowl made of wood. The *ijálá* chanter likens Ògún to *ikin*; Ògún's eminence as a king in his lifetime is compared to the eminence of *ikin* in Ifá divination, and Ògún's crown is compared to that of the *ikin* represented by its ornamented lid.

17. Line 21 alludes to iron in the form of a hoe-blade. Since Ògún's primary emblem is iron, therefore, as a farmer tills the soil with a hoe and the hoe digs up or cuts many earthworms in the process, Ògún eats "two hundred earthworms without feeling sick at all."

18. *Ọṣùṣú*: a thorny, trailing plant which forms dense thickets here described as "heaps." Ògún is metaphorically called *òṣùṣú* because of his roughness and dangerousness—qualities possessed by *òṣùṣú*.

19. Ìjẹbú woodland is mentioned simply as an example of a war theater. Ìjẹbú is an area of Yorubaland that is close to the coast. It was often invaded by the Ibadan warriors in the nineteenth century. As each warrior carried a gun made of iron, the warrior represented Ògún.

20. Ògún . . . not *oògùn*: This is a play on words for humorous effect. The *ìjálá* artist thus emphasizes the identity of the personage to whom his verbal salute is addressed. *Oògùn* means "medicinal charm"; the artist chooses to mention this because its consonants and vowels are identical with those in Ògún, whereas the tones on both words are dissimilar, and there is a difference of meaning.

21. Fágbèmí is the personal name of the Head Priest of the Ifá cult in Lagos Municipality who was present on the occasion of the *ìjálá* artist's performance and to whom the homage was paid.

22. Àjànàkú is the Head Priest's surname.

23. *Àràbà* is the traditional title for the Head Priest of the Ifá cult in a particular area.

24. "Offspring of *Lágúnádé*": This is a quotation from the verbal salute to the *Olówu* lineage to which the Àràbà belonged.

25. 26, 27, 28. *Àmàdú, Alùtótó, Ẹgbẹdi Òwu*, and *Arọwáyán* are the names of some of the royal ancestors (*Olówu* lineage) of the Head Priest previously named.

29. *Ogúnróunbí*: The name of another ancestor of the same *Olówu* lineage.

30. Two naked swords and two horns of a buffalo represent the goddess Ọya in her temple. The connection between Ọya and the buffalo is that Ọya is the goddess of the River Niger and buffaloes, in herds, frequent the River Niger along the savannah section of its course.

31. The phonaesthetic word *jàgàjígí* in the Yoruba text captures the visual impact of the various items with which the hunter bedecked his tunic.

32. *Ọgbẹgún* is the pet name of the hunter's wife; it means one who has a full body and is robust and beautiful.

33. *Akọdá*: The fourth in order of precedence among the major Ifá priests in Ọyọ Area.

34. *Aṣẹdá*: The fifth in order of precedence among the major Ifá priests in Ọyọ Area.

35. *Kódẹnlẹgẹ*: A rare Yoruba name for Almighty God. Its etymology is unclear.

36. *Ọlálọmí*: Using metonymy, the artist names the principal lineage ancestor of his partner, whose Muslim name is Gbàdàmọ́ṣí.

37. *Orí* is each individual's personal divinity when conceived as an object of worship. In terms of the individual's experience, it represents the person's predestined lot in life.

38. Ògún worshippers believe that since iron ore is mined from the earth, swearing by the earth is as sacred and effective as swearing by Ògún himself.

39. *Eégún*: Ancestral spirits, as an object of worship, represented by masqueraders.

40. Embodied spirits: demons, nymphs, dryads, and so on.

41. *Èéwó*: mashed, boilt yam pieces mixed with palm oil.

42. Ògún *deliberately* fell off his seat slowly.

43. This is the reference to the incident at Ìrè. In remorse, Ògún is here said to have cut off pieces of his own flesh and munched them. It is *not* connected with the incident at the smithy.

44. *Adìgbòlẹgbọ*: The nickname of one of Ògún's ancestors; the name means "He who dashed himself against *ẹgbọ*" (a certain useful plant).

45. *Eníràn* is a term used by the *ìjálá* artist to describe Ògún as a "Trouble-Lover"; the word is a dialect rendering of 'oní + òràn' ("one who has trouble" literally).

46. *Enirè* is a dialect rendering of Onírè (Lord or king of Ìrè).

47. *Mọnílọ́lá* is the personal name of the *ìjálá* artist's father; it means "This child has a share of honor."

48. Of course this is anthropomorphic. In reality the tradition holds that Ògún accepts a sacrifice: "*Ògún gbà.*"

49. Should an affray somehow occur at a wedding celebration, this kind of multiple death can result from the use of knives and daggers.

50. *MÒgún* = *imu Ògún* = Ògún's place. Since the inhabitants of Ìrè annually hold a grand Ògún Festival (*Ọdún Ògún*) in memory of Ògún's exploits in the town during his lifetime, Ìrè may rightly be described as "Ògún's place."

51, 52. *Mogbe* = *imu ogbe* = a place where cocks' combs abound. *Ìlákùkọ́* is the name of a village; it means "Where the people have cocks." Therefore, the village may rightly be called "a place where cocks' combs abound."

53. Ìlógbò town is 13 kilometers from Ìnísà in Ọṣun area. "Ògún passed through Ìlógbò" is another figurative way of saying "An internecine strife burst out in Ìlógbò."

54. Line 20 was said in the voice of ordinary speech by the *ìjálá* artist's pupils, in reply to his question in line 19. This reply is an ornamented "Yes." The ornamentation lies in the use of a proverb which alludes to the *Ẹlúkú*, which is a type of ancestral spirit (represented by a masquerader) in the Ìjẹbú area of Yorubaland. The masquerader is very friendly with children and he gets them to sing, giving the lead by first singing the main melody.

55. Farmers on distant farms where they are resident for a few months before coming home (to their town) for a festival find solace in worshipping trees traditionally held sacred, for example, *Ìrókò, Àràbà, Akòko, Àyàn*, and others.

56. *Ìgalà*, bushbuck: The bushbuck's coat has several vertical stripes down its sides. These stripes are like the stripes formed by palm fronds around Ògún's waist.

57. *Alárá* is the title of the king of Ará, a town now known as Arámọkọ in Ondo State of Nigeria.

58. *Onírè* is the title of the king of Ìrè; the huge ram is presented as an extra after the traditional dog has been offered in sacrifice to Ògún.

59. Ìkòlé is a town now in Ekiti Yoruba territory. The snails offered to Ògún are additional to the dog.

60. *Ẹlẹ́mọnà* is said to be the title of the king of Imọnà, a town now extinct in the Ekiti Yoruba area.

61. *Akìrun* is the title of the king of Ikirun, a town in the Odò Ọtin District north of Oṣogbo.

62. River Ago is a local river near the *ìjálá* artist's hometown, Oṣogbo.

63. *Àjíkẹ́*: Tradition holds that this is the *oríkì* name of Ògún's favorite wife.

64. *Òrìṣà-oko*: the goddess of agriculture. Ògún is her lord and master because a variety of iron implements (Ògún) is a *sine qua non* for the farmer's work that she is to bless.

65. See legends 1 and 2 in Babalọla (1966). An inference is drawn that Ògún once reigned briefly at Ilé Ìfẹ.

66, 67. The point being made is that for a sacrifice to be offered to Ògún, his devotees harass neither the hare nor the bullfrog (both having dainty meat) but rather the dog, whose meat is Ògún's favorite delicacy.

68, 69. The song urges the hunters to remember to participate in the hunting trip in the high-grass parkland in the evening of the Ògún Festival day after they have eaten the meat of the dog offered in sacrifice to Ògún.

70. There are famous Ògún shrines and festivals in Ìrè and Ibadan (Ọyọ State); also in Ondo and Ikarẹ (Ondo State).

References Cited

Babalọla, S. A. 1966. *The Content and Form of Yoruba Ìjálá*, Oxford: Oxford University Press.

———. 1968. *Ìjálá*, Lagos: Federal Ministry of Information.

———. 1975. "The Delights of Ìjálá," in *Yoruba Oral Tradition*, Wande Abimbọla (ed.), Ile Ifẹ̀: University of Ifẹ̀.

'Bade Ajuwọn

8

Ògún's Ìrèmòjé: A Philosophy of Living and Dying

O ral traditions maintain that the god Ogun led four hundred and one Yoruba divinities when they descended to earth at Ifẹ-Oodaye, the exact location of which we are, today, not sure. These traditions also state that Ogun helped the divinities to survive in their initial settlement on earth and to effect harmony among themselves as they struggled with new and unforeseen circumstances. Ogun's ability to direct the various activities of the other divinities emanated from his philosophy that one must display courage and heroism in living and in dying while serving one's fellow men. For Ogun, the only means of achieving honor in life was to live up to this philosophy. The leadership ideals associated with Ogun have been preserved in ritual and oral traditions associated with hunting and warfare, both of which Ogun enjoined his followers to know and to perform. Today, one of the best sources for examining them, and the one on which this essay concentrates, is *Ìrèmòjé*, a corpus of poetic chants sung at funeral ceremonies, also known as *Ìrèmòjé*,[1] held for deceased hunters.

Of the various traditional rites of passage for the dead which are still observed in West Africa, ceremonies attached to the Yoruba hunter's guild appear to be among the more widespread. Other death rites are performed by religious groups such as those devoted to Ṣango (the god of lightning and thunder) or Ifa (the divination oracle) of Nigeria; by the Ẹlẹgbara worshippers of the People's Republic of Benin; or by occupational guilds, including the Yoruba and Hausa calabash carvers of Nigeria or the Ewe cloth weavers of Ghana. The funerals for deceased members of each of these groups are the sole concern of members. By contrast, the death rites for Yoruba hunters are a full community affair. Nearly everyone in a traditional Yoruba community is in one way or another connected to Ogun and likes to have a hand in a ceremony which honors the deity who gave to the world its first divine model-performance for a leader.

The communities from which the data in this study come are Ọyọ, former capital of the Yoruba-speaking peoples' largest precolonial empire, and towns surrounding it. At its peak, c. 1780, the Ọyọ Empire stretched from the Niger River in the north to the sea in the south and from Dahomey in the west to the Benin border in the east. It is thought that hunters' guilds were spread throughout this area, and that they welcomed and protected fellow hunters in their travels. That being the case, the traditions associated with the guilds were no doubt widely circulated and understood. In fact, knowing the traditions was possibly a "password" for gaining acceptance in a strange place. Today, the geographical core of the old empire is preserved as Ọyọ state, one of twenty-one states in Nigeria. It embraces one of at least a dozen Yoruba-speaking subgroups, each of which has its own dialect and historical traditions. Part of the reason that we may speak of them collectively as Yoruba is that some common traditions were disseminated across subgroup boundaries by such travelers as the hunters.

The Ìrèmọ̀jé Tradition

Oral traditions concerning the origin of hunters' death rites state that when Ogun was on earth he taught men the art of hunting and warfare. He organized and trained hunters in occupational guilds and then established rules and regulations to guide them in all facets of their professional, religious, and social activities. For the entertainment of himself and his followers, he also established two sets of poetic chants, one called Ìjálá, to be performed on various occasions, particularly Ogun festivals,[2] and the other Ìrèmọ̀jé.

During the latter part of Ogun's life on earth he was greatly concerned that the hunting profession and its traditions be preserved after his departure. He feared the loss of his cherished hunting charms, and, more importantly, the Ìrèmọ̀jé chants, which preserved the philosophy which was central to him and to his way of life. Consequently, Ogun consulted the Ifa oracle, who counseled him to order the hunters to perform the Ìrèmọ̀jé at the final funeral rites for their departed colleagues. It was Ifa, it might be noted, who christened the chants as Ìrèmọ̀jé, the etymology of which is unclear. Thus Ogun directed guild members to perform the chants henceforth, warning them that this final observance was to be taken as a sacred religious duty. Failure to perform this duty would place a deceased hunter in a state of peril in which he would not be able to find his proper place among the ancestors. It is this injunction to which the chanters of *Ìrèmòjé* refer when they say:

1   Ọdẹ yòówù o ku,[3]
2   Tá a bá ṣèrèmòjé ẹ̀,
3   Ọ̀dọ̀ Olúmọkin ló ń lọ.
4   Ọdẹ yòówu tó ṣídẹ lọ,
5   Tá à bá ṣèrèmòjé ẹ̀,
6   Tòun tegbére ni ọ́ jọ máa jẹ.

1   A hunter who dies,
2   For whom *Ìrèmòjé* is performed,
3   Shall join *Olúmọkin*[4] in heaven.
4   A hunter who dies,
5   For whom *Ìrèmòjé* is denied,
6   Shall join the company of demons.

The effect of the message is such that the children of deceased hunters often double their pace in arranging *Ìrèmòjé* performances for deceased parents. This, then, is the way the *Ìrèmòjé* ritual performance became an intimate part of the Yoruba hunters' way of life.

While the observance of *Ìrèmòjé* has divine justifications and sanctions, it also has a number of important social functions. For one thing, when word is spread that an *Ìrèmòjé* is to be performed, members of Yoruba hunters guilds gather from far and near, from villages and towns, to commune, socialize, and renew their ties to one another as well as to renew their loyalty to the hunters' traditions and ethics. For another, the *Ìrèmòjé* ritual performance provides guild members with an opportunity to mourn collectively their loss and, as Van Gennep showed to be the case in death rites throughout the world, to reintegrate the remaining members of the society with one another. The *Ìrèmòjé* marks the termination of the deceased's membership in his earthly occupation, and thus the performance signals to the public that he has ceased hunting— an important step, since it is a bad omen for the living and the dead to "hunt," that is, to consort, together. As a way of marking the separation of the living from the dead, *Ìrèmòjé* chanters sing:

1   Ìgbà mĩ,
2   Ìgbà mĩ,
3   Ká má tùún jọ règbẹ́ pọ̀ mọ́.

1   In future,

2   In future,

3   Stop going a-hunting with us.

It is believed that this chant represents Ogun's own order to the deceased to refrain from ever hunting again with his living colleagues and, instead, to take up his earthly profession in heaven. There he will be exposed to superior hunting skills, as imparted to him by Ogun.

Finally, despite the closure that the funeral ceremony puts to the social relationship between the survivors and the deceased, the actual performance is believed to bring the living into the company of the deceased hunter for one final tribute, and into the company of Ogun himself.

The *Ìrèmọ̀jé* Performance

The *Ìrèmọ̀jé* ritual performance is usually held in an open space outside the house of the deceased. It begins at about 10 p.m. and continues until dawn. The general audience—including farmers, blacksmiths, barbers, drivers, and other users of iron implements—ordinarily is seated in a large circle, with the hunters separating themselves from the others by taking their places on woven mats spread on the ground. The hunters' drummers sit at one corner of the circle so that they can easily be seen by the *Ìrèmọ̀jé* chanters (fig. 8.1) at the opposite corner, and by the audience. The members of the deceased's family sit at their left. The seating arrangement enables the drummers to salute each set of participants as a group.

The focal point of the assembly, at the center of the ring, is the hunter's paraphernalia, arranged on a forked post so as to represent the deceased himself (fig. 8.2). The paraphernalia includes his hunting clothes and personal equipment, such as a dane gun, flint, powder, cutlass, and knife. The effigy is intended to be an impersonation of the deceased. It has been reported that in other cases a living impersonator briefly appears and calls farewell to the assembled group.[5] Whichever is the case, the impersonation is the means chosen by the living to bring the deceased into their company for a farewell meeting.

An assortment of items is tied to the hunter's effigy. It symbolically represents the earthly role of the hunter and, simultaneously, the distinctive qualities of his deity, Ogun. Many of these items come from the kit which is taken to the forest where the hunter expects to spend long periods in solitary pursuit of game. One set of items consists of foodstuffs. The most prominent are roast beans, Ogun's favorite food (perhaps because they can be preserved for several days and eaten cold); red palm oil, the color by which he is, incidentally, known; ground pepper (evidence of the hunter's vitality); guinea pepper (an important item in hunter's charms); and salt (to preserve the hunter's catch). A second set of items represents forest products: fresh palm

FIGURE 8.1. *Ìrèm̀ọ̀jé* chanters.

FIGURE 8.2. The deceased hunter's paraphernalia is displayed as the centerpiece of the *ìrèm̀ọ̀jé* performance.

kernels and fresh palm fronds (màrìwò). The palm is a special tree in the Ogun tradition. It provides food (its oil) and wine (Ogun's favorite beverage). It provides fuel (the palm kernels) for the smithy. And it provides the "clothes" (i.e., the màrìwò) of Ogun—clothes which he wore when he emerged from the forest and which signaled his role in bringing civilization— the Iron Age—to humankind. The clothes of Ogun are used to decorate his shrines, or as a sign along a path that indicates it leads to the shrine of another divinity. A third set of items consists of the iron tools of the hunter and other, random, pieces of iron. They represent more explicitly the fact that Ogun was the deity who introduced metal and metallurgy. A fourth set includes an assortment of magical charms which ensure the hunter's survival when he encounters dangerous situations in the forest and which aid him in tracking and killing game. Ogun is believed to be the divinity who controlled the mysteries of hunting charms and who gave them to the hunters. Finally, there is a set of items which represent other professions, but which the hunter must employ when he lives alone in the forest. The significance of these items is explained when we examine the Ìrèmòjé chants themselves.

The ceremony is presided over by the commander-in-chief of the hunters' guild, the Aṣipadẹ. When Ogun was on earth he appointed the Aṣipadẹ as the senior member of his titled chiefs, conveying to him his powers and instructing him to act as his personal representative. The Aṣipadẹ is, therefore, entitled to tell his colleagues when to go hunting, to war, or to the farm, and, indeed, when to carry out a number of outdoor activities in which guild members are collectively engaged. One of them is the Ìrèmòjé ceremony, and in this context the Aṣipadẹ directs the seating arrangement, the chanting of dirges, and the accompaniment of drummers. During the Ìrèmòjé performance, the Aṣipadẹ is thought to become Ogun himself and, therefore, he is offered respect and deference which exceed the normal amount given him at other times. Anyone who disregards the Aṣipadẹ's orders at funeral ceremonies, in effect, disregards Ogun himself. Even the drummers, who normally are an uncooperative group of people, readily obey the guild leader in this ritual context.

The personality exhibited by the Aṣipadẹ ideally mirrors the personality of Ogun. This is in keeping with a widespread belief that devotees' personalities should resemble the personalities of the deities they follow. Ogun is fierce, his eyes fiery, and his mannerisms harsh. The Aṣipadẹ is expected to reveal the same qualities. Similarly, the devotee is expected to exhibit Ogun's character traits: bravery in war, skill in hunting, and virtue in morals. Only a man who displays these traits is eligible to hold the title of Aṣipadẹ. The following Ìjálá chant sets forth some of these expectations:

1   Ẹni tí ò gbónágbònàgbóná,[6]
2   Kò le è jAṣipadẹ.
3   Bẹ́ẹ̀ lẹ ni tí ò lógùngùn bí àrònì,

4   Kò leè jAṣípadẹ.
5   Ẹni tí ò láyàa yìnbọnjẹ,
6   Mo ní kò leè jAṣípadẹ wa.
7   Èmi láyàa yìnbọnjẹ.
8   Mo lè kerin lójú.
9   Mo lè pẹfọn níjà.
10   Mo lè jAṣípadẹ.

1   A person who is not ferocious,
2   Cannot be installed Aṣípadẹ.
3   A person who does not possess charms like àrọnì,[7]
4   Cannot be installed Aṣípadẹ.
5   A person who cannot commit suicide by the gun,
6   I say, cannot be installed Aṣípadẹ.
7   I am brave to the point of committing suicide by the gun.
8   I can challenge an elephant.
9   I can challenge a bushcow.
10   I can be made Aṣípadẹ.

Ìrèmòjé performances restate these expectations to inspire the assembled crowd and to instruct youthful hunters who aspire to hold the Aṣípadẹ chieftaincy title and to follow the lead of Ogun himself.

Ìrèmòjé Themes

The themes of Ìrèmòjé can be placed under two divisions: those which focus on life, and the ideal way to live it, and those which focus on death and its inevitability. Several themes are elaborated upon within each division, and they convey the Ogun philosophy. I now turn to those themes.

Ogun did for humans what he did for the divinities: he showed them the way to live on earth. This role is emphasized in the following praises sung to Ogun by the Ìrèmòjé artists:

1   Ògún Lákáayé.
2   Oṣìn Mọlẹ̀.
3   Òòsà tó sọgbó dilé,
4   Òòsà tó sògbẹ́ dìgboro,
5   Òòsà tó sàkìtàn dọjà.

1   Ògún, Chief Lákáayé.[8]
2   Chief Oṣìn Mọlẹ̀.[9]
3   The deity who made the forest his home,

4   The deity who made the forest-heart into a township,
5   The deity who made a refuse pit into a market.

As the praises suggest, Ogun was an innovator, a founder, and a leader, each role demanding self-reliance.

Ogun's life in the forest, the life which is stressed in the *Ìrèmọ̀jé*, is the kind of life which brings out the need for self-sufficiency. It should be pointed out, however, that Ogun was a marginal divinity who lived half of his life in the wild and disorderly state of nature (the forest) and the other half in the orderly state of human existence (the township). Of these two kinds of life, Ogun best loved that in the forest and wished to instill in his followers the qualities which would produce that same devotion as well as the self-assurance and versatility expected of a leader.

Before going to the forest, Ogun gathered all of the materials he would need to sustain himself for long periods of time. These materials, then, form the bulk of the items which are usually attached to the hunter's effigy at the center of the funeral ceremony. The gear includes items representing the many professions hunters are required to know if they are to sustain themselves when they are alone. During the *Ìrèmọ̀jé* performance an item representing a profession is taken separately from the effigy, displayed to the audience, saluted by the living hunters, and praised by the chanters. For example, a tool represents Ogun as the carpenter who builds his hunting lodge; medicine represents Ogun as the physician who heals his wounds; a pot represents Ogun as the cook who prepares his meals; and preservatives represent Ogun as the chemist who cures his meat.

The kinds of tributes given to the hunter's equipment are illustrated by the following two excerpts taken from *Ìrèmọ̀jé* chants. The first is sung as a needle is held up to public view; the second accompanies the display of the hunter's mending thread:

A.
1   Ògúnjìnmí ọwọ́ọ̀ rẹ́ tajáa bàbáà rẹ.[10]
2   Abẹ́rẹ́ wọnú ọ̀fin ó ráá poo.
3   Abẹ́rẹ́ ò ní balẹ̀ ó ró gbọ̀ngbọ̀n.
4   Abẹ́rẹ́ ọdẹ,
5   Tí fi í lẹsọ nínúu 'gbó rèé oo.
6   Àrà mọ̀ jí èlèè.
7   Òwú dúdú ọdẹ náà rèé o o,
8   Àrà mọ̀ jí èlèè.

1   Ògúnjìnmí,[11] you have caught your father's dog.[12]
2   A needle that falls into a pit is lost forever.

3   A fallen needle will never give a loud sound.
4   Here is the hunter's needle,
5   With which he mends his clothes in the forest.
6   Attending hunters awake.
7   Here is the hunter's black thread,
8   Attending hunters awake.

B.
1   Ṣòkòtò ni mo bọ̀,[13]
2   N ò bọ dígòóò mi.
3   N jọ́ọ mo bá bọ dígbóò mi,
4   Ìyọnu ni í ṣe.
5   Ojú pọ́ndẹ ńjù a firàwé dáńá.
6   Gbogbo ẹ̀ ò dùn mí, bí i dígòó mi tọ́ya.
7   Kẹ̀kẹ́ ta dídùn aṣọ lèdidì èèyàn.
8   Dìgòó ọdẹ náà rèé oo,
9   Àrà mọ̀ jí èlèè.
10   Atare ọdẹ náà rèé oo,
11   Àrà mọ̀ jí èlèé.

1   I wear a pair of trousers,
2   I do not wear my hunting outfit.
3   Whenever I wear my hunting outfit,[14]
4   This signifies trouble.
5   In the forest, a poor hunter will make fire with dry leaves.
6   While I least regret other losses, I feel the most my torn hunting outfit.
7   A thread well-spun makes clothes that make humans handsome.
8   Here is the hunter's outfit,
9   Attending hunters awake.
10   Here is the hunter's guinea pepper,
11   Attending hunters awake.

The needle (lines 2–4 of A) and the thread (line 7 of B) indicate that the hunter must master the skills of the tailor so that he can mend his torn clothing and protect himself from cold weather and the discomforts of insect bites while he is alone in the forest. Such instruments, however small, contribute to a hunter's comfort and the ease of his forest life. This is why the needle is praised as a thing which appears so insignificant that "it can be lost forever" (line 2 of A) but which, in truth, has great value, i.e., "hunters awake."

A more important consideration is that a hunter's outfit plays a significant role in the actual chase (lines 2–6 of B). The hunters wear special clothing during trying moments—when there is danger in the forest or when an important attack is about to be mounted. The hunter relies on his outfit to conquer magically the game he stalks and to ensure his own survival and success. Parts of the hunter's special outfit can be seen in the sculpture of a Yoruba hunter (fig. 8.3). The hat is the most prominent item the artist has portrayed here; it contains magical materials in the long pouch (hanging down the hunter's back) which protect the wearer and ensure his survival in the next world. Special charms also are tied to the hunter's dog and hung around the hunter's waist and neck. Should the hunter's outfit become torn, it cannot serve him adequately. But the hunter cannot turn back. The Ìrèmọ̀jé makes this point with considerable emphasis:

1   Kò pa, kò walé,
2   Ọkọ Àkútè.

1   He who catches not, dares not return home,
2   Husband of Àkútè.[15]

As we see, even if the hunter is unable to repair his clothing (if the needle and thread are lost), he must persevere with courage, for he dare not return home without catching a respectable amount of game.

All in all, the performance which accompanies the presentation of hunter's gear is designed to convey several messages to the audience. One is that the hunter is a versatile member of the community. Another is that the lonely, self-reliant life of the hunter is a sacrifice made by him for the well-being of others.

A second theme in the Ìrèmọ̀jé performance which concentrates on the exemplary life focuses on manliness and three virtues which an ideal male member of society is expected to exhibit during his lifetime: heroism, courage, and bravery. The following are examples of heroic praises, known as oríkì, sung at Ìrèmọ̀jé performances:

1   Kìnìún igbó kìjikìji
1   Lion of the thick forest.

2   Ajẹ́ ogun Jalumi
2   Witch of the Jalumi war.

3   Iku Ogun
3   Death of war.

4   Elégbèje Àdó
4   One who owns a thousand and four hundred gourds of charms.

FIGURE 8.3. A Yoruba hunter and his hunting dog. Charms are tied to the dog's neck. The hunter wears charms around his waist, neck, and arm. The hat has materials inside to ensure the hunter's survival in the forest. (Wood sculpture, University of Ife Museum.)

The chanters devote a large portion of their presentation to describing the heroic exploits of the deceased person in terms such as these. The praises refer directly to the hunter who is being honored, to hunters and warriors in general, and to Ogun himself.

So that he may deserve public salutes such as these after his death, it is believed that each hunter strives to challenge and kill courageously the fiercest forest animals: lions, leopards, and bushcows. Part of his honor also comes from being able to face game with skill, perseverance, and patience.

Traditionally a hunter automatically became a warrior—usually a scout—in time of conflict. Hence he also strove to face and to fight wars bravely. The hunter who sought honor and fame in warfare was a man who quickly took up his arms and went to battle with speed and vigor. The following saying describes some of the qualities expected in a hunter-warrior:

1   "Gbà mí, gbà mí," kò yeégún,
2   "Ibi ogún lé mi dé rèé; kò yọdẹ."
3   "Gbà mí, gbà mí," kò yọ́ọ̀sà,
4   "Ibi ẹrán lé mi dé rèé," kò yọdẹ.

1   It is a paradox for masqueraders to call for help from humans,
2   For a hunter to say, "This is how far war drove me," is unbefitting.
3   It is a paradox for a deity to call for help from humans,
4   For a hunter to say, "This is how far game drove me," is unbefitting.

In this saying, the hunter-warrior is compared to the divinities, for neither man nor god can call upon his inferiors for help in the face of danger.

Manliness is not simply a matter of *emulating* the divinities, manliness also is linked to *using* divine power. The following chant tells us that the hunter who has noble goals is the hunter who owns charms:

1   Ògúndíyà Akítíẹpẹ,[16]
2   Ìkà ògàn tíí bo 'ra rẹ̀ẹ́ mọ́lẹ̀.
3   Báwí, bàwì, báwí,
4   Mo ní ẹ ma ṣe b'Ogùúndíyà wí.
5   Ìran ọdẹ ní ti í lápó.
6   Ọdẹ tí ò lápó,
7   Ọdẹ tí ò lájàbò,
8   Kò leè sọdẹ erin.
9   A tóńtórí ọdẹ ẹfòn lájàdì.
10   Odẹ tí ò lájàbò lọ́ọ́ọ́,
11   Tòun tobìnrin ni wọ́n jọ ṣọgba.
12   Èmí légbé.

13   Èmí sì lájàbò.
14   Mo láfẹ̀ẹ̀rí pẹ̀lú.
15   Mo láyẹ̀ta ọdẹ.
16   Ode tí ò ní wọ̀nyí, oo,
17   Láwujọ obìnrin ló gbé ń ṣọdẹ.

1   Ògúndíyà Akítíẹpẹ,[17]
2   A wicked thorn that buries itself.
3   Reprimand, reprimand, reprimand,
4   I warn you not to reprimand Ògúndíyà.
5   It is the hunters' tradition to own apó.[18]
6   The hunter who does not possess apó,
7   The hunter who does not possess àjàbò,[19]
8   Can hardly be a hunter of elephants.
9   Neither can he be a hunter of bushcows at Àjàdì.[20]
10   The hunter who does not possess àjàbò,
11   Is like a woman.
12   I have egbé.[21]
13   I have àjàbò.
14   I have àfẹ̀ẹ̀rí.[22]
15   I also have the hunter's ayẹta.[23]
16   The hunter who does not own these,
17   Is a hunter in the midst of women.

One secret behind the hunter or warrior's professional success in life is related, then, to his ability to use charms to his own advantage. Such supernatural aids represent another theme in the Ìrèmòjé chants and, as indicated,
are part of the gear which is displayed at the funeral.

When Ogun was on earth, he, too, possessed many charms; he used them
to control humans and to perform miraculous deeds. He used his charms to
hold an enemy to ransom, render a lion and other wild animals feeble, heal
the sick with immediate effect, make himself invisible in the face of a charging
animal, float on water, or become immune from attacks made by enemies
wielding cutlasses or knives. His most powerful charms consisted of special
iron armlets which could divert the course of bullets away from himself and
toward another direction. Figure 8.4 is a brass sculpture of a hunter going
to war with an iron armlet on his right arm. This armlet and the other charms
of Ogun were marks of high status and authority—a signal of manliness, without which, as the Ìrèmòjé remind us, the hunter is powerless, like a
woman.

The belief that charms are essential to success remains strong today in situations of confrontation despite the introduction of modern weaponry and its
efficacy. An excellent example of the continued relevance of this belief comes
from the Ibadan area (part of the precolonial Ọyọ Empire), where in

FIGURE 8.4. A Yoruba hunter going to war, riding a horse and armed with a dane gun. He wears a metal armlet. (Brass sculpture, University of Ife Museum.)

1968–1969 a large number of relatively low-income groups of people, mainly farmers, joined to protest government tax levies and other unpopular policies which the common people felt were unfair. The protest became known as the Àgbékòya Uprising, that is to say, "farmers rebel against oppression and punishment."

One of the leaders of the uprising was the Olu Ode, head of the senior members of the hunters' guild of a community under the jurisdiction of municipal Ibadan; another was the Jagun Ode, head of the junior members of another nearby guild. Under the leadership of their professional hunters, large numbers of very low-income farmers, hunters, and laborers were organized and communications channels were established for staging a series of demonstrations designed to harass police and military forces which had been deployed by the government to control the situation.

The significant point about the Àgbékòya Uprising in this context is that the hunters were armed not only with weapons (certainly less plentiful or efficient than military weapons), but more important, in the public view, with charms and iron armlets. Up to 3,000 protestors, led by the hunters, staged demonstrations in the city of Ibadan, singing war songs and incantations. As was later written:

> Many stories were told by terrified policemen and soldiers of, for example, 'the ground rising and falling in waves' when patrols were ambushed, and of men being deformed or injured without being touched by bullets or matchets.[24]

In the armed confrontations which took place during the Ibadan demonstrations, between eight and eleven government officials, military, and police were killed; and up to forty rebels and some thirty-five unidentified civilians were killed. Elsewhere in Yoruba divisions, where the protest had spread, there were some seventy-five deaths, mainly among civilians.[25] In the end, local leaders were called upon to restore peace and, in so doing, they effected a settlement in which the tax levy was lowered significantly. Throughout Ibadan, the hunters were credited with bringing victory to the Àgbékòya rebels—a victory which, it was believed, was won with the powers of Ogun and the charms he had left to his followers.

The theme of living an exemplary life next finds specific expression in the lifetime achievements of the deceased hunter whose funeral is being held. The following Ìrèmòjé is addressed to the deceased hunter:

1   Baálé iléè mi,[26]
2   Arálágbe má sàá,
3   Olóbèé tèmi nìkan.

1   The head of my family,
2   One who never runs away on sighting a beggar,
3   My breadwinner alone.

In this case, the chanter—a woman—secured information about the deceased—his kindness to the down-trodden and his concern for the well-being of his family—from his wife, and then composed a chant based on it. Ìrèmǫ̀jé chanters strive to present the virtues of the deceased to the assembled audience.

But all is not praise at the Ìrèmǫ̀jé performance. While the close relatives of the departed hunter are eager to assuage their sorrow in verbal compliments, Ogun instructed his followers to objectively assess the deceased's achievements. Ìrèmǫ̀jé artists are able to interject balance in their praises because they are not closely related to the deceased. One of the conventions they use in describing the failings of the deceased is to do so with humor. A light touch relieves emotional tensions while it injects a note of realism. The following chant illustrates the kind of humor which is used:

1   'Mǫdé ìí gbẹ̀nu lǫ́wǫ́.[27]
2   Ẹnuù rẹ́ rún ju tiwa lǫ.
3   Àbǫ́ ǫ̀ mǫ'hun tí ń be?
4   Àbǫ́ ǫ̀ mǫ'hun tí ń be?
5   Jawajawa léti bí àgbà 'sǫ̀nà.
6   A birun ń 'mú bí òbò 'sàlẹ̀.
7   A bikun ń 'mú bí òkùnrùn àgùtàn.
8   Ìbà ńlẹ̀ n tóó máa lǫ.
9   Lóòótó nikú já wa lódòdò àwa lǫ.
10   Ǫ̀ràn náà jǫ bí ẹrín lójúù mi.

1   Boy, would you shut up your mouth.
2   Your mouth stinks worse than ours.
3   Are you not aware of what is happening?
4   Are you not aware of what is happening?
5   See the stripes at his ears are like those of an old carver.
6   See the whiskers by his nose are like those of a vagina.
7   The mucous in his nose is like that of an ailing sheep.
8   I salute you before I proceed.
9   Indeed, death deprived us of our flower.
10   In my view, the occasion is one for laughter.

The chanters make vulgar remarks as a way of entertaining the audience and assuaging the grief of the bereaved. Hence the chanters mock one another and hurl insults—neither of which is taken seriously. In fact, the chanters carry on a friendly verbal duel which extends from one occasion to another and from time to time in the same performance. Finally, tension is relieved through dancing on and off throughout the night.

All things considered, the greatest test of human courage and the most im-

portant consideration in evaluating the personal lives of deceased hunters is
to determine how well they react to difficulty. The magnitude of one's misfortunes or losses, or their frequency, is not important when compared with
one's reaction to them. The overall message of the *Ìrèmòjé* with respect to
the exemplary life is that manliness rests on one's capacity to bear the vicissi-
tudes of bad events without dismay.

Our second division in the *Ìrèmòjé* themes concentrates on the inevitability
of death. These chants are intended to instruct the living in the way they
should face death and what they should expect after it.

To begin, the chants state that death is cruel. It nips in the bud lives that
are flowering and not just lives that have begun to fade. Untimely death is
treated in the *Ìrèmòjé* by a recurrent use of flower symbolism, as in the
Ìrèmòjé immediately above, and as in the following chant:

1   Irókòó lọọ,[28]
2   Àkànbí loo.
3   A à rÁKànbí mọ́.
4   Ọmọ Adéyẹmọ.
5   Ikú já wa lódòdó àwa lọ.
6   Lóko-lódò a ò rónílé,
7   A ò mọ 'bi onílé filé 'lẹ̀ lọ.

1   Irókò is deceased,
2   Àkànbí[29] is deceased.
3   We no longer see Àkànbí any more.
4   Offspring of *Adéyẹmọ*.[30]
5   Death has cut off our flower.
6   Here and there, we no longer see the house-owner,
7   We do not know where the house-owner went.

A cruel death is one which unexpectedly deprives the community of a valued
member. The flower quite naturally stands for man's mortality; the suddeness
of death is likened to cutting a flower (or a tree) in bloom.

The sense of deprivation and cruelty of death also is expressed in house
symbolism. In addition to the above allusion to the empty house (lines 6 and
7), the following *Ìrèmòjé* also relies on an empty house theme:

1   Mo kílé òò.[31]
2   Ilé ọ̀ jẹ́ oo.
3   Háà! mo sàgò sílé,
4   Ilé ọ̀ fọhùn.
5   Mo wọ́lé bẹ́ẹ̀ n ò bérò mọ́.

6   Ń bo lonílé ìí wà?
7   Ibo ló a lọ òoo?
8   Ilé tó ti kún télẹ̀ ń kọ́,
9   Ilé ti sọ̀gangan ọ̀nà tákéé sọ férò,
10 Ilé ìí gbẹ̀kan ò ooo.

1   I salute the house.
2   There is no answer.
3   Alas! I greet the house,
4   There is no answer.
5   I enter the house to find no more people.
6   Where is the house-owner?
7   Where has he gone?
8   A house that was once full of people,
9   That was a point of direct call for many,
10 Has become desolate and unhappy.

When death takes away a member of the community, the house may be full
of inhabitants, but the absence of one resident creates an emptiness among
those who remain. Death therefore is equated to "pulling down" the house—
that is, the binding structure which holds the community, the hunters' guild,
or the family together.

   Death is more cruel when it is a "bad death." Not even the most potent
charms can ward off a bad death, as the *Ìrèmọ̀jé* warn:

1   Àjùwòn Àkànbí,[32]
2   Ọdẹ n bó o légbéé.
3   Kì í sẹ pódẹ ò légbé.
4   Ọdẹ n bó o lájàbòò.
5   Kì í ṣe pódẹ ò lájàbò.
6   Egbé lọdéẹ́ fi í sọkọ erin nínúu 'gbó.
7   Àjàbò lọdẹ́ sìí fí sọkọ ẹfọ̀n níjù.
8   Ṣùgbọ́n bíkú bá dé,
9   Ikú wọn ò megbòo 'gi.
10 Mè gbẹbọ.
11 Mè gbòògùn.
12 Kò sí 'gbà tá ò ní kú.
13 Ikú ẹléyà nìkàn ni ọ̀ dáa.

1   Àjùwọ̀n Àkànbí,[33]
2   Hunter, I thought you had *egbé* magic.
3   It is true you have.

4 Hunter, I thought you had a * àjàbò* magic.
5 It is true you have.
6 Egbé is used by hunters to capture elephants in the game-forest.
7 *Àjàbò* is used by hunters to conquer lions in the game-forest.
8 But when Death comes,
9 Magic cannot serve as an antidote.
10 Sacrifice cannot ward off Death.
11 Magic cannot ward off Death.
12 Death is the inevitable end of man.
13 Bad Death alone is what we pray against.

Just as a warrior must defend himself against the enemy, the living must battle to avoid a bad death and the forerunners of a bad death. This battle is waged on many fronts, as it were, and is vividly portrayed in the following chant:

1 Ikú kọ̀ dá pa,[34]
2 Bẹ́ẹ̀ ni kò dá jà.
3 Ọmọ Ogun rẹpẹtẹ ló kó loojú Ogun.
4 Ó rán kọ̀ rán,
5 Ó rán mẹ́tàdín lójúù mi gbangba.
6 Àrùn lọ rán saájú.
7 Ẹ̀gbà ló rán tẹ̀lé e.
8 Ó rófò.
9 Ó répè.
10 Ó rẹ́wọ̀n lójúù mi gbangba ló ṣe.
11 Ni Baba ọdẹ́ wá domi akọ̀kọ́ nùùù,
12 Omi atan ni wọ́n ń mu.

1 Death does not kill alone,
2 Nor does he fight singly.
3 He goes to war with plenty of warriors.
4 To count the forerunners he sends to war,
5 He sends about seventeen in my presence.
6 He sends *Disease* first.
7 He sends *Paralysis* next.
8 He sends *Loss*.
9 He sends *Curses*.
10 He sends *Imprisonment* in my presence.
11 Death finally comes to kill the hunter's father,
12 Who now drinks of heavenly water.

Man is the lone warrior who is pitted against death's team of warriors. The warrior team, collectively known as *ajogun*, consists of "malevolent supernatural powers" or supernatural "war lords."[35] Death himself is one of the *ajogun*. Together with the others, he polices the world and protects it from human beings who violate the ethics and mores of society—the values which Ogun espoused and which we already have examined.

At the same time a bad death is to be avoided, death itself is inevitable. The *Ìrèmọ̀jé* are explicit in this regard:

1   Kọ̀ sẹ́ni tíkú ò leè pa.[36]
2   Ẹ má bìínú ọmọ̀ọ̀ 'Rókò.
3   Kọ̀ sẹ́ni tíkú ò leè pa.
4   Bí ó ti pẹ́ tó,
5   Bí ó ti yá tó,
6   La ò tíì mọ̀.
7   Ó dá mi lójú,
8   Ẹ kúù 'fojú ní pẹ̀kun ẹ kú ewu.

1   Death has full control over human life.
2   Be consoled, offspring of 'Rókò.[37]
3   Death has full control over human life.
4   How late,
5   Or how soon,
6   Is what we know not.
7   I am sure,
8   To everyone, birth and death salutes will be paid.

It is with these comforts in mind that death can be taken as a normal occurrence. As such it must be faced courageously. The following *Ìrèmọ̀jé* instructs the bereaved in how best to face the death of a valued member of their community:

1   Bọ́dẹ bá kú,[38]
2   Ọdẹ kì í sunkún.
3   Ọdẹ kì í sẹ̀jẹ̀,
4   Ìrèmọ̀jé Ògún lọdẹ fi í ṣàárò ara wọn,
5   Kẹ́ní ọ́ gbón róhun mú dira.

1   When a hunter dies,
2   His colleagues never weep.
3   They never shed bloody tears,

4   They chant Ogun's *Ìrèmòjé* to mourn his death,
5   And the wise will draw inspiration therefrom.

This chant also infers that the "wise will draw inspiration" by learning how to face their own death. Manliness and courage are thus displayed not only in the manner in which one faces the death of others but also in the preparations one makes for one's own death.

   Humans are subject to an inevitable, controlled cycle of life and death. They may take succor in the fact that on completing the cycle they will be honored in death as they were honored in life. Honor, however, cannot be found in material acquisitions. The *Ìrèmòjé* make this clear:

1   Ebi kì í jé á pawó àná mó òò,[39]
2   Àlàdé omo Obíèsan.
3   Mo fé kó o máa gbó dáadáa.
4   Odún nìí màá raso.
5   Èmîí màá rèwù.
6   Odúń méta òní ma dágbádáa sányán.
7   Lóríi kílàkílò ni 'kú bá ni.
8   Ògúndélé, òrun dèdèèdè bi ohùn arò.

1   One cannot make savings in the face of hunger,
2   Àlàdé, offspring of Obíèsan.
3   Listen to me attentively.
4   This year, I will buy one type of clothing.
5   Next year, I will buy another type of clothing.
6   Year after next, I will buy still another type of clothing.
7   As man continues his relentless struggle, Death will catch up with him.
8   Ògúndélé, rest in peace.

Whether or not man can save, or buy many types of clothing, death does not allow him to take earthly acquisitions into the next world. Rather, life must be spent enjoying its pleasures, not in hoarding them: "One should not be a miser to one's stomach." This philosophy is contained in the next *Ìrèmòjé*:

1   Ńjó e rí kéré,[40]
2   E je kéré.
3   Ògúnjìnmí, a-lé-ràá-wègi lo,
4   A-lé-toolo já lumi,

5   Ńjọ́ ẹ rí họ̀mù,
6   Ẹ jẹ họ̀mù.
7   Ọjọ kan ń bẹ
8   A á sùn a ò ní jí mọ́.
9   Eyín ìjòbì a deyín ìjawùsá.
10   Eyíin jẹranjẹran a deyíin fọ́ọgunfọ́ọgun.

1   When you have little,
2   Eat little.
3   Ògúnjìnmí,[41] who chases 'Ràá[42] into the thick forest,
4   Who chases Toolo[43] until it drops into the river,
5   When you have plenty,
6   Eat plenty.
7   A day will come
8   When we will sleep never to wake again.
9   Teeth that hitherto chewed kolanut will grind walnut.
10   Teeth that hitherto chewed meat will break bones.

Man must, in many ways, be an opportunist and, as the *Ìrèmọ̀jé* instruct, make the most of each day, each morsel, each small reward. A proverb is quite explicit in this regard:

1   Ibi táyé bá gbé bá ni là á jẹ ẹ́.
2   Bí òjò ń pa ọ́, máa tọ̀ sí ara.

1   Whenever you have the abundance of life, don't miss it.
2   As rain drenches you, empty your bladder as you go along.

In the final analysis, honor in life comes from living it to its fullest and taking advantage of each opportunity.

   Death cannot be considered as a finality, however. It is a gateway to another kind of life: the life of an ancestor. The *Ìrèmọ̀jé* thus move from the solemnity of death to the joy of another kind of existence. The following excerpt from the *Ìrèmọ̀jé* instructs the living concerning immortality:

1   Mọ pọsẹsẹ-pọsẹsẹẹ,[44]
2   Ọwọ́ọ̀ mi ọ̀ bÁkànbí mọ́.
3   Babaá wá diná ọ̀run kò tiẹ̀ kú mọ́.
4   Babaá wá sí tiẹ̀ dòòrùn,
5   Eyí ta ó fi sásọ gbẹ kalẹ̀.
6   Àkànbí ire lálẹ̀dé ọ̀run.

1 I trotted and trotted,
2 I couldn't reach Àkànbí any more.
3 Our father has been transformed into a heavenly light which never
      dies.
4 Our father has even been transformed into a sun,
5 Whose rays shall dry our clothes.
6 Àkànbí, rest in peace.

Deceased hunters who become ancestors are thus a source of light; they permit no obscurity. The "sun" refers to all of those souls who have displayed sufficient energy while on earth that they may thereafter illuminate the spirit world.

The deceased who become ancestors are also likened to trees:

1 Baba àwá ti dìmùlẹ̀.[45]
2 Wọn ti digi àlóyè,
3 Èyí tí ò leè kú mọ́,
4 Èso wẹẹrẹ ni wọ́n ń so.

1 Our father is now an ancestor in whom to confide.
2 He is a transplanted tree that thrives,
3 A tree that no longer dies,
4 But bears countless fruits.

An ancestor is like a "transplanted tree" in that he has demonstrated an ability to "take root" in a new setting. He "thrives" in that he has been resurrected in the countless descendants who have been left on earth to reproduce in the generations yet to come. In Yoruba belief, children who resemble their deceased forebears, usually grandparents or parents, are a reincarnation of their souls, which have been reborn in them. This belief is symbolically represented by the effigy of the dead hunter, which is, as we have seen, the central figure at the ceremony. The ancestral role of the deceased members of society is shown in an ability to live on in the spirit world and to direct, influence, and even control human activities from afar. It is this belief, then, which enables the deceased hunter to return to his colleagues for a final farewell.

Conclusion

The philosophy of Ogun, as conveyed to us by the Ìrèmọ̀jé, contains three important tenets with respect to the model existence. The first is that humans are essentially alone. The solitary existence of Ogun and his hunter-followers is, in many ways, a metaphorical solitude. Humans must be self-reliant. The good life, the honorable life, the exemplary life is one in which the individual can meet his own material needs. This attribute is economically summed up with the presentation of the seemingly insignificant needle and thread. The ideal life is, all in all, one in which the individual faces his ordeals—be they ordeals of living or of dying—through his own inner strength.

The second tenet is that the ideal individual takes a leadership role. In this respect the warrior motif comes to the fore in the Ìrèmọ̀jé, for it is through this theme that leadership is most clearly portrayed. The role played by the Aṣipadẹ in the funeral ceremony is a living reminder of the leadership role expected of the Ogun follower. The Aṣipadẹ looks out for the participants, seeing to their needs and guiding them through the ritual. Charms, moreover, also are symbolic representations of leadership in the form of manly valor, and they remind the assembled witnesses that the ultimate source of that valor lies in the power which comes from supernatural forces. By using the charms, the hunter-warrior is better able to protect, defend, guide, and provide for others, especially the members of his community and his family. The charms contain the message that the leader who defends his own people is a person who knows how to control himself and his foes.

The third tenet is that man will be judged by his own achievements. The accomplishments which carry the greatest weight are those which are won in the service of others. Each individual, say the Ìrèmọ̀jé, is responsible for his own success. The amount of courage and heroism one is able to bring to the complex problems and confrontations of life must be mixed with a certain amount of opportunism, vigor, and lust for life. Each of these ingredients contributes toward the individual's achieving his own kind of greatness and his own kind of honor. His immortality lies, then, in his heirs' memories of his achievements.

In Yoruba society, the death of a hunter is an occasion for reinforcing the values associated with an honorable life. The hunter's funeral communicates these values through the oral traditions which are contained in the Ìrèmọ̀jé funeral dirges, through the ritual performance enacted by the Aṣipadẹ, and through the many symbolic representations placed at the center of the gathering. By means of each of these elements the members of a community periodically renew their acquaintance with, and reaffirm their commitment to, the philosophy of Ogun. As we have seen, it is a philosophy designed to embrace the ideals associated with a "good life."

NOTES

1. They are also known as Ìpà. See also Simpson 1980:33.
2. See chapter 7 for an examination of the Ìjálá.

3. Chanted by Làmídí Abóníkaba at an *Ìrèmọ̀jé* performance at Ọ̀yọ́ in 1975.
4. Olúmọkin: another name for Ògún.
5. See also Simpson 1980:36–37.
6. Chanted by Làmídí Ògúndíyà at an *Ìrèmọ̀jé* performance at Apinni, Ọ̀yọ́.
7. Àrọ̀nì: An imaginary elf, believed to possess immense charms, who can become invisible at will.
8. Lákáayé: Ògún's cognomen, meaning "the deity whose influence spreads around the world."
9. Ọ̀ṣin Mọ̀lẹ̀: Ògún's chieftaincy title, the meaning of which is now obscure.
10. Chanted by Làmídí Abóníkaba at Ọ̀yọ́ in 1975.
11. Ògúnjìnmí: A hunter's name, meaning "the god Ògún blesses or favors me."
12. This means that the hunter is like a dog in that he is very clever and stealthy.
13. Chanted by Adebayọ at Akeètàn, Ọ̀yọ́, in 1972.
14. Dígòó is the hunting outfit. It consists of short trousers equipped with charms and worn by hunters specifically to attack and magically gain victory over any charging game animals.
15. Àkútè: The wife of a one-time heroic hunter.
16. Chanted by Adebayọ at Akeètàn, Ọ̀yọ́, in 1972.
17. Ògúndíyà: Personal name. Akítíẹpẹ: A nickname describing a tough, hardy person.
18. Apó: Quiver for arrows.
19. Àjàbò: Charm to render a challenger weak and unable to fight with vigor.
20. Àjàdì: A high, bushy hill in the Ọ̀yọ́ area.
21. Egbé: A charm which enables the holder to fly away from danger.
22. Àféèrí: A charm which makes the holder invisible.
23. Ayẹta: A charm which diverts bullets away from the human target.
24. Beer 1976:194–95.
25. See Beer 1976:162, 190, 194, 245–52.
26. Chanted by Ògúnyóyin at Ọ̀yọ́ in 1976.
27. Chanted by Láníyàn Àwuùbẹ́ at an *Ìrèmọ̀jé* performance at Àpínni, Ọ̀yọ́.
28. Chanted by Àjàlá Adebayọ for Pa Ìrókò at Akeètàn, Ọ̀yọ́, in April 1972.
29. Àkànbí: The offspring of Adéyẹmọ.
30. Adéyẹmọ: A previously deceased heroic hunter.
31. Taken from dirges chanted by Olókòtó for Ògúndélé at Akeètàn, Ọ̀yọ́, in 1976.
32. Taken from dirges chanted for Pa Ògúnọle by Atóyèbí at Àpínni, Ọ̀yọ́, in 1975.
33. Àjùwọ̀n Àkànbí: Another deceased hunter.
34. Taken from dirges chanted by Lamidi for Ògúndélé at Akeètàn, Ọ̀yọ́, in 1976.
35. See Abimbọla 1973:50.
36. Taken from dirges chanted for Pa Ògúndáre by Atóyèbí at Agúnpopo, Ọ̀yọ́, in 1975.
37. Rókò: A previously deceased hunter.
38. Taken from dirges chanted by Láníyan for Pa Ìrókò at Akeètàn, Ọ̀yọ́, in April, 1972.
39. Chanted by Atóyèbí while performing *Ìrèmọ̀jé* for Pa Ògúndélé at Akeètàn, Ọ̀yọ́, in 1975.
40. Taken from dirges chanted by Adebayọ for Pa Ìrókò at Akeètàn, Ọ̀yọ́, in 1972.
41. Ògúnjìnmí: A previously deceased heroic hunter.
42. 'Ràá: A shortened name of Ìrákúnnúgbá, a very aggressive game-animal; the Western Hartebeeste (*Bubalis Major*).
43. Toolo: A fast-moving but easily charging game-animal; a member of the deer family (unidentified).

44. Taken from dirges chanted for Pa Ògúndípẹ̀ by Olokoto at Àpáàrà, Ọyọ, in 1976.
45. Taken from dirges chanted by Lamidi for Pa Ògúndípẹ̀ at Àpáàrà, Ọyọ, in 1976.

References Cited

Abimbọla, Wande. 1978. "Yoruba Traditional Religion," in *Contemplation and Action in World Religions,* Yusuf Ibish and Ileana Marculescu (eds.), Seattle and London: University of Washington Press, pp. 218–42.
Beer, Christopher E. F. 1976. *The Politics of Peasant Groups in Western Nigeria*, Ibadan: Ibadan University Press.
Simpson, George E. 1980. *Yoruba Religion and Medicine in Ibadan*, Ibadan: Ibadan University Press.

Margaret Thompson Drewal

9

Dancing for Ògún in Yorubaland and in Brazil

D

ance is an integral part of African ritual.[1] Addressing metaphysical beings or powers, it is a poetic, non-verbal expression continually created and re-created by countless performer/interpreters over generations. In its formulations of time, space, and dynamics, dance transmits a people's philosophy and values; it is thought embodied in human action. A primary vehicle for communicating with the spirit realm, it is at the same time perceived to be an instrument of the gods through which they communicate with the phenomenal world. As such, ritual dance is an unspoken essay on the nature and quality of metaphysical power. Indeed, for the Yoruba, dance—in certain contexts—is metaphysical force actualized in the phenomenal world.[2]

In western Yorubaland this is dramatically illustrated in ritual dances associated with Ògún, the deity whose quick, aggressive actions may bring violent death and destruction or, by contrast, may bring the birth of children. It is also evident in dances of Candomblé in Bahia, Brazil, where during the early nineteenth-century Yoruba captives were sold into slavery (Pierson 1942:35) and where, as a result, the influence of Yoruba culture, and of Ògún, is strong (Bastide 1978:66, 205–206, and 253–55). To place these ideas about dance into a broader Yoruba philosophical context, the following discussion considers the Yoruba concept of metaphysical power and its more well known relation to utterances.

The power of utterances has been widely documented in Africa (cf. Ray 1973; Peek 1981) and in Yorubaland (Prince 1960; Beier 1970:49; H. Drewal 1974; Verger 1976–77; and Ayoade 1979:51). Prince observes, for example, that among the Yoruba "to utter the name of something may draw that something into actual existence . . . not only within the mind and body of he who utters and he who hears the word, but also in the physical world as well" (1960:66). And Ayoade points out, "to the initiated the sound of the words is the audible manifestation of its innate force" (1979:51). In certain contexts, voicing action verbs literally activates dynamic forces. Thus Verger reveals that, in Yoruba incantations (*ọfọ̀*) chanted during the preparation or application of medicines (*òògùn*) to invoke the dynamic essences of all their ingredients, a monosyllabic action verb drawn from each ingredient's name is pronounced following that name to set the ingredient into action. For example:

1   ewé ọ̀ọ́yọ́ àjẹ́ bá wa yọ àrùn kúrò n'ìhà
2   ewé awùsá sà àrùn ìhà
3   ìyẹ́ agbe gbé àrùn ìhà kúrò
4   ìyẹ́ àlukò kó arun ìhà kúrò

1   *ọ̀ọ́yó àjé* leaf chase away (*yọ*) the disease of the flank for us
2   *awùsá* leaf heal *(sà)* the flank disease so it may go away
3   *agbe* feather carry *(gbé)* the flank disease outside
4   *àlukò* feather pick *(kó)* the disease out of the flank (Verger 1976–77:254)

Verger suggests further that appellations are attributed to ingredients based upon particular actions described by verbs used in formulating them. It is thus the action or, more accurately, the *acting* verbs inherent in names and incantations which, when voiced, enable them to mobilize the inner essence of a spirit or force. Beyond this, however, it is the sound qualities of the acting verbs which make them dynamic.

The sound qualities of verbs, nouns, adjectives, and adverbs in Yoruba incantations often correspond to the dynamic qualities of actions in the natural environment. In the following invocation, utterances simulate actions in evoking the way an Egúngún spirit called Àgàn becomes manifest.[3] Serving as a formula for bringing the Egúngún festival into the world (*ayé*) (H. Drewal and M. Drewal 1983:2–4), this invocation uses an analogy to rainfall, playing upon its dynamic qualities—not just one quality, but a whole repertoire of qualities—to convey the spirit's elusiveness. Like rain, the spirit Àgàn comes to the world qualitatively in a myriad of ways:

1   Mo dé wẹ́rẹ́wẹ̀rẹ́ bi eji orì alẹ́
2   Màrìwòoo! Àgànóoo!

3   Mo dé kùtùkùtù bí ejí òwúrọ̀
4   Màrìwòoo! Àgànóoo!
5   Mo dé pápàpá bi ejí ìyálẹ̀ta
6   Màrìwòoo! Àgànóoo!
7   Ojú alág̣bẹ̀dẹ kò tó'lẹ́ arọ́
8   Màrìwòoo! Àgànóoo!
9   Ojú amọ̀kòkò kò tó'lẹ̀ amọ̀
10 Màrìwòoo! Àgànóoo!
11 Mẹ̀mẹ̀mẹ̀ nigbe ewúrẹ́
12 Màrìwòoo! Àgànóoo!
13 Bọ̀bọ̀ nigbe àgùtàn
14 Màrìwòoo! Àgànóoo!
15 Mojí lóòrọ̀ kùtùkùtù
16 Mogbé inini ọ̀run w'aiyé
17 Mo wọ̀ rùrùrùrù
18 Màrìwòoo! Àgànóoo!
19 Mo dé t'ogbó t'ọ̀gọ t'àkọ̀ t'idà
20 Màrìwòoo! Àgànóoo!
21 Gbámù! Òfo!
22 Gbámù! Òfo!
23 Gbámù! Òfo!
24 Amamamamamamama!
25 Ẹ má a wá!
26 Ẹ má a wá!
27 Ẹ má a wá! (Recorded in Ilaro, 1977)

1   I come wẹ́rẹ́wẹ́rẹ́ [small, quick, and light, i.e., drizzling] like the early
      night rain
2   Màrìwòoo! Àgànóoo!
3   I come kùtùkùtù [forceful and quick, i.e., pouring] like the early morn-
      ing rain[4]
4   Màrìwòoo! Àgànóoo!
5   I come pápàpá [large, heavy, slow sporadic drops] like the rain at sun-
      rise
6   Màrìwòoo! Àgànóoo!
7   The eyes of the blacksmith cannot see underneath the ground of his
      shed
8   Màrìwòoo! Àgànóoo!
9   The eyes of the potter cannot see the inside of clay
10 Màrìwòoo! Àgànóoo!
11 Mẹ̀mẹ̀mẹ̀ cries the female goat
12 Màrìwòoo! Àgànóoo!
13 Bọ̀bọ̀ cries the female sheep
14 Màrìwòoo! Àgànóoo!

15   I get up early in the morning
16   I bring dew from the otherworld to earth
17   I become *rùrùrùrù* [all pervasive, literally the sound of walking over
         dewy grasses]
18   *Màrìwòoo! Àgànóoo!*
19   I come with cudgels, a sheath, a sword
20   *Màrìwòoo! Àgànóoo!*
21   Grasp it! Nothing's there!
22   Grasp it! Nothing!
23   Grasp it! Nothing!
24   Amamamamamamama!
25   Be looking! We are looking!
26   Be looking! We are looking!
27   Be looking! We are looking!

That Yoruba acknowledge a relationship between the dynamics of speech and the dynamics of action is evident in their verbal characterizations of dance, particularly in the use of evocative words, or what Babalọla (1966:67–68) calls word-pictures, words which by their very sound and intensity evoke mental pictures or images. Hence, a dance for the ancient female deity *Oòduà*, perceived to be cool, patient, and calm, is described by Ọ̀họ̀rì Yoruba as gentle (*ijó jẹ́jẹ́*). In addition to its definition—gentle—the sound *jẹ́jẹ́* is evocative. Its oral dynamics in this context evoke light, moderately and evenly paced, effortless motion. In contrast, a dance associated with the god of thunder and lightning is described by an Ègbádò priestess as being very powerful (*ijó kíkan kíkan tó l'abgára*), literally "a dance performed *kíkan kíkan* with forcefulness." *Kíkan* connotes a forceful release of energy as if under pressure (personal communication, Rowland Abíọ́dún, 1981). Like *jẹ́jẹ́*, the phrase *kíkan* simulates verbally the effort quality of the dance, that is, one in which a dominant motif is raising (*kí*) and percussively dropping (*kàn*) the shoulders repetitively, i.e., *kíkan kíkan*. *Kí* is quick, sharp, and high (or up) in tone; *kan* is forceful, full, and heavy, dropping in tone. The dance further evokes, in its speed and thrust, the dynamics of lightning and thunder—in that order—associated with Ṣàngó. In fact, from this perspective, the image of lightning and thunder can be seen, like the analogy to rainfall illustrated above, to derive meaning from its actual dynamic qualities, qualities which in turn reflect the nature of Ṣàngó's own power.

In Yoruba thought, there is a direct correlation between the dynamic qualities of both dance and oral performance and power known as *àṣẹ*. According to Beier (1970:49), "Yoruba believe strongly in the power of the word, or rather in a mysterious force called ashe . . . that quality in a man's personality which makes his words—once uttered—come true." One Yoruba singer alluded to this concept of voiced *àṣẹ* in referring to certain songs he performs which have efficacy because, when voiced, they operate as "wind (èfúùfù) combatting wind"; that is, the force exerted in voicing a song *acts upon* other forces permeating the world that are believed to be creating a particular situation (cf. H. Drewal 1974). Going a step further, Verger (1964:16) states that *àṣẹ* is "the principle of all that lives or acts or moves . . . everything which exhibits power, whether in action or in the winds and drifting clouds, or in passive resistance like that of the boulders lying by the wayside."[5]

In its broadest sense, *àṣẹ* is metaphysical power. It has been translated as "authority" or "command" (Abraham 1958:71), "a coming to pass . . . effect; imprecation" (Crowther 1852:47).[6] However, when Yoruba speak of an individual with *àṣẹ, aláṣẹ,* a person with authority, they usually mean one with innate metaphysical power who by virtue of this power maintains complete and awesome control over spiritual realms and, by extension, over social ones. In and of itself, *àṣẹ* has no moral connotations; it is neither good nor bad, positive nor negative (Verger 1964:16). It is the principle of realization (dos Santos 1976:71). It is absolute power and potential, present not only in utterances, but in all things—rocks, hills, streams, mountains, leaves, animals, sculpture, ancestors, gods, and actions. It is through voiced power, or *àṣẹ,* that devotees of Ògún call him and seek his advice. It is also with voiced *àṣẹ* that they bring him into the phenomenal world.

For the Yoruba, evidence of the presence of *àṣẹ* in the various things of the natural and supernatural realms is displayed in their qualitative aspects. Thus Yoruba define and classify plants used in medicines by taking into account their odors, their colors, their textures, their responses when touched, and their effects upon those who touch them (Verger 1976–77:249). According to Warren et al. (1973:ii), "If one asks herbalists why they select certain ingredients [for their medicines] one learns that it is because they are bitter or sweet, red or black, hard or slimy, or that they possess some other quality." The qualities of inanimate objects, such as leaves, rocks, ores, or other natural elements, as Warren and Verger indicate, are inherent in their tastes, textures, shapes, and colors. Animated beings such as humans and animals express innate power in their behavior, that is, in their everyday actions and utterances.[7] In performative phenomena, such as in ritual utterances and dance, these qualities are expressed dynamically through patterned time. To a great extent, utterances and actions carry this power precisely because they are intrinsically dynamic.

If oral recitations possessing *àṣẹ* invoke supernatural forces, bring them into existence, and set them into action, then dance represents more literally the materialization of those forces in the world. It is through dance, through what Langer (1953:187) refers to as "a play of powers made visible," that metaphysical forces become manifest. Nowhere is this relationship between words and actions more explicit than in the verbal and kinetic exertions associated with the deity Ògún, the hot, vengeful warrior who kills with quickness and directness.

The Dynamics of Ògún

The *àṣẹ* personified by Ògún is driving force—that which thrusts into new realms, breaks new ground, and achieves the ordinarily unachievable. Ògún represents accomplishment, exploration, and innovation (Barnes 1980:7, 28–29). He penetrates the frontiers of the unknown—the forest, the battle-ground, and the fringes of society. He both benefits mankind and on occasion destroys parts of it, and in his quests he is insatiable, tenacious, and unyield-ing. His path is often fraught with unexpected hazards. It is Ògún's nature to be quick, direct, and strong. Whether creative or destructive, his dynamic can be characterized as explosive.

Many of Ògún's symbols, such as the *àgbaadù* snake, represent his *àṣẹ*. Small and black, with a red stripe on its neck, the *àgbaadú* or *òṣúùró* snake reportedly is very quick, vicious, and deadly and, because of its small size, is able to attack people completely by surprise.[8] Iron also embodies Ògún's *àṣẹ* (cf. H. Drewal, chapter 10). Consistent with the nature of his power, iron implements when used by people to perform work demand actions of quickness, forcefulness, directness, and an explosive release. Like Ògún's acts, these acts can be creative, but they can also be destructive, whether by intent or by accident. Working with iron, man thus partakes of Ògún's dy-namic force. Hence, human action can be seen to derive ultimately from met-aphysical force, or *àṣẹ*. Indeed, this relationship between human action and metaphysical force to a large extent accounts for the need of people who use iron implements to sacrifice to Ògún. Individuals revitalize Ògún through sac-rifice so that they may partake of that vitality and manage it safely.

Ògún's *àṣẹ* can, therefore, be heard and observed. It is expressed physically and audibly in the dynamics of dance and oral performance. Both dance and utterances are physical exertions which express attitudes toward time, space, weight, and flow (Bartenieff 1980:51).[9] Some combination of quickness, forcefulness, and directness expressed in an explosive release of energy recurs frequently in Ògún's performative imagery; these same qualities are also al-luded to in the physical and behavioral properties of the many objects and beings, like iron and the *àgbaadú* snake, which make up his symbolic com-plex. The following analysis of the dynamic qualities of oral texts and dances specific to Ògún demonstrates how they display the *àṣẹ* of Ògún.

One of Ògún's dominant images is that of destruction. Barnes, in fact, views Ògún as "a metaphor for the dangerous and destructive powers of man-kind" (1980:28). An oral praise poem reinforces the destructive image:

1   O p(a) ọkọ s(i) oju ina
2   O p(a) aya s(i) madiro
3   O p(a) wọn wẹrẹwẹrẹ sa l(i) (o)de
4   Ogun ni ẹjẹrengun ile alaigbọran

5   O gbe ori olori sawisa
6   O wo (o)ko oloko rojo rojo
7   O pọn (o)mi si (i)le fi ẹjẹ wẹ
8   Ogun l(i) ọn jẹ agbe (i)rin omo pa omo
9   Sare m(u) omi wa o pa meje
10 Ọkunrin giri bi ẹni ṣi lẹkun
11 O pa s(i) otun o ba otun jẹ
12 O pa s(i) osi o ba osi jẹ

1   He kills the husband before the fire,
2   He kills the wife in the foyer,
3   He kills little ones as they flee outside.
4   Ogun is the *ẹjẹregun* leaf in the house of the proud, fierce man.
5   He seizes the head of another freely,
6   He stares at the penis of men.
7   With water in the house he washes with blood.
8   Ogun who makes the child kill himself with the iron he plays with;
9   While carrying water he kills seven (people).
10 Man trembles like someone who opens the door.
11 He (Ogun) kills on the right and destroys on the right,
12 He kills on the left and destroys on the left. (Verger 1957:176, my
    translation)

The action verb *pa*, to kill, is common in praise poetry and invocations
for Òguń, and its dynamic in oral performance is analogous to the visible dynamics of movement. Hence the oral expression can be subjected to the same
analytic treatment that is given to physical effort.[10] The verb *pa* pronounced
in oral texts conveys a blow which is spatially direct, sudden, and powerful,
executed with an explosive release. In this volume (chapter 2), Armstrong
uses the spelling *kpa* to underscore the vocal force of the Yoruba "p" sound.[11]
Its repetition, *"Ó pa ọkọ. . . . Ó pa aya. . . . Ó pa wọn wẹrẹwẹrẹ"* (lines 1–3)
and so on, conjures up an image of Òguń with cutlass in hand slashing out
at those around him. Indeed, one of his most widely known praises is, "He
killed them with one blow (instantly)" (*Ó p'awọn bere kojo*). This verbal
image is enacted physically in Ilaro, where, on certain occasions, a hunter
possessed by Òguń rushes through the town, cutlass in hand, and decapitates
any dog in his path with one stroke of his iron blade. Another invocation for
Òguń declares:

1   Ó pa oko síbi iná
2   Ó pa aya si bálùwẹ̀
3   Ó pa omo pa ìya
4   Adamolore kège kège

5   Kùtùkùtù l'òguń ba
6   Àiyí gọlọtọ s'oko oloko
7   Ekun oko eke wo

1   He kills the husband near the fire,
2   He kills the wife in the bath house,
3   He kills the child, kills the mother.
4   Sword-cuts-off-heads *kège kège*.
5   Early in the morning, Òguń met them;
6   They were found stone-dead in the farm of another farmer.
7   Ogun will punish those who don't fear him. (Olúpọnà 1975)

The phrases above play upon harsh *p* and *k* sounds pronounced with explosive energy. They possess a dynamic that is unleashed in the act of pronouncing them, and convey force through the effective patterns of stress placed on consonants, words, or phrases, that is, the combination of tone, speed of syllables, vocal force, and flow—all of which combine to simulate physical effort. Again, the word *pa* (kill) is direct, quick, and explosive. In another phrase containing a word-picture, "Sword-cuts-off-heads *kège kège*," the image of heads rolling is conveyed. The sound *kège* has a heavy, sluggish quality and, when repeated, suggests continuous motion. The syllable *kè* interrupted by the sound of *ge* followed by a short pause and repetition sets up a rhythm which evokes an image at once horrific and humorous, that of a heavy, irregularly shaped sphere—the head—rolling after the quick, powerful thrust of Òguń's cutlass. It is evident from these examples that Yoruba have a great sensitivity to dynamic qualities and that they use them quite deliberately in verbal performance—and, as we shall see, in dance—to evoke, and thus ultimately to invoke, the vital force of Òguń.

Throughout Yorubaland there are many different Òguń dance styles. For the purposes of this paper, however, one distinct style and its context will be discussed: Òguń possession trance dance associated with a ritual festival for the gods in western Yorubaland. A comparison then will be made with Òguń possession trance dance in the Yoruba-derived Candomblé houses of Bahia, Brazil.[12] These examples provide us with insight into the role of dance and the significance of its dynamic qualities in ritual. Using the body as an expressive instrument, the Òguń dancer evokes, and thus invokes, the actual dynamic qualities which constitute the essence of the god and accomplishes this by manipulating and controlling time, space, energy, and flow in accordance with traditional precedent.

Possession Trance in Western Yorubaland

Invocations, praise poetry, music, and dance are essential to nearly all Yoruba ritual in which spiritual forces are actualized. Invocations and drumming performed before the onset of possession trance both in Yorubaland and in Brazil serve to bring Ògún into contact with devotees. Through dance, spiritual forces materialize in the phenomenal world. The god is said to mount (*gùn*) the devotee (*eléégún*, literally, "one who is mounted") and, for a time, that devotee becomes the god. Temporarily, then, the animating spirit of the deity (*èmí òrìṣà*) displaces that of the individual being mounted (Ọsitola 1982). Whatever the priest does from the moment he enters the trance state is thought to represent the god's own actions. Among the Yoruba, possession trance states are expressed through the medium of dance. To my knowledge, there is no instance of possession trance among the Yoruba which does not occur as dance or in association with dance.

Spirit mediumship is the most significant role of a priest. The uniting of devotee and deity into one image often causes some confusion for researchers who, for example, try to establish the identity of figures represented in Yoruba sculpture. Sculpture represents the union of the priest and deity in the depiction of the former with the costumes, hairstyles, and paraphernalia identified with the latter (M. Drewal 1986). Likewise, these identical fashions are observable in ritual dance. It is through dance, however, that the priest brings the active deity (not a symbolic representation) into the phenomenal world for the community. To become possessed by the gods is, therefore, the primary role of the medium.

As in all initiations into priesthoods throughout Ẹgbádò and Ọhọrí areas, Ògún devotees go through extensive training, which in large part is devoted to preparing them for spirit mediumship. They metaphorically die and are reborn. According to Verger:

> An initiation always begins with a symbolic death and resurrection which marks the novice's break with his past and shows his birth into a new life consecrated to the deity. . . . During the period which separates the day of resurrection from that on which the novice receives a new name, . . . [the novice] seems to lose all reason, he is plunged into a dazed state of mental paralysis; he has forgotten everything, no longer knows how to speak and talks only in unintelligible sounds. The novice in this state is called *Omotun*, new child (1954:337).

Mediums become differentiated in the particular dances, music, and songs attributed to their personal deities and in their performance styles. Throughout Ẹgbado and Ọhọri areas, however, there is consistency in the practice, initiation, and training of mediums, as well as in the broad style of entering trance. The novices' clothes are taken away, their heads are shaved, and they are secluded in a dark shrine, where they must remain quiet and still for some weeks. During this period, the head is bathed regularly in the *àṣẹ* of the deity, made up of an amalgam of leaves, blood of animals, and pulverized minerals (Verger 1954:324 and 1969:n.2, p. 65). Furthermore, the *àṣẹ* of Ògún is rubbed into incisions made in the shaven head. This is thought to fix the power of the deity in the head of the devotee and to stimulate possession

trance. The initiate is now known as *adóṣù*, one who has received the medicine, or *òṣù*, of the god. Later, special hairdos are worn by the newly initiated
to identify them with their particular god and to show that this is a head endowed with power. Finally, the devotee receives a special new name which
suggests Ògún's hold or claim on the initiate, such as Opelajumiedebo,
"The-one-who-kept-late-and-came-speaking-a-new-language," or Omulel'o-
kiti, "The-one-whose deity-carried-her-to-Omolu's-mound (shrine)." Both
names refer to possession trance; the first refers to a ritual language spoken
during trance which reflects the dialect of the Òhọrí Yoruba subgroup from
which this particular Ògún practice spread, and the second refers to the notion that Ògún took charge of or claimed a devotee by carrying her to
Omolu's shrine. The verb here implies that she was "carried" via a trance
state.

In possession trance performance, the left side is stressed to symbolize the
spirit realm. Ògún mediums in Yorubaland carry iron implements in their
hands, often in their left hands.[13] Likewise, the priest of Ẹlẹ́gba, the divine
messenger, carries a cudgel in the left, and the priest of Ṣàngó also carries
in the left a staff representing a neolithic axe of paired thundercelts (M.
Drewal 1986). The left in Yoruba society is used in many other ritual contexts: inside the Ògbóni lodge on special meeting days, Ògbóni members
greet each other and guests with the left hand;[14] when *òjẹ̀* don the Egúngún
masquerade they step into the cloth with the left foot;[15] and deities greet the
community with the left hand, that is, the possessed priest, whose head has
been mounted by the deity, greets the community with the left, as illustrated
in figure 9.1, in which Ògún shakes left hands with a kneeling female.

These contexts of lefthandedness have a common purpose. In every case
they involve spiritual communication. As one devotee put it, "The right is
used by men; the left is used by the gods." Hence, when one enters the
Egúngún cloth to make the Egúngún spirit manifest, one must step in with
the left foot, and when offering a gift or sacrifice to deities one presents it
with the left hand.

The prevalent interpretation in the literature on the Yoruba of the unclean,
antisocial left hand is misleading in that it does not allow us to perceive the
importance of the left for spiritual communication in a ritual context. The
left is reserved for ritual and must not, therefore, be used in ordinary social
discourse. In this way the sacred is kept separate from the profane to protect
the integrity of both worlds at once (Hertz 1973:7); as Yoruba would put it,
the world (*ayé*)—a domain where people reside only temporarily—is ritually
separated from the otherworld (*òrun*), a metaphysical realm of permanent
existence. Seen from this perspective, it is then possible to understand why
the social use of the left is unacceptable and even considered to be deviant
behavior.

Hand-held objects particular to Ògún and carried in the left hand inevitably signal a possession trance context, when the deity mounts the head of his
priests. The priest literally becomes Ògún, and whatever the possessed priest

FIGURE 9.1. Draped in *mariwo*, a priestess possessed by Ògún shakes the left hand of a kneeling woman. Igbogila, Nigeria, 1978.

says and does is taken to be Ògúń's own words and actions. In the left hand, possessed priests carry objects symbolic of the god's powers, the iron blades of Ògúń, the cudgel of Ẹlẹ́gba, the bow and arrow of Ọ̀ṣọ́ọ̀sì, or the thundercelts of Ṣàngó. These power symbols in the left hand signal a visitation from the spirit realm, but at the same time they assert the authority and the responsibility of the medium to be the god's conduit in this world.

In any ritual where iron or iron implements are required, particularly in blood sacrifices performed with iron blades, Ògúń must be dealt with first, for iron itself is Ògúń. It represents Ògúń's vital power, his capacity for quick, forceful, overt action concretized in iron tools and implements of all varieties (cf. H. Drewal, chapter 10). Iron implements are a symbol of Ògúń's worldly accomplishments, whether those accomplishments are destructive or productive, whether they involve the iron cutlasses, arrows, and guns of warfare, automobiles and motorcycles, the blades of circumcision, the hoes of farming, or the adzes and knives of carving. Iron implements and Ògúń get things done quickly and forcefully. That is the nature of their power. Thus, while iron implements carried by the mediums symbolize Ògúń's nature and his dynamic potential, the left hand which wields them speaks of his ability to penetrate the phenomenal world allowing devotees to tap his force.

In western Yorubaland, a religious group whose principal deity is Omolu, an earth deity in charge of contagious diseases, especially smallpox, believes that all deities, including Omolu, have their own Ògúń and their own Ẹlẹ́gba (also known as Èṣù, the trickster). Ẹlẹ́gba is the divine mediator who must receive the first invocations and sacrifices; he is the "god of the crossroads" who makes initial contact with other gods on man's behalf. He personifies the intersection of the world and the otherworld. Ògúń, on the other hand, represents the path itself. He facilitates Ẹlẹ́gba by "clearing the way." Therefore, ceremonies which involve Ògúń often place him first in the ritual order together with Ẹlẹ́gba, the divine mediator.[16] Ẹlẹ́gba and Ògúń work hand in hand. Informants explain that, as the god of iron, Ògúń is first to enter and clear the bush where the shrines of all the other deities are installed (*Ògúń ló ṣàlè f'òrìṣà dó*)—a way of saying that without Ògúń no other deities can be worshipped on earth. He is in front, unyielding and "courageous like the road" (*Anaya pátá bí ọ̀nà*). As an ambitious, courageous warrior he is determined to go first. This is communicated explicitly when, during a procession to the bush, the site of Omolu's shrine on the outskirts of town, the female medium possessed by Ògúń Igbó, "Ògúń of the Bush"—shown in figure 9.1 wearing palm frond vestments—charges to the front of the line intent upon commandeering the group. Consistent with his perceived personality, Ògúń acts quickly, directly, and forcefully. His inclination to rush forth quickens the pace of the entire group. Because Ògúń's courage and tenacity can place the female medium, who is mortal, in great physical danger, attendants continually restrain her from fully asserting Ògúń's prerogatives.

Dancing for Ògun in Western Yorubaland

In Igbogila, an Ẹgbádò community northeast of Ilaro toward Nigeria's western border, a religious group that combines many olórìṣà, literally "owners of deities," performs rituals for those deities every five days (every four days by a Western count).[17] These are essentially danced rituals, the primary object of which is possession trance. Deities represented among the olórìṣà cluster around and symbolize the realm of the bush. In order of their ritual performance, they are Ògun, Eyinlẹ, Ìrokò, Ondo, Omolu, and Ẹlẹgba.[18] Eyinlẹ (Erinlẹ) is a deity associated with streams and hunting; Ìrokò is a bush deity associated with the African teak tree of the same name. Omolu appears to be the dominant deity in this group; he is the god of contagious diseases, particularly smallpox. Not specifically identified with the bush, however, is Ondo, the deified founding forefather of the town of Pobẹ in Benin (R.P.B.).[19]

In the shade of a large tree, the group sets up chairs for its own members and for spectators. The mediums, with shoulders bare and chests bound with cloth, stand side by side to open the ceremony and invoke Ẹlẹgba, by placing their left feet forward (fig. 9.2). Attention is focussed on the spiritual (left) side, since what is to follow is direct communication with the spirit realm. The mediums slowly and repetitively place their left feet forward, returning each time to their starting position with both feet side by side. Turning to face the opposite direction, they repeat the exercise. With this formulaic opening, they then form a circle, dance counterclockwise, invoke each deity in the aforementioned order, and sing his praises (fig. 9.3). The songs, the dances, and the drum rhythms are particular to each god or set of gods. The song determines what the drums play and how the devotees dance.

After a process of honoring and invoking each deity in song and dance, beginning with Ògun, the mediums break out of the circle, and the drums again invoke Ògun. Ògun's mediums gaze downward; their dance movements diminish. A change in attitude occurs, from outgoing and playful to concentrated, serious, and inwardly focussed. As if bound to the spot, the mediums stop moving their feet (fig. 9.4); upper torsos veer to the side; heads drop; and left knees quiver, causing their bodies to tremble. The priests in this state are called "horses of the gods" (ẹṣin òrìṣà). Attendants rush to straighten their cloths and bind their waists and breasts tightly (fig. 9.5), in much the same way a rider saddles a horse, pulling the straps tightly to secure the saddle in place, for Ògun must "mount" (gùn) and ride his medium. At this point, the mediums are fully transformed into the deity. They repeatedly lick their lips in an agitated fashion. Their upper torsos drop, the heads roll back, and eyes roll upward (fig. 9.6). Attendants quickly close the mediums' eyelids and bring their heads forward. The final sign that Ògun is present is signaled when the medium emits a deep guttural yell. It is said that when the god mounts

FIGURE 9.2. With bare shoulders, the mediums stand side by side to open the ceremony, invoking Ẹlẹ́gba by placing their left feet forward. Igbogila, Nigeria, 1978.

FIGURE 9.3. Dancing counterclockwise in a circle, the mediums invoke each deity one by one. Igbogila, Nigeria, 1978.

FIGURE 9.4. As if bound to the spot, the possessed medium entering trance stops moving her feet, and her upper torso and head veer to the side and drop forward. Igbogila, Nigeria, 1978.

FIGURE 9.5. Attendants rush to straighten the cloth of the newly possessed medium and bind it tightly to her waist and breast much in the same way that a rider saddles a horse. Igbogila, Nigeria, 1978.

FIGURE 9.6.   Four mediums become possessed by Ògúṅ simultaneously. The one on the far left is prepared to dance, awaiting a cue from the musicians. Initially their upper torsos drop slightly forward, and their heads often roll back as their eyes roll upward into the sockets (third medium left). An attendant closes the eyelids of the medium second from the left, bringing her head forward.

FIGURE 9.7.   With hands placed on her hips, an iron pincer in her left, a medium possessed by Ògúṅ takes a giant step, leading with the whole left side of her body, as she makes her way to the gathered crowd. Igbogila, Nigeria, 1978.

FIGURE 9.8. A possessed medium greets members of the audience with "*Ẹ kú o!*" Igbogila, Nigeria, 1978.

the medium's head he roots the medium's feet to the earth; thus, attendants release the possessed mediums by slapping or stepping on the tops of their feet. The possessed mediums then take giant steps, leading with the whole left side of their bodies, and make their way to the gathered crowd (fig. 9.7). Hands are placed on the hips, and knees and feet are lifted and extended forward. After greeting the entire assemblage with *"Ẹ kú o!"* (fig. 9.8), the mediums sing, dance, and pray. Ògún in this way directs the drummers.

During the performance, spectators give money to Ògún and the drummers. The amount ranges from several cents to one dollar with an average of about twenty cents. By "spending money" (*níná'wó*) for Ògún, spectators receive special recognition and blessing from him. In a sense they invest in his dynamic power, and in return they receive the benefit of that power.

More than one Ògún priest may be possessed simultaneously (fig. 9.6), but only one comes forth at any given time to sing. An Ògún may step forward to sing, for example:

1   I am afraid of everybody.
2   But if anybody claims to be higher than Ògún,
3   I shall lower him down (Verger 1969:60).

A ceremony's progression is spontaneous in that the mediums decide on the spur of the moment which song to sing, and this in turn determines what the drums play and what dance is performed. Likewise, the mediums determine at what point they will stop a dance and begin a new one.

The Ògún mediums perform several dances, which are rhythmically and visually distinct, and these can be in any order as long as they are appropriate to Ògún. In none of the dances are the mediums' orientations in the dance space predetermined; rather, they tend to scatter themselves and face any direction. Further, they do not relate to each other physically. They dance simultaneously, yet independently.

As noted above, Ògún mediums carry various instruments in their hands to identify the power of their deity. Iron blades of various descriptions evoke Ògún's role as hunter and warrior; miniature flintlock guns suggest similar ideas; miniature iron pincers evoke the work of the blacksmith. In figures 9.9 and 9.10, for example, Ògún mediums (Olóògún) each carry an iron spade in the left hand. In this context, the mediums usually carry a combination of implements in both hands, which are held rather statically, moving only in response to active shoulders. Whatever the particular combination of instruments, one is usually iron. Ògún's presence then is implicit even before the onset of possession trance. The implements speak of Ògún's acts; the dance on the other hand evokes the dynamics required for those acts.

Ògún's dances express the nature of his vital force. In all of them, the head is calm; in contrast, the shoulders are active, especially the shoulder blades or scapulae, which are repetitively raised and lowered, a special characteristic of Ọ̀họrí style dancing.[20] Known as èjìká, a term which refers both to the shoulders and the movement associated with the shoulder blades, these gestures have an amazing range of dynamic possibilities, from gentle and subtle to forceful and exaggerated, and from fluid and smooth to sharp and angular (fig. 9.9). As performed by Ògún, however, they are distinctly forceful, quick, sharp, and exaggerated, in keeping with his explosive manner. The èjìká of the thundergod Ṣàngó is performed similarly to convey similar attributes of power (M. Drewal 1986). Knees are flexed, and torsos are pitched forward from the hips at approximately a 45 degree angle. From this position, and with active shoulders, a number of different stepping patterns and rhythms are performed. These patterns are fairly short, often in counts of four, and repetitive.

Ògún's dances range from extremely rapid to moderately paced. The most moderate of them conveys a stalking dynamic. Its overall quality can be characterized as cautious, that is, a combination of hesitancy and determination. The movement bursts forth with a quick, strong step, and is then held back, restrained for an instant before it bursts forth again; a third step exhibits an even more sustained movement with a final large burst of energy that ends in a crouching position, again held (fig. 9.10). The medium steps on one foot and places the other slightly to the back side in a wide stance, pausing for an instant in a very deliberate fashion. Stepping then on the other side, she repeats the pattern. On the third step, instead of placing the foot, she slides it past the other; it skims the ground, then goes out and around so that the medium changes direction toward the sliding foot. The slide is suspended and, at the last possible moment, in time to the music, the medium lunges forward in a slight crouch onto the other foot. This position is held again in a long pause to give it emphasis. Thus the medium steps: &1 hold, &2 hold, &3_slide 4 hold, and so on. The implements carried by the mediums are held motionless in front of the torso. While there is a clear emphasis on pauses and sustained movements, these are interspersed with strong bursts of energy which are sudden and emphatic that ultimately evoke an overall dynamic of stalking.

Another of Ògún's dances uses similar elements to produce slightly different qualities and rhythm. It, too, has a stalking dynamic. But this time the medium takes three long, low strides at a pressing pace and then with a catch step either continues in the same path or changes direction; thus, stepping 1 2 3&4; 1 2 3&4. With each step, the scapulae jump forcefully outward and upward and then plunge emphatically in again, thus double-timing the feet. The forcefulness and directness of this dance give it a feeling of determination. No matter which way Ògún travels, he does so with a sense of pressing urgency and self-confidence.

In both dances, Ògún is forceful. In the first, restraint combined with bursts of energy evokes both force and quietude and conveys a sense of caution.

FIGURE 9.9. Back view of a medium possessed by Ògúń, carrying an iron blade in her left hand. Her shoulder blades pop out forcefully in rhythm to the lead drum. Igbogila, Nigeria, 1978.

FIGURE 9.10. Carrying iron blades in the left and a carved miniature dane gun in the right, "Ògúń" (foreground) bursts forth in a crouching position—held for an instant in a very deliberate fashion—in a step that evokes stalking. Igbogila, Nigeria, 1978.

In the second, he is the epitome of Ògún as a driving force. Pursuing a direct path quickly with long, low strides, he is "courageous like the road," as his praise name recalls.

A third and final dance, the *àgèrè*, can be performed both for Ògún and for Eyinlè, who is also found widely throughout Yorubaland.[21] The name refers at once to the dance and to a traditional hunter's drum (Abraham 1958:30), even though any one of a number of different drums can play the *àgèrè* rhythm and accompany the dance. *Àgèrè* can be performed anytime either Ògún or Eyinlè is honored. For example, it can be performed by the hunter/warrior association during rituals at the shrine of Ògún Ilu, also known as Ògún Àjobò, that is, the Ògún for the Town, or the Ògún Everybody Worships Together;[22] by priests of other deities, like Sàngó, during rituals in which Eyinlè is invoked; and by certain masquerades known as Eléyinlè (Owners of Eyinlè), who dance during Egúngún "performances of miracles" (*ap'idán*) (cf. Drewal and Drewal 1978:34–35, pl. 15). While the first two dances are fairly localized within western Yoruba groups influenced by the Ohóri, the *àgèrè* Ògún appears to be more widespread, often associated with Oyo-derived institutions, although this may be the result of a historical melding of traditions from different regions.

The *àgèrè* has a quality distinct from the others. Its rhythm is rolling: one foot essentially remains in place while alternately the other foot shifts backward and forward and backward and forward—each time assuming full body weight. After the second forward step, the moving leg then becomes the stationary one so that the sequence is repeated on the other side. If the dance progresses at all, it does not travel far. This dance in different contexts is performed with varying degrees of energy. Female caretakers of Eyinlè shrines, who are not necessarily mediums, dance it very gently with small, easy steps, whereas Ògún mediums in possession trance perform it powerfully with large leg gestures so that, instead of a rolling feeling, it jumps. Quickness and forcefulness in combination once again speak of Ògún's innate power.

As mediums begin to tire from being "ridden" by Ògún, an attendant stretches out their arms over their heads (fig. 9.11). When Ògún finally leaves the female medium's head, he withdraws suddenly. Her body tenses all over (fig. 9.12) and, if near a spectator, she grabs hold tightly. Attendants must be ready to catch the medium and help her to the sidelines to be seated, or the medium will have a difficult time coming out of the trance state. With the attendants' aid, the medium leaves the performance space, and a number of measures are taken to clear her head and return her to normalcy. Attendants pour gin over the medium's head and rub it in to revive and alert the inner head; they blow into the ears and onto the top of the head (fig. 9.13), press the base of the neck, press their foreheads against the medium's forehead, stretch the medium's arms upward and then place them on the knees, and pull the legs forward by the big toes, all the while calling the medium's special name bestowed at initiation.

The medium revives as if from a deep sleep and sits quietly gazing into space.

Dancing for Ògúń in Bahia[23]

In Bahia, initiates of Candomblé go through a ritual death and rebirth (Herskovits and Herskovits 1942a:10 and 1942b:273). They are secluded for three to twelve months; their clothes are taken away, never to be worn again, and their heads are shaved (Pierson 1942:286–87); they are innoculated on their heads with sacred cuts to infuse them with the vital force of their deity (Herskovits 1943:501); the head is further washed regularly in a solution of leaves and other natural ingredients to attract and stimulate the vital force of the deity (Verger 1955); and the initiates are given new names (Herskovits 1943:501; Verger 1954:337). During this time, the devotees learn, among other things, the songs and dances of their particular deity. This spiritual re-treat serves to dedicate the devotees to their deities and to prepare them for receiving the vital force of their god through possession trance (Omari 1984:23) (fig. 9.14).

Among the Ketu and Nago Candomblé houses, danced ceremonies known as *obrigação* begin publicly as the "daughters of the gods" enter the *barração*, the ceremonial house, accompanied musically by the drummers.[24] Holding their two fists together in a manner in which one holds a horse's reigns while riding, the daughters enter single file to a rapid cadence with small cantorlike steps, the *mae de santo* (literally, "mother of the saint," the female head of Candomblé) in the lead.[25] The entrance is said to represent a horse and to serve the purpose of dispatching Exu, god of the crossroads, for Exu is "a messenger boy" (*menino de recado*) between men and the gods. The horse is a symbol of mediation, a symbol which recurs in possession trance when the mediums are said to be literally the "horses" of the gods.

With tiny, quick steps, the devotees circle counterclockwise and, as the *mae de santo* reaches the spot closest to the front door, she raises her arms toward it and, crossing her two index fingers at a right angle, makes the sign of the crossroads, the metaphorical intersection between the world and the spirit realm. Twice more, she steps back, whirls around quickly, and gestures toward the door, crossing her index fingers to open the ritual, that is, to mark the time and place to begin spiritual communication.

When the devotees have formed their circle, they invoke the gods with three chants each, beginning with Ogun. This segment of the ritual is known as a *xire,* the same as the Yoruba word *şiré,* indicating "a play" or "an enter-tainment" for the gods, for it is the purpose of this portion of the ceremony to coax the gods from their otherworldly domain into the phenomenal world. The *mae de santo* sings in Yoruba, *A xire Ogun o! A xire Ogun!* "We play for Ogun oh! We play for Ogun!" The devotees join in the chant and dance. Led by the *mae de santo* and accompanied by the drums, the devotees honor

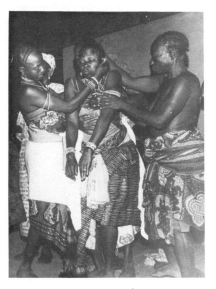

FIGURE 9.11. As a medium begins to tire from being "ridden" by Ògun, an attendant stretches her arms and torso. The medium carries iron pincers. Woman in background, left, carries iron gongs and Ògun sword. Ẹgua, Nigeria, 1978.

FIGURE 9.12. When Ògun finally leaves the head of the medium, he withdraws suddenly. Her body tenses all over as attendants hold her tightly. Igbogila, Nigeria, 1978.

FIGURE 9.13. A man leans over to blow on top of an Ògun medium's head to clear it as attendants support her. Igbogila, Nigeria, 1978.

FIGURE 9.14. The "coming out" (*saida*) of a newly initiated medium. Ipitanga, Bahia, Brazil, 1974.

and invoke the gods one by one.[26] After Ogun comes Oxossi, god of the hunt; Osanyin, god of herbalism; Omolu, god of disease; Nana, goddess of deep water; Oxumare, goddess of the rainbow; Yewa, goddess of water; Yemanja, goddess of the salt water; Oxun, goddess of fresh surface water; Yansan, goddess of wind and war; Xango, god of thunder and lightning; and Oxala, god of creativity.

When the devotees have finished invoking the gods, the *mae de santo* starts again and this time the devotees begin to fall into a trance. They kick off their shoes, and they begin to quiver. Their upper torsos and heads drop forward, and their chests rock back and forth rapidly in short, sharp motions. Sometimes a devotee may become instantly possessed, as if suddenly struck with the full force of the deity. This is visibly communicated by an unexpected burst of energy from the devotee which seems to thrust her out into space, body rigid, and which sends attendants scrambling to keep her from falling or landing on other participants. Attendants adjust the possessed's cloth by tying it tightly around her breasts, in the case of female deities like Yansan, Oxun, and Yemanja, or, in the case of males, either over the left shoulder or over both shoulders, crisscrossing on the chest (Omari 1984:22); they also assist the "horses" until they have regained control and are transformed into the deity. Fully possessed, the mediums prostrate themselves before the drummers and the *mae de santo* and, as the manifestation of the deity, greet the spectators. In trance the possessed mediums stand with hands either on their hips or folded behind their backs. After dancing to a song associated with the deity, the possessed mediums are led out of the dance enclosure. The particular god honored at any given ceremony determines which other gods will "visit"; thus, if Xango is honored, his wives—Oxun and Yansan— are likely to visit and, if Omolu is honored, chances are his mother, Nana, will make an appearance.[27]

A break in the ceremony occurs while attendants prepare the mediums in the clothes of the deities. When ready, the deities form a single line led by the *mae de santo*. In the ceremonies in which Ogun visits, he always comes first. A slow processional song is played by the drummers as the *mae de santo* sings,

Ago, ago l'ona.

Make way, clear the way.

The line of deities enters slowly. As the Herskovits's (1942b:277) recall, "First comes the god of war, in green, wearing as a male deity, lace-edged pantalettes, a short wide skirt over them, dagger in hand, a sash about the waist tied in a wide bow, a brilliant cap as of a prince in an Arabian Nights tale."

The dances which characterize Ogun, in contrast to those performed in western Yorubaland, are mimetic. They act out in a stylized way Ogun fighting with his cutlass. Crucial to this mime, however, are the dynamics of

Ogun's actions, and indeed this is what seems to capture the imagination of observers. Thus:

> The outward manifestations of the ecstasy of the children of Ogun, god of war, are much more forceful than those of the children of Oxun, goddess of fresh water. The former have something of the brutality of armies in battle, some of the hardness of steel, while the latter have a liquid, amorous quality— the fascinating sensuality of lazy rivers or still lakes sprinkled with sunlight. (Bastide 1978:377)

Whether or not Ogun carries a scythe or a sword:

> He brandishes it with eyes closed, slashing about wildly on all sides in his dancing. Sometimes, in a thrilling mock duel, he will fence with an agile devotee who has nothing but her bare arms to use as weapons. Such a brave daughter will be rescued from him, just in time to prevent injury, by being drawn away from the fray by several alert *ekedes* [assistants]. (Leahy 1955:9)

This dance, reflecting the nature of Ogun's vital power, is quick and direct with an explosive thrust.[28] As Ogun, the medium slashes, but does not do so "wildly on all sides." Inclining his body toward a diagonal, he takes two large steps, closes his feet to change to the opposite diagonal, and repeats the pattern in the opposite direction. While his stepping carries him back and forth diagonally forward, his bent arms, which carry metal blades (*espada*), slash powerfully in opposition up and down in the direction of the diagonally inclined torso and in time to the quick paces of his feet. As one *mae de santo* (Olga do Alaketu, 1974) explained: "He eats raw [food] and doesn't throw anything away; he kills, eats, and doesn't throw anything away, doesn't repent for what he has done" (*Ele come cru e não lança; ele mata, come e não lança, não se arrepende do que faz*).[29] Ogun moves between the seated audience and the drums, and, when reaching one or the other, spins around forcefully and returns in the opposite direction. Olga do Alaketu called this dance *pada Ogun* (1974), perhaps "Ògún's return" (Abraham 1958:539).

There is a popular story in Yorubaland about how Ogun sank into the ground alive leaving a long chain emanating from the spot and instructing his people that, if they ever needed him to defend them, they should pull on the chain that he left anchored in the earth. To test Ogun's allegiance, one day a citizen tugged on the chain, and Ogun came out slashing with his cutlass, in the process decapitating his own townspeople. Realizing what he had done, he vowed never to return. The *pada* Ogun of Brazil may relate to this well-known Yoruba motif of Ogun's absolute aggression, for it is said to represent gestures of war (*gestos dos guerreiras*).

Another of Ogun's mimes is similar to dances for other "hot" or dueling deities, such as Xango and Oxossi, called *ecu* (Pierson 1942:304). Two people face each other: two Oguns, or Ogun and another "hot" deity or other participant. Slightly shifting the right foot backward in four counts while pivoting on the left, and then repeating on the other side, each dancer prepares for a mock duel. Then, the dancers shift their bodies slightly from side to side alternately kicking the feet backward. All the while facing each other, they thrust their cutlasses, carried in the right hand, back and forth laterally, cutting across the left wrist in a rapid cadence in time to the music.

Sometimes the preparatory steps described above can be used to lower the knees to the ground to a seated position. From that position, sitting on their knees, the dancers move their torsos in a circular direction so that, at its farthest extent backward, they are practically lying horizontally on the ground. After circling one way and then the other, the dancers slowly work their way back to a full standing position in the same fashion as they descended. Such dances express Ogun's identity as a warrior.

It is perhaps significant in the Brazilian context, where the Yoruba language is no longer well understood, that the dances are mimetic, representing Ogun in a literal way. With the possible exception of a few elders, devotees are unable to give translations of Yoruba-derived songs; rather, they prefer to explain the dances which accompany the songs (M. and F. Herskovits 1942a:12; Binon 1967:165). In the Bahian context, where the oral liturgy is only vaguely understood by its users, dance can define and characterize the deity in a more precise way than the oral texts. Thus in addition to stressing *how* Ogun operates, that is, his dynamic qualities, the dances in Bahia become more literal by miming precisely *what* Ogun does.

Bastide felt that "Ogun's persona as a brutal and aggressive warrior and beheader . . . won out" over that of hunter, blacksmith, or farmer in Brazil, where he has become more widely known as the patron deity of slave revolt (1978:254). Indeed, warrior plays and dances are traditionally popular in Brazil, where they have become odd mixtures of elements from the *cucumbys*, the *congos*, and the *quilombo*—mystery plays patterned after the Portuguese *autos* (Portuguese mystery plays)—which usually depicted battles between two opposing groups (Ramos 1939:111). An 1888 illustration (fig. 9.15) in a book by Mello Moraes Filho shows a group of Os Congos performing a war dance which appears to be quite similar to the mock battle in which Ogun mediums engage. Moraes Filho states,

> In transit, following a religious litter, a struggle ensues between the two lines of blacks, that were in dispute, defending themselves, ...
> And, fighting each other with iron swords, making complete turns and cadencing the flanks, the *Congos* advancing in procession, singing, in heat of battle, in bitterly contested combat:
>
> *Fire on the earth,*
> *Fire in the sea,*
> *That our queen*
> *Us has to help!* . . .
> (Moraes Filho 1888:95)

FIGURE 9.15. A nineteenth-century illustration shows
Brazilian Os Congos dancers performing a war dance
similar to the mock battles staged by Ogun mediums.
Adapted from Mello Moraes Filho (1888).

As in performances of the *congos* and *quilombos*, Ogun engages in mock combat in which two people face each other wielding swords. Ogun dances, as well as *quilombos* performances, symbolize slave revolt (Ramos 1939:110; Bastide 1978:254). Since these mystery plays tended to be mimetic and preceded the Candomblé by nearly a century, it is quite possible that Os Congos, *cucumbys*, and/or *quilombo* war dances were appropriately grafted onto the Yoruba war deity Ogun.[30] Further evidence for this suggestion lies in the Portuguese-inspired costumes worn by the possessed mediums. Like the older Os Congos' costumes, the vestments of Ogun, as well as other male deities, consist of a long tunic, belted by a wide sash, over full-legged pantalettes.

By the same token, the *àgèrè* dance, which is associated with hunters and is performed to honor Ògúń and Eyinlè in Yorubaland, appears to have been incorporated into the repertoire of dances for hunting deities Oxossi and Yansan in Bahia. In Bahia, Inle (Eyinlè) represents an aspect or quality of Oxossi (*qualidade*).[31] Thus, as Bastide (1978:254) suggests, Ogun's persona as hunter seems to have dropped out in favor of his persona as warrior, or rather seems to have been usurped by Oxossi, who in Yorubaland is also traditionally a hunting deity.

Ògúń in Western Yorubaland and Brazil: A Comparison

There are marked similarities between ritual performances for Ògúń in Igbogila, Nigeria, and in Bahia, Brazil. Like those in Igbogila, cult groups or Candomblés in Bahia honor diverse Yoruba deities collectively during a single ceremony. The rites of initiation are similar too, including symbolic death and rebirth, seclusion, and practices of taking away the clothes, bestowing new names, shaving and bathing the head, and embedding medicines to stimulate possession trance. After honoring Ẹlẹ́gba, both groups dance in a counterclockwise circle to invoke each of the deities in sequence with a minimum of three songs each. In addition to Ẹlẹ́gba, other deities represented in the cult group of Igbogila which are also found in Bahia are Iroko, Omolu, and of course Ògúń. Inle, the Bahian version of the Yoruba deity Eyinlè, is considered a manifestation of Oxossi—both are associated with hunting. In Yorubaland and in the more traditional cult houses of Bahia, Ògúń is always invoked first after Ẹlẹ́gba, and explanations for his coming first are much the same: he "opens the way."

Devotees of Ògúń in both places carry instruments symbolically associated with the deity. The sword is more common in Brazil, but in Nigeria Ògúń mediums also carry iron pincers, spades, flywhisks, or miniature guns. Although Ògúń is acknowledged in Brazil to be the god of iron, the cutlasses carried by the possessed mediums are made of laminated chrome, as are many of the ritual instruments of Candomblé which require metal. Emphasis on the left in the context of possession trance is not as evident in Brazil as in Yorubaland. Yet, Pierson (1942:289) notes that, when a deity wishes to take leave of the ceremony, he clasps left hands with another participant tightly.

The style of the onset of possession trance is quite similar, including the practice of greeting members of the audience individually, keeping the hands on the hips, and exaggerated stepping. In Brazil as in western Yorubaland the possessed devotees are called the horses of the gods.

A further comparison may be made in the marked distinction between dance which serves to invoke spiritual forces and dance which follows the invocation and represents the materialized force itself. Both in Yoruba country and in Brazil the distinction is made in terms of dynamics. In Bahia, when devotees invoke the deities at the beginning of the performance, gestures are minimalized. Rather than portraying the deities fully, they merely give an indication of the movements which represent them. Thus Ògún's large, forceful movements are reduced to small, vague, effortless gestures. In a subtle way, index fingers that serve as cutlasses offer a gross understatement of underlying warlike intent. This minimalization of movement conserves energy for the long service which culminates in possession trance, when the deities are given full expression. For as the horses of the deities, the devotees are ridden hard. Nonetheless, the marked difference between dances performed as invocations and as actual possession serves to concentrate energy in the part of the dance which actualizes the deity.

The important point here is that the dances, however understated, were nevertheless performed. Like liturgical texts, the import of which is not always fully understood by listeners, their significance lies in their actual performance. Whether or not the dances are literally understood, the performance is thought to carry power. What is vital, then, is the actual effort—the verbal and kinetic exertions which, when minimally stated, invoke metaphysical forces but, when fully asserted, activate and even embody those forces. Both in Brazil and in western Yorubaland, the dances which manifest Ògún indeed reinforce the verbal images of him in myths and praise poetry. They show him to exert explosive force—powerful, quick, and direct.

Conclusions

Because dance and oral performance express, and are even thought to conduct, spiritual force, an analysis of the use of dynamics in ritual is essential to our understanding of the total religious framework of the Yoruba; it allows us to perceive the gods as power personified, each embodying a particular locus of dynamic qualities which remain coherent and consistent no matter the context. By focussing on *how* deities act (the qualities of their actions) as distinguished from *what* they do (the acts themselves) it is possible to resolve apparent contradictions in their personalities. We can go beyond the creative/destructive dichotomy and examine the wellspring of power that underlies both creation and destruction: Ògún's *àṣẹ*. The dynamic configurations expressed in Ògún's dances and verbal arts serve as models of and for humans so that, as Bartenieff (1980) puts it, they may cope with the environment. Through ritual performance, people tap and use power that is appropriate for meeting life's demands.

NOTES

1. The data for this paper were gathered during fieldwork in Nigeria in 1975, 1977–78, and 1982 and in Bahia, Brazil, during the summer of 1974. The 1982 research trip was sponsored by the National Endowment for the Humanities (RO-20072–81–2184). I wish to thank in particular the *Olóriṣà* of Igbogila, Nigeria, for welcoming me at their rituals. I am also indebted to Joçelina Françisca Barbosa of Ile Olga do Alaketu, Matatu, Salvador, for teaching me the Candomblé dances for the deities, and Olga do Alaketu and Antonio Agnelo Pereira, Elemaso, Ile Caşa Branca, Salvador, for discussing Candomblé ritual and dance with me. Special thanks also go to Juana and Didi dos Santos and to Pierre Verger for many courtesies during my stay in Bahia. I also wish to thank Rowland Abiodun for reading and commenting on this paper and Henry John Drewal, who assisted in all phases of this project.

2. In Yoruba thought, the phenomenal world is *ayé*, usually translated simply as world. *Ayé* is a domain where people reside temporarily. In addition it includes a number of spirits who can become manifest in human or animal form. The realm of the gods and ancestors is known as *ọrun,* a permanent otherworldly reality. The relationship of *ayé* to *ọrun* is expressed in the proverb "The world is a market, the otherworld is home" (*Ayé l'ọjà, ọrun n'ilé*).

3. Egúngún refers to masquerades which honor the ancestors in Yorubaland and also to the society which produces them. Cloaked in cloth and embellished with other items such as carved masks, bones of animals, or feathers, they are thought to be spirits manifest in the world (*ayé*).

4. *Kùtùkùtù* means "early in the morning" and, in this context, also evokes the quality of the rain. It conveys the dynamic of just beginning something; it implies an initiating action which has not yet reached its full potential (personal communication, Rowland Abiodun, 1982).

5. Rudolph Laban's theories of effort are based on similar kinds of observations. Thus, "the weighty power of a rock with its visible potential for impact speaks of the tremendous impetus with which it might plunge into the valley as an avalanche. The grace of a plant speaks of the readiness to move which drives a flower out of its stem from which fruit and new seed will sprout. . . . Animal movement speaks of the fine adaptations with which a particular species has immersed itself into its surroundings to fit increasingly finer, more differentially into the workings of nature" (Laban cited in Bartinieff 1980:1).

6. For the most elaborate discussions of *àṣẹ*, see Verger (1964), dos Santos (1976), and M. and H. Drewal (1987).

7. For a discussion of behavior as it relates to concepts of inner power, see H. Drewal (1977).

8. Informants say this snake is the Black Mamba; however, Abraham (1958:153) points out that "the Spitting Cobra (Blacknecked Cobra) is often wrongly called the

Black Mamba." Indeed, salmon-pink and black cross-bars, according to Abraham, usually alternate on the underpart of the Spitting Cobra's neck and front part of its body.

9. Utterances express attitudes toward time, space, weight, and flow audibly through the combination of: 1) speed of sounds or syllables, 2) their degree of directness—whether they are voiced in a straightforward manner or are gliding, 3) their vocal force or thrust, and 4) their flow—whether the stream of energy is free-flowing or bound, held back, or restrained.

10. In analyzing movement and its corollary oral expression, I follow Laban and Lawrence, who identified four factors which, in varying degrees, combine to produce effort or dynamic qualities: exertion (from light to strong), control (from fluent to bound), time (from slow to quick), and space (indirect or direct). In the authors' view: "A person's efforts are visibly expressed in the rhythms of his bodily motion. It thus becomes necessary to study these rhythms, and to extract from them those elements which will help us to compile a systematic survey of the forms effort can take in human action" (1947:xi).

11. However, I have followed the practice of the Department of African Languages and Literatures at Ọbafemi Awolowo University (see, for example, Oyelaran 1976–77).

12. Candomblés are Afro-Brazilian cult groups organized for the worship of African deities, primarily those of the Yoruba (see Omari 1984).

13. The right hand sometimes carries percussion instruments shaken initially to invoke the god and ultimately to pronounce àṣẹ, àṣẹ, àṣẹ, "so be it," in response to prayers. As one participant in traditional Yoruba religion noted, "When townspeople hear the bells and gongs of the priest performing ceremonies inside his shrine, they will be saying in their homes as they are working, 'àṣẹ, àṣẹ, àṣẹ' to accompany the ringing in support of whatever the priest is saying." Lending efficacy to prayers and invocations, the sound of the bells helps to induce possession trance and later in the ceremony to enforce the words of the gods, spoken through the mediumship of the priest.

14. Ògbóni is a society of elders which functions as a governing body together with the king. For more information on Ògbóni, see Morton-Williams (1960) and H. Drewal (in press).

15. Òjẹ̀ is the name given to members of the Egúngún society.

16. This holds true in the United States among practitioners of Yoruba religion who were originally trained by Cubans (Edwards and Mason 1985:iii). Thus, at sacred ritual parties (bembe) for Yoruba deities in the New York metropolitan area, drummers begin by saluting Ẹlẹ́gba first and then Òguṅ. For an American practitioner's perspective on Òguṅ, see Edwards and Mason's booklet (1985:16–20), written primarily for English-speaking initiates of Yoruba religion.

17. The cult is found in an Ègbádò town, but it originated among the Ọ̀họrí Yoruba. Thus devotees sing and pray in the Ọ̀họrí dialect. The Ọ̀họrí Yoruba live on the border between Nigeria and Benin (R.P.B.) in the area of the Kumi swamp. Because of their relative inaccessibility during the rainy season, they are considered by their neighbors to be among the most conservative Yoruba. Their dialect is quite distinct. The members of this cult group indicate that their practices had earlier roots among the Gùn (Ègùn), an Àjà-speaking people of southern Benin (R.P.B.). The deity Omolu is said to have come from Gun country and, indeed, one of Omolu's dances is called ègùn Omolú, meaning the Omolu of the Ègùn people, who, according to cult members, are from Àjàṣẹ́ (Porto Novo).

18. Although Òguṅ is the dominant deity in this cult group, any medium can join, and thus conceivably any deity can be included. Other deities represented within the

group are Ṣàngó and Ọya, whose priests are no longer possessed, because they have grown too old and feeble to perform.

19. For another ceremony which features the deity Ondo, see M. Drewal (1975).

20. Western physicians refer to this movement as "winging of the scapulae," which implies a neurological disorder and a lack of control. However, these movements performed in western Yorubaland, quite to the contrary, are superbly controlled. Not only can they be performed with a wide range of dynamics, but they also can be intentionally varied rhythmically.

21. For more details on the deity Eyinlè (Erinlè), see Thompson (1969) and Babalọla (chapter 7).

22. One of the association's titleholders, Aṣípa, holds a position on the king's council of chiefs. The society was probably at its peak during the nineteenth century, when during the Yoruba civil wars hunters became warriors to defend the town.

23. The analysis of Candomblé dance comes from observations of 14 ceremonies in 6 different houses during 1974. For consistency, the English spelling of Ògún is used throughout, without tone marks.

24. *Obrigação* are analogous to *bembe* in the Cuban Lucumi, or Santeria, tradition, which are now held in the United States by Hispanic peoples as well as both black and white Americans.

25. Saint here is a euphemism for an African deity. In Brazil, Catholic saints have been syncretized with African deities. To a large extent, this occurred to mask Candomblé during a time of religious repression (Omari 1984:14).

26. For a discussion of the role of the drums and drummers in Candomblé, see Herskovits (1944).

27. This is also the case in Afro-American *bembe*, sacred parties held for the Yoruba deities.

28. Tempo is one of the factors that make up dynamic qualities thereby helping to characterize the vital force of deities. Behague notes in his examinations of Candomblé songs that "the idiosyncrasies attributed to a given orixa (whether young or old, temperamental or peaceful, and so on) influence the tempo of such songs" (1975:75). As in the Old World, the song determines the drum music, which in turn sets the pace of the dances.

29. Lépine (1981:23) presents some personality traits that are common to Ogun mediums, suggesting at the same time that after initiation they become more like the deity. It seems clear that one's personal deity licenses the expression of certain distinctive personality traits associated with that deity. And dance is one of the mechanisms through which Ogun power is expressed and felt.

30. According to Pereira da Costa (cited in Ramos 1939:106), the earliest documented date of a Congos or Cucumbys is June 24, 1706. This is found in a document belonging to a religious association in the town of Iguarassu in Pernambuco; whereas, Carneiro (1954:48) calculates a date of circa 1830 as the foundation of Candomblé. Furthermore, Ramos says of the *quilombos* of Palmares, formerly a community of runaway slaves who banned together in collective resistance, that their plays recall "the opposing camps, the dances, chants, struggles ending in capture, intrigues and trickery and finally the siege of the Negro position and with its fall, the reenslavement. . . . When the queen is introduced into the plot, there seems to be a close relationship between these plays which I have called *quilombos* and the Congo plays" (1939:110). Moreover, in a revised reprint of Moraes Filho's 1888 work, Câmara Cascudo observes (1979:72, n.28) that the performance of Os Congos is very similar in detail to that of "os 'Mouriscos'" (Moors) associated with processions on São João's Day in Portugal. Such warrior dances involving battles with swords as part of Catholic processions, he suggests, can be traced to fifteenth-century Europe.

31. These shifts in emphasis and fusions in Brazil reflect the need to systematize deities from diverse locations in Yorubaland who have similar attributes in order to show how they actually are integral parts of one unified system.

REFERENCES CITED

Abraham, R. C. 1958. *Dictionary of Modern Yoruba*, London: University of London Press.

Ayoade, J. A. A. 1979. "The Concept of Inner Essence in Yoruba Traditional Medicine," in *African Therapeutic Systems*. Z. A. Ademuwagun, J. A. A. Ayoade, I. E. Harrison, and D. M. Warren (eds.), Waltham, Mass.: Crossroads Press, pp. 49–55.

Babalọla, S. A. 1966. *The Content and Form of Yoruba Ìjálá*, London: Oxford University Press.

Barnes, Sandra T. 1980. *Ogun: An Old God for a New Age*, Philadelphia: ISHI.

Bartenieff, Irmgard, with D. Lewis. 1980. *Body Movement: Coping With the Environment*, N.Y.: Gordon and Breach, Science Publishers, Inc.

Bastide, Roger. 1978. *The African Religions of Brazil: Toward a Sociology of the Interpenetration of Civilizations* (Helen Sebba, trans.), Baltimore: The Johns Hopkins University Press.

Behague, Gerhard H. 1975. "Notes on Regional and National Trends in Afro-Brazilian Cult Music," in *Tradition and Renewal: Essays on 20th-Century Latin American Literature and Culture*. M. H. Forster (ed.), Urbana: University of Illinois Press, pp. 68–80.

Beier, Ulli. 1970. *Yoruba Poetry*, Cambridge: Cambridge University Press.

Binon, Giselle. 1967. "La Musique dans le Candomblé," in *La Musique dan la Vie*, Tome 1. T. Nikiprowetzky (ed.), Paris: pp. 159–207.

Carneiro, Edison. 1954. *Candomblés da Bahia*, Rio de Janeiro: Editorial Andes (2nd ed. revd.).

Crowther, Samuel. 1852. *A Vocabulary of the Yoruba Language*, London: Seeleys.

do Alaketu, Olga, Mae de Santo. 1974. Interview, Matatu, Salvador, Bahia, August 17.

dos Santos, Juana E. 1976. *Os Nago e a Morte: Pade, Asese e o Culto Egun na Bahia*, Petropolis: Editora Vozes.

Drewal, Henry J. 1974. "Efe: Voiced Power and Pageantry," *African Arts* 7(2):26–29, 58–66.

———. 1977. "Art and the Perception of Women in Yoruba Culture," *Cahiers d'Etudes Africaines* 68(37–4):545–67.

———. In press. "Meaning in Oshugbo Art among Ijebu Yoruba," in *Festschrift*, Ethnologisches Seminar, B. Engelbrecht and R. Gardi, (eds.), Basel: Universität Basel.

Drewal, Henry J., and Margaret T. 1983. *Gẹlẹdẹ: Art and Female Power among the Yoruba*, Bloomington: Indiana University Press.

Drewal, Margaret T. 1975. "Symbols of Possession: A Study of Movement and Regalia in an Anago-Yoruba Ceremony," *Dance Research Journal* 7(2):15–24.

———. 1986. "Art and Trance among Yoruba Shango Devotees," *African Arts* 20(1):60–67, 98–99.

Drewal, Margaret T., and Henry J. 1978. "More Powerful Than Each Other: An Egbado Classification of Egungun," *African Arts* 11(3):28–39, 98–99.

———. 1987. "Composing Time and Space in Yoruba Art," *Word and Image* 3, 4.

Edwards, Gary, and John Mason. 1985. *Black Gods—Orişa Studies in the New World*, Brooklyn: Yoruba Theological Archministry.

Herskovits, Melville J. 1943. "The Southernmost Outpost of New World Africanisms," *American Anthropologist* 45(4):495–510.

———. 1944. "Drums and Drummers in Afro-Brazilian Cult Life," *The Musical Quarterly* 30(4):477–92.

Herskovits, Melville, and Francis Herskovits. 1942a. "Afro-Bahian Religious Songs," (Album XIII Notes), *Folk Music of Brazil* issued from the Collections of the Archive of American Folk Song, Library of Congress Music Division.

———. 1942b. "The Negros of Brazil," *The Yale Review* 32(2):263–79.

Hertz, R. 1973. "The Pre-eminence of the Right Hand: A Study in Religious Polarity," in *Right and Left: Essays on Dual Symbolic Classification*, R. Needham (ed.), Chicago: University of Chicago Press, pp. 3–31.

Laban, Rudolph, and F. C. Lawrence. 1947. *Effort*, London: Macdonald & Evans.

Langer, Suzanne K. 1953. *Feeling and Form: A Theory of Art*, New York: Charles Scribner's and Sons.

Leahy, J. G. 1955. "The Presence of the Gods among the Mortals: The Candomblé Dances," *Brazil* 29(4):4–11.

Lépine, Claude. 1981. "Os Estereótipos da Personalidade no Candomblé *Nàgó*," in *Olóòrìşà: Escritos sobre a religião dos orixás*, C. E. M. de Moura (coordinator and trans.), São Paulo: Editora ÁGORA, pp. 11–31.

Moraes Filho, Mello. 1888. *Festas e Tradições Populares do Brasil*. Rio de Janeiro: H. Garnier. [Reprinted in 1979 with preface by Silvio Romero and revisions and notes by Luís da Câmara Cascudo. São Paulo: Editora da Universidade de São Paulo and Livraria Itatiaia Editora.]

Morton-Williams, Peter. 1960. "The Yoruba Ogboni Cult in Oyo," *Africa* 30:362–74.

Olúpǫnà, A., Aşǫgún. 1975. Interview, Ibaiyun, November 13.

Omari, Mikelle Smith. 1984. *From the Inside to the Outside: The Art and Ritual of Bahian Candomblé*, Monograph Series, no. 24, Los Angeles: Museum of Cultural History, UCLA.

Oşitola, Kolawole, Babaláwo. 1982. Interview, Ìjèbu-Òde, July.

Oyelaran, Ọlasope O. 1976–77. *Seminar Series*, no. 1 (2 vols.), Ifę: Department of African Languages and Literatures, University of Ifę.

Peek, Philip M. 1981. "The Power of Words in African Verbal Arts," *Journal of American Folklore* 94(371):19–43.

Pierson, Donald. 1942. *Negroes in Brazil: A Study of Race Contact at Bahia*, Chicago: University of Chicago Press.

Prince, Raymond. 1960. "Curse, Invocation and Mental Health among the Yoruba," *Canadian Psychiatric Association Journal* 5:65–79.

Ramos, Artur. 1939. *The Negro in Brazil*, Washington, D.C.: Associated Publishers.

Ray, Benjamin. 1973. "'Performative Utterances' in African Rituals," *History of Religions* 13(1):16–35.

Thompson, Robert F. 1969. "Abatan: A Master Potter of the Ęgbado Yoruba" in *Tradition and Creativity in Tribal Art*, D. P. Biebuyck (ed.), Berkeley: University of California Press, pp. 120–82.

Verger, Pierre. 1954. "Rôle Joué par l'État d'Hébétude au cours de l'Initiation des Novices aux Cultes des Orisha et Vodun," *Bulletin Institut Fondamental d'Afrique Noire* 16(3–4):322–40.

———. 1955. "Bori, Première Cérémonie d'Initiation au Culte des Òrishàs Nàgó à Bahia au Brésil," *Revista do Museu Paulista* (São Paulo), n.s., 9:269–91.

———. 1957. "Notes sur le Culte des Orisa et Vodun à Bahia, La Baie de tous les Saints au Brésil et à l'Ancienne Côte des Esclaves en Afrique," *Mémoires de l'Institut Fondamental d'Afrique Noire*, no. 51.

————. 1964. "The Yoruba High God—A Review of the Sources," Paper prepared for the Conference on The High God in Africa, Ibadan, December 14–18.

————. 1969. "Trance and Convention in Nago-Yoruba Spirit Mediumship," in *Spirit Mediumship and Society in Africa*. J. Beattie and J. Middleton (eds.), N.Y.: Africana, pp. 50–66.

————. 1976–77. "The Use of Plants in Yoruba Traditional Medicine and its Linguistic Approach," in *Seminar Series*, No. 1, Part I, O. O. Oyelaran (ed.), Ifẹ: Department of African Languages and Literature, University of Ifẹ, pp. 242–95.

Warren, Dennis M., A. D. Buckley, and J. A. Ayandokun. 1973. *Yoruba Medicines*, Legon: The Institute of African Studies, University of Ghana.

Henry John Drewal

10

Art or Accident:
Yorùbá Body Artists and Their
Deity Ògún[1]

Yorùbá who live and work with iron (*irin, ògún*) are also worshippers of Ògún, the god of iron. Iron is Ògún. Ògún lives in his followers and they in him, a reciprocal relationship which can be documented in the lives of Ògún devotees. In considering the attributes of Ògún, iron users, and iron itself, and then in focusing upon body artists, this essay explores the way art, tools, and techniques express the presence and impact of Ògún in Yorùbá life and thought.

The Attributes of Ògún

A cluster of traits portrays the essence or life force (*àṣẹ*) of Ògún. Among these are physical force, hotness, quickness, directness, sensuality, firmness, and tenacity. For some he is known as *Ògún onígboiyà*, "Ogun the brave one" (Ògúnole 1973). Ògún's mode of operation implies no moral connotations; it is neither bad nor good, negative nor positive. It is not how he operates, but what he does, and when, that determines whether people consider him harmful or beneficial. On one hand, Ògún's quickness or impatience can result in hasty, careless, irrational behavior causing wanton destruction. This dangerous side of Ògún evokes images of hot violence, vengeance, blind rage, and indiscriminate destruction for, more than anything, Ògún is associated with bloodshed; he is "the one who is steeped in blood," *a-mọ̀-kúkú l'ẹ̀jẹ̀* (Oluponọn 1975). One widespread tale recounts his arrival in a town where the inhabitants offended him by what he considered to be an inhospitable reception. In a blind rage, Ògún began to destroy everything. Not until the appropriate offerings (dog, snail, oil, and soothing leaves) were made and his praises sung did he come to his senses and realize that he was killing his own people.[2] Thus, when he is ignored, angered, or affronted, Ògún destroys indiscriminately. Yet, appropriate rituals can avert destruction and calm him by turning his àṣẹ to beneficent ends.

In other circumstances, Ògún's anger may be justified. He judges and punishes liars, thieves, arrogant fools, and others viewed as antisocial:

1   Ògún a dájọ́ b'obinrin l'oyún àbòsí f'ọkọ rẹ̀.
2   Ògún a-dá-jọ́. (Fadare 1975)

1   Ògún will judge if a woman conceives without the knowledge of her husband [commits adultery].
2   Ògún will judge.

He acts as arbiter of human actions, especially those involving matters of deceit. As one priest explained: "If someone stole something and that person is in a lorry, that motor will simply kill the person. . . . Ògún will kill him there. Anytime you see something that belongs to another, you must not take it, otherwise you will be killed by Ògún" (Oluponọn 1975). Ògún in his better moments is firm, forthright, and, above all, honest. He is direct and straightforward in his actions, and demands the same of his followers. Truthfulness is one of Ògún's qualities. More than anything, he hates thieves and liars, those whom the Yorùbá would describe as going "zig-zag."[3] Thus, in the courts of contemporary Nigeria, òrìṣà worshippers swear their oath of truthfulness by putting their lips to a piece of iron and invoking Ògún's name.

Besides punishing wrongdoers, Ògún facilitates interactions between humans and supernatural forces. Worshippers of various cults frequently assert that Ògún is essential for the creation of any altar to otherworldly beings (ará ọ̀run). "Anywhere you are going to put any idol [shrine] on earth, Ògún will first of all work there. We Yorùbá have the proverb, Ògún lo ṣálẹ̀ f'òrìṣà dó, meaning 'Ògún is the one who clears the place where a shrine for the gods is established'" (Oluponọn 1975). Ògún, in this positive, creative aspect, symbolizes order: he makes possible the worship of the supernatural forces as much as he allows the creation and maintenance of roads, bridges, fields, and homes, all of which are essential for the survival and well-being of humans.

Ògún is also involved in procreation. He gives life as dramatically as he takes it away. Ògún presides over the beginning of life and the cutting of the umbilical cord, and he is there at the end, for "Ògún is the hoe that opens the earth (to bury you)," *Ògún okoko yeri ogu* (Verger 1957:193). His praise poetry is often graphically sexual in nature:

1 O ṣe'pọ̀n janna bi'mọ s'ilé Ijanna.
2 A gbọ́ s'okó lùku oko èrò ọjà! (Legbe 1971)

1 He made his penis lengthen to father a child in the house of Ijanna.
2 We heard how the penis struck those in the market!

Other, more pungent images were collected by Verger (1957:177).

1 O bu rin bu rin fi ọwọ ba okó idi rẹ.
2 Boya o ti ku?
3 O ri ki okó yi wọle ko ku kiki epọn
4 Kiki epọn o di ofo.

1 He entered deeply and touched his hand to the base of his cock.
2 Perhaps it was inactive?
3 He found that his penetrating penis was active except for his testicles.
4 Except for his testicles which were emptying.

Ògún's sexual prowess may perhaps be lauded because of his links with the origins of circumcision and excision. These are recorded in a myth from Kétu and summarized here:

> God put Ògún and a woman, Olùrè, on earth but Olùrè wanted to travel there alone. She set out and came to a large tree that had fallen across the path. She returned to God (Ọlọ́run) and asked him to have Ògún cut the tree. While he was chopping the tree, Olùrè was sitting nearby with her legs apart. A piece of wood flew up and accidentally lodged in her vagina. When the path was cleared, she continued on her way but the wood caused so much pain that she returned to Ọlọ́run and Ògún and asked that it be removed. Ògún asked if she would marry him and she accepted. If he had been more patient, it would have been women who asked men to marry them. Ògún removed the piece of wood. A scar remained and this was the origin of excision. . . . Ògún had sex with Olùrè but because his sperm did not come out quickly enough, he cut the foreskin of his penis, and this was the origin of circumcision. (Verger 1957:144)

The deity, infamous for bloodshed, violence, and destruction, is at the same time famous for taming nature, sustaining culture and the worship of the gods, and facilitating the very act of creation itself. He castrates as well as circumcises.

Ògún's personality implies certain kinds of actions. Images of his speed resound in praises such as "Ògún killcd them instantly [all-at-one-blow]," *Ògún pa wón bèrè kójó*. This quickness reveals his legendary impatience. The thrust of his penis, euphemistically referred to as a knife (*òbè*), is direct and forceful. Like hard, sharp, powerful, and direct blows of a flashing iron implement, Ògún's actions are judged as negative when done without reason or justification, or positive when they intentionally ensure the survival and well-being of a person or community. Ògún is like a double-edged sword: wielded with rationality it can be an efficient tool, but when out of control it can cause mayhem. Ògún's image, like his *àse*, is multidimensional. Literally on the edge between control and irrational anger, Ògún's potentiality must be activated with caution and care. Such concerns are important for all Ògún worshippers, and they are paramount for body artists.

Iron Users and Ògún

The attributes of Ògún are, in many ways, mirrored by all his followers who live and work with iron. To a large extent, this is due to certain fundamental Yorùbá beliefs and practices concerning a person's relationship with particular supernatural forces. Two primary factors govern a person's or a group's worship patterns: divination and descent. The first, divination, discloses the forces, natural and supernatural, affecting individuals and prescribes appropriate ritual actions, including the honoring of particular divinities or ancestors. The second, inheritance, is perhaps the more common means of acquiring a god, for the Yorùbá believe that one's right, authority, and obligation to honor a particular divinity are transmitted through the blood's life force from generation to generation. Individuals explain this by saying, "It is in our life blood from the founder; it is our foundation." It is therefore assumed that anyone born into the lineage has an inherent spiritual affinity with a particular deity or group of deities. By extension, such innate affinity means that the person may exhibit some of the same propensities or capacities as the god.[4] In addition, individuals within the lineage are believed to share certain personality traits, which are often described in the lineage praise poems (*oríkì*) (see Babalola 1967) and which may derive ultimately from lineage divinities. This same logic applies to professions presided over by different divinities; Òrúnmìlà for diviners, Òsanyìn for healers, Olókun for beadworkers, or Ògún for ironworkers, for these, like worship patterns, are generally inherited. As the Yorùbá say, *Òwú ti baba ba gbòn ni omo fi o rán*, "The cotton carded by the father will surely be sewn by the children" (Olabisi 1975:23). As a group, ironworkers partake of an Ògún ethos.

Within this broad group, however, are a number of "branches" of Ògún, each with its own special concerns which arise from the nature of its iron-related activity. Carroll (1967:79) notes some of these branches and the implements which are their symbols: (1) Ògún Onìré, (2) *ògún* of the house (knife), (3) *ògún* of the farm (hoe), (4) *ògún* of the hunters (gun), (5) *ògún* of the carvers (tools), (6) *ògún* of the blacksmith (anvil), (7) *ògún* of the face-mark cutter (knives), (8) *ògún* of the torrent (outdoor shrine of Ògún), and (9) *ògún* of the lorry-driver (truck).[5]

The various branches within the Ògún complex fall into three broad groups depending upon where and how iron implements are used. They are in the realm of the forest, within the borderland between the bush and the community (the farms), and at the center of culture, that is, the bustling towns and markets. In the first group are the hunters, warriors, and palm-wine tappers, whose iron implements are varied: spears, guns, arrows, swords, spiked clubs (*orukùmò*), chained club (*gaman*), and knives, cutlasses, and axes. In the second group are the farmers, whose cutlasses, axes, and hoes first clear the bush and till the earth, and the ironworkers, who mine and smelt with their picks, shovels, prongs, pokers, hooks, prickers, and hammers. In the third group are the blacksmiths, with their hammers, anvils, pokers, tongs, and shears, who fashion all manner of utilitarian implements as well as exquisite sculpture in iron for the cults of Ògún, Ifá, Òsanyìn, Eyinlę, Òşóòsì, and Òrìşà Oko; the wood-carvers, with their axes, adzes, and knives; the barbers, with their razors; and the body artists or *olóòlà* (literally, "those who make marks [in human flesh]"), with their delicate blades. All are engaged in work which, both dangerous and physically demanding, requires courage and strength—attributes dominant in Ògún's imagery. Yet artists need more. They also need skills such as the ability for finesse, concentration, control, and especially dexterity. The Yorùbá define an artist (*onísọna*) as one who is a "skilled designer" (cf. Abraham 1958:522). The term *onísọnà* consists of *onísę ọnà*, "one-who-controls/presides-over-the-creation-of-art." Art *ọnà*, for the Yorùbá, encompasses notions of nonfunctional elaboration and enhancement of a thing (like embroidery on cloth) and craftsmanship (H. Drewal 1980:9). Nowhere is such skill more important than in the work of body artists, for they cut lines in human flesh.

The Nature of Iron and Iron Tools

Generations of Yorùbá ironworkers and users have forged a complex body of knowledge about iron, about its potential as well as its dangers, and about its properties, both physical and spiritual (see Bellamy 1904; Adéníji and Armstrong 1977). The nature of iron as a substance recalls the nature of Ògún and those who work with iron.

Iron possesses a number of inherent qualities that set it apart from other substances. Probably its most dramatic characteristic is its ability to undergo striking transformations. It has a capacity to possess radically different properties while still maintaining its "iron-ness." As the ore responds to the intense heat of the smelter, the iron locked within it begins to emerge. During the process of separation and purification, the metal begins to glow. It is an intensely hot, reddish, and unstable substance that can become liquid as quickly and dramatically as it can become white, hard, cold, and unyielding. These changes are evocative of Ògún himself. Later, heat, hammering, and cool water alter the metal's temper, producing objects of strikingly different characteristics. They range from being as brittle as glass to being as pliable as fresh wood. This dramatic capacity to undergo radical changes in temperature, color, and temper constitutes iron's essence. This is its inherent potential.

Tools fashioned and used by humans further define the inherent physical qualities of iron. The attributes of tools and the manner in which they are handled convey an image of overt physical force. In general, it is men who wield instruments of iron.[6] The domain of iron is the domain of men and elaborate prohibitions prevent the intrusion of women at various stages in the ironworking process (Adéníji and Armstrong 1977:41–43). Making and using iron implements require actions which are direct, quick, and strong, and this is evident in the form of the objects themselves.

Many iron tools, despite diversity in form and function, have in common a sharp edge designed to penetrate cleanly and directly in order to accomplish a task efficiently. For example, spears or arrows pierce the hides of animals, hoes till the soil, and adzes cut wood. These man-made tools possess a particular duality: the more efficient the cutting edge of the implement, the more potentially dangerous it becomes and the more control must be exerted. All involve the potential of creation and destruction simultaneously. Like the potentials and problems introduced by computers in our own age, iron offers enormous possibilities as well as dangers for society, alternatives which are embodied in iron as a sacred substance.

Iron as a Sacred Substance

Iron's potential gives it a sacred status.[7] The innate qualities of iron are a manifestation of its àṣẹ, a metaphysical concept central to all Yorùbá thought and action. Àṣẹ is present in all that exists—things, persons, supernatural forces, sounds, and gestures (cf. M. Drewal, chapter 9). Iron possesses that supernatural force. Hence, objects made of iron are not only primary symbols of Ògún, they *are* Ògún. An Ògún devotee reveals this philosophical concept when he describes how an Ògún altar is established:

> When a shrine is called Ògún, it is Ògún. It becomes Ògún once you have placed two pieces of iron together and poured oil on it. The shrine needs food to be active. Then you can offer prayers to it. As soon as it is put together

it stays Ògún, and will be Ògún forever after. By dismantling the iron, one takes Ògún away. (Barnes 1980:37)[8]

The essential elements are two or more pieces of iron, sacrifices, and the voiced prayers of humans.[9] The iron on the shrine is not only the "witnessing object" that, as Verger explains (1964:17), is the "support" of the altar or shrine, but also it contains the life force or àṣẹ of the divinity. Examples of other such objects hosting intensified àṣẹ are the thundercelts or neolithic axes (ẹdùn àrá) on Ṣàngó shrines, and the river pebbles (ota) on Ọya, Eyinlẹ̀, and Ọṣun altars. When iron is present on a shrine, it must be ritually "fed" with the blood of animal sacrifices, palm oil, palm wine, gin, water, kolanut, snail's fluid, or other substances, all of which activate and exalt the deity.

The importance of sacrifice is brought out in well-known praises to Ògún such as the following invocation from Porto Novo:

1   Ògún alake ni jẹ aja
2   Ògún onigbajamọ irun ẹni ni jẹ
3   Ògún olola wọn jẹ ẹjẹ
4   Ògún alapata ẹran ni jẹ. (Verger 1957:194)

1   *Ògún alake* eats dog
2   Ògún of the barbers eats human hair
3   Ògún of the body artists drinks blood
4   Ògún of the butchers eats meat . . .

Different branches of Ògún require particular kinds of sacrifices. Ògún Aláké, the Ògún of warriors/hunters, prefers dog, whose blood is poured upon the iron and stone altars of the deity. The iron razors of the barber consume human hair, while the iron instruments of body artists drink blood of a client. The same is true for the tools of the carver, for "Ògún of the carvers consumes the blood [sap] of wood" (Ògún *gbẹ̀nàgbẹ́nà jẹ ojẹ̀ igi*) (Oluponọn 1975). The term *ògún* in this and other verses cited earlier is used in a double oonoo to mean the deity *und* the iron implement, for they are inseparable. Supervised by the god of iron, the work carried out by iron-using professionals constitutes, in a sense, sacred activity since it provides nourishment for iron, for Ògún's àṣẹ.

The proper "feeding" of iron also requires prayer. These praises and invocations contain àṣẹ to assure that what is asked will come to pass (cf. M. Drewal, chapter 9). The importance of sacrifice and human voices is clear in all aspects of iron work, from mining, to the siting of a Yorùbá smelter, to the elaborate rituals required when a smelting furnace is lit. Before digging, miners place palm wine, the fluid of a snail, and kolanut on the spot and offer prayers to Ògún. As Adéníjí and Armstrong (1977:11) explain, they serve to ensure success in finding good iron ore and in preventing the hole from "collapsing upon them." Additionally, the miners must bear no one ill will (literally, "bad inside") (*kò gbọ'dọ̀ ní inú búburú sí ẹnikẹ́ni*), not commit adultery, nor steal (Adéníji and Armstrong 1977:13).

Similar spiritual concerns emerge in siting a smelter. A smelter must not be so close as to disrupt society, yet never so far as to prevent society from controlling it. As Adéníji and Armstrong (1977:19–21) explain:

> . . . one must go to build the smelting house in the bush; but it must not be far from the place where many people live or where Ogun stays and hears (the) voices (of human beings). [The reason for this siting of the smelter is] if the sound of people's voices does not penetrate inside the hearth of the smelter, the iron which is being smelted inside it will become dumb (*yó'yadi*); that is that this iron will not become iron that rings but rather slag (*ìdàrọ́*)—which means that this iron is still-born (*èyí ni pé irin náàá ya àbíkú*).

In other words, earth turns to iron only through human intercession. Hands, minds, and voices transform a natural substance into a functional, "living" cultural artifact.

The rituals attending the establishment of a smelter become more elaborate when the smelting fire is lit. The smelter constitutes a shrine to Ògún and the fire, like the heat of the deity, is sacred. In the powder that ignites the furnace, the smelters mark the sign for Ògún (Ògúndá Ìrẹtẹ̀) that comes from the Ifá divination lore. This sign and its verses denote "victory" (Abimbọla 1976:30) and celebrate success in the face of danger, an association which is appropriate to a deity who revels in battle. Then the ironworker straddles the "mouth" of the furnace with a red cock in his left hand, a mixture of pepper and red and white kolanut in his mouth, and his eyes closed, and begins to recite incantations (*ọfọ̀*) to Ògún:

1 Ìbà Ògún, Oníporin Ayé
2 Ìbà Ògún, Oníporin Ọrun
3 Ìbà àgbààgbà mẹ́'ta, ìporin
   ìgbà ìwá ṣẹ̀
4 Ògún dá'kẹtẹ̀ ní pópó
5 Ọ́ rawọ́ agada ibéjé ibéjé
6 Iná giri-giri nínú ada
7 Oòrùn giri-giri òkè
8 Iná sunṣu àri jẹ
9 Oòrùn sunṣu àsun lòlùbọ́
10 Iná giri-giri inú ada
11 Akùkọ rẹbẹ̀-rẹbẹ̀ Ògún fún ọ rèé!
12 Kírin ó pò!
13 Kírin ó jiná
14 Wọnrọn-wọnrọn-wọnrọn! (Adéníji and Armstrong 1977:30–33)

1   Homage to Ògún, the Iron-Smelter of the World (3 times)
2   Homage to Ògún, the Iron-Smelter of Heaven (3 times)
3   Homage to the three patriarchs, iron-smelters when existence began!
        (3 times)
4   Ògún put on a big straw hat in an open place
5   He spun the sword as a warning, as a warning! (3 times)
6   The blazing fire in the furnace, (3 times)
7   The sun shining brightly above; (3 times)
8   Fire cooks the yam so it is edible, (3 times)
9   The sun cooks the yam so it wilts [and is inedible] (3 times)
10 Blazing fire in the furnace, (3 times)
11 Here is the red-red cock which Ògún presents to you! (3 times)
12 So let the iron be well-smelted,
13 Let the iron be well heated
14 To ring well and long! (3 times)

The cock's crow is said to carry from this world to the afterworld (tó kọ jáyé kọ já'run). It is likened to a palm frond (amọ̀) "separated from death" (tàbí tó bákú lamọ̀). The allusion to the palm frond (amọ̀ or mariwo), an important Ògún symbol, refers to its continued life as thatching or dressing for shrines after it is cut from the tree. Amidst these invocations, the smelter sacrifices the cock and pours its blood over the Ifá sign, lights a bundle of reeds with flint, and ignites the furnace while reciting the secret names of fire over the blaze. Finally, he climbs on the furnace platform and vigorously blows pepper and kolanut over the smelter as further prayers are voiced (Adéníji and Armstrong 1977:29–31). Through the ritual, humans shape, control, and change raw power into socially useful power.

The supplications voiced by the followers of Ògún have one major theme: protection from physical harm. More specifically, they ask to be spared from "accidents" caused by iron that has gone out of control, like a careening lorry or a wayward axe blade. Essentially, these prayers appeal to Ògún to ensure that iron is used to benefit humanity. This is graphically illustrated at annual Ògún rites in Ifẹ̀ and Ileṣa known as Ìbọgún or Ìbéjá, when devotees must sacrifice a dog by decapitating it with a single, swift stroke of a sword. They must emulate the quick and precise actions of Ògún himself, who kills instantly. Failure to accomplish this act shows a lack of efficiency and control; the rite is, therefore, unacceptable to Ògún.

The major themes from Ògún rituals are repeated in his symbols. Ògún's symbolic colors, red and white, represent the extremes through which iron goes (hot/cold, liquid/solid, brittle/pliable). Red connotes heat (fire, forge), violence (anger), impatience, and bloodshed. The leaves used in preparations for Ògún, such as ọdúndún and rinrin, are said to "cool" the heat of Ògún (Verger 1976–77:249). One Ògún devotee (Alabe 1975) explained the predominance of red in Ògún symbolism as follows: "When a man takes a blade to make marks, you won't see white water come out of the person's body. The blood will be red . . . Ògún is using something which is red." Awolalu puts it another way:

> Since Ògún is believed to be fiery, things offered to calm his anger include snail and palm oil. Before a child is circumcised . . . the body-fluid of the snail is sprinkled on him, especially on the part of the body to be incised. After circumcision, the knife used for the purpose is put in a plate in which there is plenty of palm oil. (1973:86)

Ògún's red may also refer to the lateritic soil of Yorubaland and the rust that forms on unused iron. Both connote the absence of man. In contrast, white evokes man's intercession, for Williams (1974:99) notes that iron is considered to be "worn white with use." Likewise, the white fluid squeezed from the snail soothes both the cuts made by Ògún and Ògún himself, and white semen possesses life-giving potential. Cool white balances the heat of red by symbolizing the eternal effort to control and channel the enormous powers of iron and Ògún.

Yorùbá Body Marks: Types and Significance

For the Yorùbá, lines in flesh are primordial. Pointing to the palm of his hand, one tattooer commented, "God made a proverb saying, 'open your hand, here are lines'" (*Ọlọrun pa sò'we sile pe lagba ga yin ọwọ, ilà ni*) (Fadare 1975). From this fact of creation, humans evolved the art of cutting patterns in flesh. The symbols associated with Ògún and iron resonate in the art, tools, techniques, and personalities of body artists.

Marks and Identity

Lines on a person signify many things. Some marks localize a person in time and space, indicating indelibly an individual's place and condition in a broad cultural and ontological system. The practice of using marks for this purpose, probably ancient among the Yorùbá,[10] seems to have been especially important during the nineteenth century, a period of widespread conflict between Yorùbá and their neighbors as well as among various Yorùbá ethnic subgroups who engaged in slave-raiding on a massive scale (see Johnson 1921; Ajayi and Smith 1964; Smith 1969).[11] Immediate visual identification became crucial, as one elder recalls:

> In the ancient days . . . during the wars long ago, if any children (without marks) were carried away by the enemy, we could not recognize them later if they were found because there were no marks . . . therefore if I have my own mark then I put it on my children and if I see them, I know that they are my own children. . . . This happened during the wars [which] caused them to have to make marks. (Fadare 1975)

This is of course only a partial explanation, because facial marks generally distinguish ethnic subgroups and not lineages (fig. 10.1a, b). In some cases, however, marks signified members of royal households (both masters and slaves) (Johnson 1921:106). In other cases, divination determined that a child receive no marks at all (Faleti 1977:26). Facial scarifications may therefore be remnants of religious practices or political allegiances which have, over the last two centuries, undergone significant changes.

Face and body scarifications communicate other biographical facts about a person, including conditions of birth. Children called àbíkú (literally, "those born to die"), mischievous spirit infants who plague their mothers by being born and then dying soon after, are sometimes marked with a distinctive sign such as three scars on the shoulder (Houlberg 1976). If and when they are reborn, they are recognized and treated appropriately to encourage them to remain alive. Other marks indicate the presence of younger siblings or relations. Adepegba (1976:56–57) notes the practice of sympathetic scarification (èjè gbígbà). When a child undergoes circumcision and cicatrization, his relatives have cuts made to remind them to handle the child gently.[12] The marks are also believed to ease the child's pain. Other cicatrices may indicate inherited occupations, such as three lines on one cheek and four on the other to identify a mark-maker. A person's cult membership may be evident from tattoos or scarifications, like a double thundercelt on the arm of Ṣàngó worshippers. Among the Ọhọri Yorùbá a large jagged zigzag mark from the ear to the corner of the mouth (fig. 10.1c) called òṣílùmí is a "mark of sorrow" to denote the loss of someone very dear to the person (Ògúnole 1973).

Marks and Well-Being

A large variety of body markings have curative or protective associations. Two types, circumcision and excision, are performed as initiation rites in many African societies, but among the Yorùbá they are done primarily for reasons of health and procreation. The elderly olóòlà Fadare (1975) explained that dirt can collect under the foreskin, causing an infection known as èèta (cf. Abraham 1958:167). Too, he said, a circumcised penis is easily washed and "better" for intercourse. His explanations recall Ògún and the myth given above that accounts for the origin of circumcision. Excision, as explained by Yorùbá males, allows intercourse to be more "enjoyable" for the woman since removal of the clitoris (ọba inú ayé, "king-inside-the-world"), which can enlarge and extrude, causing discomfort, allows the female freedom of movement (Alabe 1975). Once again, the explanation for this operation accords with the myth.

Other types of marks on the body are curative. Herbal doctors, priests of the god of herbalism, Ọsanyìn, as well as body artists administer a large number of medicines via incisions on the body (see Warren et al. 1973). The placement of the incisions corresponds with the intended effect of the medicines to be inserted. Thus, short vertical marks under the eyes (gbẹ́rẹ́ ojú) of some

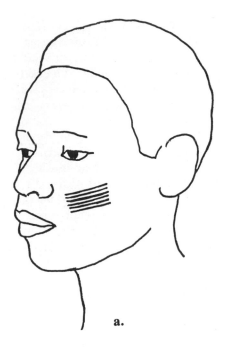

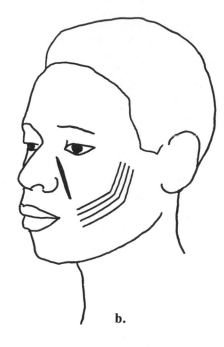

a.   b.

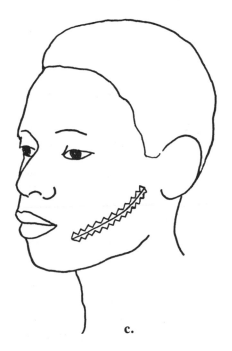

FIGURE 10.1.   a—Ẹ̀fọ̀n Yorubá
marks consist of many, closely
spaced lines that are said to be
"split open" (là). After Abraham
1958:301;
b—The four kẹ́kẹ́ marks of Ọ̀yọ́ and
Ẹ̀gbádò Yorùbá and the single
oblique cicatrice (bààmuń are broad
and bold. After Abraham 1958:300;
c—The Ọ̀họ̀rí Yorùbá face mark
òṣílùmí indicates sorrow for the loss
of a loved one.

c.

children signify that medicines have been inserted to prevent the child from trembling, a condition believed to be caused by the sight of spirits (Faleti 1977:24, 25). An olóòlà explains: "The mother or parents will prepare a medicine and bring it to the olóòlà who will then put it in the cicatrices he makes on the child and in this way prevent the child from dying" (Ògúnole 1973). The medicine ẹrọ àgbà ì-ná, literally "relief from that which is obtained and not spent" (i.e., the acquisition of money that disappears without producing tangible results), is rubbed into cuts made around the wrists of both hands. Medicine for severe headache is put into three cuts in the forehead (Warren et al. 1973:2, 3, 69), and medicine to prevent snakebite is put in an incision that encircles the left ankle: it must be renewed after the person kills a snake (Tereau and Huttel 1949/50:11). Medicine to protect one from the destructive invocation of another person is inserted in a "cut in front of the patient's ear" (Prince 1960:73), while medicines to make a curse effective (àfọ̀ṣẹ) are rubbed into a cut below the lower lip, so that "when the individual wishes to curse he licks his lower lip and whatever he says will come to pass" (Prince 1960:68). Similarly, the singer of ìjálá chants (for hunters) has incisions near his mouth for the insertion of medicines to give him courage and aid his memory (Babalọla 1966:68–86).

Such substances also facilitate the worship of the gods. Those initiated into cults for the gods must be prepared to receive, without danger, the spirit of their deity in order to become mediums in rituals of possession. To accomplish this, incisions are made in the cranium of the devotee and substances which activate the vital essence of àṣẹ of the god are inserted and sometimes signified by a patch or tuft of hair known as òṣù. The deity can now enter the properly prepared spiritual or inner head (orí inú) and possess the medium (adóṣù).[13] Substances inserted into the heads of devotees for Ògún, the one who clears roads and fields, "open the way" for contact between the world and the otherworld.

Marks of Beautification

The accomplished body artist also creates complex and intricate tattoo cicatrice designs known as kóló for men and especially for women. Kóló consist of very short, shallow, and closely spaced hatch marks (wẹ́nẹ́wẹ́nẹ́) that form linear designs into which a colorant (usually charcoal or lampblack) is inserted. The healed cuts produce a matt black pattern with a low-relief rippled texture against a semi-glossy, dark skin surface (fig. 10.2). These elaborate patterns are judged primarily in terms of aesthetic properties, that is, how successfully they enhance the appearance of the wearer.[14] They constitute the ultimate test of the visual acuity, sensitivity, technical ability, and creativity of an olóòlà. Informants without exception stress aesthetics when discussing kóló: "We are making designs, art (A nṣe ọ̀nọ̀n) . . . to make a person famous (gbajúmọ̀n) [literally, '200 faces know him']" (Ògúnjobi 1975). Another informant puts it this way: "It [kóló] has no reason, just for funning

. . . just to make *fáàrí*, to make *yọ̀nga*" (Fadare 1975). *Fáàrí* and *yọ̀nga* connote ostentation, showing off, or boastful behavior like strutting or swaggering (Abraham 1958:205, 688). The emphasis is clearly on the visible display of the enhanced and beautified human body. As the *olóòlà* Ògúnole remarks, *kóló* "is in order to embellish, to make one beautiful, illustrious (*a fún yín ṣògo*) with marks. The women do it to enhance their beauty."

Placement

While both males and females adorn themselves with *kóló*, women have by far the most varied and numerous designs placed on different parts of their bodies. The most common sites for women's *kóló* are face, neck, chest, abdomen, back, arms (upper and lower), back of hands, calf or lower leg, and thighs. Men have *kóló* on the face, neck, and arms. These sites are not in order of importance, for the client decides where patterns should be placed. Rather, the placement of designs seems to suggest an awareness of differing degrees of visibility. Face, neck, arm, and hand designs for women are fully public and highly visible (fig. 10.3); patterns on the back, chest, and abdomen, however, are somewhat more restricted though still often visible in public (figs. 10.4, 10.5); but patterns on the upper thigh, intended for intimate friends or a spouse, are basically private (fig. 10.6a).

Motifs

The designs formed by the hatching process (*wẹ́nẹ̀wẹ́nẹ́*) consist of a small number of lines and shapes that are altered and recombined to create a wide range of distinct yet subtly differentiated configurations. Zigzag lines are a pervasive element whose alteration and placement create a series of individual motifs; one is called "legs of a cripple" (*eruku arọ*). The diamond, the zigzag line flattened and mirrored, produces a design called "cowries" (*ẹṣa*). The diamond shape in a different combination with additional lines produces a motif called "lizard" (*arágba/alángba*). The triangle (sometimes referred to as *onígun mẹ́ta*) is identified by its placement, usually in a border or "closing" motif, which is then called "arrow" (*ọfà*). The hemisphere, a subtly rounded triangle, is also found in "closing" motifs. The circle, called simply "o" or "ho," may be embellished with radiating lines. The names assigned to some of the most basic lines and shapes—for example, "legs of a cripple"—seem to be based only in part on a visual correspondence with the subject represented. The primary objective of the semantic association appears to be the labeling of motifs to facilitate the identification and transmittal of imagery.

These visual units can be combined to create more complex representations of flora, fauna, and cultural objects. An early account (Burton 1863:104) describes how "The skin patterns were of every variety . . . tortoises, alligators, and the favorite lizard, stars, concentric circles, lozenges, welts. . . ." Only one example of flora, the palm tree (*igi ọpẹ̀*), has been documented (fig. 10.6b), although other motifs resemble leaf forms. Fauna are, by far, the

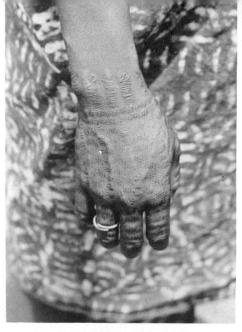

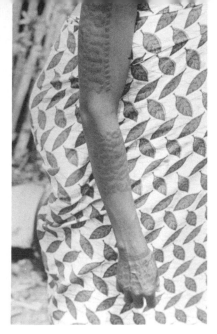

FIGURE 10.2. Tattoo cicatrice design (*kóló*) on the back of a hand showing lines of hatch marks (*wẹ́nẹ́wẹ́nẹ́*) darkened by lampblack or charcoal that produce a slightly raised, rippled texture on smooth skin.

FIGURE 10.3. *Kóló* designs on the arm and hand of a woman.

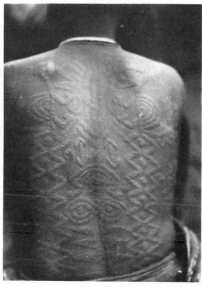

FIGURE 10.4. Elaborate *kóló* design on a woman's back showing two ostriches (*ògòngò*) at the shoulder blades. Pobe, Benin, pre-1948. Photograph #C48-1784-567 by G. Labitte, courtesy of the Phototheque, Musée de l'Homme, Paris, France.

FIGURE 10.5. Elaborate *kóló* design on a woman's back showing two ostriches (*ògòngò*) at the shoulder blades. Photograph #70037, courtesy of the Field Museum of Natural History.

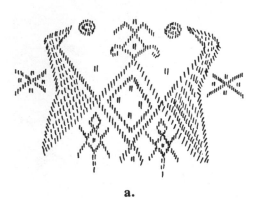

a.

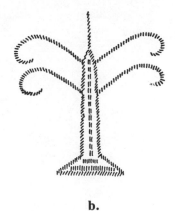

b.

c.

d.

FIGURE 10.6.
a—The *kóló* design called "husband sits on lap" (*gbókó létan*) is usually placed
   on a woman's thighs;
b—*Kóló* design of a palm tree (*igi òpè*);
c—*Kóló* design of lizards (*alángba*) and chameleons (*agèmọ*) in a larger design;
d—*Kóló* design of a king's crown (*adé ọba*).

most consistently represented. They include specific species of birds such as ostrich (*ògòngò*), vulture (*igún*), dove (*àdàbà*), or simply a generalized form of bird in a larger composition; lizard (*arágba, alángba*) (fig. 10.6c), snake (*ejò*), chameleon (*agẹmọ*), centipede (*ọ̀ọ̀kùn*), and butterfly (*labalábá*). Cultural items include forms with religious connotations such as *ẹ̀ta Ògbóni*, the name given to a divination sign, a Ṣàngó dance-wand (*oṣé Ṣàngó*), a Muslim writing board (*wàláà*), the sign known as "moon of honor" (*oṣù ọlá*), and an amulet (*tírà*); symbols of status—a crown and title staff (fig. 10.6d); objects of everyday use like a comb (*òòyà*), *ayò* game-board, scissors, and the Y-shaped blade of the *olóòlà*; more contemporary images such as a wrist-watch or an airplane (*ọkọ̀ òkè*); and calligraphy, such as the name or initials of a client or a fiancée, or proverbs and prayers.[15]

Tools of the Body Artist

The tools of the body artist are unlike those of farmers, blacksmiths, hunters, and warriors in an important way: they are extremely small and light-weight (fig. 10.7). On the far right is the blade used in circumcision. Its twisted iron shaft allows a firm grip by the *olóòlà*, and the slightly curved and wide blade allows a smooth, continuous cut of the foreskin. The blade next to it is for excision.[16] The two blades on the left are for scarification. These double-edged spear-shaped blades are suitable for longer, deeper marks. In contrast to them is the most delicate of all the instruments, the one in the center, for making the elaborate *kóló*. It is a Y-shaped tool with two sharp, narrow blades at the top.[17] The design of these instruments is suited to small, refined, and delicate effort rather than large, gross manipulation. The absence of wooden handles emphasizes this fact, for these instruments are meant to be held not with the hand, but rather with the thumb and fingers. The design admirably suits the function, allowing for precision and sensitivity, since the width of the cutting edge facilitates short, fine lines. Doubling the blades allows the *olóòlà* to work rapidly and continuously without having to change or sharpen the instrument. Another significant feature is the squared shaft, which allows the artist to maintain constancy in the alignment of the blade since the cuts are parallel marks placed close together. Thus, the very form of the body artist's implements conveys a concern for controlled manipulation of iron. But more than this, the blades embody the canons of dexterity—precision, firmness, and delicacy.

Like all iron implements, the blades of the mark-maker are sacred. The procedures used in their manufacture include certain strict rituals (Faleti 1977:26). The blacksmith is said to "create" (*pa*) the blades, a verb which connotes the performance of a magical, highly skillful act (Abraham 1958:538). The client provides a snail, a pigeon, and soothing leaves (*rinrin* and *ọ̀dúndún*). When the instruments are finished, the blacksmith bathes them in a mixture of the leaves, snail fluid, and the blood of the pigeon for three days before they are given to the body artist. The mark-maker repeats the same procedure and, on the seventh day, he polishes them white with the potion as he chants the following invocation:

1   Ògún niyi lọwọ alagbẹ̀dẹ
2   Abẹ ma niyi lọwọ oníkolà
3   Ire mi mbe l'ekulé mi. (Faleti 1977:26)

1   Ògún is here handy for the smith
2   Blades are here handy for the mark-maker
3   My fortunes are at the back of my house [with my shrine for Ògún].

The care taken with the body artist's implements also reveals their sacredness. The blades are carefully wrapped and tied in a red or white cloth, Ògún's symbolic colors (Fig. 10.7). They are kept with other ritual items that are essential for success; kolanuts (top, far left), for all invocations to Ògún, and fan-shaped objects or "badges" of the mark-makers known as atáàmù (below blades). One informant explained, "They are like a license from the ancient days. . . . If they [body artists] walk about the town [holding them] . . . people will say, 'That is the person who is making marks.' . . . If you don't have them you won't come from the foundation of [be a legitimate] olóòlà" (Fadare 1975). Blood and other scarificial residue cover these objects, both of which have large iron rings on their handles and one has iron rings around its perimeter.

Techniques of the Body Artist

Two skills are important to the body artist. The first is an ability to create marks which differ subtly yet significantly from each other. Such proficiency distinguishes the accomplished body artist from a mutilator. The second is an ability to work with speed. An accomplished olóòlà can perform a variety of cutting operations. To a large extent, the skills he uses in each operation are reflected in the terminology used to designate specific cutting techniques and distinct types of cuts.

Each cutting operation has its own term: (1) circumcision (dá'kó) and excision (dábò), (2) scarification (ilà), (3) medicinal incision (gbẹ́rẹ́), and, the most demanding of all, (4) the creation of intricate kóló patterns. In circumcision and excision, flesh is cut (dá). This same verb is used in the context of tapping palm wine (dẹmu, dá ẹmu) through an analogy to a cut around something and the release of fluid, whether sap, blood, or semen.

In facial scarification, different cutting techniques produce a variety of visual and textural qualities (fig. 10.8). Yoruba terminology distinguishes these

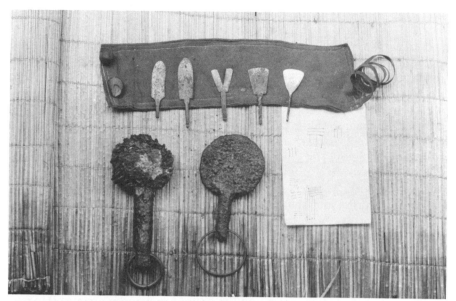

FIGURE 10.7. The tools and ritual implements of the *olóòlà*. Top left to right: kolanuts, two blades for cutting face marks (*àpálílá* and *ọmọ*), Y-shaped double blade for cutting *kóló* designs, circumcision blade, blade for making marks on the neck (*eke*). Bottom left to right: two badges of the body artist (*atáàmù*), drawings of various face and neck marks done by the artist, Y. Fadare. Ìláró, Nigeria.

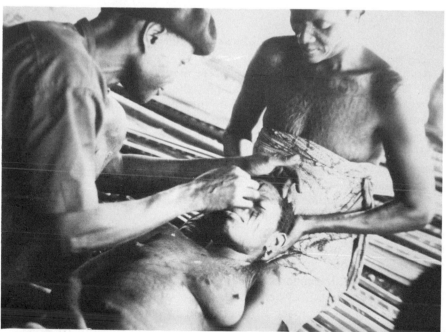

FIGURE 10.8. The body artist A. Ogúnole demonstrating how he cuts face marks on a client while she is steadied by a friend who has elaborate *kóló* designs on her upper chest. Isose, Benin (R.P.B.).

types of cuts from others and reveals that there is a high degree of sophistication in the definition of lines and linear patterns. Thus *şá kẹ́kẹ́*, or, literally, "to slash *kẹ́kẹ́* marks" on a person, indicates broad, bold and highly visible lines; making the same pattern less distinct and visible is indicated by a different cutting verb (*wà*) and a different name for the marks (*gọ̀mbọ́*). Other verbs that distinguish subtle differences in technique are *kọ* (to cut) *turé* facial marks, *bù* (to cut or tear) *àbàjà* marks, and *là* (to split open) Ẹ̀fọ̀n marks (Abraham 1958:301) (fig. 10.1b). Medicinal incisions have their own terminology. The verb *sin* is used to denote cuts (*gbẹ́rẹ́*) made for the expressed purpose of inserting some substance. This same verb is used for *kóló*, when colorant is inserted into shallow cuts.

The tattoo cicatrices executed by the *olóòlà* require the most elaborate and refined technique. The term for the lines formed by the hatch marks (*wẹ́nẹ́wẹ́nẹ́*) suggests a number of visual, tactile, technical, and aesthetic qualities: slenderness (*wẹ́*), indicating short, closely spaced parallel lines (Thompson 1973:49); smallness (*wẹ́wẹ́*), implying linear delicacy; and *wẹ́lẹ́wẹ́lẹ́*, conveying a pleasing rippled texture on the skin (Anonymous 1937:228). Speed of execution is also imperative in the creation of *wẹ́nẹ́wẹ́nẹ́* marks, for colorant must be inserted before the blood flows or coagulates and the cuts close. As one *olóòlà* explains, "If the first one [blade] is no longer sharp we begin to use the second" (Alabe 1975). Speed in cutting, like the swiftness of Ògún, is crucial.

Body Marks and Ògún

Kóló motifs appear to have little direct association with Ògún, although there are some exceptions. For example, the palm tree (fig. 10.2b) is the source of the oil and wine preferred by this divinity. Palm-wine tappers are devotees of Ògún. It is also the source of the palm-frond midrib, *mariwo*, a dominant Ògún symbol. Cultural items of metal, such as scissors, the *olóòlà*'s blade, a wristwatch, and an airplane also appear. It seems more likely, however, that these motifs express prestige, identity, or aesthetic preference as much as they do Ògún.

Circumcision, excision, and *kóló* all have a clearer link with Ògún as expressions of sensuality. As indicated, the first two, according to male informants, make intercourse "better" for males and more "enjoyable" for females. *Kóló* are explicitly erotic in intent. Dark, textured patterns in low relief on a smooth, flat surface have both a visual and a tactile appeal. Witness the playful comments of one *olóòlà*: "A woman with marks all over her body is very fine . . . when we see a girl with marks and she is (naked), we boys can easily approach her and begin to play and rub her body with our hands . . . if we see [the marks] and glance at the body, the weather will change to another thing [we will become sexually aroused]!" (Ògúnjobi

1975). Ògún is thus linked to these marks in that he ensures human reproduction not simply by facilitating intercourse but also by encouraging it.

Tattoos and scarifications evoke Ògún in another implicit but important way—as rites of passage. Although they are not ritually celebrated, the body marks indicate changes in the wearer's status. As with initiation ceremonies, they also are tests of the subject's strength. Comments about *kóló* are explicit in this regard. Sometime before puberty, a person chooses to have these marks, at least in part, because of the way society regards them. One informant describes how people praise a woman covered with body designs with words like "she is very courageous" (o ni láyà dáadáa) or ridicule one without marks with "she is a coward" (*ojo ni*). *Kóló* announce that the bearer is brave and strong enough to endure pain in order to enjoy society's admiration. Thus it is said, "With pains and aches are marks made on us, we become beautified by them only when they are healed" (*Tita riro ni a nkolà, bi o ba sàn tán ni a to di oge*) (Faleti 1977:27).

The prevalence of body markings may be due in part to concepts of the human body and of the person. According to Morakinyo and Akiwowo (1981:26, 36), the Yorùbá "concept of the person . . . , vis-à-vis body-mind relationship, is a unitary one. The body is the mind . . ." and Yorùbá assess an individual's personality from both physical appearance and behavior. In light of this, elaborate body markings are viewed as proof of courage, fortitude, and strength. All of these are highly valued. They are personified by Ògún and body artists.

Body Artists and Ògún

The *olóolà* is an extension and manifestation of Ògún in a number of ways. First, he brings order to society by providing temporal, spiritual, and spatial markers at various points in a person's life. The severing of the umbilical cord is the initial act of defining an individual. Circumcision and excision follow after the child is named, that is, when it is regarded as part of human society. These operations define and anticipate the child's sexual role. Sometime later, divination may require other incisions to identify a special child, such as an *abíkú*. Once a child's survival seems likely, facial scarifications indicating social identity are incised, and others, indicating occupations, cult affiliations, and initiations, may be added. In making indelible signs, the mark-maker gives visual expression to Yorùbá concepts of the self as a part of an embracing cultural and cosmological system. Like Ògún, who creates order by transforming the forest into farms and cities, and who tames society by judging disruptive individuals, the *olóolà* helps to create order by visibly placing individuals in a larger social and cosmic universe.

Second, the body artist sustains culture by providing for the physical and spiritual well-being of individuals. The curative inoculations ensure survival.

Others are designed for protection against enemies, or for facilitating contact with the supernatural realm; they enhance a person's potential for dealing with the often inexplicable forces in the world.

Third, the *olóòlà* is a cultural innovator. As an artist, he contributes his aesthetic sensibilities by embellishing human flesh with beautiful, creative patterns. Itinerancy among Yorùbá body artists, a tradition of some antiquity, fosters such innovation and leads to the rapid dispersal of motifs over a wide area.[18] Several artists recount their frequent trips to distant markets where they observe, adopt, and adapt new patterns. Some (Fadare and Ògúnjobi 1975) develop "portfolios," notebooks of motifs and patterns observed and recorded during their travels, which they carry with them and show to prospective clients. Literacy has also caused body artists to innovate. Many of them, even those unable to read, introduced calligraphy into Yorubaland. They learned to inscribe the letters of the Yorùbá alphabet, names, sentences, and proverbial expressions on the bodies of their clients. Fostering as well as responding to changing aesthetic preferences, body artists have continued to develop new patterns.

Finally, the personality of body artists expresses most clearly their relationship to Ògún. *Olóòlà* seek the qualities of patience and composure. One describes the ideal artist as having "a cool, patient character (*ìwa tútù àti súùrù*). He must not be excitable but friendly, attractive, and approachable (*ń fa ni móra*). He must not drink liquor or palm wine, because if he drinks a lot he won't be able to do the marks well. He may penetrate too deeply and instead of making a design he will just make a big wound." Precise control by the mark-maker is the difference between art and accident. Precision is possible only when an artist exhibits self-control as well as control of his medium.

The need for self-control in the face of danger is a theme that is central to Ògún. All Ògún followers confront danger, but the challenge for a body artist is fundamentally different from that faced by a hunter or warrior. The latter faces death or injury at the "hands" of his prey, be it animal or human. The former faces danger that is within himself. Carelessness and cowardice can result in disaster; they must be avoided at all costs. He must strive to emulate the finer attributes of his god—firmness and bravery—in order to achieve success. The irreversible nature of his work demands courage, confidence, and, above all, precision. An *olóòlà* is reminded of this each time he invokes Ògún with the praise:

1   Ògún, iyan kan bí ọgbẹ́
2   Anaíyà páta bi ọna

1   Ògún, the one who is like a big scar [wound]
2   The courageous one is like the road

The scar, the road, and Ògún are alike. None can be changed. An informant explains, "if the blade should turn, mistakenly turn, you can't say 'make another one' . . . it can't be cleared [removed] . . . if three or four marks are put in the place, they are there until the end of a person's life, they can't be cleared again" (Fadare 1975). Another adds, "The road is always there. It never moves. No matter what traffic comes along, truck or car, it does not budge. It is courageous."

In Yorùbá thought, the cosmic realms of world (*ayé*) and otherworld (*ọrun*) are distinct but not separate. They penetrate and influence each other depending upon the quality of communication established and maintained between humans and spirits, gods, and ancestors. One affects the other, and vice versa. Such beliefs shape in significant ways people's thoughts and actions. People not only contemplate divine forces, they manipulate them—sometimes praising, sometimes emulating, other times scolding or blaming. Such closeness between devotee and deity forges a clearly definable ethos that shapes as well as reflects various facets of a person's life. The examination of those who work with iron, specifically body artists—their myths, rituals, materials, implements, techniques, and personalities—shows this to be true. Embodying many of Ògún's attributes, they boldly incise beautiful, indelible lines in human skin with firmness, speed, and precision. In thus forming their concepts of Ògún and actualizing them in their lives, body artists have helped to create the world of Ògún that in turn has shaped Yorùbá culture in distinctive ways.

NOTES

1. Fieldwork for this study was carried out among the Ọhọrí and Ègbádò Yorùbá in Benin (R.P.B.) and Nigeria in 1973, 1975, and 1977–78. I wish to express my gratitude to The National Endowment for the Humanities, Cleveland State University, and the Institute for Intercultural Studies for their generous financial support; the Institutes of African Studies, Universities of Ìbàdàn and Ifè, and the Nigerian Museum for providing research affiliations; Rowland Abiọdun and especially Margaret Thompson Drewal for their editorial suggestions and insights; and to the Yorùbá individuals who patiently shared their thoughts on Ògún and body arts. Unless otherwise indicated, all drawings and photographs are by the author.

2. Cf. Verger 1957:142; Beier 1956:29; and Awolalu 1979:32 for other versions. English translations from Verger 1957 are by the author.

3. Ògún's primacy in matters of honesty is evident in another of his symbols, young palm leaves, the "cloths of Ògún" known as *mariwo*. These are often tied on bundles of harvested crops or firewood left unattended along the roadside by their owners. These fronds announce, in effect, "Ògún will punish (kill) those who steal." Similarly, *mariwo* placed at the entrances to sacred sites or private places signals a warning to the uninitiated and the unwelcome that the path cleared by Ògún for a certain purpose should not be misused and that just retribution at the hands of Ògún will follow.

4. Verger (1957) has noted the same phenomenon. More recently Morakinyo and Akiwowo (1981:32–35) discuss heredity and the gods as important factors in the formation of a person's personality (èdá èni).

5. Williams (1974:304) gives a slightly different list: (1) those who use knives or other iron tools within the community, (2) palm-wine tappers, (3) farmers, (4) hunters, (5) Ògún Onírè, ruler of Ìrè, (6) blacksmiths, and (7) all other worshippers of Ògún. In the Òhòrí community of Ibaiyun, the Asògún (head of the Ògún worshippers) identifies the categories as blacksmiths (Ògún Alágbèdè), body artists (Ògún Olóòlà), carvers (Ògún Gbénàgbénà), and towns where Ògún is the major civic deity (Ògún Ìlú, Ògún Onìre, Ògún Ajobo) (A. Oluponon, interview, November 14, 1975).

6. However, certain qualifications should be noted. Faleti (1977:27) states that ". . . a woman whose father is a mark maker can be taught how to and she can make marks. But the daughter of a mark maker who marries a lay man cannot teach her child to make marks." In 1975, I was told by the head of the body artists at Ìláró (Fadare) that the Ìyálóde, leader of women and a titled elder of the community, was sanctioned to perform all rites in his absence.

7. The material and spiritual aspects of any substance are for the Yorùbá inseparable. It is for this reason that persons swearing oaths of truthfulness say "May Ògún/ iron kill me if I lie" as they touch a piece of iron to their foreheads or lips.

8. See Williams 1974:78–100 and Barnes 1980:8–30 for discussions of the sacred iron complex in Africa and among the Yorùbá.

9. Williams (1974:39–40) makes the similar point that "spirit and matter are seen as coterminus. 'Simply anything can become a god,' a Yoruba informant once remarked. 'This button' (pointing to the dashboard of the car in which we were), 'it only needs to be built up by prayer' . . . all matter is dormant spirit with potential expression as a good or evil force depending on the manner of its propitiation. . . ."

10. A number of Ifè terra cotta and copper sculptures (ca. 1100) and Òwò terra cottas (ca. 1400) depict elaborate scarification patterns, some closely resembling nineteenth and twentieth century Yorùbá marks. An Ifá divination tray now at the Ulmer Museum and collected at Allada in the early seventeenth century (possibly Yorùbá, but probably Aja) depicts male and female figures with elaborate face, chest, and neck scarifications.

11. Based on data received from an Ìjèbu Yorùbá informant, d'Avezec (1845:55–59) recorded that the tradition of tattooing ("ella" [ilà]) and circumcision were done by a specialist known as alakila.

12. Faleti (1977:24) notes the same practice, which he calls gba èjè fun. A photograph by T. J. H. Chappel in the Nigerian Museum Archives (#41.1.A.30) documents a similar practice among the Egun/Ègbádò Yorùbá in which a large triangular pattern of keloids are made on the abdomen of an elder sibling to complement the incision of facial marks on the younger, for it is said that, "if an older child is marked at the same time, the baby will not suffer such pain." This triangular scar pattern is identical to keloid designs on abíkú statuettes of Aja people discussed by Merlo (1975).

13. For detailed analyses of the symbolic significance of Yorùbá projections from the top, see M. Drewal 1977, 1986.

14. An Ègbá Yorùbá praise poem graphically recounts the aesthetic impact of such marks: A hunter's wife had elaborate designs known as gbegbéèmu put on her abdomen while her husband was away. When he returned, he was so taken by the sight of his wife's beauty that he stopped short, thunderstruck, and in so doing accidentally dropped his loaded gun, which exploded, killing him! (Faleti 1977:23–24)

15. For illustrations of these kóló see H. Drewal 1988.

16. Faleti notes that the difference in size of these two instruments is "to afford an easy and quick recognition during an operation," but more important they differ

because "of a taboo that the female's must not be used for a male, or the male's for a female. If this happens, the subject will be prone to promiscuity" (1977:26).

17. A similar blade used by an itinerant Yorùbá tattooer at Ìlọrin was documented in 1912: "The cutting edge was indented in the middle, thus giving the blade two sharp angles with which the incisions were made" (MacFie 1913:122).

18. For a discussion of itinerancy and its implications for African art history, see H. Drewal 1977.

References Cited

Abimbọla, Wande. 1976. *Ifa: An Exposition of Ifa Literary Corpus*, Ibadan: Oxford University Press.

Abraham, R. C. 1958. *Dictionary of Modern Yoruba*, London: University of London Press.

Adéníji, D., and R. G. Armstrong. 1977. *Iron Mining and Smelting*, Ibadan: Institute of African Studies, Occasional Publications, no. 31.

Adepegba, C. 1976. "A Survey of Nigerian Body Markings and Their Relationship to Other Nigerian Arts," unpublished Ph.D. dissertation, Indiana University.

Ajayi, J. F. A., and Robert Smith. 1964. *Yoruba Warfare in the 19th Century*, Cambridge: Cambridge University Press.

Alabe, A., body artist. 1975. Interview, Igbeme, November 19.

Anonymous. 1937. *A Dictionary of the Yoruba Language*, Oxford: Oxford University Press.

Awolalu, J. O. 1973. "Yoruba Sacrificial Practice," *Journal of Religion in Africa* 5(2):81–93.

———. 1979. *Yoruba Beliefs and Sacrificial Rites*, London: Longman.

Babalọla, S. A. 1966. *The Content and Form of Yoruba Ìjálá*, London: Oxford University Press.

———. 1967. *Awọn Oríkì Orílẹ*, Glasgow: Collins.

Barnes, Sandra T. 1980. *Ogun: An Old God for a New Age*, ISHI Occasional Papers in Social Change, #3. Philadelphia: ISHI.

Beier, Ulli. 1956. "Before Odudua," *Odu* 3:25–32.

Bellamy, C. V. 1904. "A West African Smelting House," *Journal of the Iron and Steel Institute* 2:99–126.

Burton, Richard. 1863. *Abeokuta and the Cameroon Mountains*, 2 vols., London: Tinsley Brothers.

Carroll, Kevin. 1967. *Yoruba Religious Carving*, New York: Praeger.

d'Avezec, M. 1845. *Notice sur le pays et le peuple des yebous*, Paris: Librairie Orientale de Mme. Ve Dondey-Dupre.

Drewal, Henry J. 1977. *Traditional Arts of the Nigerian Peoples*, Washington: Museum of African Art.

———. 1980. *African Artistry: Technique and Aesthetics in Yoruba Sculpture*, Atlanta: The High Museum of Art.

———. 1988. "Beauty and Being: Aesthetics and Ontology in Yoruba Body Art," in A. Rubin (ed.), *Arts of the Body*, Los Angeles: Museum of Cultural History.

Drewal, Margaret T. 1977. "Projections from the Top in Yoruba Art," *African Arts* 11(1):43–49, 91–92.

———. 1986. "Art and Trance among Yoruba Shango Devotees," *African Arts* 20(1):60–67, 98–99.

Fadare, Y., head of the mark-makers. 1975. Interview, Oke Ibese Quarter, Ìláró, November 6.

Faleti, A. 1977. "Yoruba Facial Marks," *Gangan* 7:22–27.

Houlberg, Marilyn. 1976. Personal communication, November 4.

Johnson, Samuel. 1921. *The History of the Yorubas*, Ibadan: Ibadan University Press (1969 edition used).

Legbe, A., diviner and Èfè singer. 1971. Interview, Emado Quarter, Àyétòrò, April.

MacFie, J. W. S. 1913. "A Yoruba Tattooer," *Man* 13:121–22.

Merlo, Christian. 1975. "Statuettes of the Abiku Cult," *African Arts* 8(4):30–35, 84.

Morakinyo, O., and A. Akiwowo. 1981. "The Yoruba Ontology of Personality and Motivation: A Multidisciplinary Approach," *Journal of Social and Biological Structures* 4:19–38.

Ògúnjobi, body artist and town head. 1975. Interview, Igbeme-Ile, November 19.

Ògúnole, A., body artist. 1973. Interview, Isose, Ọ̀họ̀rí, May 5.

Ọlabisi, O. 1975. In *Dimensions in Black Art*, H. Drewal (ed.), Cleveland: Cleveland State University, p. 23.

Oluponọn, A., Ògún priest. 1975. Interview, Ibaiyun, Ọ̀họ̀rí, November 14.

Prince, Raymond. 1960. "Curse, Invocation and Mental Health among the Yoruba," *Canadian Psychiatric Association Journal* 5:65–79.

Smith, Robert. 1969. *Kingdoms of the Yoruba*, London: Methuen.

Tereau and V. Huttel. 1949/50. "Monographie du Hollidge," *Études Dahoméennes* 2:59–72 and 3:10–37.

Thompson, Robert F. 1973. "Yoruba Artistic Criticism," in *The Traditional Artist in African Societies*. W. L. d'Azevedo (ed.), Bloomington: Indiana University Press, pp. 19–61.

Verger, Pierre. 1957. "Notes sur le Culte des Orisa et Vodun à Bahia, La Baie de tous les Saints au Brasil et à l'Ancienne Côte des Ésclaves en Afrique," *Mémoires de l'Institut fondamental d'Afrique Noire*, no. 51.

———. 1964. "The Yoruba High God—A Review of the Sources," Paper prepared for the Conference on The High God in Africa, Ibadan, December 14–18.

———. 1976–77. "The Use of Plants in Yoruba Traditional Medicine and Its Linguistic Approach," in *Seminar Series,* no. 1, Part 1. Ọ. Ọyelaran (ed.), Ifè: Department of African Languages and Literature, University of Ifè, pp. 242–95.

Warren, Dennis M., A. D. Buckley, and J. A. Ayandokun. 1973. *Yoruba Medicines*, Legon: The Institute of African Studies, University of Ghana.

Williams, Denis. 1974. *Icon and Image*. New York: New York University Press.

CONTRIBUTORS

'BADE AJUWỌN is senior lecturer in the Department of African Languages and Literatures at the Ọbafemi Awolowo University (Nigeria), having gone there from Indiana University, Bloomington, where he received his Ph.D. and later was a Fulbright visiting scholar in 1984–85. He is author of *Funeral Dirges of Yoruba Hunters* (1982) and many articles on oral traditions of the Yoruba-speaking peoples.

ROBERT G. ARMSTRONG, an anthropological linguist, spent most of his career in West Africa. After retiring as Director of the Institute of African Studies, University of Ibadan (Nigeria) in 1983, he joined the staff of the University of Nigeria at Nsukka, where he remained until his death in 1987. Among his many writings were a *Dictionary of Idoma*, more than sixty articles, and five volumes of edited essays. In addition he translated six Nigerian books into English and produced numerous recordings of oral literature.

ADEBOYE BABALỌLA is the author of a pioneering study of oral poetic traditions in West Africa, *The Content and Form of Yoruba Ìjálá* (1966), and 15 other books, texts, and collections, many of which are published in Yoruba. He is emeritus professor and head of the Department of African Languages and Literatures and a former dean of arts at the University of Lagos. The government of Nigeria recently conferred one of the highest national merit awards given to academicians on Prof. Babalọla for his prolific work on oral literature and for his leadership in standardizing the Yoruba language. In addition to scholarly works, he has written and published in Yoruba a play, a novella, and collected poems.

SANDRA T. BARNES is professor of anthropology at the University of Pennsylvania. Her research and publications have focused on African urbanism, religion, politics, and history. She is the author of *Patrons and Power: Creating a Political Community in Metropolitan Lagos* (1986) and *Ogun: An Old God for a New Age* (1980). She is preparing a study of cultural and social pluralism in precolonial West Africa.

PAULA GIRSHICK BEN-AMOS is on the faculty of the Department of Anthropology at Indiana University and has taught at the University of Pennsylvania and at Northwestern University. She has published extensively on the cultural background, symbolism, and history of the arts of the Benin Kingdom. Her writings include *The Art of Benin* (1980) and *The Art of Power: The Power of Art, Studies in Benin Iconography* (1983, with Arnold Rubin). She is currently working on an historical overview of the study of African art.

KAREN MCCARTHY BROWN has carried out extensive research in Haiti and in New York City on Haitian Vodou. She is Professor of the Sociology and Anthropology of Religion in the Graduate and Theological Schools of Drew University and has been a member of the Center for the Study of World Religions at Harvard University on two occasions. Her articles have focused on Vodou and the role of women in religion. Her book, *Mama Lola: A Vodou Priestess in Brooklyn*, is forthcoming.

HENRY JOHN DREWAL, professor of art history and former chair of the Art Department at Cleveland State University, has recently spent two years as an Andrew W. Mellon Fellow in New York's Metropolitan Museum of Art. His research into the culture of the Yoruba-speaking peoples has resulted in many publications. His books include *Traditional Art of the Nigerian Peoples* (1977), *African Artistry: Technique and Aesthetics in Yoruba Sculpture* (1980), and (with M. T. Drewal) *Gelede: Art and Female Power among the Yoruba* (1983).

MARGARET THOMPSON DREWAL is a performance theorist who has worked among the Yoruba-speaking peoples of Nigeria and their descendants in Brazil. Her publications have dealt with the interconnections between the arts in ritual performance. She has authored (with H. J. Drewal) *Gelede: Art and Female Power among the Yoruba* (1983) and guest-edited a special issue of *TDR: Performance Studies* on ritual performance in Africa (1988). Apart from these works, she has also published on George Balanchine, Isadora Duncan, and the Rockettes. She has recently joined the faculty of the Department of Performance Studies at Northwestern University.

RENATO ORTIZ is with the Graduate Program of Social Sciences at São Paulo's Catholic University, and he recently spent a Fulbright year at Columbia and Notre Dame Universities. He prepared his Ph.D. at the École des Hautes Études en Sciences Sociales, Paris, *La Mort Blanche du Sorcier Noir*, also published in Portuguese in 1978. As a student of Brazil's emerging religious traditions and spokesman for its popular culture, Ortiz has published widely in Brazil, France, and the United States. His books include *A Consciência Fragmentada* (1980), *Cultura Brasileira e Identidade Nacional* (1985), and *Cultura Popular: Românticos e Folcloristas* (1985).

JOHN PEMBERTON III, a student of religion and art in southwestern Nigeria for more than 15 years, is the author of many articles and (with William Fagg) *Yoruba: Sculpture of West Africa* (1982). He is Crosby Professor of Religion and Andrew W. Mellon Professor of Humanities at Amherst College (Massachusetts). In conjunction with Margaret Drewal and Henry Drewal, Pemberton is carrying out a long-term examination of civic ceremonies and ritual cycles among Yoruba peoples under a grant from the National Endowment for the Humanities.

INDEX

(Because conventions vary, and authors differ in their use of them, tone markings are not included in this index.)

Abimbọla, W., 144–45n.56, 197n.35, 198, 242, 259
Abiọdun (King of Ọyọ), 58
Abiodun, R., 202, 229n.4
Abomey (Dahomey), 23n.3, 42, 53, 59; *map*, 40
Abonikaba, L. (Iremọje artist), 197nn.3, 10
Abraham, R. C., 58, 61, 143n.38, 145, 203, 219, 224, 229–30n.8, 232, 239, 245, 246, 248, 251, 254, 259
Achade (Achade Boko) (sorcerer), 71, 74, 79, 81
Achievement, 204; lifetime, 196; worldly, 210
Adebayọ, A. (Iremọje artist), 197nn.13, 16, 28, 40
Adeniji, D. A. A., 30, 34–35, 52, 61, 239–43 *passim*, 259
Adepegba, C., 245, 259
Adetoyi, A., 140n.6, 141nn.13, 21, 143nn.41, 43, 145
Adewumi, S., 139n.2
Ado (Nigeria), 49; *map*, 40
Afọbaje. See Ila, chiefs; Kingmakers
Agbẹkọya Uprising, 187
Agɛ, concept of, 37n.1
Age (earth deity), 30, 37n.1, 50
Agèou Hantò (Ogou spirit), 80, 83, 88n.12
Aggression: in actions, 199; military, 39, 44; as Ogou power, 79, 83; in Ogun traditions, 14, 55, 57; in possession, 55, 57, 68, 79, 84, 199. *See also* Civilization
Agiri, B. A., 142nn.24, 28, 145
Agriculture, 30, 35, 39, 46, 55, 165
Ajayi, J. F. A., 47, 50, 61, 244, 259
Ajilete (Nigeria), 42; *map*, 40
Ajuwọn, B., 8, 12, 15, 16, 51, 173, 261
Akande, O. (Ọbatala priest), 142n.36
Akinjogbin, I. A., 50, 51, 61, 144n.55, 145
Akintoye, S. A., 50, 51, 52, 61
Akiwowo, A., 255, 258n.4, 260
Akure (Nigeria), 49, 50; *map*, 40
Alaafin (King of Ọyọ), 47, 57–58
Alabe, A. (body artist), 243–44, 245, 254, 259
Alao, R. O. (Ijala artist), 161–62
Allada (Kingdom of), 49, 67, 258n.10
Alleyne, P., 24n.9
Amali, S. O. O., 35, 38
Amulet of Ogum (film), 100
Ancestors, 31, 67, 72, 85, 156, 170n.39, 194–95, 257; house of, 67; as masqueraders, 144nn.52, 56, 170n.39, 229n.3; as protective spirits, 72; rites for, 133, 134, 135, 143–44n.46; sacrifices for, 139
Anger (Ogun theme), 3, 19, 73–76, 78, 82, 84, 86, 236

Angola, 91
Anike, A. (Chief of Women), 143n.39
Animals, 30, 33–34, 35; *illustrated* in body marks, 249–50; *pictured* in brass sculpture, 56
Animal symbolism, 48, 127, 128. *See also* Bird, imagery; Dog; Elephant
Antonio das Mortes (film), 100
Anvil, 55, 58; *pictured*, 56; ritual uses, 52
Aphrodite, 23, 24n.8
Ardra. *See* Allada
Argentina, 10
Argyle, W. J., 47, 50, 61, 144n.55, 145
Aribuki, G. (Ijala artist), 169nn.3, 7
Armstrong, R. G., 5, 16, 23n.1, 29, 31, 38, 61n.14, 205, 239, 259, 261
Art. *See* Batik; Body art; Carving; Chromolithographs; Dance; Ijala; Iremọje; Iron, art; Oriki; Praise poetry; Sculpture; Songs; *Vèvè*
Artists, 8, 18, 46, 235–57 *passim*; creativity of, 256; mobility of, 8, 51; sculptors, 160; skills, 239; vocal, 147. *See also* Carvers; Ijala; Iremọje
Aṣẹ (power), 112, 123–25, 128, 131, 199, 202–04, 207, 230n.13, 238, 240–41; in body marks, 247; concept of, 229n.6; in crown, 128; manifestations of, 124, 240, 241; medicinal, 124–25, 207–08; of Ogun, 229, 235–36; royal, 124, 131, 143n.38. *See also* Power
Ashanti, 50–51; *map*, 40
Aṣipa (Ashipa) (Ogun cult chief), 47, 231n.22
Aṣipade (hunter leader), 178, 196
Asiwaju, I., 142n.24, 145
Atkinson, J., 24n.11, 25
Atoyebi (Iremọje artist), 197nn.32, 36, 39
Authority, 138, 203; competition for, 132; locus of, 131; sacrality of, 137, 203. *See also* Kingship, divine
Avery, D. H., 4, 25
Awẹ, B., 47, 52, 55, 61
Awolalu, J. O., 244, 257n.2, 259
Awori (Yoruba sub-group), 42
Awuubẹ, L. (Iremọje artist), 197n.27
Ayandokun, J. A., 234, 260
Ayeni, W. A. (Ọrangun of Ila), 120, 128, 139n.2
Ayoade, J. A. A., 199–200, 232

Babalọla, A. (S. A.), 6, 8, 16, 17, 18, 147, 148, 156, 165, 169n.1, 171n.65, 172, 202, 231n.21, 232, 238, 247, 259, 261
Babayemi, S. O., 60n.5, 61
Badagry (Nigeria), 42, 49, 50; *map*, 40
Bahia (Brazil), 92, 199, 206, 220–28
Baixo espiritismo, 91
Balogun. *See* Ila; Warriors, chiefs
Bandeira, C., 92, 98, 101
Barbers, 160, 241